National Identity and Democracy in Africa

Edited by
Mai Palmberg

The Human Sciences Research Council of South Africa,
the Mayibuye Centre at the University of the Western Cape and
the Nordic Africa Institute
1999

© The Publishers and the authors, 1999

All rights reserved. No part of this publication may be reproduced or transmitted in any form or by any means, electronic or mechanical, including photocopy, recording or any information storage and retrieval system, without permission in writing from the publisher.

Published in Sweden by the Nordic Africa Institute 1999
ISBN 91-7106-453-2

Published in South Africa by the Human Sciences Research Council and Mayibuye Centre of the Universtity of the Western Cape, 1999
ISBN 0-7969-1901-1

Language checking: Elaine Almén
Cover design: Alta Benadie

Printed in South Africa by Capture Press 1999

Table of Contents

Preface 5
Introduction 8

Part I. Inventing the Nation's past

Kimani Gecau, Harare
History, the Arts and the Problem of National Identity:
Reflections on Kenya in the 1970s and 1980s 19

Siri Lange, Bergen
How the National Became Popular in Tanzania 40

Svend Erik Larsen, Odense
The National Landscape—a Cultural European Invention 59

Raisa Simola, Joensuu
The Question of Identity during the Nigerian Civil War (1967–1970)
in the Fiction of Flora Nwapa and Ken Saro-Wiwa 80

Part II. Identities and Transformation

Ousseina Alidou and Alamin Mazrui, Columbus, Ohio
The Language of Africa-Centered Knowledge in South Africa:
Universalism, Relativism and Dependency 101

Horace Campbell, Syracuse
War and the Negotiation of Gendered Identities in Angola 119

Zimitri Erasmus and Edgar Pieterse, Cape Town
Conceptualising Coloured Identities in the Western Cape
Province of South Africa 167

Maria Olaussen, Åbo
Intimate Transformations: Romance, Gender and Nation 188

Mai Palmberg, Uppsala
From Masters to Minorities: The Swedish-speaking Finns and
the Afrikaans-speaking Whites 203

Part III. The South African Experiment

Brendan P. Boyce, Durban
Nation-Building Discourse in a Democracy 231

Gerhard Maré, Durban
The Notion of 'Nation' and the Practice of 'Nation-Building' in
Post-Apartheid South Africa 244

Robert Mattes, Cape Town
Do Diverse Social Identities Inhibit Nationhood and Democracy?
Initial Considerations from South Africa 261

Michael Neocosmos, Gaborone
Strangers at the Cattle Post: State Nationalism and Migrant
Identity in Post-Apartheid South Africa 287

Rupert Taylor, Johannesburg and Don Foster, Cape Town
Advancing Non-Racialism in Post-Apartheid South Africa 328

Petra Smitmanis, Stockholm
Select annotated bibliography 342

About the authors 350

Preface

The Mayibuye Centre of the University of the Western Cape and the Nordic Africa Institute are located many thousand miles apart, one in Bellville near Cape Town in South Africa and the other in Uppsala near Stockholm in Sweden. But the distance in geography is outweighed by the proximity in ideas.

Sweden is the country which perhaps gave the most extensive and constructive assistance to the struggle against apartheid in South Africa, while the Mayibuye Centre is itself an outcome of that struggle. In different ways both institutes have set as their tasks to document and analyse the changes in Africa in ways which produce results that make a difference to contemporary perceptions and debates.

Cooperation between us was thus natural. This book bears witness to the first step in wider collaboration on themes of common interest, notably the international support to the struggle against apartheid. The first joint conference organised by the Mayibuye Centre and the Nordic Africa Institute forms the basis of this book. We have worked on it with the aim of having it finished for the second joint conference of our institutes, to be held in 1999 to highlight, discuss and celebrate the Nordic support to the liberation of southern Africa.

The chapters of this book are all revised versions of selected contributions to the conference entitled "National Identity and Democracy" held from March 14–16, 1997 at the University of the Western Cape.

The objectives of the conference were:

- to bring together scholars from Africa and the Nordic countries to further future collaboration and scholarly exchange between young and advanced scholars
- to provide a forum for the meeting of scholars from various disciplines involved in research on national and cultural identities
- to facilitate the exchange of ideas between academics, cultural workers and political activists

– to highlight the issues involved in the formation of national identity, with a focus on South Africa but including comparative experiences.

An invitation was distributed widely especially in South Africa, the Nordic countries and those African countries with which the convenors had scholarly contact. Ninety seven proposals were sent in and were vetted by a committee of scholars from the University of the Western Cape and the University of Cape Town, together with the coordinator of the research project on "Cultural Images in and of Africa" at the Nordic Africa Institute, Mai Palmberg. Thirty four proposals were accepted for presentation at the conference representing a wide variety of experiences, nationalities, and universities from South Africa, other African countries, the Nordic countries, and scholars in Europe and North America.

We are very grateful to the Swedish International Development Cooperation Agency (Sida), particularly its cultural section, without whose support the conference would not have been possible. We would like to express our gratitude towards the Human Sciences Research Council (HSRC) of South Africa for deeming the conference and this book of sufficient interest to be a partner volume in their series on nation-building and identities.

We would also like to thank all those from the Mayibuye Centre and the Nordic Africa Institute who helped with the organising. A special thanks to Mike Abrahams, special coordinator of the conference, and to Susanne Östman and Petra Smitmanis, assistants to the research project on "Cultural Images in and of Africa" at the Nordic Africa Institute. Susanne Östman has since done a great job in preparing the manuscripts for printing, while Petra Smitmanis compiled an annotated bibliography on the theme of national identity, which appears at the end of this volume. Mai Palmberg has been responsible for the work with the authors on the revision of the papers chosen for inclusion in this volume.

In his opening statement to the conference, the Minister of Justice of South Africa stated that it was the objective of the new South Africa to recognize diversity and the importance of building a national identity at the same time, while professor Colin Bundy, then Dean of Social Sciences at the University of the Western Cape stressed that issues of national identity require rigorous analysis, and Swedish Ambassador Bo Heinebäck pointed at the dilemma of the mobilisation of national identity containing seeds of both good and bad. We hope that this selection from a successful conference will contribute to elucidating the dialectics and thus avoid the pitfalls.

Uppsala and Cape Town, September 1999

Barry Feinberg *Lennart Wohlgemuth*
Director Director
Mayibuye Centre The Nordic Africa Institute

Introduction

"This is not a contribution to nation-building. I hope it helps disrupt nation-building." These words by film-maker Zackie Ahmat gave a kick-start to the discussions at the international conference on "National Identity and Democracy" held at the University of the Western Cape in Bellville, South Africa 14–18 March, 1997.

Ahmat's understanding of nation-building was the kind of cultural homogenisation ordered from above which has been the rule in many countries all over the world, and also in Africa. In these cases nation-building has been a hypocritical cloak for the cultural hegemony of the elite of one cultural group. The provocative remarks by Ahmat were made in connection with his showing of a controversial film which sets out to wrest the heritage of the Afrikaans language from conservative whites and transfer it to the large number of coloured people whose mother tongue is Afrikaans.

Through the title of the conference the organisers wanted to invite a discussion both on the insight that building a nation and building democracy are not necessarily twins, and on the risks of the misuse of power in the name of the nation. Or as the Swedish ambassador, Bo Heinebäck, said in an opening speech: How do we avoid the negative exploitation of "we-ness"?

South Africa is an extreme case of the usurpation of national identity by one minority group, the white Afrikaans-speakers. This group saw themselves as the true South Africans, at least until Verwoerd's time, when the Afrikaner project was turned into a white project, thus increasingly including the English-speaking whites. The black majority was suppressed through a more or less artificial division into ethnic groups, each given an extremely artificially constructed set of "homeland" territories, while the Indians and the Coloureds were accorded no territories, but were covered by a number of rules setting them above the black majority and below the whites.

Given this history it would not have been surprising if majority-ruled South Africa had taken the same road as so many African countries have in the past, instituting a policy of denying all cultural divisions, and accusing all those who claim minority rights or want to organise on a cultural/regional basis of "tribalism". Instead, the new South Africa, has gone to the other extreme, declaring eleven languages as national languages, and setting up a political system with a complex mixture of centralism and federalism.

One can argue that cultural pluralism enshrined in the South African constitution is merely a result of expedient political compromises. The emergent majority, the ANC with its largely black following but with a mixed leadership and a non-racial stand, needed to compromise with at least three other major players in the field. There was the Zulu-based Inkatha movement and its leader Mangosuthu Buthelezi. There was the ruling party since 1948, the National Party, still very much with its base in the Afrikaner population. There was also the Freedom Front, a party of extreme Afrikaners who still took part in the elections of 1994. One could equally argue that one of the few earlier examples in Africa of a similar recognition of cultural differences, Ghana under Nkrumah, was also more a product of political expediency than a matter of principle. But how many principles have not emerged because of the force of circumstances?

The background is most probably a mixture of tactical and ideological considerations. The fact is that in the new South Africa the line taken is a combination of building unity in a new nation and recognition of cultural pluralism. This reality, and the fact that it follows an unprecedented long popular struggle for democracy makes it particularly interesting to discuss the premises and prospects. The fact that South African scholars had been isolated for so long from most of the rest of Africa gave an added impetus to organising the conference in South Africa, as a meeting-place for South African, other African and Nordic scholars.

The conference was organised jointly by the research project "Cultural Images in and of Africa" at the Nordic Africa Institute, and the Mayibuye Centre of the University of the Western Cape. For the former it was a follow-up of studies on the formation of cultural identities, launched in November 1995 with a conference on "Facing Ethnicities in Africa" in Åbo/Turku, Finland. For the latter it was an opportunity to contribute to the discussion of South Africa's future on the basis of its solid documentation and knowledge of the history of the struggle. Out of 29 papers presented at the conference we have made a selection for this book of those that we believe will best further the continued scholarly discussion of identities, and the concepts of nation and democracy.

Scholarly debates usually have their pace-setters, to whom every subsequent contributor to the debate must relate. In the discussion on the theories of trade one can hardly bypass Adam Smith, one of the forefathers of classic economics. The much more recent but equally topical scholarly discussion on the construction of and relations between nations has its own A. Smith who cannot be bypassed. This is Anthony D. Smith. He does not put forward bold theses, but his works have deserved their place as summaries of "the state of the art" in the field. They are clearly argued, erudite overviews with global dimensions and lucidly written. No wonder that his books are often on the course list of university textbooks as gateways to the field, which, in fact, I found was the case at the University of the Western Cape at the time of the conference.

Let us therefore use Anthony Smith's book *National Identity* as a reference point to place the contributions in this volume in the discussion on the theme.[1]

'National identity' according to Anthony D. Smith is founded in culture, in contradistinction to the concept of nationalism, which is a political movement. 'National identity' involves both cultural ideas (such as ideas on common ancestry or history), and cultural symbols, (such as monuments, poetry, architecture). A special category of people, the intellectuals, are needed to articulate the ideas and create new symbols of the assumed old common roots.

A primary task for intellectuals and artists in the heyday of nationalism in the 19th century was thus to provide the cultural paraphernalia of that period's nation-building. One can add that an important task today is to question and analyse that very same project in order to sort out what should be discarded and what should be saved. The present book is part of this endeavour.

We soon encounter difficulties, however, if we use Anthony D. Smith as a guide. These shortcomings are not his alone, but characterise much of the thinking on modern nations. On the one hand

---

1. Anthony D. Smith, *National Identity*, Penguin Books, Harmondsworth 1991.

Smith writes with an ironical tone about the myth of nationalism and its central idea "that nations exist from time immemorial, and that nationalists must reawaken them from their slumber to take the place in a world of nations."[2] But when he treats the concept "ethnicity" the tone is not one of distance but ambivalence. He says he is placed between the two extremes of those who find a primordial quality in ethnicity, which "exists outside time", and those who see ethnicity as "situational", dependent on the individual's situation and open to instrumental manipulation by competing elites.[3] The perspective he adopts stresses "the historical and symbolic-cultural attributes of ethnic identity".[4] In fact, he does see the origin of nations in ethnic communities (or *ethnies*) despite the fact that he does not underwrite the nationalist myths that they have always existed.

On this point Smith is largely irrelevant for the discourse on national identity in modern Africa. The modern states were the results of colonial rivalries, partition conferences and conquests. The resulting map frequently meant that the areas of an ethnic group straddled the borders of more than one colony, and even more frequently several ethnic groups found themselves in one and the same country.

It seems more helpful to turn to another oft-quoted writer on the theme, Benedict Anderson, whose book title *Imagined Communities* has become almost a household term.[5] But let us remind ourselves that "imagined communities" did not for Anderson mean "fabricated" or "invented". His starting point is the rather obvious fact that the nation, defined as "an imagined political community" is imagined "because the members of even the smallest nation will never know most of their fellow-members, meet them, or even hear of them, yet in the minds of each lives the image of their communion."[6] And he adds that all communities other than primordial villages with face-to-face contact are in fact imagined.

---

2. Ibid.:19–20.
3. Ibid.:20.
4. Loc.cit.
5. Benedict Anderson, *Imagined Communities* , Verso, London and New York 1992. (The book was first published in 1983, the revised and enlarged edition in 1991.)
6. Ibid.:6.

This is far from Ernest Gellner's view that nationalism works under false pretences, and invents nations where they do not exist.[7] Yet Anderson gives much more room than Smith does to a sympathetic account of how in fact new nations come to be imagined. For Smith nations without a basis in an ethnic community do not have a solid foundation. For Anderson the creation of genuine feelings of national identity in post-colonial Third World countries spring from a complex intertwining of schooling and administrative systems in the formation of new bilingual elites.[8] His examples are mainly from Asia, but here a vast field remains to be researched on Africa. There have been far too many assumptions that only ethnic identification patterns are genuine, and that national identity is a shallow invention.

For Smith Africa is an anomaly. He writes of sub-Saharan Africa:[9]

> the ruling élites, who may often have been recruited from a dominant *ethnie* or coalition of ethnic groupings, were tempted to fashion a new political mythology and symbolic order not only to legitimate their often authoritarian regimes, but also to head off threats of endemic ethnic conflicts and even movements of secession. In these cases the state is utilized to fashion the 'civil religion' whose myths, memories, symbols and the like will provide the functional equivalent of a missing or defective dominant *ethnie*.

Note here how close Smith comes to Gellner's perspective—for different reasons—that nationalists entertain false pretences. Certainly there is in Africa (but indeed just as much elsewhere) the danger of one group, whether ethnically defined or not, creating a 'civic religion' to mobilise a sense of collective community, which in reality is a cover for nothing less than collective elite projects.

Some of the papers in this volume describe such processes, notably the paper by *Kimani Gecau* on how that section of the Gikuyu elite, which assumed political power with independence set an intellectual agenda which gave no room for popular projects. Culture with a capital C was identified as the culture of the former colonial power, Great Britain, and the heritage of resistance from the rebellion in the 1950s was toned down. This is a fascinating case study of the struggle over symbols of national identity, "struggles over what history to tell".

---

7. Referred to in loc.cit.
8. Ibid.:chapter 7 (pp. 113–140).
9. Smith, 1991:41.

In much of the writing on national identity there is an assumption that nationalism and democracy go hand in hand. Smith does not hold this simplistic view. Nor is he really interested in democracy, perhaps because he so firmly believes that the only real basis of national identity must lie in an ethnic community. He includes "common legal rights and duties for all members" and "a common, mass public culture" in the list of fundamental features of national identity.[10] National identity is here placed in the age of mass education and universal conscription.

The thought that national identity could be based on democracy is not discussed in Smith's book on national identity. His concern is the lack of congruence between state and nation, and he refers to Walker Connor's estimate from the 1970s that only about 10 per cent of the states could claim to be nation-states in the sense that the state boundaries coincided with those of the nation and that the total population of the state shared a single ethnic culture.[11]

Much of this volume, in contrast, rests on a conviction that the multi-ethnic state is here to stay, that ideas other than myths of ethnic origin can and must be the ideological basis of the imagined community of those living in a given state, and that these are not poor substitutes for the unifying ethnic community which is lacking.

Svend Erik Larsen discusses one of the symbols of nationalism found in the production of intellectuals, the idea of the national landscape. He discusses how the metaphor of the landscape has been used to express nationalist emotions, but also to express a sense of belonging by expatriates, as when Karen Blixen writes of "her" Kenya. He suggests that the use of the landscape metaphor has nothing to do with democracy, and that perhaps in South Africa democracy itself will provide a more constructive metaphor for national identity.

The use of cultural symbols to create national unity is also the theme in the paper by *Siri Lange*, who describes how a particular kind of musical show, intended to extol the nation, turned into an important prop of popular culture. The shows were stripped of their mes-

---

10. The others being "an historic territory, or homeland", "common myths and historical memories", and "a common economy with territorial mobility for its members". Ibid.:14.
11. Ibid.:15.

sage from above about national unity, but instead they became much more effective tools for creating national identity by their cross-ethnic popularity.

The idea of a nation-state where state borders and ethnicity coincide presupposes one single ethnic identity. As we have seen this is realistic in only one tenth of all existing states. In all others, ethnicity and national identity alone, make for dual identities. When gender is taken seriously, we have multiple identities. Generation, life experience (such as years in exile), and education abroad or in an educational system modelled on foreign ideals provide further sets of identities that compete with or colour the formation of national identity. Aspects of identity have not previously entered much into the discourse on national identity. But the discourse on identities has surged to attention with the post-modernist rejection of the idea of grand designs in history, which accords individuals fixed roles and boundaries.

Whether post-modernist or not, the analytical tool of multiple identities, helps us understand social change. Three papers here deal explicitly with this theme. *Zimitri Erasmus* and *Edgar Pieterse* reflect on how to conceptualise the identities of the coloureds in South Africa. After an analysis of three major discourses on coloured identities in South Africa, they reject attempts to assign to this group an essentialist fixed-for-all identity. At the same time they criticise "the discourse of denial" which describes coloured identity as solely an imposed label. Identities are relational, they are different at different times, and they are contested, and hence, unstable. It is on diverse and constantly reinterpreted experiences that a new South African national identity must be built, they conclude.

Robert Mattes arrives at some interesting conclusions in reviewing surveys from the first two years of the New South Africa. They reveal that most South Africans adapt a sectarian (racial, ethnic, linguistic, religious) identity rather than a secular, South African one when asked to give their own spontaneous, self-described identities. Yet at the same time, other questions find almost consensual pride among South Africans in being South African. The propensity to adopt a secular or sectarian self-described identity is unrelated to how much pride one exhibits in the common national citizenship. In contrast to conventional wisdom this suggests that group-based identities are not necessarily inimicable to developing a strong, widely held sense of citizenship and national identity, (i.e. a non-ethnic sense of nation).

Mai Palmberg adopts a consciously voluntaristic approach by saying that an identity image which has been created can be remoulded. She suggests that the Afrikaans-speaking whites, or those accepting the change, could now re-create the image they had once created and projected for the time of the laager. She compares them with another group who had to change "From Masters to Minorities", the Swedish-speaking Finns who on universal suffrage in 1907 were deprived of their political dominance, and had to take on a role as good hyphenated Finns.

Language plays a crucial role both as identity marker and as the medium for national symbols. In most of Africa the role of the metropolitan languages makes for an extraordinary situation, where the national identity is developed through a language medium which is not the mother tongue of anybody in the country. This situation has provoked a language debate which has raged for many decades. On the one hand, we find many who base their support for the use of the languages of the former colonial masters on arguments of expediency, or by saying that "language has no nation". Benedict Anderson underwrites this argument when he says: "Nothing suggests that Ghanaian nationalism is any less real than Indonesian simply because its national language is English rather than Ashanti"[12] and that "language is not an instrument of exclusion: in principle, anyone can learn any language."[13] In this volume *Ousseina Alidou* and *Alamin Mazrui* take a contrary line, and argue against the acceptance of English as the most favoured language in the new South Africa, arguing that this cannot be combined with the need for a growth of Africa-centred knowledge.

Smith uses the term "demotic" for popularly based nationalism. Democracy as a political system of government and participation in the political process does not, however, figure much at all in his book *National Identity*. For him the development of national identity is a modern phenomenon because it comes at a time when the means of

---
12. Anderson, 1992:133.
13. Ibid.:134.

mass mobilisation are available for governments, through mass education, mass propaganda and universal conscription.

To create a sense of "we-ness" also requires an establishment of borders and exclusion. In South Africa this process has reappeared on the agenda since a legitimately elected government came to power in 1994. The migrant workers from neighbouring countries, and unemployed so called "illegals", especially from Mozambique, have been pointed at as unwelcome foreigners. The paper by *Michael Neocosmos* deals with one migrant worker group, those from Lesotho, with historically deep roots in the South African society. But more than a contribution on the current processes of exclusion and inclusion his paper is a study on different ways of constructing identities, from above by the state or from below by the people themselves. Neocosmos concludes that there is no democracy at play in dealing with the 'foreigners' in South Africa.

Why does the state need a strong national identity in its citizens? One aim for the state mobilisation around national values is to make the members of the imagined community respond to the call-up in times of war against some "them". This call is usually directed to the male members of society, but equally significant is the willingness among the women to bear the burdens of the home front.

Raisa Simola gives an account of two Nigerian authors, Ken Saro-Wiwa and Flora Nwapa, writing on the civil war between the federal government and secessionist Biafra in the late 1970s. Neither the stories by the authors, nor the ironical twists with which they tell them, witness to great success at winning hearts and minds for the war effort. Is this an indication of the failure to construct the nation-state in the multicultural setting in Africa, or is it a sign that intellectuals are not necessarily available for nationalist projects?

Horace Campbell writes about another war situation, the long war in Angola. He elucidates how the women are the major force for peace, and the main source of strength in the war-torn society.

Inclusion, exclusion, and citizenship have a gender aspect so often ignored in the past, and not yet squarely on the research agenda. Maria Olaussen illustrates this by analysing how the representation of womanhood within a romance theme changes with the changing circumstances of nation-building. The analysis focuses on two novels,

Bessie Head's *The Cardinals* and Nadine Gordimer's *None to Accompany Me*, and points to the central and often unacknowledged links between sexuality and nationalism.

Nationalism and racism in their construction of "we-ness" have often coincided. But both Smith and Anderson are keen to distinguish the two phenomena. Smith notes that the concept "ethnic group" has too often been confounded with the concept "race". This, he says, is[14]

> because of the widespread influence of racist ideologies and discourses, with their purportedly 'scientific' notions of racial struggle, social organisms and eugenics. In the hundred years from 1850 to 1945 such notions were applied to the purely cultural and historical differences of *ethnies*, both inside Europe and in colonial Africa and Asia, with results that are all too well known.

Anderson devotes a short chapter to racism, and also contends that racism and nationalism are altogether different: "...nationalism thinks in terms of historical destinies, while racism dreams of eternal contaminations...."[15] The dreams of racism actually have their origins in class ideologies, he writes, rather than in those of nation.

The end of *apartheid* in South Africa has been heralded as the victory over racism. Indeed the legislation specifying different rights and prohibitions for different people in terms of race ascription is no longer applicable. But this is not all there is to racism, *Rupert Taylor* and *Don Foster* point out. All too often, and not only in South Africa, "race" is taken as a fact of life that we have to relate to, despite the fact that no scientific basis of the concept of "race" has been established. An effective non-racialism requires some new thinking, they write.

"Rainbow nation" was proposed as a metaphor for the new South Africa, first by the then Archbishop of the Anglican church, Desmond Tutu, and then by President Nelson Mandela in his inauguration speech in Pretoria in May 1994. On a general level the metaphor is a beautiful symbol for a new attitude towards the various groups making up South Africa, each welcome to add colour to a multiethnic country. Surely equality, tolerance and pluralism were the values intended in the metaphor. But one does not have to be the devil's advocate to ask whether the respect for other groups is built on safe demo-

---

14. Smith, 1991:21–22.
15. Ibid.:149.

cratic ground. Are there not pitfalls in accepting ethnic groups as significant social actors? There is first of all a mistaken notion that it is easy to define who belongs to a particular ethnic group, and who does not. In the second place, when ethnic groups are given political power it means that some authority within what has been defined as a named ethnic group is given the power to speak on behalf of others. This almost inevitably means strengthening authoritarian, patriarchal and undemocratic structures.

These are some of the questions raised in the papers by *Gerhard Maré* and *Brendan Boyce*. They are both wary of the tendencies of the state to foster a national identity from above. While both recognise the need to redefine national identity and seek some sort of unity, they raise questions about the nation-building concept and its historical stress on uniformity. Maré even questions whether nation-building as a project is desirable, and thinks that any attempt to build one single political identity will be doomed. He offers as an alternative "a wide notion of democracy", including a united effort towards social justice.

South Africa certainly deserves continued attention, both for the aspects of novelty it brings into the formation of national identity, and for the necessity to monitor whether indeed the building of national identity and democracy can go hand in hand or not. On a more general level we have seen how the authorities on national identity, Anthony D. Smith and Benedict Anderson, do have much to tell us, but also leave us largely without analytical tools when it comes to Africa. More research is needed on "the special cases" represented by Africa. This volume contributes to that enterprise. Perhaps in the end we will find that the special cases, which do not have such neatly fixed and ethnically bound identities, will be found to be more normal than what is seen today as normal and typical.

Uppsala, September 1999

Mai Palmberg

History, the Arts and the Problem of National Identity: Reflections on Kenya in the 1970s and 1980s

Kimani Gecau

In Zimbabwe, a popular singer has sung that "Zimbabwe yekahuya ne hondo" (that is, 'Zimbabwe' came through the war of liberation from colonialism). However, in Kenya this statement could not be made so confidently about the country's post-colonial identity. A debate, involving both artists and historians, has continued over whether the Mau Mau war of liberation contributed to the making of a Kenyan national identity or not. As Lonsdale (1992:265) pointedly remarks "at the heart of Kenya's modern history broods the enigma of Mau Mau". In spite of its contribution to bring Kenya freedom the memory of Mau Mau "disturbs more Kenyans than it inspires, it divides them". The tendency then has been to try to devise "codes of oblivion to suppress such division, like all other states that claim to be nations". This, however, has created a problem in the mobilising of history and the arts for the establishment of a national identity in Kenya.

History and the related cultural and symbolic forms which come with it are, of course, central in the construction of national identities. As Anderson (1991) and Burke (1993) argue, nations as imagined communities are cultural artefacts which have a historical specificity. Thus struggles for either domination or freedom are also struggles over what history to tell; what history is to become dominant, who is to be glorified and who is to be vilified. The re-telling of histories therefore accompanies efforts at decolonisation and nation-building (Ranger, 1983:41). In the new nations, for example, the history of struggle against colonialism becomes one of the points of reference in building the nation providing the symbols and sensibility of what it means to be a national and giving account of how the collective—the 'imagined nation'—has, through its efforts moved from one phase of its historical development into another—from its people being subjects to their becoming citizens.

History and culture or processes of signification are themselves inextricably linked. The concept 'the nation' is in fact made evident through the circulation of symbolic forms and the holding of national events which assume a more or less ritualistic aspect. The day that the people achieve their nationhood, with the symbols that come with this, is celebrated in elaborate annual commemorative ceremonies and in song and dance. Those sports competitions between 'our' national team and other teams from other nations become metaphors of nation competing against nation. These popular festivals and occasions help in the construction of a national identity and a sense of community and are strengthened when the media turn them into media events of national significance.

History and the arts are therefore important in constituting a 'knowable community'—of including some people and excluding others; of defining those who share in the history and the life represented by the arts and also in recreating 'otherness'. This leads to a necessity to understand how history and the arts represent reality and their inclusions and exclusions in the processes of identity formation. However, in a society divided by class, race, gender and ethnicity there may not be one history and one kind of art. In addition there are also what we may regard as universal values that come with history and the arts in so far as these are about human beings seeking to further humanise themselves and their lives. Hence history and the arts assume meanings and resonance far outside their geographical localities and may transcend time and space and specific exclusionary identities. In any case struggles for independence as quests for freedom and justice are themselves manifestly universal and they provide the new and modern historical contexts in which to build nations and national identities.

Our interest in this discussion is to briefly show how historians on the one hand and people in literature and the theatre on the other came to debate what constitutes a national history. This debate goes back to the discussions over the need to change the literature syllabus in 1968, the subsequent changes in the syllabus, debates over the interpretation of the Mau Mau by historians and literary figures (specifically in Ngugi's work) and the development of popular theatre with themes based on history. These discussions are connected to the formation of identities and to the struggles for democracy in Kenya. The discussions have also brought to scrutiny the role of cultural institutions and cultural producers (including intellectuals and their products—led by national historians and artists). The implicit concerns are whether the nation-building project in Kenya has been informed by a clear operative cultural policy especially in regard to the philosophy, aims and goals of national education, the media and other cultural institutions, and in the role that the arts and humanities are expected to play in the formation of identities and hence in national development.

CHANGES IN THE LITERATURE SYLLABUS

In September 1968 the acting head of the English Department at the University presented a paper which was concerned with possible developments in the Arts Faculty and how they related to the then English Department. Three lecturers Awuor-Anyumba, Taban Lo Liyong and Ngugi wa Thiong'o questioned the assumptions behind his proposals that (in their own words) "the English tradition and the emergence of the modern west is the central root of our consciousness and cultural heritage. Africa becomes an extension of the west, an attitude which, until a radical reassessment, used to dictate the teaching and organization of History in our University." (Ngugi et al, 1972:146).

They instead proposed that in our studies we place Kenya, East Africa, and then Africa in the centre so that we can view other cultures in relation to our literature and to ourselves. This would help in the understanding and appreciation of the important role literature has played in "the African renaissance". It further said:

> All other things are to be considered in their relevance to our situation, and their contribution towards understanding ourselves.... The primary duty of any literature department is to illuminate the spirit animating a

people, to show how it meets new challenges, and to investigate possible areas of development and involvement.

A study of literature and language should be located at the local, Kenyan, African, African-American, Third World and European sensibilities in roughly such an order of inter-connectedness. This then was not rejecting the western cultural stream and its contribution to language and literature in Kenya and elsewhere, but enriching the study of literature in Kenya with other streams which had also contributed to the making of a Kenyan culture.

Significantly, in keeping with this argument, they were to suggest that we study "our oral tradition which is our primary root". Their understanding of this tradition, however, linked it with what has now come to be known as popular culture—that of songs sung in "political rallies, in churches, in night clubs by guitarists, by accordion players, by dancers, etc." (Ngugi et al, 1972:147). This would ground the student in a literary tradition that would help in the student's appreciation of modern written literature from Africa and from the rest of the world. Implied in this was also a desire to not only change the canon but also the way that literature was taught. The discussions over these proposals were to continue into the 1970s and were to lead to the creation of a new Department of Literature with a new syllabus and orientation in 1973. This debate was also to lead to a prolonged debate and change (though temporary) in the secondary schools syllabus which was to be finally implemented in 1980.

DEVELOPMENT OF THEATRE

The 1968 statement had also identified theatre as important for study and development, "since drama is an integral part of literature". This led to the inclusion of courses on drama and theatre-in-education in the new syllabus. Theatre performances were to become a strong feature in the new department and were to be consolidated with the establishment of the University Free Travelling Theatre that annually toured schools and communities nation-wide, "taking theatre to the people". In turn, this was to stimulate theatrical activity in schools and communities. As a result, the Kenya Schools Drama Festival became a national event involving almost all schools and colleges in festivals at district, provincial and national levels. Its continued existence to this day, in spite of official censorship, has led to the production of predominantly original plays, many in Kiswahili, and to the emergence of what we may consider a national theatrical tradition and culture. This has been strengthened by the development of community based theatre which was inspired by the changes in theatre and literature in the 1970s. The best known example of this theatre is the Kamiriithu Community Educational and Cultural Centre's Theatre Project which was to inspire the formation of other community based groups many of which are still active.

The significant unresearched aspect of these developments therefore is the effect of this popularisation of the arts and the involvement of people of different social backgrounds as performers and audiences. This has happened alongside developments in popular songs some of which have been influenced in their themes by the plays. Another significant influence of these activities is on how writing and literature came to be practised. For example, the involvement of Kenya's leading writer, Ngugi wa Thiong'o, in these activities was to lead to the further development of his own ideas and perceptions which were to influence his writings (see for example Ngugi, 1981). This involvement was to lead to Ngugi's one year detention in the last year of Kenyatta's reign (Kenyatta died in August 1978). Hence his work since the mid-1970s seeks to depict the role of ordinary people in history and to recapture collective memory and experience. He thus moves from seeing history as made by the fortunes of the elite to an understanding of it as the product of human beings acting collectively to transform their natural and social world as they also transform themselves. (See for example his introduction to Wa Kinyatti, 1987). His involvement in the theatre at Kamiriithu and his move towards a more popular view of history was also to lead to his writing in his Kikuyu language. How this has affected the production and reception of the popular arts is also a matter for further research.

RESPONSES TO THE CHANGES

We may clearly understand the changes in the literature syllabus and the move towards more popular forms of literature, theatre and music as quests for symbolic forms that would be at the centre of constituting a national identity (see Gramsci, 1985). However, experiences of colonialism and the Mau Mau were to leave legacies which have influenced not only how the changes in the literature syllabus were received but also how history and the future of Kenya are understood. The responses, in particular those of the historians, may be best understood within this wider context. Basically there were two tendencies in these responses. Some tended to suspect Marxism as the inspiration behind them while others somehow saw in the changes a strong desire by those involved in the changes to continue and consolidate the hegemony of the Kikuyu ethnic group.

'MARXIST' INTERPRETATIONS

There were those who saw these changes as either Marxist inspired or intended to lead to Marxism (see for example *the Weekly Review*, of 7 January 1983 and Ngugi, 1981). This interpretation is consistent with the evoking of the communist bogey against most struggles for national liberation in this century. In Kenya charges of communism have been levelled at anti-colonial activities since the 1920s. Some, for example Cox (1965:59), were to link the Mau Mau with communism. After independence Kenya was deeply implicated in cold war politics and anti-communism became official policy. This is to be seen in the tendency to dismiss as communist those who have opposed the government in the name of more democratic practices since the days of the Kenya People's Union in the late 1960s (Odinga, 1967) to the Mwakenya underground movement of the 1980s.

As a way of responding to this challenge in 1969, the Kenyatta government mobilised "Kikuyu ethnicity to defend it against the threat of radical (i.e. Marxist) opposition" whose home was seen to be located among the Luo people (Lonsdale, 1992:218). This entailed oathings which were a vulgarisation of the symbolism of Mau Mau. A popular Kenyan politician of Luo origin, Tom Mboya, was assassinated and later in the same year there was a confrontation between Kenyatta and Odinga in Kisumu, the capital of Nyanza province—the home of the Luo people. There was shooting and people died. These events were to have an important influence in the future political developments in Kenya where the non-Kikuyu were to increasingly interpret events in terms of Kikuyu attempts at hegemony while those Kikuyu opposed to the turn of political events saw this as the work of a minority class among the Kikuyus (see Ngugi's *Petals of Blood* for an interpretation of this). A popular Kikuyu politician, J.M. Kariuki, who had been a Mau Mau detainee and had written a book called just *Mau Mau detainee* was to say that he did not want to see a Kenya of ten millionaires and ten million beggars. He was to be murdered in 1975 in circumstances which have yet to be explained.

'TRIBAL' INTERPRETATIONS

A dominant trend, however, among historians was to understand the changes within a context of 'tribal' politics and the intended continuation of Kikuyu hegemony. This may be explained as reflecting the continuation of the effect of colonial encouragement of divisions along ethnic lines, the massive propaganda mobilised against the Mau Mau, fears over a possible Kikuyu hegemony arising out of the same propaganda, concerns over a just redistribution of resources and a need for unity through attaining a single national identity. Each one of these aspects was to influence those historians whose responses were consistent with official interpretations of history. There is need therefore to say a few words about each.

Colonial control rested on isolating ethnic groups from each other and re-inventing the 'tribal structures' within the geographical boundaries (reserves) allocated each group. The colonial state also consciously encouraged and kept politics at the local and tribal level and sought to avoid colony-wide nationalist organisations (Berman, 1990:302–304). The Mau Mau itself was to create deep cleavages where some people from other ethnic groups, alongside the Kikuyu 'homeguards', were to be used to defeat the movement. Others of the 'homeguards' took over the jobs and the land of those who were in detention.

Political organisations were banned during the Mau Mau war. After the unbanning during decolonization political parties were allowed, but only at district level. All-Kenyan national parties were allowed only just before independence. Therefore, the two 'national' parties—the Kenya African National Union (KANU) and the Kenya African Democratic Union (KADU)—were really coalitions of district organisations bringing together local bosses, each with their own constituency. Barkan (1992:169) explains these as "typically clientilist organisations created by individual candidates to mobilise support among the members of their ethnic groups".

This had far reaching consequences on the relationship between the state and the people which is reflected in the metaphor used in Kenyan political discourse when politicians are expected to deliver their people and constituencies to the ruling centre in return for favours. After taking over from Kenyatta in 1978, Moi's rule was to be based more on his personal pronouncements which did not invite discussion. His aim was not to mitigate class inequities but ethnic and regional ones (Barkan, 1992). In fact as his adviser, Ngweno, was to tell the World Bank, the official belief was that 'Big Tribes' and not 'Big Men' were the cause of mismanagement in Africa (*Weekly Review*, 25 January 1991).

PROPAGANDA AGAINST THE MAU MAU

As well as using propaganda to make the Mau Mau appear communist, it was also depicted as a disgusting atavistic movement out to destroy the civilization built by colonialism. The Mau Mau was thus referred to as an unpleasant aberration, a disease which those fighting against it were trying to cure. At the same time other tribes were warned to keep away from the Kikuyus so as not to contact this disease (Berman, 1990; Alot, 1982:32–33; *the Corfield Report* of 1960). Michael Blundell was to describe those who were supporting Kenyatta during political campaigning at this time as unwashed with that strong smell mixed with human perspiration which I have already described, wearing dirty odoriferous monkey skin hats and speaking quickly and intensely with the adenoidal intonation of the Kikuyu. They were almost like the inhabitants of an underworld; devoid of human virtues, greedy for the main chance and treacherous to a degree .... (Blundell, 1964:291)

In the same breath, as it were, the Mau Mau came to be linked to quests for Kikuyu hegemony. As late as 1960 Governor Sir Patrick Renison said of Kenyatta and Mau Mau that:

Here was an African leader to darkness and death .... He planned for Kikuyu domination, he was an implacable opponent of any cooperation with other people, tribes or races, who live in Kenya. (Mboya, 1986:44–45)

Significantly the Kenya African Democratic Party (KADU), whose then Secretary General was the present Kenya's president Daniel Arap Moi, initially formed a minority government in a coalition with the New Kenya Party, a white settler's grouping led by Michael Blundell. The Governor explained the formation of this minority Government as a way of overcoming Kikuyu attempts to enforce domination "over those who did not accept such domination, in what was called Mau Mau" (Mboya, 1986:45–6). Blundell who was to exert a lot of influence in the new Kenya at this time believed then that it was necessary to agree to work with those Africans who "had accepted the ideas and standards which we were trying to plant in Africa" as opposed to the Mau Mau whose "technique" led to the "dreadful debasing of the human mind". To him the Mau Mau was an anti-British (read 'anti-civilisation') Kikuyu revanchist movement:

It is important to realise that the Mau Mau leaders were fighting to unite the Kikuyu people. Once this was achieved they hoped to destroy British influence and secure Kikuyu domination throughout the country in its place. (Blundell, 1964:147–8)

Christian leaders and home guards—those who had accepted British influences—prevented this insidious aim and thus saved Kenya from the Mau Mau. (Blundell, 1964:169)

In words that sound ironic today, Blundell says that those in KADU were "pledged to the same political objectives as Ronald Ngala (their leader)—the creation of a society which is democratic, non-totalitarian and based on individual freedom" (Blundell, 1964:324). Ronald Ngala, the then leader of KADU is described as a person who

> appeals to the men and women of all the smaller groups and tribes who are seeking a leader without a pronounced tribal image. He is essentially a sincere, dedicated man, who profoundly believes in the principles of discussion and is firmly opposed to the one party system, or what we might call the parliamentary autocracies of the African scene. (Blundell, 1964:233)

THE NEED FOR UNITY AND ONE IDENTITY

Given the cleavages and conflicts that Kenya had gone through by the time of independence in 1963, it was understandable that the leaders sought to build a unified and stable nation. In any case Kenya inherited the familiar problem of nation-building in that, like other ex-colonies, her boundaries were arbitrarily drawn, enclosing within them a multi-ethnic population. This was however also a time of the modernisation ideology which came with its binariness such as traditional/modern; literate/illiterate; African/Western and so on. There was therefore what we may call an official tendency influenced both by this and also by colonial perspectives to give people a fixed identity according to their 'tribe' and to refuse to accept that Kenyans could be differentiated and identified by more than this one primary identity.

Cohesiveness and unity were said to be the basis of progress and they inevitably entailed that a homogenised nation be built, one that would speak in one voice—that of the President (who is also said to be the symbol of national unity). The political leader's job was therefore understood as that of moving people from being tribalists to their becoming nationalists; from their having many vernacular languages to having one national language and so on. It was further assumed that a people's political identity is formed on the basis of their 'tribe'. This has led to the notion that pluralism in politics leads to tribalism and is hence bad for a nation. Further, the existence of 'tribes' is equated with 'tribalism' (and the term is used with no shame). This inevitably means that ethnic diversity is understood among these circles as synonymous with conflict and disunity.

This emphasis on the residues of the precolonial in our identities ignores the deep changes that have come into our societies since the colonial period. We could, for example, speak of class, profession and occupation, gender, age, and religious identities among other things. Some of these have created forms of social consciousness and other solidarities that may cut across regional or ethnic boundaries. The official fixity even overlooks the unequal and uneven exposure to culture through schooling and the media. Further this privileging of one identity has made it difficult to deal with the diversity of culture, political opinion and so on. It has in fact been at the heart of the crisis in the formation of what has been desired as a single and homogenous national identity based on a political community and accepted rights and obligations.

Further, the implicit official approach defines people according to their assumed biological, not social, make up. By emphasising primary identities such as language and geography in exclusion of other identities it leads ethnic groups to think in terms of 'us' who are distinct from 'others' of Kenya's ethnic groups. It also makes what are small differences between these groups loom large through exaggeration and emphasis. This has further strengthened the 'blood and soil' essentialist understanding of identities so that in the official quest for homogeneity, in a politically repressive context that refuses other ways of constructing oneness, serious ethnic conflicts have occurred (see for example the Amnesty International Report of December 1995). This is a sad reminder that collective identities cannot be invented or constructed at will.

CONCERNS OVER REDISTRIBUTIVE JUSTICE

Behind the anxieties of the small groups were concerns about the sharing out of the natural resources and what the smaller groups grouped under the KADU thought was a socialist programme by KANU that would nationalize private property. This fear, however, seems to have been more the expression of the fears of the white settler mentors of KADU who had developed an implacable hatred of KANU and what was assumed to be its communist background.

Nonetheless the linking of communism with 'tribalism' in discussions over power and redistribution of resources was to become a regular feature—more or less metaphors—in Kenya.

At independence, Kenya inherited inequalities and unevenness in regional and intra-regional development leading to inequalities between ethnic groups and classes. In fact most of the struggles in Kenya have been around this. Over the years there has been a perception that inequality was rife and that there were some ethnic groups, notably the Kikuyu, who were being favoured over others . 'Counting the heads' of senior employees and their 'tribal' origin in order to prove or refute allegations of 'tribalism' became almost routine in parliament and in the daily press from the 1960s (Gertzel et al., 1969:37–52). The shrillest pitch was reached in the early 1990s when even those who campaigned for more democratic political changes were accused of being 'tribalists'. Such changes were suspected of seeking to bring back Kikuyu domination.

THE HISTORIANS' VIEW ON MAU MAU

The changes in the literature syllabus were thus being enacted in what were gradual but fundamentally important shifts in the popular perception of a crisis in the relationship between the state and the citizenry, and a growing polarisation around ethnic and class identities. These factors were also to influence debates over the Mau Mau and the arts in the mid-1970s.

The historians were clearly influenced by these discussions. In response to the interpretations of history and of the Mau Mau among some arts practitioners and historians, one of the trajectories in the then dominant interpretation of the Mau Mau was to pose the question whether it was an ethnic or a popular nationalist movement.

Official versions of history usually leave out collective history and memory from which a people find their stories and voices to tell who they are. This is true of the disputes over Mau Mau as well. Apart from the Mau Mau being mainly a movement of the smaller property owners and the propertyless among the Kikuyu, it was not elitist. Hence concern over the recognition of the legitimacy of the Mau Mau as a successful nationalism which brought about a new nation is also seen as a recognition of a popular movement, a popular history and the right of the popular classes to participate in nation-building. As we have seen the official myth of Mau Mau was to represent it as disruptive. In any case the modernisation ideology holds that only the elite who are modern and western can lead in nation-building.

The elitist tendency in the arguments against Mau Mau may be seen in the words of professor Ogot whom I quote at length. In his introduction to the special issue of the *Kenya Historical Review* he laid down the main areas of disagreement between those who shared his views and those who wished to see the Mau Mau in a positive light. He first invoked the idea of objective history and need for rigour in the definition of terms; for scholarly analysis as opposed to what he refers to as polemical out-pourings. He then went on to make a clear distinction between Kenya nationalism and Mau Mau. The general Kenyan nationalist movement, he argues, "had followed the general pattern found in many Third World countries. Its ideology was liberal, rational and nationalistic. It operated within the colonial economic system". In other words the nationalists had qualities of modernity. Mau Mau "was more of a short-lived break" in this "peaceful development of nationalism in Kenya". Ogot goes on to describe the Mau Mau as

> in fact, an attempt by the Kikuyu masses, the landless, the disinherited squatters and urban lumpenproletariat—to found a revolutionary movement. Mau Mau lost the war, the revolutionary movement died, and its incipient radical ideology was rejected by the nationalists in both KANU and KADU who continued from where KAU [Kenya African Union] had left off. --- Having completely rejected the Mau Mau ideology, the nationalists agreed to join hands with the former colonial masters to *disabuse* the former Mau Mau adherents of their *misguided* ideas .... It should therefore be evident that despite the lip service usually paid to Mau Mau by the nationalists in Kenya, its ideology had been rejected by 1960. (Ogot, 1977:170) [Italics added]

The problem with the Mau Mau then was that it was violent and was not nationalist but 'tribal'. Its rituals especially were tribal. Ogot asks: "The problem after 1956 then was that how does one develop a nation from a base that is so developed tribally?" He then refers to Robert Buijtenhuis who in his *Mau Mau: Twenty Years After* had argued that while Mau Mau was a tribal movement it was not hostile to other ethnic groups in Kenya and was rather a case of "tribalism serving the nation".

> In the same book, Buijtenhuis eventually realises this dilemma and admits that Mau Mau could eventually become a negative factor in the process of nation-building. His argument is that he cannot see how a movement which denies non-Kikuyu a role in the independence struggle can be the focus of Kenyan nationalism. In any case, we are to a large extent merely indulging in the politics of nostalgia. The Mau Mau ideology, as I have argued, was already rejected by 1960 by the nationalist forces. How can we then regard Mau Mau as the basis of Kenya nationalism? This is a painful conclusion. (Ogot, 1977:172)

Thus there was another aspect which was to become very important in the efforts of the arts and history to domesticate the colonial legacy—that of the opposition between the new dominant political and economic elite and the popular classes. At the heart of the problem is the question of the agents who would reconstruct society after independence: "scarcely anybody imagined that the reconstruction of society might lie in the hands of the mass of ordinary people; they had been cut off from their past and were incapable of devising a future". Ordinary people were thought to have lost capacity for political judgement and to be easily manipulable by their political leaders. The Mau Mau and the ordinary people in it could not restore the lost soul of a people and a nation. Only an elite, sure of itself could do so (Lonsdale, 1986:20). Interestingly, the early and young Ngugi shows the Mau Mau heroes as tragically flawed and the elders as too tradition bound. Only the young educated elite could lead others to the light.

WHOSE INTERESTS?

The debate over Mau Mau therefore is a debate not only on legitimacy but on whose interests are going to be served during the independence period. This is clear from the following statement by a historian professor Mwanzi (*Weekly Review*, 5 October, 1984:39). After accusing Ngugi of plagiarising, lacking philosophy or theory of society, being a very poor writer, and suffering intellectual poverty, he went on to say:

(Ngugi's) falsification of our history had become apparent. Ngugi had been a champion of well rehearsed orchestrated falsehoods. One of these had to do with what he regards as the place of Mau Mau in the history of this country, especially in relation to independence. The other has to do with the meaning of that independence. His views on these two issues were rejected by us at the conference. The reasons for this rejection were simple. One was summarised by Professor Ogot. In his words, the argument about Mau Mau as advanced by Ngugi is an argument about who should control who, or who should take the largest share of the national cake. In this way Ngugi and those he represents use Mau Mau as an instrument of tribal domination.

The intellectuals hostile to the Mau Mau thus make it appear as if they are speaking in the interest of the minority tribes against the hegemonic interests of the Kikuyu. But by invoking a tribal nationalism they wish to effect a horizontal alliance, making it appear as if everyone within a given ethnic group is a social equal—and equally a victim of the Kikuyus (or Kalenjins). This obscures the equally problematic vertical relationships between classes.

The historians take their argument further that the Mau Mau was not national; that Mau Mau was a break in the peaceful evolution towards independence. In other words, Mau Mau delayed the coming of independence instead of facilitating it. This argument goes against the now accepted understanding of what happened at decolonisation. Thus Hobsbawm (1994:221) argues that it was the weaknesses of Portugal's "uncompetitive, backward, politically isolated and marginalised metropolitan economy" which made it necessary to continue to exploit African resources through direct control: "However, Paris, London and Brussels (the Belgian Congo) decided that the voluntary grant of formal independence with economic and cultural dependence was preferable to lengthy struggles likely to end in independence under left wing regimes". Thus they pursued what Hobsbawm calls "prophylactic decolonization".

Significantly, South Africa and Southern Rhodesia which had substantial white-settler populations like Kenya, chose to go Portugal's way. The reasons why Kenya did not go the same way lie in the specific character of colonialism in Kenya and the struggles within the country since the 1920s. There is however, good reason to state that the Mau Mau (which Hobsbawm regards as "a substantial popular insurrection and guerrilla war") played a role in the course of events in Kenya. The fact that both Southern Rhodesia's (Zimbabwe's) and South Africa's decolonization was delayed till 1980 and 1994 respectively and until there were popular insurrections and guerrilla wars should warn us to reconsider Ogot's and Mwanzi's faith in peaceful negotiations in those colonies with a substantial number of white settlers.

Indeed the Kenyan settlers consistently struggled for self government (as in Southern Rhodesia and South Africa). It was only the struggles of African people against this that made the colonial office not grant this independence. In the mid-1950s colonial officials spoke of another generation of 20–25 years of colonial role in Kenya (Berman, 1990:377). Spencer (1983:98) also notes that in spite of the heightened crisis, the colonial situation in fact did not allow for the option for discussions. Till the onset of the Mau Mau the white population of Kenya did not know what was going on around them among the African population and they continued to believe that Kenya would be a 'white man's country' for generations to come and that conditions were indeed brightening. To them the Kenya Africans were an uneducated, quarrelling lot whom the Government could easily control. Berman (1990) and Spencer (1983) thus offer a good discussion on the limits of the politics of discussion and collaboration.

Furedi's (1989) study of the Mau Mau was to lead to a conclusion which links the Mau Mau and its past with the current crisis in land and identity in Kenya:

> Unlike subsequent political movements, it put into question the existing socio-economic structures of society. Despite its restricted regional constituency it provided the most extensive foundation for collective action and participation than had existed in Kenya hitherto. Subsequent nationalist parties like the Kenya African National Union, or the more populist Kenya People's Union, were formally more 'national' than Mau Mau. But these parties were essentially the restricted organizations of middle-class or capitalist politicians rather than movements for collective mobilization and action. The hunger for land and related concerns that provoked squatters to revolt are motives that still preoccupy millions in Kenya. But with a balance of classes, and in particular with the strengthening of the African capitalist class, such grievances have the character of purely local affairs. Consequently, at least for the time being, the landless and the rural and urban proletariat do not count as a political factor. The brief entry for these groups into the center of the

political stage in Kenya was the historical significance of Mau Mau. (Furedi, 1989:18)

Indeed what has been lacking in Kenyan history as in its politics is the people who are the essential constituents of the nation. These are denied a presence so as to legitimate the continued internal and international unequal relations.

However, the developments in Kenya in the 1970s, the arts were moving towards the nationally popular. This included a re-discovering of the popular character of the anti-colonial struggles and their informing heroism, hopes and values. Indeed at independence there is a felt need for official history to move towards this popular history for professional historians to "tell the stories the people dream of but cannot put words to" (Ranger, 1982:45). In any case, the expressions of popular cultures continue insisting on the presence of the people as historical subjects who have certain understandings about their relationships with history, with each other and with the state. These popular forms of expression are also chronicles that mediate popular experience and constitute a very important element in the circulation of ideas and formation of opinion outside the official and mainstream media and channels. The latter are, in fact, often interrogated by the popular discourses. In any case, people do have intellectual and artistic needs and in real life they continue, through their songs, stories and other forms of communication to tell themselves stories of who and what they think they are. At the artistic and aesthetic level, these constitute an imaginative popular vocabulary which provides a subjective aspect in the construction of identities.

CONCLUSIONS

The discussions on Kenya's political history in the 1970s and 1980s crystallised into two main views. There were those who agreed with Ngugi wa Thiong'o, and those who agreed with the prominent historians. They had different interpretations on two questions: Firstly, the question of the redistribution of resources, and secondly the place of the Mau Mau in Kenya's history.

Clearly the question of the redistribution of resources in Kenya and who is to do this and who is to be the beneficiary have been a major influence in politics, the writing of history, representations in the arts and in nation-building. What in fact the official approach has done is to create a myth of 'tribes' obscuring the fact noticed by Lonsdale (1986) and Berman (1990) that ethnic nationalism and Kenyan territorial nationalism are both creations of both the colonial state and the new literate middle classes who wished to use ethnic nationalism in the same way as the colonial state had done—as a means of controlling the ordinary people and the future of the country. A major concern among this group has been how to maintain the clientelist patronage system and the sources of their power and wealth.

However, as the ethnic killings in the 1990s and the current realities in Kenya show there is still great need for forging a Kenyan political community. This should involve both 1) political integration, which refers to the progressive bridging of the elite-mass gap on the vertical plane in the course of developing an integrated political process and a participant political community and, 2) territorial integration, which refers to the progressive reduction of cultural and regional tensions and discontinuities on the horizontal plane in the process of creating a homogeneous territorial political community (Coleman and Rosberg quoted in Sklar, 1967:2).

Official Kenya's error is the belief in creating a homogeneous culture from above. In any case there are only a very few countries in the world with a homogenised culture. There are those states which have been able to contain cultural diversity and those countries with potential or actual struggle (Tomlison, 1991:73–4). Instead of the tendency toward exclusions, nation-building is in fact the art of extending economic, political, cultural or symbolic boundaries and making diversity appear as a positive good not a basis for 'otherness'.

Further, the concept of 'nation' embodies the principle where government has legitimacy only if it is a form of national self-government, that is, a political expression of the nation. It is important that the new leaders must be able to establish themselves as symbols of the nation, and they should therefore espouse the democratic aspiration of those whom they lead and be ready to be "called to account by a people whose civic rights are grounded in a common culture and language of mutual responsibility" (Lonsdale 1986:20). This makes it necessary to understand struggles for independence such as the Mau Mau as a coming together of national and social struggles. It is of course here that the question of human rights and hence democracy becomes important. For the ordinary person's major wish is to be materially secure while also being human and enjoying guaranteed civic rights.

However, as the recent ethnic conflicts in Kenya have shown, the achievement of social justice and civic rights is difficult without, at the same time, the building of a sense of 'Kenyanness'. This crucially depends on a sense of a shared history, not on biological or even abstract cultural aspects, for as Lonsdale says: "in so far as (nations) exist at all and they are not entirely imaginary, they have been created by common history rather than a common lineage of descent...." (Lonsdale, 1986:19-20). Such a historical approach also entails deliberately turning the inherited geographical space into a social and cultural space within which the development of various cultural identities (including national identity) could take place.

The efforts to change the literature syllabus and to develop the arts in Kenya in the 1970s thus offer an example of how the creation of a national identity could be reconsidered in a context which includes the aspirations of Kenya's people for freedom, dignity and the right to belong to their own nation.

REFERENCES

Africa Watch (July, 1991), *Kenya: Taking Liberties*, Washington DC, Human Rights Watch.
Africa Watch (November, 1993), *Divide and Rule: State Sponsored Ethnic Violence in Kenya*, Washington DC, Human Rights Watch.
Alot, M. (1982), *People and Communication in Kenya*, Nairobi, Kenya Literature Bureau.
Amnesty International (July, 1987), *Torture, Political Detentions and Unfair Trials*, London, Amnesty International Secretariat.
Amnesty International (December, 1995), *Torture Compounded by the Lack of Medical Care*, London, Amnesty International Secretariat.
Anderson B. (1991), *Imagined Communities: Reflection on the Origin and Spread of Nationalism*, London, Verso.

Baldick C. (1983), *The Social Mission of English Criticism, 1848–1932*, Oxford, Clarendon Press.

Barkan, J.D. (1992), "The Rise and Fall of a Governance Realm in Kenya" in Göran Hydén and Michael Bratton (eds.), *Governance and Politics in Africa*, Lynne Rienner Publishers, Boulder & London.

Berman, B. (1990), *Control and Crisis in Colonial Kenya: The Dialectic of Domination*, London, James Currey.

Blundell, M. (1964), *So Rough a Wind*, London, Weidenfeld & Nicolson.

Björkman, I. (1989), *Mother Sing for Me: People's Theatre in Kenya*, London, Zed Press.

Burke P. (1993), *The Art of Conversation*, Cambridge, Polity Press.

Cabral, A. (1980), *Unity and Struggle: Speeches and Writings*, London, Heinemann.

Corfield F.D. (1960), *The Origins and Growth of Mau Mau: A Historical Survey*, Nairobi: Colony and Protectorate of Kenya: Sessional Paper No. 5 of 1959/60.

Cox R. (1965), *Kenyatta's Country*, London, Hutchinson.

Furedi, F. (1989), *The Mau Mau War in Perspective*, Nairobi, London and Athens, Heinemann, James Currey and Ohio University Press.

Gertzel, Cherry; Goldschmidt, Maure; Rothschild, Donald (1969), *Government and Politics in Kenya: A Nation-Building Text*, Nairobi, East African Publishing House.

Gramsci, A. (1985), *Selections from Cultural Writings*, London. Lawrence and Wishart.

Himbara, D. (1994), *Kenyan Capitalists, the State and Development*, Nairobi. East African Educational Publishers.

Hobsbawm, E.J. (1977), *The Age of Capital, 1848–1875*, Harmondsworth, Penguin.

Hobsbawm, E.J. (1994), *The Age of Extremes: The Short Twentieth Century, 1914–1991*, London, Abacus.

Lonsdale, J. (1986), "Mau Mau Through the Looking Glass", *Index on Censorship*, February 1986, Vol. 15 No. 2, pp. 19–22.

Lonsdale, J. and Berman B. (1992), *Unhappy Valley*, London, James Currey.

Mboya T. (1986), *Freedom and After*, London, Heinemann.

Mwanzi, H. (1984), "Men of Literature and Kenya's History" in *Weekly Review* (Nairobi), 5 October, 1984.

Ngugi wa Thiong'o, Owuor-Anyumba, Lo Liyong (1972), "On the Abolition of the English Department" in Ngugi wa Thiong'o, *Homecoming*, London, Heinemann.

Ngugi wa Thiong'o, (1981), *Detained: A Writer's Prison Diary*, London Heinemann.

Ngugi wa Thiong'o, (1986), *Decolonising the Mind*, Harare, Zimbabwe Publishing House.

Ogot B.A. (1977), "Introduction" and "Politics, Culture and Music in Central Kenya: A Study of Mau Mau Hymns, 1951–1956" in Ochieng, W. and Janmohammed, K. (eds.), *Kenya Historical Review (Special Issue: Some Perspectives on the Mau Mau Movement)*, Vol. 5 No. 2, 1977.

Ondinga, O. (1967), *Not Yet Uhuru*, London, Heinemann.

Phillipson, R. (1992), *Linguistic Imperialism*, Oxford, Oxford University Press.

Ranger, T. (1983), "Revolutions in the Wheel of Zimbabwean History", in *Moto Magazine*, December 1982/January 1993, Vol. 1, No. 8, pp. 41–45.

Sklar, R.L. (1967), "Political Science and National Integration—A Radical Approach", in *The Journal of Modern African Studies*, 5, 1, pp. 1–11.

Spencer, J. (1983), *James Beuttah: Freedom Fighter*, Nairobi, Stellascope.

Tomlison, J. (1991), *Cultural Imperialism*, London, Printer Publishers.

Wa Kinyatti, M. (ed.) (1987), *Kenya's Freedom Struggle: The Dedan Kimathi Papers*, London & New Jersey, Zed Books.

Weekly Review, Nairobi.

Young (1990), *White Mythologies and the West*, London, Routledge.

How the National Became Popular in Tanzania

Siri Lange

The leaders of any multicultural state face the challenge of constructing a cultural policy that can support their national project. This paper presents the cultural policy of the socialistic one-party state in Tanzania after independence. It discusses some of the unplanned results of the policy and suggests how these independent developments may indeed form a base from where the construction of national identity can take place in the present democratic society. One of the most significant unintended results is a growing inter-ethnic commercial popular culture. The paper draws on an MA dissertation submitted in 1994.[16] Fieldwork in Dar es Salaam was conducted in 1991, 1992 and 1995.

THE ONE-PARTY STATE AND THE QUEST FOR A NATIONAL CULTURE

When Tanzania (then Tanganyika) won her independence in 1962, President Julius Nyerere set out to create a genuinely African Socialism, the policy called *ujamaa*. This philosophy was based on the idea that the social system of Africa's traditional societies, "tribal socialism", could be brought up to a national level after independence. Not only the social system, but also the performing arts of the traditional societies were to be transformed for national purposes. A national culture, built on elements from tribal expressive arts, was to help Tanzanians to develop the same kind of identification with the nation as they supposedly had with their tribal homelands. The cultural policy

---

16. Lange, 1995.

was also part of a *cultural decolonization*, as expressed by Nyerere when he informed the parliament that he had set up a new ministry; the Ministry of National Culture and Youth:

> Of all the crimes of colonialism there is none worse than the attempt to make us believe we had no indigenous culture of our own, or that what we had was worthless (...). I have set up this new ministry to help us regain our pride in our own culture. I want it to seek the best traditions and customs of all our tribes and make them part of our national culture.[17]

The Tanzanian leaders wanted to seek back to their own roots, to create a national culture that was theirs, but at the same time, the tradition to be created should also be complimentary to the western tradition; different, but of the same worth. This meant that certain traditions did not fit in. "Primitive" traditions like body tattooing were actively discouraged by the government,[18] and great pressure was put on pastoralists to change their ways of living and dressing, in order to make them part of modern, agricultural society. In 1966, the Regional Commissioner simply banned the Masai initiation of young men to warrior status.[19] The rational argument for this law was to put an end to the warriors' raiding of their neighbours' cattle.

The same Commissioner, however, also initiated "a campaign against the Masai and Waarusha habit of daubing themselves with red ochre", as well as "forbidding them to walk about naked, or even wearing their customary simple shuka", habits that could not be said to hurt their neighbours.[20] What it did hurt, was the self-respect and pride of the leaders of the state, men who wished to see Tanzania as a modern state in the company of equals in the international community. The Nationalist, in its support of the new laws, stated: "The primitive image of East Africa will no longer exist" expressing precisely this wish to communicate equality with the "civilised" states.

Marriot, in his article "Cultural policy in the new states" discusses the dilemmas new nations face when seeking their own identity:

> As the recent historic pasts of nearly all new states are troubled, the cloudier glories apparent through ancient history, archaeology, or

---

17. Nyerere, 1967:186–7.
18. Mbughuni, 1974:55.
19. *The Standard*, 30 November 1966.
20. *The Nationalist*, 20 November 1967.

mythology are everywhere preferred. Where these vistas are not open, as more commonly in the states of younger civilisation, then attachment to the future itself regularly becomes the main orientation in time.[21]

And this is exactly what happened in Tanzania. Tanzanians had no great tradition from which to create their national culture. There was little to build on from the past, with the approximately 120 ethnic groups each having their own histories and myths, traditions and heroes. None of them were substantially larger than the others, and there was no attempt by the Tanzanian authorities to re-define "tribal histories" to be the history of the nation. It was the *political system* itself which came to constitute the main base of the national culture. A tight bond was formed between the Party and the nation by use of rhetoric and symbols. The Ujamaa policy was a new-born tradition, but it had the qualities the authorities had been looking for: it cut across ethnic lines, it was unique for Tanzania, and it was attracting attention and recognition in the world community. It was highly modernistic, presenting a picture of a glorious future with African socialism, and yet it still had an element of nostalgia, claiming to build on a pre-colonial tradition of egalitarian villages.

The socialist political system was declared the very basis of the culture (in a similar way as in China and the USSR), to such a degree that the concepts of politics, ethics and morality became almost synonymous. In contrast to this, most European countries had emphasised religion in their nation-building rhetoric. The reason why Tanzania did not do so, was not dogmatic Marxism on the part of the leaders, many of whom were fervid believers, but the lack of one single religion. The use of literature in the struggle for national integration was similarly hindered by the fact that the Swahili poetry had a strong Islamic content.[22]

Many of the local traditions were inapplicable to the creation of a national culture, but ironically enough, some quite foreign elements seemed less problematic. To help Tanzania develop its performing arts, the People's Republic of China invited 20 boys and girls to train in acrobatics in 1965. The youths returned after four years with Chinese kites and baskets, adding a new and lasting touch to the Tan-

---

21. Marriot, 1963:55.
22. Westerlund, 1980.

zanian national culture. That these new elements came from China, and not from the West, was probably an important precondition. It was the former colonial powers which were the "significant others" whom it was important to create a distance from.

POLITICAL USE OF TRADITIONAL PERFORMANCE

Not only acrobatics were borrowed from China, but also the notion of "Cultural Revolution". All works of arts were to support the revolution. Traditional dances were seen as an especially potent way of enlightening the people, since most dances included songs and many of the local cultures had a rich tradition of using dance-songs as a major means of communication. Moreover, traditional dances were readily at hand for fulfilling Nyerere's vision of taking the best from all the tribes and making it part of the national culture. The newspapers supported him in the task: "(N)o ngoma should belong to one tribe. What are called tribal dances now should be transformed into national ngomas".[23]

During the first ten years of independence, dance troupes performing "traditional" national dances were established at all schools and in many other statal institutions and factories. The traditional songs in local languages were replaced by new lyrics in Swahili propagating the ujamaa-policies as well as praising the political leaders:

Mwalimu Nyerere alisema	The teacher Nyerere said
Tushike jembe	Let us take the hoe
tulime mashamba	and work on the fields

Habu gamba Nyerere	Nyerere said
habu gamba	he said
Tukajiunge mashamba ya ujamaa	Let us work together on ujamaa fields

The political use of the performing arts was ideally meant to educate the people, many of whom were illiterate. Most songs with a political

---

23. *The Nationalist*, 10 November 1967.

content, however, turned out to be pure propaganda songs for the Party and its leaders, like the one below:

Chama chama	Party Party
Chama chama chama	Party Party Party
Baba Nyerere	Father Nyerere
Watanzania tunafurahi	We Tanzanians are happy

Both songs were collected among cultural troupes in Dar es Salaam in 1992. Whereas the old songs often used figurative language, were humorous and had a narrative structure[24] the new ones were less poetic. The role of the new songs was not so much to entertain or give aesthetic pleasure, as to help build socialism. The political songs propagate the government policies with a minimum of literary techniques. They are easy to understand for anyone who knows Swahili. The traditional songs, in contrast, can often be fully appreciated only by the members of that specific ethnic group or locality. This is not only due to the use of local languages. Such songs often build on oral literature like proverbs and local myths, and a full understanding presupposes familiarity with this literature.

In other cases the songs do not have their themes from specific oral literature, but figurative language is used to communicate words of wisdom. This is the case in the Sindimba dance song below by a non-commercial group in Mtwara. The song is in the Makonde language.

Mumba woo	That spear
Uyahike ngongolo	You have lost it
Nancheta akamwi ng'uku paluvla	The fox has caught a chicken
watepanawe	in the courtyard
Kwiyo, kwiyo, kwiyo, kwiyo	Kwiyo, kwiyo, kwiyo, kwiyo
Watepanawe	In the courtyard

The first stanza is a way of telling people that "You don't always get what you want". In the second, the fox is used as a metaphor for people who have a habit of doing bad and evil things, like stealing.

---

24. Songoyi, 1990:23.

Other songs use subtle language to hide from children their real meaning. An example is the final stanza of a Lingokwa dance song, also in the Makonde language:

Namkogoya akule kwetu	In the swing over there at our
akule anyoke	place
Nyapule aliulele mwene	Nyapule hurt herself
kupweteka nanga	but she doesn't feel the pain
Akule kwetu akula	Over there at our place

The swing is here a metaphor for having sex. That the girl was hurt indicates that she had been a virgin. A song like this is compatible with the erotic movements of the dance. In most cases, however, the erotic dances were accompanied by political songs so that song and movement expressed completely different things: they were no longer an integrated whole.

STATE CONTROL, AND THE FAILURE OF DANCE AS A NATIONAL SYMBOL

Traditionally, *ngoma* songs (ngoma denoting the musical event as a whole) have commonly been used for social critique and local gossip, something which made people at all levels think twice before they broke social taboos. Political criticism is absent from the modern ngoma songs. Why are the songs silent on controversial political issues? The fate of the Sukuma singer Kalikali may shed light on this situation. In 1964, three years after Independence, he composed a song called "Slavery has not ended":

Ukwitawala	We have really got
twitawalile	Independence
A bana Tanganyika	The people of Tanganyika
Nghana twitawalile	Truly we are independent
Bakulumbaga	They are giving thanks to
witawaji	independence
Abo bali na milimo mitale	The ones with big jobs
Abo balipandika magana	The ones who earn hundreds
Buli ng'weji buli ng'weji	Month after month

Al'abalimi ba buluba	But the growers of cotton
Nduhw' iyakupandika	Have nothing to gain
Litingag' ili busese	Slavery has not ended
Ililima lyingile	As the planting season comes
Tubyulima buluba	The price falls
Buguji bushike	Son of Mbagule
Guchel' umpango	We are fattening other people
Tuliginya sumba	They are really eating
Ng'wana Mbagule	Looking at watches is their
Ming'wana gakwigutaga	only job
Kulola ha sa kwesa	And blowing their noses
Na kumigija mu shitambala	With handkerchiefs

(Songoyi, 1990:57–58)

After this song, Kalikali was given a warning by the local and district leaders, but he continued to compose critical songs and he was finally arrested and detained. After two months, he was released by an order from the President. The detention proved an effective way of silencing Kalikali's criticism. After his release, he changed the content of his songs, making them compatible with the Party ideology, in the idiom of praise-singing. In 1979 he was awarded a radio from the party leaders as a sign of appreciation of his songs.

According to Songoyi, the experiences of Kalikali are typical of what other singers have experienced in Tanzania.[25] It is therefore scarcely surprising that political criticism should be absent from the songs of the dance groups. They employ self-censorship on controversial matters, and praise the Party and its leaders in order to win goodwill. The role of the government run Radio Tanzania as a gatekeeper for the distribution of music in the country should also be mentioned. Up to 1993 there had been no private or independent radio-stations in the country, no TV broadcasting on the mainland and hardly any recording studios outside Radio Tanzania. The Muungano Cultural Troupe has had three ngoma-songs on the radio. Two of those three were praise-songs.

The new political songs were meaningful to people as long as they believed in the message; but when they realised that the Ujamaa pol-

---

25. Songoyi, 1990:11.

icy did not bring the promised wonders, the songs appeared to many people as empty phrases. Although the national culture was to be representative for the whole nation, it soon turned out that many of the nationalised dances came from the same area. At the National College of Arts in Bagamoyo, 10 out of 20 dances are from the southern zone, one of the six geographical zones of the country. The other zones are represented by one, two or three dances each.

The north, represented by the Chagga (and Haya), and the south, represented by the Makonde, can be seen as two opposite poles in the country. The south is a stigmatised area, an "undeveloped" place which people from other regions shun.[26] Due to early establishment of mission schools, and early incorporation into the capitalist economy, people from the north are strongly over-represented among the educated elite,[27] and to many of them, traditional dance represents remnants from a primitive life. This was one reason why Nyerere's vision of a cultural revolution, a cultural revival involving national pride in traditional dance, could not succeed. The southern dances *entertain* people, but as long as they represent a stigmatised area, and are seen as basically indecent by many, they cannot function as a symbol of national pride—least of all for members of the upper classes.

In countries where the creation of a national culture was more successful than in Tanzania, like in some of the European nations in the late 18th century, the reified culture may not have been any more representative than in the Tanzanian case, but the nation-builders in these countries were more lucky in their choice of symbols. They managed to find symbols that a majority of the population could identify with, often by a process where the symbols first were adopted by the elite and later embraced by the common people as well.[28]

---

26. *Daily News*, 11 June 1992; *Sunday News*, 31 May 1992.
27. Hetland, 1988.
28. Berggreen, 1994 [1989].

FROM NATION-BUILDING TO POPULAR CULTURE

The venture of establishing a genuine socialistic cultural policy to a large degree failed, but the policy triggered a development in the field of performance which went far beyond the intentions of the nation-builders. In the early 1980s, commercial, multi-ethnic cultural troupes grew up in the country, entertaining the low-income masses of the cities with shows including acrobatics, nationalised traditional dance, as well as a genuinely new and syncretistic cultural form; popular theatre.

The commercial troupes were modelled on the cultural troupes established by the government. In addition to the National Troupe, there were in the 1960s and 70s cultural groups at most state-owned companies. The groups encouraged the spirit of community, and promoted the company. The dancers and musicians were workers at the company, their performances were mostly free, and they represented their region in national competitions etc. In Dar es Salaam however, the companies started assuming patronage over troupes of full-time artists who were performing commercially at the same time as they were advertising the company. The troupes were sometimes transferred from one company to another, and it did not take long before groups were formed independently of any institution, being run on a purely businesslike basis.[29] The groups were inter-ethnic, but predominated by artists from the southern part of the country.

The political songs had become a convention of the genre, and the commercial cultural groups composed the same type of propaganda songs as did the national troupes, despite the fact that many of the artists felt quite indifferent about the Party. Lihamba explains the situation in this way:

> Since the Arusha Declaration some of the cultural groups have been actively used by national and regional politicians to display "Tanzanian Culture" in a manner which the groups have expressed as amounting to "political exploitation". (...) They felt that they had to obey the politicians' orders because of fear of repercussions if they did not comply. Continued political favour was seen as necessary for their survival.[30]

---

29. Songoyi, 1988:31 [1983].
30. Lihamba, 1985.

Songoyi, in his thesis "Commercialisation, its impact on traditional dances" has the following to say about the political songs: "There is nobody among the audience who wants (needs) to hear what a dance song is saying. To most people, movement is all that matters". [31] The movements which entertain multi-ethnic audiences the most are the erotic ones. The result is that the cultural groups are even more biased to dances from the south than are the national troupes, as this is an area where these movements are especially developed. Many of the dances are traditionally performed at special occasions only, such as during initiations, and by groups of single-sex dancers. In their attempts at drawing large audiences however, the commercial cultural troupes outdo each other in extending the limits of common decency.

By 1984, only three years after the first commercial troupe was established, there were more than 40 cultural troupes in Dar es Salaam.[32] The groups usually have a contract with the social halls or bars to perform on a certain day every week. The groups thus rely on the income from the tickets at the door, while the owner of the hall benefits from the increased sale of beer and soft-drinks. Over the years, many groups have been disbanded due to lack of economic viability, but the relative success of this new genre was due to the fact that such troupes met an unsatisfied need for entertainment in the city.

Urban life, characterised by a distinction between work and leisure, had created a market for entertainment, but up to 1980 there had been few options for Dar es Salaam dwellers in this respect. There was at the time no television broadcasting on the Tanzanian mainland (the first TV station was established as late as 1994), and the films which were shown at the cinemas were either European or Indian. Theatre performances were rare and usually staged at the university campus outside town, while the dance-nights in clubs and bars were too expensive for most people and not suitable for children or single women.

---

31. Songoyi, 1988:31 [1983].
32. Lihamba, 1991:274.

Some communities, like the Makonde, had and still have a rich and entertaining ritual life in their urban "villages",[33] but for the large majority the traditional performances were something which they had left behind in the rural areas. There was thus a market for commercial performing arts, and the commercial groups tailored their performances to the rhythms of urban life, performing at neighbourhood social halls in the break between housework or wage labour ending at around 3.30 and the evening meal at around 8 pm.[34]

POPULAR THEATRE AND ITS RELATIONSHIP TO TRADITIONAL PERFORMANCE

To start with, the commercial groups were *ngoma* troupes, performing dance only. It did not take long, however, before one of the groups introduced five-minute plays, *vichekesho* (the things that make one laugh) to give the dancers time to change costumes. This genre had evolved over several years, inspired by the Western drama introduced to East African schools as early as the 1920s, and by American comedy films popular in the 1940s and 1950s. Mlama writes about these plays:

> The Vichekesho share some characteristics with Italian Comedia Dell'arte. They make use of satire, irony, ridicule and the comic sense to comment on certain aspects of life and often to make the audience laugh and ridicule evil. Although they provoke laughter they are often very serious comments on incorrect and unacceptable behaviour.[35]

The plays proved popular, and the other groups soon followed the example of the inventive troupe.[36] During their first decade of existence, the groups have developed their shows into a four-hour long performance consisting of four different art genres: ngoma, taarab, acrobatics (*sarakasi*) and theatre. The theatre plays are called *maigizo* (sing. *igizo*), and differ from the *vichekesho* genre in being much longer. They usually last for about an hour. In other respects, the plays have kept the central characteristics of the *vichekesho*. They are farce-like plays depicting and discussing the social realities of urban life, com-

---
33. Johansen, 1996.
34. Plane, 1996.
35. Mlama, 1983.
36. Plane, 1996.

monly with a clear moralistic message. The theatre gives the audience the feeling that what they see on stage is in fact their *own life*, in a dramatised, exaggerated version.

Thematically the plays cover problems like poverty, teenage-pregnancy and the changing family relations following modernisation and urbanisation. Rural-urban migration, and the problems one may encounter in the city are a common theme. As part of my study, I interviewed 104 persons who were attending cultural shows. 73 of them stated that they came from various up-country regions, and 70 had had their primary education in another place than Dar es Salaam.

Gender antagonism is commonly featured, often coupled with the conflict between in-laws and blood-relatives. Typically, a male protagonist's wife does not want her husband to share his resources with a poor relative coming from up-country. She will break all kinds of taboos in order to get her will through, and she destroys the relationship between her husband and his kin. The drama form gives the onlookers an emotional experience of the social values of their society by showing what it would be like if the rules were broken.

Through theatre, social problems are brought up that may otherwise be hard to talk about. Victor Turner holds that theatre and other cultural genres are developments which societies will produce as they grow in scale and complexity. He argues that there is a close resemblance between rituals in traditional societies and theatre in modern societies.[37] Traditional and modern performance have in common that they deal with problematic sides of the society in a time (and often place) which is clearly distinguished from "normal" time. This frame opens up for reflexivity; "the capacity of human beings to distance themselves from their own subjective experiences, to stand apart from and to comment upon them".[38]

When comparing written sources about the various forms of traditional performance in Tanzania with the urban popular theatre, I found striking similarities, both in form and content. Mlama, writing about the Kaguru,[39] Haram, studying the Meru,[40] and Johansen who

---

37. Turner, 1982, 1985.
38. MacAloon, 1984:11.
39. Mlama, 1981.
40. Haram, 1992.

works with the Makonde, all describe how traditional performance has theatrical and didactic aspects. When young Makonde girls go through their initiation, older women perform mimical plays for them. Among other things, the girls are warned not to be dazzled by seemingly rich suitors, who may well turn out to be poor and in bad health.[41] A play with the very same message was staged by one of the cultural troupes in 1992. Also the need to avoid unwanted pregnancies, and the idea that in-married women are treacherous, are themes that traditional performance and popular theatre have in common.

THE MEANING OF CULTURAL PERFORMANCE

When the government decided to revitalise traditional performance after independence, they concentrated on traditional dances. One reason for this, as already mentioned, is that the dances were readily at hand for fulfilling Nyerere's vision of taking the best from all tribes and making it part of the national culture. Another reason for choosing dance, and not drama, which is also part of traditional performance, may be the fact that dance would fit well into the international convention of "folklore".

Folklore troupes are used the world over to welcome foreign guests, as well as to entertain at public holidays and feasts. As discussed earlier, the Tanzanian leaders were eager to seek back to their own roots, to create a national culture that was *theirs*; but at the same time, they wanted something which could be acknowledged as complementary to the Western tradition. The concept "complementarization", meaning that phenomena from different cultures are acknowledged as different, but of the same worth, was introduced by Eidheim who studied the stigmatized Sami (so-called "Lappish") people of Norway in the early 1960s. Eidheim demonstrated how Sami leaders, as part of their strategy to achieve equality between Sami and Norwegians, re-codified aspects of their culture to make it more comparable to the values of Norwegian culture.[42]

---

41. Johansen, forthcoming.
42. Eidheim, 1987 [1977].

One of the dances to be nationalised in Tanzania was Ukala, a dance of the Zigua people of Tanga region. Maguluko writes that traditionally, this dance "is performed annually to appease the spirits". It may also be performed "if a member of the community falls sick with an undiagnosed disease, or other abnormalities".[43] In its nationalised form, however, Ukala does not relate to "abnormalities" or conflicts in the society. It is performed at any random time by national or commercial troupes to entertain a (paying) audience. When the commercial groups address conflicts of today's urban society, they do this through the performances of theatre plays, not by traditional dances.

During fieldwork, I found that theatre was more popular than the dance genre. People told me that they preferred theatre because they learned something from the plays. What they learn is the central moral codes of their society, and the popular theatre in this respect carries on a central element from traditional performance. Coplan writes that "common experience and perceptions based upon shared values and understandings provide the context within which any performance becomes aesthetically, emotionally, and socially meaningful".[44] The theatre plays are meaningful to the multi-ethnic urban audience exactly because they relate to what these people have in common, regardless of ethnic and religious background.

The dances never lost their ethnic affiliation despite active nationalisation efforts, and during interviews I found that most members of the audience preferred a dance of their own ethnic group. Dance as entertainment was unable to fulfil the reflexive role that theatre later did because it was forced into a convention of political praise. Frederick Cooper, suggests that people in Africa may "develop cultural alternatives to the sterility of officially sponsored hymns to the glories of traditional African society".[45] This is an interesting perspective for understanding the development of popular theatre in Dar es Salaam. In contrast to the dance songs, there is no political propaganda in the theatre plays, and no attempt to make the plays appear "traditional". Its very nature is syncretistic, incorporating freely ele-

---

43. Maguluko, 1991:49.
44. Coplan, 1986:156.
45. Quoted in Barber, 1987.

ments from Western and Indian movies; it seems indeed to be open to anything that increases its popular appeal.

Barber says about popular culture in Africa that it is recognised by just this syncretism, and that some see this as "a deplorable corruption of the authentic culture".[46] Traditional dance, even its commercialised form, is seen as more "authentic" and African than popular theatre by the general Tanzanian public. I shared this view, before going deeper into the material. Now, however, I would argue that the dances taken out of their original context constitute a new and modern performative genre just as the popular theatre does, and that neither is more *traditional* than the other.

Ngoma, the traditional musical event including music, dance and mime in an integrated whole, has in the modern sphere crystallised into various performative genres. In the true nature of popular culture, the new cultural fields will continue to develop in the years to come. Soon after the first TV broadcasts were started in mainland Tanzania in 1994, the popular theatre was screened as locally produced "soaps" reaching new audiences in addition to the live performances in bars. The locally produced soaps are far more popular than the imported ones.[47] One obvious reason is that few among the ordinary people speak English (the local soaps are all in Swahili), but just as important is the fact that the locally produced soaps relate to the lived reality of the people who watch them.

The commercial popular culture in present day Dar es Salaam is an unplanned result of the socialistic cultural policy of the one-party state after independence. There are reasons to believe that this independent, unofficial culture indeed has the potential for working for the good of nation-building, albeit at a different level than Nyerere and his cultural planners envisaged.

DEMOCRACY—AND A NEW FORM OF NATIONALISM?

Up to 1992, CCM was the only legal party in Tanzania. The first democratic election took place in 1995, CCM remaining in power. A

---

46. Barber, 1987:10.
47. *New African*, February 1996.

friend of mine had this to say about the democratisation process: "It is not easy. It is like walking in the darkness". She was 32 years old, born at the time of Independence, and had grown up with ujamaa. Other informants expressed fears that Tanzania now would face problems of ethnic revitalisation and national disintegration, like they had seen in several of their neighbouring countries.

With the era of multi-partyism, one of the most difficult tasks is to untangle, both practically, and in people's minds, the link which was so carefully forged between the Party and the national symbols during the first years after Independence. The concept of Ujamaa replaced *Uhuru* (freedom) as the uniting power and symbol, and a tight bond was formed between the Party and the nation by use of rhetoric and symbols. This is reflected in an atlas for use in schools, published as late as 1987.[48] The first page has the title: "Our Country Tanzania" (*Nchi Yetu Tanzania*). The very first symbol presented is the flag of the CCM party. Under it, the Tanzanian national flag and the national emblem are presented side by side. The principal symbol of the national emblem is a burning torch, symbolising hope and unity. Every year since Independence a burning torch has been raced around the country by the Party's youth organisation.

In 1992, the Party's youth organisation handed the Uhuru Torch Race over to the government, as a neutral institution.[49] Several of the National Days that have been connected to the Party, have been reconsidered. 5 February, for instance—the "birthday" of the CCM party, which is also the day of the Arusha Declaration, is no longer celebrated as a national holiday. The artists of the cultural troupes have composed new songs to go with their dances. They are no longer supposed to support the CCM party and its leaders trough their art.

What are Tanzanians to build their new nationalism on? Luckily enough, the Tanzanian nation has indeed consolidated during the past thirty years. The question is whether Tanzania really needs the kind of nationalism that the leaders attempted to construct after Independence. Eriksen suggests that nationalism is a dual phenomenon, with formal nationalism connected to the demands of the modern

---

48. Wizara ya Elimu, 1987.
49. *Daily News*, 25 August 1992.

nation state on the one hand, and the informal nationalism in civil society on the other.

Formal nationalism is connected to "national symbols and practices associated with the state, such as the flag, the national anthem and the national mottos". Informal nationalism on the other hand, which Eriksen exemplifies as religious festivals, carnivals and international sports events, is different from the formal nationalism, "which is far removed from the constitution of individual identity in everyday life, and which therefore does little to mitigate the potentially disintegrating effects of ethnicity". He continues by stating that "informally constituted cultural institutions have firm roots in the immediate experiences of people, and can therefore more easily contribute to the production of shared meanings".[50]

It may thus be, that the by-product of the Tanzanian cultural policy, the unofficial commercial popular culture, plays a more important role in nation-building than anyone has imagined. Political leaders and the educated elite have dismissed it on the ground that it has been "motivated by survival instincts and financial gains rather than professionalism in their work".[51] But just the fact that their goal is to attract as many customers as possible, regardless of background, makes the popular theatre troupes underplay ethnic and religious differences while elaborating on problems that the urbanites have in common. Musicians too, like Remmy Ongala, articulate sentiments that may seem threatening to the political leaders, but which at the same time offer Tanzanians new shared metaphors which they may use to communicate about their lived experience. One example is Ongala's 1994 hit *Kilio cha samaki*. The song describes in figurative language how the suppressed masses are exploited by the leaders and the then governing party CCM. When "Remmy" performed this song at a football stadium with the president and vice-president present, onlookers in their thousands responded by cheering him.[52]

It remains for further investigation to empirically scrutinise the degree to which ethnically and religiously neutral popular culture indeed represents common references which in an indirect and per-

---

50. Eriksen, 1993:10–11.
51. Lihamba, 1991:274.
52 *New African*, May 1994.

haps unconscious way may help Tanzanians to develop their feeling of oneness at a time when the once unbreakable link between the one-party state and the nation no longer exists, and conflicts centred around ethnic revitalisation and religious polarization seem to be on the increase.

REFERENCES

Articles and books

Barber, Karin. 1987. "Popular Arts in Africa", in *African Studies Review*, Vol. 30, No. 3.
Coplan, David B. 1986. "Ideology and tradition in South African black popular theatre", in *Journal of American Folklore*.
Berggreen, Brit. 1994 [1989]. *Da kulturen kom til Norge.* Oslo: Aschehoug.
Eidheim, Harald. 1987 [1977]. *Aspects of the Lappish minority situation.* Oslo: University of Oslo, Oslo Occasional Papers in Social Anthropology, No. 14.
Eriksen, Thomas Hylland. 1993. "Formal and informal nationalism", in *Ethnic and Racial Studies*, Vol. 16, No. 1.
Haram, Liv. 1992. "Sexual behaviour and gender relations among the Meru peasants of northern Tanzania: The case of a ceremonial dance with three scenes depicting love-play, birth and care of the newborn child". Working paper, Department of Social Anthropology, University of Bergen.
Hetland, Atle. 1988. *Survey of institutional and individual academic links.* Working document, NORAD, Dar es Salaam.
Johansen, R. Elise B. 1996. "Kunnskapsforvaltning og makt i et kjønnsperspektiv" in *Norsk antropologisk tidsskrift*, No. 3, 1996.
Johansen, R. Elise B. Forthcoming. *The secrecy of sexuality: Female initiation rituals among the Makonde.* Department of Social Anthropology, University of Oslo.
Lange, Siri. 1995. *From nation-building to popular culture: The modernization of performance in Tanzania.* Bergen: Chr. Michelsen Institute (Report 1995:1).
Lihamba, Amandina. 1985. *Politics and theatre in Tanzania after the Arusha Declaration 1967–1984.* Ph.D. dissertation, University of Leeds.
Lihamba, Amandina. 1991. "The Role of Culture", in J. Hartman (ed.) *Rethinking the Arusha Declaration.* Copenhagen: Centre for Development Research.
MacAloon, John J. (ed.). 1984. *Rite, drama, festival, spectacle: Rehearsals toward a theory of cultural performance.* Philadelphia: Institute for the Study of Human Issues.
Maguluko, Frank R. C. 1991. *Continuity and change in traditional dances: A case study of Mdumange and Ukala dance.* B.A. thesis, Department of Arts, Music and Theatre, University of Dar es Salaam.

Marriot, McKim. 1963. Cultural policy in the new states, in Geertz (ed.) *Old societies and new states*. New York: Free Press.

Mbughuni, L.A. 1974. *The cultural policy of the United Republic of Tanzania*. Paris: Unesco Press.

Mlama, Penina M. 1981. Digubi: A Tanzanian indigenous theatre form, in *The Drama Review*, Vol. 25, No. 4.

Mlama, Penina M. 1983. *Tanzanian traditional theatre as a pedagogical institution: The Kaguru theatre as a case study*. Ph.D. dissertation, University of Dar es Salaam.

Nyerere, Julius. 1967. *Freedom and unity*. London: Oxford University Press.

Plane, Mark William. 1996. *Fusing Oral and Literary Practices: Contemporary Popular Theatre in Dar es Salaam*. Ph.D. dissertation, University of Wisconsin, Madison.

Songoyi, Elias M. 1988 [1983]. *Commercialization, its impact on traditional dances*. B.A. thesis, University of Dar es Salaam. Published by Rådet for folkemusikk og folkedans, University of Trondheim.

Songoyi, Elias M. 1990. *The Artist and the State in Tanzania*. M.A. thesis, University of Dar es Salaam.

Turner, Victor. 1982. *From ritual to theatre: The human seriousness of play*. New York: Performing Arts Journal Publications.

Turner, Victor. 1985. *On the edge of the bush: Anthropology as experience*. Tuscon: University of Arizona Press.

Westerlund, David. 1980. "Traditional African cultures and national culture in Tanzania", in *Antropologiska studier*, Vol. 29.

Wizara ya Elimu Tanzania. 1987. *Atlasi kwa shule za msingi Tanzania*. Macmillan.

Periodicals

"Ministry posts 11 doctors south", *Daily News* (Dar es Salaam), 11 June 1992.

"Vijana wants government to oversee torch race", *Daily News* (Dar es Salaam), 25 August 1992.

"National ngomas", *The Nationalist* (Dar es Salaam), 10 November 1967.

"The Masai", *The Nationalist* (Dar es Salaam), 20 November 1967.

"Remmy Ongala", *New African* May 1994.

"Rise of the African soap opera", *New African*, February 1996.

"No more initiations for Masai moran", *The Standard* (Dar es Salaam), 30 November 1966.

"Working in the South", *Sunday News* (Dar es Salaam), 31 May 1992.

The National Landscape—a Cultural European Invention

Svend Erik Larsen

THROUGH THE PARK

Nadine Gordimer's short story "The Ultimate Safari" (1991) is told from a child's perspective: what he sees, what he is able to understand, what he is able to put into words. His village in Mozambique is being threatened by war and his family and 200 other villagers try to escape. After a strenuous tour led by a local guide they arrive at another village where people speak the same language, and they settle down—as refugees and in tents, but this is better than war.

The shortest way to safety runs through the Kruger Park. The boy does not know when he is in or is out of the park or why it is something specific. He is simply crossing a familiar landscape with its plants, rivers and animals. Dangerous maybe, but known. "[...] it was like the bush we'd been walking through all day [...] I didn't know we were away" (Gordimer, 1994:145, 151). In the new village he cannot help being "surprised to find they speak our language; [...] That's why they allow us to stay on their land. Long ago, in the time of our fathers, there was no fence that kills you, there was no Kruger Park between them and us, we were the same people under our own king, right from our village we left to this place we've come to" (ibid.:151).

He knows, however, that the Kruger Park *is* something special: The real dangers are not only the animals, but fences, police, wardens and laws forbidding you simply to trespass or find food on the terrain. From fear of being captured his group has not even time to wait for his grandfather who disappears in the dark. The park, he notices, is made for white people, and that some of his folks "used to leave home to work in the places where white people came to stay and look at the animals" (ibid.:145).

He does not understand why it is so, but he registers that the Kruger Park *does* something to his people and himself. It separates people of the same language; it turns his land into a white people's place and, most notably, it changes their own position: although their "country is a country of people, not animals" they have to "move like animals among animals" (ibid.:145, 146). In their new village "Some white people came to take photographs of our people living in the tent—they said they were making a film." (ibid.:152). They are but animals among animals, inborn elements of a wild landscape, or they stand out as objects of entertainment or of foreign people's political agenda. When they cross the park they are forever displaced—"There is nothing. No home" is the grandmother's final words to the white film crew (ibid.:153). The park is not just a slice of land, but a decisive physical and cultural barrier.

This conclusion is far beyond the boy's capacity to make his insights explicit. But in a motto to the story, the heading of a newspaper advertisement Gordimer gives us a key to reading his quasi-innocent discourse. It also contains the title of her short story and runs as follows: "The African adventure lives on ... you can do it! The ultimate safari or expedition with leaders who know Africa. (Travel advertisement, *Observer*, 27 November 1988)" (Gordimer, 1994:143). This short description, addressed to white tourists, covers also, ironically, the boy's experience of his ultimate safari. Thereby the text acquires a double structure that allows us to see its critical dimension. The boy's only vague perception of what is going on behind the surface is contrasted to the heading's reference to the organized disneyfication of the wild landscape that turns it into a profitable tourist industry, displacing local people or reducing them to props in the scenery of wilderness.

In his analysis of conservation policies in Africa, especially in Kenya, Roderick Neumann quotes British park authorities: parks are supposed "to be reserved as natural habits both for game and human beings in their primitive state", say British Park authorities in 1955 trying to prove the reality of the European dream of a pristine Eden (quote from Neumann, 1995:160). Neumann also explains how there is a contradiction in the eradication of traditional land use practices (especially use of fire) which are prohibited inside the park, and supported outside by "the government's development schemes", a contradiction that became detrimental to nomadic people like the Masai who had to constantly cross the new boundary, ironically widening "the symbolic and ecological gap between the landscapes of production and consumption" (ibid.:161). With the term 'ironic' Neumann both grasps the actual conflict in relation to the landscape and the subjective experience of it, the latter aspect being developed more subtly in the story stressing the problem of identity and belonging.

Thus, between the advertisement serving as motto and the boy's story there is the real landscape with people, parks, animals, tourists, wildlife conservationists, bandits, villages etc., a complex sign of this relation between physical surroundings and cultural identity and of the interwoven levels of consciousness, rendered to us through the ironical twists of the story. The landscape becomes in fact the main character, emphasized at the end when the boy, now 11 years old, hears his grandmother remark that they will never have a home. He decides to go back to his home, maybe his lost mother and grandfather will be there. With the landscape as its medium the text lays open the ambiguities in what it is and what it takes to belong to a place, a theme that on a larger scale is essential in nation-building.

The story was written during the new nation-building period of South Africa, but it reflects, through specific historical conditions, a universally important relationship between landscape and cultural identity. It seems a valid enterprise to redefine the landscape stripped bare of its layers of dispossessing colonization and domestic repression and redefine its meaning in support of the unity of the new nation. The identity of people, of nature and of democracy should be seen as interchangeable identities, a dream reflected in the natural metaphor of the Rainbow State.

Such an attempt, easily justifiable as it may seem, has a history that is far from innocent. It is mainly the history of the European nation states. The actual borderlines between African states replicate by and large the boundaries between the major European nation states; the imported democratic ideals are European derivatives; and the attitude to and the use of the landscape in conservation and production is heavily influenced from Europe. Therefore, the parallel between South Africa and Europe in the process of nation-building is highly relevant (Davidson, 1992). In this paper I shall focus on the ambiguous and mainly negative role the interpretation of landscape had for the merging of nation and democracy, mainly with reference to literature in a Scandinavian context.

NATION-BUILDING

From the late 18th century and onwards Denmark together with many European countries was engaged in a process of nation-building after the Napoleonic wars. A new group of nations came into being after World War I, and yet another group followed the collapse of the Soviet Union. But the political and ideological components remained very much the same: the same logic and the same pitfalls in new contexts that allowed for repetitions of the same conflicts. Of course, many of the new nations or would-be nations, as in today's former Yugoslavia, had existed for hundreds of years, but under very different conditions and institutionalized forms. They are and were engaged in a struggle to redefine the country as a nation in a new geographical, political, economic and cultural context as an answer to preceding conflicts. Nation-building has never had a peaceful background.

In the first and prototypical phase of nation-building Europe was burning during the Napoleonic wars, feudal empires—like Denmark—were crumbling, economic advantages and disadvantages changed drastically among the European regions, the outline of a new urban-industrial area began to be visible on the horizon, and new secular ideologies redefined collective and individual identities with new conceptions of language, ethnicity, religion, social power, education etc.

In this complex transitional process, the national landscape played a fundamental role in the formation of national identities, both on a collective and an individual level. In the national ideologies growing out of romanticism, especially in the German realm, language and landscape were the basic constituents of national identity, the first one defining and expressing the latter, presenting it as the natural foundation of the nation. Of course, landscapes existed before they were constructed as national landscapes and before nationalism emerged as a dominant geopolitical ideology. They were there as God's nature, a complex of signs constituting the Great Book of Nature, or they were there as an artistic creation, especially in painting. They were also considered as regions submitted to a feudal order governed by a common law. But as national landscapes, with a major impact on national identity, they were a later invention, shaped between the French Revolution and the Vienna Congress as a response to the complex historical transition.

The typicality of landscapes or of landscape uses—such as, for instance, a certain type of forest and forestry—were not regarded as simple facts shared by nations belonging to the same climatic zones, but were turned into symbols of national specificity with an impact on national character and thereby on national identity. And strong symbols they are, because whatever meaning they acquire they are also always out there in their undeniable material presence—you walk in it, you live from it, memories of it are inscribed in your body as well as in your mind. Painters and writers received standing ovations when they gave artistic form to this idea in visual or verbal texts, and their imagination materialized later on in concrete landscapes like natural parks, nature reserves or preserved cultural landscapes. Brochures on these natural wonders from the national tourist agencies, also those of South Africa, have perpetualized and commercialized these landscape views, more often than not stressing their national character. Of course, criticism of this development has run parallel to the development itself, as suggested in Nadine Gordimer's short story.

It is, however, important not to forget that in Europe the national landscape was amalgamated with a national ideology before democratic constitutions and institutions were created (the USA being an exception) and, therefore, its contribution to the national identity was not necessarily shaped by a consideration for democracy. Although the national landscape has been, and is, appreciated as an integral and indispensable part of the cultural identity of democratic nations today, it does not necessarily contribute in an unambiguous and positive way to the process of democratization.

Considering how the latest development in Europe, especially in Eastern and Central Europe, re-enacts the ambiguities and intricacies of the early nation-building period of Europe, with no guarantee of democracy, there might be a message to be learned, also outside Europe, in analyzing the mechanisms and functions of the national landscape as a cultural invention. And even more so because many of the basic ideas prompting the cultural and political development of new nations, their constitutions and their fight for democracy have a European origin. Europe is on the one hand undeniably a part of the heritage of many non-European countries in a post-colonial era and, on the other hand, the reflection of the European image in the mirror of other continents will be an important element in the self-understanding of Europe, facing its own turbulence.

THE FUNCTIONS OF THE NATIONAL LANDSCAPE

The national landscape, in its material–symbolic complexity, serves three basic ideological functions in the make-up of a national identity:

1) it gives *unity* to people and place
2) it provides people and place with a common *origin*
3) it *naturalizes* the unity and the origin.

The national landscape tends to present the actual state of affairs, called a unity, as the outcome of a linear and almost purposive process, a historical destiny, and not as a complicated and partly unforeseeable process of fragmentation and breaking up, partly due to circumstantial human and non–human interventions; it tends to disguise the actual conflicts and contrasts in the national setting, especially the fact that the nations are mostly established after the breakdown of older structures and often with a reduced geographical territory; and, finally, in naturalizing the national identity, the landscape removes change, including radical change, from the definition of national identity.

The national landscape sets the national identity apart from the history it is part of. In the national landscape nation and nature become one and the same thing, both in language (*nation* and *nature* actually derive from the same word) and in the perception of political reality, where change, differences etc. are considered unnatural. On the surface, the national landscape is an active and creative force in the formation of a non-exclusive identity for all members of a nation. Nevertheless, it is more correct to see it as a reactive and partly repressive force, hiding actual conflicts and legitimizing historical boundaries on a quasi-natural basis. If nation-building is a process of belonging, involving both a redefinition of territory and of collective and individual identity the national landscape has a major function in amalgamating these factors into a unifying national identity.

Considering the standard image of Denmark as a homogeneous and democratic nation, a brief example might illustrate my point. Hans Christian Ørsted, one of the leading figures in modern science of his day due to his investigations on electromagnetism, was deeply involved in the national issue in the first half of the 19th century. In 1836 he defined and naïvely defended Danishness in this way:

> What is Danishness? Like any national character it includes, first of all, everything that defines the human being; but what makes this character a special Danish character is, naturally, the totality of the features that are more frequent in our people than in others. [...] The Danish land has a friendly nature, the enormous only reveals itself in sky and sea, and the horrifying is almost absent; only the sea unfolds now and then with terror; but numerous are the vistas where the Dane has either a wide or a smiling panorama over its blue surface. [...] Surrounded by this nature the people have lived and developed for centuries: how can we not notice a correspondence between them? I think nobody can easily deny that the Dane is good-humoured, easy-going, modest, disinclined to violence and wiles, rarely passionate. (Ørsted, 1852:50–51, author's translation)

This was written after Norway, more than three times as large as present day Denmark, was forcibly separated from the Danish kingdom by the Vienna Congress after a 700 year union, because of Denmark's alliance with Napoleon, the loser; after national bankruptcy in 1813; and after the King's denial of some sort of constitution in 1836, the year of Ørsted's paper was originally published. Thus, the national landscape was used to reduce historical complexity to natural simplicity which was part of the ideological and political make-up that naïvely led Denmark on the road toward two wars with Prussia (1848–50 and 1864), reducing the Danish territory even more. The national landscape confused the basic national agenda, giving priority to an imaginary unity over the conflicts and changes that constituted the real political agenda of the nation: health, education, urban and industrial development, new class structures, political participation etc. that grew out of the economic and political processes of the 19th century.

Ørsted continues:

> If anybody asked me: what enables me to write as a genuine Dane? then I would almost give him the same answer as if he had asked me: what enables me to be a genuine Dane in the very essence of my being? I would simply tell him thoughtfully to follow his nature: when a Dane, born and raised among Danes and having his life among Danes, follows this precept, he will automatically become genuinely Danish; only by artificiality will he deviate from true Danishness. (Ørsted, 1852:53, author's translation)

The argument is simple, its consequences complicated: in the national identity outer nature, the landscape, and inner nature, the genuine Danishness, are unified in a complete balance that works all by itself, and the two 'natures' find a common means of expression, the national language that confirms their unity. Although an explicit hostility toward foreignness, or just the lack of balance between inner life and outer landscape, is avoided, xenophobia toward domestic and foreign enemies is just next door. History is full of examples of how national awakening goes hand in hand with hostility toward inner and outer enemies, real or imagined, on the grounds of, among other things, language and ethnicity.

A pragmatic attitude to language as a means of communication you have to master to a certain degree in order to function in a society was predominant in Denmark for centuries. For centuries it was of no major concern that several kings and ministers spoke better German than Danish, as long as they performed their duties. But gradually, and especially after the adaption of the Danish Law in 1683 to apply to the whole of Denmark (then including present-day Norway), and later through the Royal Academy of Science from 1742, Danish was programmatically shaped into a modern language of administration, science, commerce and art. The ground was laid for the Romantic conception that the Danish language expressed essential Danishness. The hidden message is that national identity is there as a seed before the nation, but grows and develops because of it, not the other way round. Therefore, even if you move to another nation, the national identity you acquire will be external to you (cf. Smith, 1991:71).

Pogrom-like attacks on Jews, almost unheard of previously in Denmark, took place in 1819 in Copenhagen. An anti-German wave culminated in two disastrous wars in the mid 19th century. The propaganda around such and other events was heavily loaded with references to the non-Danishness of these groups: foreign on the soil and foreign in the language, independent of how long they had lived there and how well they spoke Danish. This essentialism is still an important component in politics and the general debate resulting both in exclusion and inclusion of people, and gives nationalism a long afterlife. When applied today in relation to integration of immigrants and refugees and other ethnic issues the excluding effects are most obvious. When applied in landscape preservation in the 20th century, aiming both at restoring natural processes and recreating cultural landscape types that contain stories of Danish cultural history, the promotion of a shared national identity is clear (for example, Ministry of the Environment, 1994).

The Landscape as Dream

The national language has both to express and promote the national identity, especially in describing the national landscape as the scene of the original national life. In this perspective, the landscape is of course more fundamental than language, being accessible to you by immediate sense perception alone, whereas it requires some learning to master the production and interpretation of landscape descriptions. This is however, a twisted argument: the immediate perception does not capture a national landscape, but just some environmental elements; only a person already informed by descriptions will 'know' that what is perceived is a national landscape.

Due to the intimate relation between national landscape, national language and national identity, literature plays a fundamental role in creating the vision of the national landscape and making it serve its ideological functions right into this century. The textual mechanism itself survives. But literature has always been an unfaithful alliance that often dissolves its own basis and thereby invites to critical reflection. By its very nature literature de-unifies and ambiguizes its objects and therefore also de-naturalizes and historizes them. In relation to the landscape this process is prompted by literature in two ways: either the landscape is stripped of any symbolic meaning, or it is loaded with meaning which is gradually undermined in the text.

From this perspective there is an illustrative connection between Gordimer's story and two texts by Isak Dinesen, a pen name for Karen Blixen. She lived for many years in Kenya as a coffee farmer, but returned to Denmark in 1931 after having lost all her money and began a successful international career as a writer. Her memoirs from Africa, *Out of Africa* (1937), open with the impressive view of the Ngong Hills:

> I had a farm in Africa, at the foot of the Ngong Hills. The Equator runs across these highlands, a hundred miles to the North, and the farm lay at an altitude of over six thousand feet. In the day-time you felt that you had got high up, near to the sun, but the early mornings and evenings were limpid and restful, and the nights were cold.
> The geographical position, and the height of the land combined to create a landscape that had not its like in all the world. (Dinesen, 1985:3)

After a long explanation of the uniqueness and the astounding beauty of the African setting, with many concrete details of trees, plants and animals, light and temperature, earth and sky, she sums up:

> Up in this high air you breathed easily, drawing in a vital assurance and lightness of heart. In the highland you woke up in the morning and thought: Here I am, where I ought to be. (ibid.:4)

Although Dinesen explicitly wants to give an image of the totality of the landscape, horizontally and vertically, she actually presents a highly selective description, including only those details that make the landscape a totality for *her*, in itself, and enable her to experience an identity in relation to the local place. The first thing to notice is that nature is more loaded with subjective purposiveness than with natural factualness. The same goes for the national landscape: it is a highly selective unity, suppressing details that contradict the naturalizing and uniform effect of national identity. It serves a human purpose, in a sense like natural resources used for farming or to excavate raw material, although on a symbolic level. The boy in Gordimer's "Ultimate Safari" also felt at home in his landscape, seeing it as "a country of people, not animals" (Gordimer, 1994:145).

Secondly, the landscape in all its splendour is not present, but absent. It is a lost landscape, only retained in memory. In fact, it has in a certain way to be looked upon as unreal, before it can be transformed or interpreted in relation to human identity, be it an individual, as here, or a national identity. The national landscape is a mindscape that is intensified by the denial of the physical reality of the perceived landscape. The mental image of human belonging, for example as the national unity, is then projected on physical landscape in order to claim that this is its basic reality.

Dinesen's text shows this discursive strategy in great detail, and with a fascinating linguistic and imaginary mastery, through metaphors and with many references to the dreamlike state she is in when she experiences the landscape—first of all it is a dream about her own place in the world, an attitude close to that of the boy in Gordimer's story, imagining himself going back to the lost village, finding his mother and grandfather and then finally being home. In both cases belonging is not a given, but a human process. In contrast to the boy Dinesen knows painfully well that she can never belong to the African landscape or any other landscape than through symbolic construction.

Thirdly, the landscape is described as containing her whole life: there is no alternative, no replacement possible. In the same way, the national landscape inscribes the members of the nation into the landscape so that they cannot escape it. It is their nature. Outside the national landscape, you live an artificial inauthentic life like Gordimer's refugees in their tents. Although Dinesen's text focuses more on a specific locality than a specific nationality, it makes visible the general conditions for combining landscape, or nature, and identity. On the one hand, the landscape is irresistibly attractive, almost seductive; on the other hand, identity is founded on the landscape only if it is made unreal, lost and seen as an artificial totality of subjective selected details. She is highlighting the role of human intervention for the creation of identity in relation to the landscape and thus reducing the importance of its immediately perceived naturalness. Gordimer's boy does not possess the reflective subtlety of Dinesen, but the motto of the story ironically points to the fact that wherever he goes his landscape is formed by the images and interests of others.

Landscape as History

A similar discursive strategy is at work in a description of a Danish landscape. The introduction to her story "Sorrow–Acre" from *Winter's Tales* (1942) presents the undulating Danish landscape before the action unfolds. The story is historically situated around 1780 in the fields and gardens of a Danish manor house.

> The low undulating Danish landscape was silent and serene, mysterious wide–awake, in the hour before sunrise. There was not a cloud in the pale sky, not a shadow along the dim, pearly fields, hills and woods. The mist was lifting from the valleys and hollows, the air was cool, the grass and the foliage dripping wet with morning dew. Unwatched by the eyes of man, and undisturbed by his activity, the country breathed a timeless life, to which language was inadequate.
>
> All the same a human race had lived on this land for a thousand years, had been formed by its soil and weathers, and had marked it with its thoughts, so that now no one could tell where the existence of the one ceased and that of the other began. The thin grey line of a road, winding across the plain and up and down hills, was the fixed materialization of human longing, and of the human notion that it were better to be in one place than another. A child of the landscape would read this open landscape like a book. (Dinesen, 1986:172)

Already in this simple appraisal of the eternal beauty of the Danish landscape that embraces the entire life of its inhabitants, certain underlying contradictions reveal that Dinesen is trying to provide us with more than a simple description. In these opening lines of her story we are invited to *reflect* upon the relation between national landscape and national identity—to *read* it—rather than just to *observe* it. Thus, in the brief quotation she both celebrates the place's boundness and the longing to get away; she both places the landscape inside the realm of human experience, language and interpretation and outside it, in a timeless transcendence.

On the following pages, before the action actually takes place, she continues to articulate two levels simultaneously: that of simple recognizability and stable, comforting identity, and that of unsolvable and thereby dynamic and destabilizing contrasts and contradictions of the landscape, related to four interwoven structures—the natural, the social, the sexual and the symbolic. They are simultaneously working in the landscape, each based on a major conflict through which the four structures are now reinforcing each other, now neutralizing each other. The landscape is over-determined by several types of natural, social and symbolic features, each of which contributes to its permanent dynamics.

Dinesen presents a landscape that only on the surface can be described as a national landscape, according to a set of fixed features. Literature brings back the landscape from nature to the history of human beings, their lives and memories. But the two landscape descriptions do not naturalize this experience. They show the ambiguous, even conflictual, character of the identity emanating from the landscape, so that we see that it is a result of human choice and of a process of change. But history means difference, also between Europe and Africa.

In the Veld

In a brief sequence from André Brink's *An Instant in the Wind* (1976) we find a marked difference both to Dinesen's and Gordimer's texts (cf. Coetzee, 1988; Gräbe, 1997). All history, memory, subjectivity is taken out of the landscape when Elizabeth is fighting her way through a completely foreign location in the far away hinterlands of the Cape region:

> Separate objects on the road caught her attention, absorbing her completely so that she became oblivious of motion altogether. A thorn tree stump with all redundant bark and softness stripped by the wind and sun, reduced to pure wood, a bare hard pattern of indestructible grain. A rock formation corroded through centuries, all sandiness and flakiness destroyed, terrifying and beautiful in its utter stillness its refusal to be anything but itself. [...]
>
> For long stretches she would wander on with her head bowed scrutinising the ground immediately in front of her feet, looking for wagon trails cut into the hard soil, flattened branches, discarded objects. Something, anything: the barest sign to reassure her that she'd really passed that way before.

> But there was nothing. Not the slightest indication or admission by the landscape that it acknowledged her, that it was aware of her. [...] Nothing. Just nothing. (Brink, 1976:160, 161)

This experience is echoed in the exiled grandmother's remark in Gordimer's text: "There is nothing. No home." Without human invention and inventiveness, without human decisions and human history, there is no human identity, neither national nor individual. To be born in a place is not enough. Identity does not grow from the ground like plants, as Ørsted would have it. Dinesen focuses on the historical processes, conflicts and human signs in the landscape that *create* our identity in it; Brink on the naked materiality of the landscape that *requires* our activity if we want to belong there and shape an identity, an activity which does not follow an already prepared programme but evolves while it unfolds. But nothing promises us that we will be able to act or succeed in our efforts.

The emptiness of the landscape is a common feature in white South African literature. The land is a place of constant confrontation, fear and fighting, not an embracing and welcoming harmonious setting. In his *White Writing* (1988) J.M. Coetzee points to a general attitude to the landscape in the farm novel and plaasroman:

> Africa is a land of rock and sun, not of soil and water [...] The landscape remains alien, impenetrable, until a language is found in which to win it, speak it, represent it. It is no oversimplification to say that landscape art and landscape writing in South Africa from the beginning of the nineteenth century to the middle of the twentieth revolve around the question of finding a language to fit Africa. [...] Is there a language in which people of European identity, or if not of European identity, then of a highly problematical South African–colonial identity, can speak to Africa and to be spoken to by Africa? [...] Many English–colonial doubts about identity are projected and blamed upon the English language itself, partly because, as a literary medium, English carries echoes of a very different natural world. (Coetzee, 1988:8)

This is Ørsted's argument once more, but turned upside down: landscape and language are separated and no collective identity in relation to the landscape is possible. Although many Afrikaans *plaasromans*—with Olive Schreiner's *The Story of an African Farm* (1883) as the first and most important example—report about the successful fight against the land, it is a fight that begins over again every day. The land is never completely cultivated.

Coetzee shows that white literature, whether in English or Afrikaans, is silent about non-white views of landscape and people. In this literature the actual work put into the landscape by the black labour force over the centuries is made invisible. And in traditional white South African literature there is no manifest knowledge of the African experience, expressed by, for example, Gordimer's boy, that you can be at home in a land that is tough and uncontrolled, but nevertheless known to you, useful and readable. The estrangement of whites vis-a-vis the landscape, Coetzee underlines, is a product of a necessary neglect of this history. But to remember it would not make any difference. It would not be a history of their belonging there.

Coetzee puts it even stronger in his chapter on "Idleness in South Africa" (Coetzee 1988: chap.1): the oblivion of the actual work of the native peoples, before and during colonial time, is a way of putting the work obligation on them and thereby evaluating settler idleness in positive terms as enabling distance to manual work and native idleness in negative terms as natural laziness that has to be disciplined and embedded in an individualized work ethic. This strategy legitimized a one-to-one relationship between the practice of colonial power and the discourse on power relations, both based on natural superiority. Instead, Coetzee suggests that the behaviour interpreted as a natural demoralizing inclination for idleness is the result of an almost institutionalized choice between two imposed evils: either you become poor and physically destroyed by working for the settlers or you become poor and displaced by not working for them. The latter is the better choice because it allows for a certain sense of feeling at home in the landscape, as manifested, for example, in the boy's attitude in Gordimer's story. This attitude is, therefore, seen as a culturally coded reaction against the colonial power to safeguard a sense of belonging. Having this interpretation of the relationship between humans and landscape as the backdrop for white idleness, this becomes a self-inflicted estrangement from the landscape and, consequently, in white colonial self-interpretation it will to be pushed aside with its reference to historical processes and not to natural differences.

The problem of neglected, or suppressed, history in relation to the landscape forms a telling parallel to a decisive difference between European and non-European nation-building. Territorial boundaries and democratic institutions framing European nation-states also have a European history from which they unfold. Ørsted claimed, that a natural sense of belonging existed prior to the nation, and was not an ideological wrapping up of a nation once born. In *National Identity* (1991) Anthony Smith likewise, but on historical grounds, terms as nationalism those ideological movements which, rooted in a specific cultural history, may end up actually forming a nation that may acquire the features of a state, including a democratic state. Therefore, the nation-state is both a specific historical product and also an embodiment of the ideal model of a nation, which serves as an ideological platform to evaluate actual nations.

Whether any nation corresponds to the model or not, in Europe the model, together with the actual nations, also as nation-states, belongs to the same cultural history that also includes specific ways in which model and reality are confronted (freedom of speech, legal systems, parliamentary systems, constitutions, human rights, etc.). If the European nation-state as an ideal model is transplanted to another historical and cultural context, it will constitute merely a formal and thereby rigid structure. When realized it imposes a territorial, political, economic and cultural structure on a region or an entire continent without being rooted in local economies, languages, institutions, literatures etc. The power of a nation designed or invented in such circumstances is conditioned by a suppression or neglect of local history, a neglect which, at the same time, disguises their formal character and thereby maintains it in its formal rigidity that ultimately leads into a blind alley. In order to keep the historical and contextual sensitivity in nation-building alive, Smith therefore, points to different nation models and to different realized types of nations as historically operational, none of which can function without fully taking into account local history prior to a nation-formation.

In *The Black Man's Burden* (1992) Basil Davidson points to the fact that there were kingdoms with self-government in Africa that might have been a basis for a specific local development of national democracies. They were not neglected by the colonial administrators, but negotiation was actively refused. In his chapter on "Shadows of neglected ancestors" his example is Ufia in present day Tanzania. He notes that "Africa's problem in becoming independent from colonial rule was not to modernize its own institutions [...] but to suppose there had been none, or none of any relevance." (Davidson, 1992:75). From the European perspective the germ of a nation could only grow in Europe and be exported when fully grown and dressed up in ideological European outfit. His point, however, is that without an active relation to some relevant local basis any nation state or democracy will be an empty shell, a formal structure. In this context landscape as supposed pristine wilderness, untouched by humans, and especially not owned by humans, is open both for exploitation and for preservation in the image of the European dream of the wild beyond the all too cultivated landscapes at home (Neumann, 1995).

The modern descriptions of landscapes in literature, when at best, express the historically determined double experience of foreign dream and indigenous reality, local use and foreign influence. Only an emphasis of such features in their non-exclusive complexity in contrast to the natural autonomy of the landscape, can make it part of a democratic vision of national identity. It will be a sign of the real conflicts and not, like in Europe, disguise of conflicts that should have been negotiated without being subsumed under one language or one harmonious unity. Democracy does not presuppose a pre-established harmony, in the landscape or elsewhere, but it is a way of making differences work.

NATIONAL IDENTITY WITHOUT A NATIONAL LANDSCAPE?

The interaction between nature and history is, on the one hand, part of a national identity because the interaction between human actions and natural processes constitutes the cultural processes, and on the other hand it transcends the national borders in today's international conventions and practices in landscape preservation. In this context the African experience, in all its cruelty and complexity, will be an antidote to the naïve re-emerging traditional nationalism in Europe with all its naturalizing propaganda in which the notion of the national landscape may reinforce its role as a non-democratic or even antidemocratic ideological device that neither serves the national identity and its democratic processes nor ecological concerns. Its public appeal has always been great and easy to communicate, but its long term effects have often been to remove human actions, history and democracy from our interaction with each other and our environment, ending up satisfying only the international tourism industry.

It would, therefore seem advisable, both at home and abroad, not to cling to the national landscape in the creation of a national identity. This does not imply, though, that the question of national identity has to be dismissed altogether. Such a conclusion would, of course, have been impossible or at least provocative for the Danes of the pre-democratic phase of nation-building. As Ørsted pointed out, the national landscape and the national identity, or character, as he phrases it, are but two sides of the same coin. This is not the case when national identity and democracy constitute an inseparable unity, and when the landscape—national or not—only plays a role for our identity on such conditions. The basic question is not: do we have a national landscape, and what does it look like? Instead, we will have to ask: what does it mean to belong to a place as part of one's identity on democratic conditions, and how does a landscape fit in?

The British politologist David Miller has addressed similar issues in his book *On Nationality*. Although the role of landscapes does not enter his discussion (or, astonishingly enough, the discussion of most others taking issue with the question of national identity, e.g. Hobsbawm, 1990; Smith, 1991), his argument is very much in line with the one I put forward. He is trying to escape the easy solutions: because a keen interest in national identity has often degenerated into destructive chauvinism, we do not need to dismiss it as an uncontrollable quasi-natural atavism or as a stable but unhappy fact of modern *Realpolitik* with which ordinary people should not interfere; furthermore, because nationalism has had some unfortunate effects in modern history, we do not need to delegitimize all questions about place-bound identity and set up a placeless cosmopolitanism as our ideal. It is legitimate, and in fact inevitable, to argue for a place-bound identity; to accept, as we saw in the Dinesen quotation above, "the human notion that it were better to be in one place than another".

Firstly, Miller claims that as humans we are social beings whose *identity* or the way we understand our place in the world, partly—but not exclusively—includes that we are inextricably part of a national grouping. In certain contexts the essentials of this grouping have to do with language, with certain institutionalized practices, with family structure etc.; sometimes we take them all together, sometimes we especially cherish one of them; and they all change over time. Nationality is a result of historical over-determination, not of a natural foundation whether related to landscape, to race or other natural or quasi-natural categories. Dinesen's and Gordimer's landscapes showed exactly this complexity, further developed in Coetzee's analysis. So, a landscape *may* be part of this whole, not as a natural foundation but as a historically developed feature which, however, is not always important.

Secondly, he insists that nations are *ethical* communities, implying mutual obligations between compatriots that may, and sometimes also ought to, embrace others. But we cannot, so Miller says, avoid having mutual obligations that are defined on the basis of a national community. Ethical obligations begin inside a closed space from which we can reach out; but we cannot start by reaching out and only then turn to the community closer to us. In that case there would be no ethics at all. The effects of globalization of politics and economics for the environment, wars and humanitarian disasters bear witness to this fact. Much post-colonial nation states are not ethical communities in that sense.

Thirdly, nations define *limits* to who I am and what I ought to do. Miller calls this the political aspect of the nation, its claim to self-determination. A nation that offers us an identity and imposes obligations on us toward our fellow nationals will have to be able to define and defend this self-determination with regard to at least the essential identity creating elements (for example language or education, or its multiethnic character, or multilingual character) and the basic obligations (for example the level of social welfare or compulsory schooling), and it must have a certain territory to exercise that self-determination in, that is certain boundaries to be respected (but not necessarily a specific landscape). Identity and obligations must have a place that can be shaped accordingly. Building a nation is to build up a combination of these three aspects.

The most essential part of the identity part of the complex is *history*: a common culture for interaction, for a memory of these actions and a shared belief in the orientation toward the future. So, building up a national identity will have to refer to institutions that carry a common history, not a common nature but perhaps a shared attitude to nature. An important task is therefore the opposite to what happened during the Danish nation-building from the late 18th century. Here the use of the national landscape as a naturalized basis for national unity repressed the actual history of the dissolution of the country and its institutions that necessarily preceded the building of the new nation as a sovereign nation state, and highlighted a story of unification.

In the post-colonial nations there was in many cases a suppression or even complete neglect of shared history and of the nation as an ethical community prior to colonial conditions. In his bold attempt to repress pessimism concerning democratic nation-building Basil Davidson takes pains to point out that the shared history is not only constituted by the content of and the glorifying stories about by-gone ages. Europe sets a negative standard for such enterprises. Shared is also the suppression or neglect of conflicts and disruptions of the past and the way ethical communities formed during the struggle dwindled. He emphasizes that ethics will only be restored through participatory practice that meets a lot of obstacles. In this respect Davidson does not see post-colonial nations re-enacting the age-old European conflictual nation-formation, but a parallel quest, on both continents and especially for England and France, for "the introduction of participatory structures within a wide regionalist framework" (Davidson, 1992:321f) with a reduction of rigid nation-state structures.

Belonging to a place is a matter of decision, not a matter of natural origin, a result of a democratic process not of its natural foundation. One of our prime obligations in a nation is therefore to institutionalize this decision in democratic institutions and learn to use and to develop them, to begin to explore history and develop fora for participation. Literature gives occasion to reflect on this obligation in its open and complex articulation of the relationship between landscape, nation and identity. In today's society our surroundings, natural or not, are bound to such decisions. If we do not develop such democratic institutions, national sovereignty will crumble, and no reference to national landscapes or national origins will be able to replace it. Democracy is a goal pursued both in Africa and Europe, but democracy is at the same time an endangered species on both continents.

REFERENCES

Brink, André (1976). *An Instant in the Wind*. London: W.H. Allen.
Coetzee, J.M. (1988). *White Writing*. New Haven: Yale University Press/Sandton: Radix.
Davidson, Basil (1992). *The Black Man's Burden. Africa and the Curse of the Nation State*. Oxford: Currey/Harare: Baobab/Nairobi: EAEP/Kampala: Fountain.
Dinesen, Isak (1985 [1937]). *Out of Africa*. New York: Vintage Books.
Dinesen, Isak (1986 [1942]). "Sorrow–Acre", *Winter's Tales*. Harmondsworth: Penguin. pp. 172–200.
Gordimer, Nadine (1994). "The Ultimate Safari", Robin Malan (eds.). *Being Here. Modern Short Stories from Southern Africa*. Cape Town: David Philip. pp. 143–153.
Gräbe, Ina (1997). *Landscape as a Troubled Space. Representations of Nature in South African Literature*. Working Paper 109. Humanities Research Center: Man & Nature. Odense University.
Hobsbawm, E.J. (1990). *Nations and Nationalism since 1780: Programme, Myths, Reality*. Cambridge: Cambridge University Press.
Miller, David (1995). *On Nationality*. Oxford: Clarendon.
Ministry of the Environment (1994). *Strategy for Natural Forests and Other Forest Types of High Conservation Value in Denmark*. Copenhagen: Ministry of the Environment.
Neumann, Roderick P. (1995). "Ways of Seeing Africa: Colonial Recasting of African Society and Landscape in Serengeti National Park", in *Ecumene* II, 2. pp. 149–169.
Smith, Anthony (1991). *National Identity*. Harmondsworth: Penguin.
Ørsted, Hans Christian (1852 [1836]). *Danskhed* [Danishness]. *Samlede og efterladte Skrifter* Vol. 7. Copenhagen: Høst. 39–58.

The Question of Identity During the Nigerian Civil War (1967–1970) in the Fiction of Flora Nwapa and Ken Saro-Wiwa

Raisa Simola

INTRODUCTION

Nigeria, the giant of Africa, is a construction of Britain, and since her independence, she has had problems which culminated in the Civil War or Biafran War. The Igbos are one of the three major ethnic groups in Nigeria and were the largest group in Biafra. Chinua Achebe has stated that although the Igbo identity has "all the time" existed, it was the Civil War which in fact created a consciousness of it.[53] Certainly, Achebe is not alone when talking about Igbo identity; for example, the prominent Igbo historian Adiele Afigbo states that "though colonial rule transformed Igbo society in many respects, it did not destroy Igbo identity or cultural soul".[54] These two statements indicate that "identity" is—at least in the case of the Igbos—something that has lasted in spite of the predicaments of colonialism and the Civil War. In addition, the extremely difficult times may even have strengthened the consciousness of belongingness to a certain ethnic group.

The Biafran War has engendered a lot of fiction, mainly by Igbo and Yoruba male writers. In this paper I will deal with the fictive writings of two Nigerian writers whose works on the Civil War have

---

53. Cited by Kwame Anthony Appiah, *In My Father's House. Africa in the Philosophy of Culture.* Oxford University Press, Oxford, 1992:177.
54. Adiele Afigbo, *Ropes of Sand. Studies in Igbo History and Culture.* University Press Limited and Oxford University Press, Ibadan, 1981:283–284.

been outside the mainstream of the Civil War writing. The books concerned are *Never Again* (1975) and *Wives at War and Other Stories* (1980) by Flora Nwapa, the first Nigerian and Igbo female novelist, and *Sozaboy* (1985) by Ken Saro-Wiwa, who as an Ogoni belonged to one of the small minority groups of Nigeria. My questions when reading these books can be simply put as follows: What is the significance of the Civil War to the Igbo and Biafran identity in these works? What is the significance of the Civil War to the human identity, seen from a female and minority perspective? Before close reading of the books, let us take a quick look at the historical background.

Nigeria became independent in 1960 and a republic in 1963; and its first president was Nnamdi Azikiwe, an Igbo. Independence was followed by a time of insecurity and corruption. The first election results of the independent state were distorted, and different ethnic groups accused one another of discrimination. The situation became worse due to oil discoveries in the Eastern Region, where the Igbos were in the majority. In January 1966 a group of Igbo officers staged a coup and the Prime Minister, Sir Abubakar Balewa, as well as some other national leaders, were killed. General Aguiyi-Ironsi, an Igbo, formed a military government. When his government abolished the federal system—that is, tried to create a stronger central government, which was opposed especially by Northern Nigerians—violent actions against the Igbos in Northern Nigeria started. In July, during another military coup, Aguiyi-Ironsi was killed. It has been argued that the aim of the coup was to retaliate against the Igbos for the January coup as well as to separate Northern Nigeria from Nigeria. The Federal system was re-established and Lieutenant-Governor Yakubu Gowon, a 32-year old Northern Nigerian, became Head of the Federal Military Government. There was intensified violence against the Igbos in Northern Nigeria, and thousands of them were killed. Survivors fled to Eastern Nigeria. Anti-Northern feelings were strong in the area, and the Military Governor, Lieutenant-Colonel Odumegwu Ojukwu, ordered non-Easterners out of the region.

On 30 May, 1967, Ojukwu declared the Eastern region independent Biafra; it encompassed several ethnic groups, of which the Igbos were in the majority. While earlier the Northern region had tried to separate from the rest of Nigeria, and the Eastern region had struggled for unity, the situation was now reversed. The civil war started in July 1967 when the armed forces of the Federation attacked Biafra. The war ended in January 1970 when Biafra was defeated.

NEVER AGAIN

The form of *Never Again*, by Flora Nwapa is that of the first-person narration with the following opening remarks: "All the characters in this collection are imaginary and bear no resemblance to anyone dead or alive". The narrator Kate is married to Chudi—both of whom are Igbos—and they have five children. The names of the places do have a resemblance to the real world; this combination of fictive characters and 'real' place names is typical of the other texts dealt with in this paper as well. The narrator tells the story after the Civil War has finished, but her story does not tackle the beginning nor the end of the war but the middle of it: the actions and atmosphere of the war itself.

We are told at the beginning of the story that Kate just wants to stay alive and as the story progresses it becomes clear that this is her main focus. She does not see any possibility of victory; and indeed she proves to be right when she predicts the fall of Port Harcourt and later the fall of her hometown Ugwuta. She predicts the fall of Biafra as well. The story concentrates on describing life in Ugwuta under the constant insecurity and fear about whether the place will be attacked by the Federal troops and whether the people should defend themselves or leave the town. Ultimately most people flee from Ugwuta; and after being refugees for some time, return to their desolated hometown.

The Ugwuta people described are Igbos, whose identity is based partly on the past that made them become Biafrans and partly on certain qualities which they think that the Igbos have. First let us have a look at the past that the Igbos share. Kate's mother puts it in this way:

> Why won't they leave us alone? We have left them in Nigeria. They said we grabbed everything; we have said: all right, you are killing us because we grabbed everything. We are not going to grab any more. We are going home. They say: now come back otherwise we will bring you back by force. And they are still killing us. They don't want us, yet they won't let us alone to fend for ourselves. That's why, my daughter, I am at a loss what to do in this war. Do they want us back, so that they can kill all of us, wipe out the whole race? (p. 27)

Kate's mother's story expresses the two important points that the Igbos share: they were harassed and killed, mainly in Northern Nigeria but elsewhere too; and when they then fled to their home area in Eastern Nigeria and planned to make their own and better future there—they founded Biafra—that was not allowed either. We may compare this with Chinua Achebe's statement that because the Nigerian government failed to protect 14 million people of Eastern Nigeria from "wanton destruction" it "rightly lost their allegiance".[55] Even Kate—who lost her belief in Biafra after Port Harcourt had fallen—states: "I had thought that Gowon was not going to fight us. I had thought that the rest of Nigeria would have been glad to get rid of the Ibos" (p. 50).

The Igbos of *Never Again* attach certain attributes to themselves. First, they consider themselves as belonging to an 'intelligent' ethnic group. (In the past, but even, today the Igbos sometimes called themselves the Jews of Africa.) The narrator states: "Before we fled from Port Harcourt we had heard that our boys had made a bomb which could sink Lagos in under twenty four hours" (p. 5). And later Kal expresses his disbelief in Nigerian science as follows: "Have they mortar bombs? Who gave them mortar bombs? They can't make a pin. Didn't you hear Gowon the other day on Radio Nigeria scolding Nigerian Scientists for their indolence? They cannot manufacture a pin. Our gallant Biafran scientists have made bombs, hand grenades, guns and shore batteries. Name it and our boys have made it" (p. 31). Secondly, a comparison of the bravery of the Biafrans and that of the Nigerian soldiers often occurs. Even if the 'bravery of the Biafrans' is used as propaganda by the Biafrans themselves, it often is 'real' in the sense that they wage war with the feeling of having a 'just' cause as defenders of their fatherland. Consequently, there is a willingness to sacrifice oneself for the fatherland if needed. Even small boys in their shorts join the army. A father may say: "I have two boys in the Army, thank God. I don't mind sacrificing them to Biafra" (p. 11). And someone sees that if the war had been only between the Nigerians and "us", "the war would have ended ages ago". The British had caused "all these troubles" by sending arms to the Nigerians. But even so:

---

55. *Morning Yet on Creation Day.* Essays. Doubleday, New York, 1975:146.

"You wait until we win. We will deal with the British" (p. 17). The belief of this man in what braveness alone can do is great indeed.

But in addition to the common past that the Igbos share and the qualities that are believed to be typical of them, the Igbos in *Never Again* divide up into two clearly different groups: those who believe in Biafra and those who don't. Or rather: those who act for the victory of Biafra—even after the defeat of Port Harcourt and Calabar—and those who have given up and just try to survive.

The former group is more visible. Besides the soldiers and civil defenders, it includes the bell man, who "every day...went round jingling his bell and assuring everybody that all was going well" (p. 29). Radio Biafra is totally for the Biafran cause, which means, for example, that it 'informs' about imaginary large numbers of dead enemies. To Ifeoma's question "Why do our people lie so much?" the narrator answers: "They are not lying. They are only boosting our morale" (p. 47). The vocabulary used is Manichean[56], or, polarized, 'black-and-white'. The Biafran soldiers are called "the gallant Biafran soldiers" and the Nigerians or Federalists are called "the Vandals" or, sometimes, "Hausas". Those Igbos who want to evacuate the town, to leave Ugwuta, are addressed as "cowards" and "saboteurs". Information which is not wanted—which may weaken the struggle for Biafra's victory—is labelled as "a false rumour".

To the narrator, official Biafran politics mainly looks like senseless propaganda. When she tells, for example, how "all able-bodied men" are summoned by the bell man and told "you should take your machetes and knives with you" (p. 49), the reader easily becomes of the same opinion that things seem desperate for the Biafrans. It really looks like sheer madness to continue the war if the youths are going to face automatic weapons with knives.

In addition many things are turned upside down. School dropouts become soldiers who use power over others, and all in all, there is looting and spying and a great deal of distrust even among the Biafrans. The following quote well illustrates the limited knowledge of people about what was happening quite close to them: "We arrived at Mgbidi. It was only six miles away from Ugwuta. There was peace.

---

56. The term originates from Abdul R. JanMohamed's *Manichean Aesthetics*. The University of Massachusetts Press. Amherst, 1983.

There was life. They hadn't the slightest notion of what we had gone through. They did not know that the enemy was six miles away, that they had occupied Ugwuta" (p. 59). And instead of helping the refugees of Ugwuta, who should be their Biafran sisters and brothers, the people of Mgbidi accuse them of being 'saboteurs'.

The discussion between Chudi, the narrator's husband, and Kal, the family friend, illustrates the two opposing views. Chudi, thinking especially of the aged and the children, says that the people should be evacuated. Kal's view, which is based on strong belief in the victory of the Biafrans, reads: "We shall fight to the last man" (p. 32). While Chudi argues his point that "it is wrong to allow men to die defenceless", Kal insists that they are going to arm them with guns. Kate, the narrator, confirms her husband's view that there were no guns; but Kal answers: "You are getting mad, Kate, and your husband too is getting mad" (p. 33).

Madness is continuing the war, Kate thinks. And since the Biafrans don't seem to want to give up fighting, the only way to end the war before the losses are too enormous is that the Nigerians defeat them as soon as possible:

> The end? Could there be an end to this ping-pong game? Secretly, I had hoped that the invasion of Ugwuta was going to be the end of the war. I had hoped that the Nigerians would hold it and thus end the war. Holding Ugwuta meant no flights to Uli airstrip, which meant no arms and no ammunition. Now we had contained them, now we had wiped them out and the war had continued. The war that nearly came to an end. (p. 83)

However, the war just continues.

There is one tendency in people's behaviour that is seen throughout the story and is emphasized at its end: people retreat into the metaphysical. Many Ugwuta people carry belief in the great Woman of the Lake, Uhamiri, with them through their agonies. But why this emphasis on a goddess at the end of the book? Doesn't the whole 'message' of the book, which mainly deals with the concrete agonies of the war, then become somewhat strange? Next I tackle this question in connection with the narrator.

In the beginning of the story the belief in Uhamiri is told in connection with Ugwuta being threatened: "The woman of the Lake would not allow it. She had never allowed the conquest of Ugwuta by water or by land or by air" (p. 4). Then at end of the book the narrator and her husband witness the desolation of the town Ugwuta. Immediately thereafter, however, the narrator also notes: "The only thing that stood undisturbed, unmolested, dignified and solid was the Lake. The Lake owned by the great Woman of the Lake. It defied war. It was calm, pure, peaceful and ageless. It sparkled in the sunlight, turning now blue, now green as the sun shone on it" (p. 84). And the whole book ends as follows:

> We turned our back to the Lake, and made for home. On our way home we met women, middle aged women in white. There was a little boy who dragged an unwilling white ram behind them. They were Uhamiri worshippers. They were going to the shrine of the Great Spirit to sacrifice to her for delivering them from the furies of the Vandals. (p. 85)

The narrator's thoughts before the concrete lake are solemn indeed; even the very end does not reveal any irony or other distance-taking from her side. It seems almost as if she was one of the worshippers herself. That is not the case, however (I leave aside the possibility that she could have suddenly converted to traditional belief).

There are Christians—many of whom are syncretists rather than 'pure' Christians—and there are those who follow the traditional religion. Kate is a Christian, but even her Christianity is somewhat syncretic; her mother then is, although a Christian, much closer to traditional religion. Kate's distance from the traditional religion is expressed in the next quote: "You went with them. Christ! Mama, did you go with them? You are no longer a Christian? You could go with the heathens to the shrine of the Woman of the Lake to sacrifice to her" (p. 38–9). Again at the end of the story the narrator distances herself from the worshippers: "Far in the distance was the gun-boat, sunk *as the people thought* not by artillery fire but by the Woman of the Lake" (p. 84; italics mine). Consequently, both the going under the skin of the Uhamiri worshippers and the distancing from them must be taken into account when interpreting the end of the story; and the order of things. Thus, my interpretation reads that Kate, who earlier made stricter boundaries between the 'Christians' and the 'heathens', in the end better understands the need of people to believe in something. The unchangeable Uhamiri who is believed to have saved the lives of many Ugwuta people serves as their mental base, the existence of which keeps them from collapsing into overwhelming, if not even fatal, desperation. Further, while the war is presented as a male endeavour, Uhamiri, the symbol of matriarchy[57], is seen as an alternative way of life.

Before making an overall characterization of the book, we need to look at the narrator once more. On the one hand, she is presented (that is: she presents herself) as 'wise': she predicts the fall of not only certain towns but Biafra as a whole. This 'knowledge' then justifies (is justified by) her behaviour. This neat story is, however, made more complex when we realize that her 'being right' does not mean that it is based on wide political awareness; nor does it mean that her few expressed political opinions will be well argued or consistent with each other as we can see in her next utterances. On the one hand she states: "We lost them (our freedom and democracy) the day that the Army took over. January 15 1966, was the day when we lost our hard-earned freedom" (p. 35). On the other hand, she is of the opinion that a "benevolent dictatorship" would be good for a nation (p. 59). Without going into the other implications here, it is enough to point out that in the former sentence she talks for "freedom and democracy" and in the latter for (even if "benevolent") "dictatorship". She wants democracy and dictatorship at the same time! Also, on the one hand she is of the opinion that Nigeria was wrong in attacking Biafra: "They should have left us in peace in our new found Biafra." But thereafter she gallops from the existence of 'oppression' easily into the 'war' and even justification of the Nigerian attack. She speculates that the idea of a Biafra where no one would be oppressed was too idealistic since there had always been oppression. Thus—she reasons—maybe there would be war inside Biafra, among the Biafrans. And she concludes: "Perhaps Nigeria did well to attack us. If they hadn't we would have, out of frustration, begun to attack and kill one another" (p. 51). Thus, the narrator offers two main options for the Biafrans: war among themselves or war between themselves and the Nigerians. Kate's view is not only pessimistic but based on very little knowledge about the Igbo, much less human, political traditions of solving pro-

---

57. See Florence Stratton, *African Literature and the Politics of Gender*. Routledge: London and New York, 1994:94.

blems peacefully. Indeed, she does not see much sense in political activity.

All in all, the story must be read as a story about a character who certainly is right in her prophesy that Biafra will be defeated, as well as in her view that "God was on the side of the battalion who had superior weapons" (p. 45), but who in general is politically quite ignorant and even naive. Further, since she sees very little sense in political activity, she prefers to avoid participating in it and concentrates on telling about its negative instead of positive aspects. In addition, against this background, her emphasis on the traditional beliefs of people as their 'survival strategy' becomes understandable. In spite of, or because of, this her human message of the waste of war is underlined. She utters her credo after having returned to her desolated hometown:

> --What folly! What arrogance, what stupidity led us to this desolation, to this madness, to this wickedness, to this war, to this death? When this cruel war is over, there will be no more war. It will not happen again, never again. NEVER AGAIN, never again.
> Why, we were all brothers--then, without warning, they began to shoot--. What was holy was desecrated and abused. NEVER AGAIN. (p. 73)

WIVES AT WAR AND OTHER STORIES

Wives at War and Other Stories is a collection of eight stories, three of which deal with the Civil War. At the beginning of this collection Flora Nwapa again makes her note: "All the characters in this collection are imaginary and bear no resemblance to anyone alive or dead."

The story "Wives at War" is composed of two different parts. The first tells about Ebo and Bisi's marriage and their growing difficulties during the war. Ebo is an Igbo man and Bisi a Yoruba woman; both of their families had opposed their "inter-tribal" marriage. The marriage "was blessed by three sons"; Bisi was "a devoted wife", and Ebo did everything to see that "his family was well provided for". "They lived happily, until the coup of January 15th, 1966, which changed everything" (p. 1). They have to leave Lagos for his home town Onitsha. His work is first at Enugu, in the Ministry of Information in the propaganda section; after Enugu has fallen, he starts working in the Department of Military Intelligence in Port Harcourt. When he determines to save his family he takes them to the heart of Igboland. Here, they are hated by the villagers as "saboteurs", and this, as much as the bombings, undermines Bisi's mental stability. Ebo manages through several lucky breaks to move the family out of the country.

The other part of the story is based on miraculously changed information and incorrect rumours: it is believed that one woman has been sent to see the Queen of England who—touched by the sufferings of the innocent Biafran children—wants to talk with a representative of Biafran women in London. The secret flight of Ebo's family is the impetus of all this imaginative storytelling. "At Umuahia, the following morning, women leaders got together for once to protest to the Foreign Secretary about their non-inclusion in the mission" (p. 9). Three women leaders approach the Foreign Secretary each one of them demanding to be sent to London as a representative of Biafran women. Only after having listened to them all do we hear the Foreign Secretary speak: "– I swear by my mother that the Biafran government received no such request from Her Majesty the Queen or from any other prominent woman in the world. What you heard is absolutely untrue" (p. 15).

The latter part of the story is a most blatant satire about the Igbo women leaders at war. Even the National Women's Club's leader, characterised as "more experienced than the other two" (p. 14), is ridiculed while trusting her "feminine intuition": "Of course the Foreign Secretary knew what she meant. Feminine intuition. That was what his wife used to win every argument" (p. 15).

When compared with the latter part of the story, the earlier part treats its characters mildly. True, Ebo gets himself extra money by illegal means since he "gave forged passes, which he got as a D.M.I. Officer, to friends and relatives who paid him in cash and kind", but he is also presented as a good husband who is devoted to the physical and mental well-being of his family. Bisi's excessive expressions are due to her being mentally "burned out". The first part of "Women at War" serves as a background for the latter part of the story. The miraculous escape of Ebo's family is made more humorous than satirical: indeed, it is the women leaders that are satirized and not Ebo who as a high official has knowledge about when to leave the collapsing country—and who thus probably manages to save his life while at the same time getting recognition as a caring husband.

*

"Daddy, Don't Strike the Match" is a story about the Okeke family: Ndidi, a maths teacher, John, a scientist who works with the Research and Production group (R.A.P.), and their children Martin, Keziah, Ifeoma and Ik. They had lived in Kano, Northern Nigeria, but because of the rumours of danger, Ndidi and the children moved to Enugu, which "was the destination of everybody in 1966 and 1967". Only "Mr. Okeke refused to leave; his wife had failed to convince him of the imminent danger" (p. 18). Somewhat later he "escaped death by a narrow margin" (p. 20). It is especially Ndidi, who was born in Kano (and whose mother tongue is Hausa even if she identifies herself as an Igbo), and her daughter Ifeoma who most miss Kano. The setting of the story is Okeke's house except at the very end where the setting is the laboratory. There is lots of talk and interaction in the house between the family members. But the basic plot is simple: Ifeoma, who tends to have nightmares which are linked with the war, says to a lab attendant who comes to fetch John Okeke's cigarettes and matches: "Tell daddy not to strike the match." Then in the lab her daddy strikes a match and "before he realised what happened, he was in the midst of a formidable fire." "It consumed Okeke and his experiment" (pp. 29–30).

John Okeke is one of those talented Igbos who has dedicated his skills to the Biafran cause. "He had contributed a lot to the defence of Biafra. He would continue to give his knowledge and time and, if need be, his life to Biafra" (p. 20). He is made a character who is worried about the well-being of his family but not at the cost of the greater whole of Biafra. To his wife he says: "Don't worry yourself too much. Millions of us are involved in this war. It is not just Okeke's family, but millions of families." He takes the role of an encourager as well: "He held her and kissed her. 'It will end. Take life as you see it. We shall survive. The suffering will end'" (p. 21). John Okeke was involved in bomb making; the following dialogue which is also the thematical crystallization of the story reveals, however, his ambivalent attitude to it.

> "Daddy," Martin began.
> "Yes." Mr. Okeke turned to his eldest son.
> "Daddy, you make bombs in the lab?"
> "Yes we do."
> "Will you teach me how to make bombs?"
> "No" Mr. Okeke said bluntly.
> "Why, daddy?"
> "They are very dangerous to make. And you remember, you told me you were going to be a doctor. You will learn to save people's lives, and not to destroy them."
> "Bombs destroy life?" Ifeoma asked.
> "Yes, don't you know?" Ik asked.
> "And daddy, you make them," Ifeoma accused.
> Mr. Okeke felt a sharp pain somewhere inside him. He had felt that pain before. When was it? He remembered but did not want to recall it. It was very painful.
> And here was Ifeoma, his own daughter accusing him. And he felt the sharp pain again. The pain he felt looking at the accusing face of the dying youth, barely two months ago. (pp. 26–7)

Ndidi and Ifeoma, the only females of the family, express their fears most openly. Ndidi is again a mother who concentrates on the survival of her children, herself and her husband. This is connected with her belief that Biafra will be defeated. With her pessimistic view on Biafra Ndidi is right and her husband with his optimistic view is wrong; also when it was a matter of whether they should leave Kano, she was right. Ifeoma, the only daughter of the family, is also made the seer of the events. But while Ndidi's concern is about her own family only, Ifeoma is the mouthpiece of human suffering without boundaries. In the end, the story proves that her childish way of not drawing a line between "us" and "them" is indeed correct: even if the bomb of her father was meant for "them", it killed and pained "us".

*

"A Certain Death" is a story about a desperate effort to survive: the narrator wants to save her brother's life whatever it takes. The brother has become suicidal since he lost his wife and two children in an air-raid. The sister-narrator is sure that if conscripted he would certainly die; the story then is about her endeavours to help her brother avoid conscription. Apart from its dramatic excitements the story concerns the fears and moral struggles the narrator faces. The end is ambivalent in its 'happiness': while the narrator succeeds in her endeavours, everything happens at the cost of another young Biafran man.

With its many details and atmosphere of anxiety, "A Certain Death" is the gloomiest of Nwapa's stories on the Civil War. Again, the beginning of unhappy events is the January 1966 coup; it was then that the narrator's husband, at the time living in the USA, asked his wife to take their three children back home from Lagos to Igboland. On their way back to 'safety', an accident happened and all the children died. In the next sentence the narrator merely states laconically: "My husband preferred to remain in the U.S.A. after this tragedy" (p. 34). Thus, with her parents and children dead, and husband absent, the narrator has only her brother, and her brother has only her.

The war is a state of chaos: "We were at war with the whole world. We were in a state of emergency. Unimportant people had overnight become Very Important People" (p. 35). In a situation of chaos, people needed scapegoats for their miseries: "Someone who lost a wife and two children in one day must be evil. He must have done something to merit the punishment. If he was not got rid of, the whole town would suffer" (p. 33). But the war was also a game: "If one played one's cards very well, one would survive" (p. 35). It is most important that one knows someone who has power; and, in this case, who is in charge of the recruits. While the first officer tells the narrator that there is no way for her brother to avoid being conscripted, another officer, her friend, promises to organize things: "I shall tick your brother's name as having fulfilled all the conditions. Never mind. There is no problem" (p. 37). The narrator gets her plans through with the illegal help of her friends—and with her money.

Those who have money buy services with it; and those who lack money, provide even macabre services in order to get the money. The young Biafran boy who goes to the army instead of the narrator's brother, does it for the money. It was also his father's wish that he earned money this way; he had done it twice already. Some people are of the opinion that "conscription is certain death. The quickest way to die. Those conscripted have no training at all. Didn't you know?" (p. 40) The harassing question in the mind of the narrator remains: the youth had replaced her brother, but would he survive?

SOZABOY

Sozaboy by Ken Saro-Wiwa is a story told by the title character, the soldierboy. The subtitle of the novel reads: 'A novel in rotten English'. The background of the education of the narrator and protagonist is told in the beginning of the second chapter or 'Lomber Two' (Number Two): he has passed the elementary six exam but could not attend the secondary school since his mother could not afford it. Indeed, the whole novel is characterized by a peculiar language—a kind of uneducated pidgin English; a glossary of six pages is provided at the end of the book. While the story of Mene, the Sozaboy, is told in a peculiar English, the novel raises the more general question of language as mediator of meanings.

The time span of the story covers from the January 1966 coup up to the end of the Civil War. The most important places mentioned are Dukana, the home town of the narrator—which is situated "at the end of the world" (p. 66)—and Pitakwa, which is another name for Port Harcourt. Lagos and Bori are also mentioned, situating the story in South Nigeria. The plot of the story reads as follows: Mene finds a nice young woman, and soon after having married her joins the army and becomes a real sozaboy. The war proves to be different than he had thought. He gets to see a lot of death. He is driven onto the side of the enemy, and after having worked some time on the wrong side, he manages to escape. Among his own people, he is ordered to be shot because of having been a 'deserter'. Again he miraculously escapes death, and continues seeking his mother and his wife Agnes. He returns to his desolated home town and learns that both his mother and wife have died in the bomb attack on Dukana. And since the Dukana people are convinced that Mene is dead and it is his ghost who has returned to the town causing continuing deaths, he flees the town.

Why did Mene decide, voluntarily, to join the army? The text offers more than one reason. First, the old Dukana comrades glorify the braveness of soldiers, and it is especially Zaza who tells about his marvellous adventures and victories—also with women—in the war against 'Hitla' in Burma. While boasting about himself, he mocks Mene and other young men who haven't joined the army. Secondly, the radio starts telling people to be ready to fight and defend themselves. Thirdly, one night the town-crier beats the drum saying that all young men shall go to Pitakwa. This is an order but once there recruiting is made so tempting that Mene makes his decision by himself; we are not told what happens to those who don't come to the same conclusion. It is the impressive outfit of the soldiers and their brisk singing and marching that hypnotize his young mind.

> Immediately, I know that this soza is wonderful thing. With gun and uniform and singing. And marching, left, right, left, right, my father don't you worry, left right, my mother don't you worry, left right. If I happen to die, right, in the battle left, never mind we shall meet again. (p. 53)

Fourth, Mene's young wife Agnes has a romantic-heroic image of an ideal husband who would defend her with his gun. And fifth, it is worth pointing out that the old 'bad' government, whose death is mentioned in the very beginning of the story, was civilian (this is implied) while by contrast, now "the new government of soza and police have come" (p. 1). Indeed, the soldier and police have a good reputation at that moment. And so it happens that for some time, the Chief Commander General becomes Mene's hero: "I think that one day I will be like that soza with spectacle, tall and fine speaking with brass band voice, enjoying myself inside fine car and fine house, giving command to small boys who are just entering into soza life" (p. 77).

Mene joins the army knowing very little about its implications. His limited understanding of the world is by and large presented through his limited language skills. There is a kind of barrier between his own language and the formal language: the formal or official language which is used when mediating information and orders is only partly understood by him.

Mene's limited understanding of the war is more concretely shown through his limited understanding of certain central concepts of the soldier. When coming back from the big recruiting tour from Pitakwa, Mene hears all the people in the lorry talking about the enemy and wonders: "The Enemy. I don't know what this person look like. Or *abi* is he like Hitla? But Hitla is white man. And the people are saying that the enemy is not very far away again. So he cannot be like Hitla" (p. 54). And the following quotation in which the idea is repeated just confirms Mene's ignorance about the concept—and his ignorance about the politics which he has just become involved with as a soldierboy. Now he has only proceeded a step forward in realising that 'fear' is somehow connected with the 'enemy'.

> But every time he (Chief Commander General) will be calling that Enemy, I begin to fear this Mr. Enemy you know. Because I am thinking he must be strong man pass Hitla sef. Otherwise why is everyone talking about him? Even the Chief Commander General is fearing this man. Why? Even sef, why all of us will join hand to kill him. Does he have many heads? What is wrong with him? 'E get stronghead? Or did he call another man's wife? Why does everybody want to kill him? All these things were wondering me as the Chief Commander General was speaking. "You boys have got excellent training. You must be brave and proud of your country." Fine fine grammar. "We shall overcome. The Enemy will be vanquished. God is on our side." (p. 78)

Later, however, he again becomes perplexed. When he is saved by the enemy and given work as a lorry driver all Sozaboy understands is that the enemy treats him well. Thus, he starts rethinking the whole concept: "So I am a fool all this time that I am wanting to kill this enemy! God of mercy!" (p. 126) And again his understanding of the concept changes when his old friends ask him to be careful because "everybody is enemy in this our war" (p. 136). And they are right: Sozaboy's final enemies prove to be people from his very own home town.

The other central concept that is totally hazy to Mene is—'the war' itself. Several times during the war, he reminds himself of Tan Papa's words "because war is war you know" (p. 76) as if this would make things more understandable for him. "War is war you know" is an explanation his 'friend' Bullet also gives to him (p. 90), and all in all that seems to be the explanation the soldiers have to be content with. Also, when the question of why they are fighting at last arises in his mind, he does not dare to ask since he remembers the advice given to the soldiers to "obey before complain" (ibid.).

There are also some 'minor' concepts that are strange to Sozaboy, all of which have been actualised by the war. One is 'a camp': "Why camp? Are they scout or what?" (p. 142) Another word is 'Red Cross'. Yet another is 'Kwasiokor': "Kwasiokor. Kwasiokor. Kwasiokor. I am telling you, I like that name Kwasiokor" (p. 143). It may also be noted that the psychological state of being extremely terrified, the state when there are 'no words' to describe the moment's feelings, engenders a stream of biblical expressions by Sozaboy:

> After the plane have disappeared, then I got up from where I was hiding. Oh Jesus Christ son of God, the thing wey I see my mouth no fit talk am. Oh God our father wey dey for up, why you make man wicked like this to his own brother? Oh Mary, mother of Jesus, pray for us to God to forgive us all our sins and not kill us like fly because of our wickedness. Angel Gabriel, please beg God if he does not want us to live, make 'e no make us only to kill us after like goat or rat or rabbit. Oh, I can never never forget what I saw that morning. (p. 111)

Besides Sozaboy's mental state of being extremely terrified, this fluency of words may imply the area where Sozaboy's linguistic skills are at their best. Religious discourse is much better known to him than the discourse of war—or the realism of warfare.

But the novel is clearly a Bildungsroman: the main theme of the book concerns how the essence of war enters into Sozaboy's understanding. He comes to see how the war makes the soldiers thieves and drunkards and liars and killers even of their own people. In fact, he gets are two important insights: first, while the concept of 'enemy' becomes complex to him, he concludes that there is no enemy proper; secondly, it is the great suffering of the refugees that makes all the war just meaningless:

> If you see how all their eyes have gone inside their head, and all their hair have become palm oil colour and they have dirty dirty rag shirt and all their bones are shaking inside their body, I am telling you, if you see all these things, and you think about them very well, you will know at once that war is very bad and stupid game. (p. 151)

It is also noteworthy that the different parties of the war are never mentioned: although Sozaboy and the Dukana people are on the side of Biafra, Biafrans or Nigerians remain unnamed. This of course emphasises Sozaboy's unawareness of the whole of politics; but it also serves the essentialist concept of the war the book offers: it is not important to mention what the parties are since the war itself, as such, is just a big mistake and confusion and the source of much suffering.

In addition to the essentialist view of the war, *Sozaboy* offers a class-based image of the society as well. In the war, the bombs are a threat to all, but the threat of hunger does not concern everybody; put simply, it does not concern those who have power and money. Chief Birabee, Pastor Barika and Manmuswak are epitomes of these people. The two first are from Sozaboy's own home town, Dukana; but because of money, they are willing to send Sozaboy to be killed, as a 'deserter'. Only fate saves Sozaboy and two other soldiers—or rather: the executioner runs out of ammunition. This scene is a culmination of Sozaboy's life in several ways. He not only learns how his own people are able to order him to be killed but the killer himself proves to be his 'friend' Manmuswak. Sozaboy learns that Manmuswak is a mercenary soldier who changes sides according to whoever pays him. What connects Chief Birabee, Pastor Barika and Manmuswak is not any ideology or vision they share but rather that they want to become fat and wealthy at any cost, that is, at the cost of others' lives. The character of Chief Birabee is already shown at the beginning of the war: he is slick towards those he thinks are more powerful than he is, but towards people under him he is patronising. However, it is the character of Pastor Barika that the war makes visible; earlier it was hidden behind his religious phrases. It is in Pastor Barika that the most ironic image of brotherly love and communal loyalty is presented.

What idea of Biafra then, does the book present? As mentioned earlier, its name never occurs. Also, it should be clear by now that for Sozaboy it was an issue too difficult to handle. But there is one scene where Sozaboy paraphrases the talk of Chief Birabee:

> – and then we shall all return home and we shall be in a new country where nobody will tief, there be no hungry again, everything will be free, from water to food, to cloth to wear to medicine to lorry and licence. And nobody will take bribe again and everyday the sun will shine long time and the rain will fall short time and the yam and maize will grow well well and everyone will get work or anything that the person want to do he can do. In short, after we have win the war, there will be life more abundant. (pp. 154–5)

The biggest irony of this image is not in its paradisiacal character or in the fact that Biafra does not win the war but in that that these words are put in the mouth of a person who is not willing to sacrifice anything at all to his little community of Dukana, to say nothing about the bigger community, Biafra. It is Zaza, Birabee and Barika who encourage Sozaboy to wage war while avoiding it themselves. It is the Chief Commander General who ultimately is responsible for sending the young boys to the front with propaganda slogans and no understanding of the framework of the war (nor does the text imply that any was ever offered). The writer's pessimistic view about the possibility of a new happy state is extremely obvious.

The only 'positive' thing in the war descriptions of *Sozaboy* is the narrator himself. He keeps his sense of morality alive by remembering the advice of his mother. He remains surprisingly innocent: he goes through the war without shooting the first shot. There is no logic in the war: both the bad things that happen to him and the miraculous escapes from the jaws of death are just absurd. The book is full of ironies. Mene is on the warfront and remains alive; but his mother and wife die in their own home. Agnes wanted her husband to become a soldier and defend her with his gun. Mene became a soldier with a gun but could not defend her. Mene wanted to be a soldier in order to become a 'big' man. In the end he has lost his mother, wife and house, all he owned; and even the Dukana people compel him to leave the town since they need a scapegoat for all their miseries. It is noteworthy, however, that after all his experiences the narrator avoids becoming insane. He keeps his sense of simple morality even in brutalising conditions—which may ultimately be a reason why he avoids psychological collapse.

CONCLUSION

The biggest difference between Nwapa and Saro-Wiwa is that the former writes as an Igbo and the latter as an Ogoni: the former belonged to the major Biafran group and the latter to a small minority people, whose attitude towards the secessionist side was quite problematic. Nwapa, as a 'typical' Igbo, emphasizes that the harassments and slaughterings of the Igbos after the military coups were the reason why the Igbos fled from different parts of Nigeria to the Igbo heartland, and, consequently, wanted to secede from Nigeria. On the other hand, Saro-Wiwa's memoirs of the war, *On a Darkling Plain: An Account of the Nigerian Civil War*—which came out in 1989, four years later than *Sozaboy*—conclude that the Ogoni people, like other Rivers' people, were the most overlooked victims of the war. As Mary

Harvan puts it: "They were conscripted to fight in a war in which most of them had no ideological or personal investment; were forced to shelter and feed Biafran troops; were marched into refugee camps as Biafran borders shrank; were called collaborators by the Igbo when federal forces recaptured Rivers-area lands; and were starved and tortured in refugee camps and in military detention. For Saro-Wiwa, these abuses epitomize the mistreatment of marginalized ethnic minorities in Nigeria."[58] *Sozaboy*'s fictionalized representation of the sufferings and ideological puzzlement of Rivers' people during this war marks an important first step in narrating historical events from an Ogoni perspective.

However, even if Nwapa looks at the war from an Igbo and Saro-Wiwa from an Ogoni position, the books under discussion share their two main themes. The biggest common 'message' of them is the cruel nature of war which makes Nwapa state its 'lesson' in the title of her novel *Never Again*, and which makes Saro-Wiwa end his whole book with the words of the protagonist: "And I was thinking how I was prouding before to go to soza and call myself Sozaboy. But now if anybody say anything about war or even fight, I will just run and run and run and run and run. Believe me, yours sincerely." The concept of war in all the writings is essentialist: cruelty is the essence of the war. The implication then is that war tends to brutalize people whatever their side; and Saro-Wiwa, who describes both parties of the war, does make this view quite explicit.

The other main theme of the writings is this: the war strengthens neither Igbo nor Biafran identity. On the contrary: while before the war people basically could trust the loyalty of their own community members, during the war things change. At one end of the spectrum there are the pro-Biafrans, whose practice of communalism was based on forced and exaggerated togetherness (propaganda) and on vague and unrealistic goals (illusions); and at the other end, the non-believers in Biafra, who cannot create a community since their view is an anomaly in the official pro-Biafran society. Further, a new 'law and order' prevails in both Nwapa's and Saro-Wiwa's books: don't trust anybody. And this attitude certainly does not nourish an identity

---

58. Mary Harvan, "Representing Ogoni: Ken Saro-Wiwa, the Ogoni Movement, and Language as Resistance". Manuscript.

based on a sense of community. However, for the individual, it is essential to maintain some identity, in order not to become lost and fragmented. This identity then is shown to be based by and large on already held beliefs (including 'theories' of scapegoats); Christian and indigenous beliefs are given a significant role in both Nwapa's and Saro-Wiwa's works.

While the essentialist anti-war image determines Nwapa's and Saro-Wiwa's descriptions, they are not interested in more detailed political questions around the Biafran war, for example, the reasons why the war began, how it came to its end, and what was the concrete work (beyond producing propaganda) of the pro-Biafrans. And they definitely do not tell what kind of images and expectations were attached to the state of Biafra (except those few satirized images given by them both): what kind of positive visions made people like Christopher Okigbo dedicate their lives 'for the Biafran cause'. But the works under discussion give a many-faceted image of the brutalizing nature of the war itself: its destructive impact on Igbo and Biafran as well as on individual identity.

THE WRITINGS UNDER DISCUSSION

Flora Nwapa, *Never Again*. Tana Press, Enugu, Nigeria, 1986 (1975).
Flora Nwapa, *Wives at War and Other Stories*. Tana Press, Enugu, Nigeria, 1986 (1980):
   "Wives at War"
   "Daddy, Don't Strike the Match"
   "A Certain Death"
Ken Saro-Wiwa, *Sozaboy: A novel in rotten English*. Longman, USA 1994. (Nigerian edition published in 1985 by Saros International Publishers, Port Harcourt, Nigeria.)

The Language of Africa-Centered Knowledge in South Africa: Universalism, Relativism and Dependency

Ousseina Alidou and Alamin M. Mazrui

INTRODUCTION

The maintenance of apartheid in South Africa depended, of course, on its ideological hegemony that provided it with some degree of legitimacy. To some extent, this entailed the subversion of indigenous systems and paradigms of thought and the destruction of the very structures that made such thoughts possible.[59] Can there be genuine democracy in South Africa when prevailing post-apartheid institutions *continue* to foster forms of knowledge that *continue* to produce inequalities which *continue* to underprivilege the African majority? Political apartheid is over; but economic apartheid seems to be well and kicking. Can economic apartheid be brought to an end—a fundamental prerequisite to a secure democratic foundation—without a complete transformation in the (re)production of knowledge?

A number of South African thinkers are indeed of the opinion that genuine democracy will have to address the politics of knowledge production, especially, as Nancy Murray observes: "The new South African government is hoping that education would be the vehicle for eventually transforming the bureaucracy and putting political democracy on a firm base by creating an aware population ... [But] change is slow to come. Schools are still operating with textbooks ... which

---

59. The denigration of African languages, customs, and political and social structures, medicinal and health care traditions, technological and other knowledge systems, was all part of the offensive against African culture. The articles in Joseph K. Adjaye's collection, *Time in the Black Experience* demonstrate that even African conceptions of time sometimes had to be subverted as a prerequisite to the establishment of a colonially-controlled capitalism.

convey the world view of the white elite" (Murray, 1997:10-11). As demonstrated in the multi-disciplinary collection on *Knowledge and Power in South Africa* (Jonathan D. Jansen, 1991), some of these thinkers now stress the need for a paradigmatic shift to Africa-centered knowledge not only as a way of (re)presenting the majority interest, but also as a means of (re)defining South African identity in the post-apartheid era.

Expectedly, language has featured quite prominently in this quest for Africa-centered knowledge. In what language(s) should it be constructed, articulated and imparted? Two contesting positions have emerged in this connection, pitting indigenous African languages, on the one hand, against imperial languages[60], on the other. There is, first, the "pragmatist" school of thought which contends that imperial languages like English can be refashioned to carry the weight of African thought. This linguistic reformation, the argument goes, would not only be the more pragmatic option, but also one that is in accord with the interests of national unity. On the other side, are the "nationalists" who argue that language determines a people's world view in a culturally circumscribed manner. The only path towards Africa-centered knowledge according to this latter school of thought, therefore, is through Africa's own indigenous languages.

We have used the concepts of "nationalism" and "pragmatism" exclusively in the linguistic sense of the terms. *Linguistic nationalism* is that brand of nationalism which is particularly concerned about the value of its own language, seeks to defend it against other languages, and encourages its use and enrichment. It is indeed possible, therefore, to be a nationalist in a broader political sense without being *linguistically nationalistic*. Many Africans, especially in the sub-Saharan region are nationalistic about their "race", ethnicity and often about their land as defined by the more recent tradition of state borders. But

---

60. The English, French, Portuguese, Italian and Spanish languages in Africa are sometimes described as "languages of former colonial masters" or simply as "ex-colonial languages". In this essay we also use the term imperial languages. An imperial language can be defined as a language which was introduced by a dominant external power and has yet to develop a substantial constituency of native speakers from the indigenous population. Among the characteristics of imperial languages is that they began from above as languages of power and at a certain level they have to be learnt formally. All ex-colonial languages are essentially imperial languages according to the above definition.

nationalism about African languages is relatively weak both in emotional and demographic magnitude in Africa as compared with the experience of India, for example, and indeed of many other Asian countries. And African nationalists who are not linguistically nationalistic in the sense defined above, tend to invoke the argument of pragmatism, i.e. the idea that Africa's linguistic complexity necessitates the national maintenance and promotion of Euro-languages inherited from the colonial experience.

In this paper we shall attempt to demonstrate that the pragmatists and the nationalists represent two sides of the same coin and do not adequately account for the historical facts of the South African situation. Instead, we propose a "dependency" paradigm which focuses on the role of imperial languages as promoters of intellectual dependency to the detriment of democratic development in South Africa, specifically, and in North-South relations in general. Our paradigm, in other words, accepts the nationalist solution without accepting its theoretical premise, and rejects the pragmatist prescription without rejecting its conception of language as a dynamic and malleable phenomenon.

ENGLISH AND THE APARTHEID AFTERMATH

In their general study of language in the African experience Mazrui and Mazrui (forthcoming) pose the question: What is the effect of the end of political apartheid for Africa as a whole? The struggle against apartheid was a pan-Africanizing experience creating a sense of solidarity among Black people across the continent and between Africa and its diaspora.

Pan-Africanism, paradoxically, often flourished through the unifying force of European languages. Figures like W.E. duBois and Marcus Garvey would never have become founding fathers of trans-Atlantic pan-Africanism without the mediation of the English language. Figures like Aimé Césaire and Léopold Sédar Senghor would not have become founding fathers of *Négritude* without the role of the French language. Racism and apartheid in South Africa helped to consolidate African solidarity through imperial languages.

But a new contradiction emerged with the end of political apartheid. Governance in South Africa itself was more Africanized almost by definition as Nelson Mandela and the African National Congress assumed control. But across the African continent the end of political apartheid was an end of one experience within pan-Africanization. A major stimulus of solidarity was defused. Pan-Africanism was wounded by its own success. In the process narrower forms of African nationalism, less dependent on European nationalism[61] began to reassert themselves. Ethnic nationalism among Black South Africans and elsewhere became a new manifest destiny. What were its implications for European languages like English?

With the end of political apartheid in South Africa, the English language has more clearly gained ground. Although South Africa has declared eleven official languages (theoretically reducing English to one eleventh of the national status), in reality the new policy demotes Afrikaans—the historical rival to English in South Africa.[62] Before the 1990s English was officially the co-equal of Afrikaans, but sometimes received fewer resources from the government within the media and within publishing. But the end of political apartheid has raised the question of whether Afrikaans should be treated in the same camp as the nine African indigenous languages. Should Afrikaans be treated as another native vernacular?

On the other hand, precisely because English enjoys greater public support, it continues to predominate in the official domains of South Africa, and will probably to expand in the less official domains of the society. As in many other countries in Africa and the world, the increasing success of English in South Africa is also partly tied America's growing cultural influence—especially in the post-Cold War period when we have moved from a bipolar world in superpower rivalry to a unipolar world dominated by the USA. Unlike the British in the colonial era who were sometimes disturbed by attempts by missionaries

---

61. The "Eurocentric" thrust in intellectual paradigms, and the Francophonie movement with its uncertain future, are examples of western nationalism. There are moments when African nationalism(s) are less of a response to the impetus of hegemonic nationalist assertions from the West, and more a product of the throbbings of local politics. We have witnessed such moments in Africa in the aftermath of colonialism in much of the continent, and of apartheid in South Africa.
62. See appendix for the clauses on languages in the new South African constitution.

to teach the "natives" English at an early age, the Americans in the neocolonial era are relentless in their efforts to spread the English language. American economic and political interests abroad have led the United States to contribute large sums of money towards the teaching of English in a number of countries (Ali Mazrui, 1989:98). And since the end of political apartheid there has been an "academic scramble" for South Africa among American universities—often with the support of funds from the US federal government—competing with each other to establish a foothold in the country's institutions of higher learning. In spite of South Africa's language policy that seems to give greater weight to African languages, there are, therefore, local conditions as well as global forces that seem to be operating to the overall advantage of the English language.

In neighboring Namibia, the choice was more clearly in favor of English against Afrikaans (Pütz, 1995; Harlech-Jones, 1990). Afrikaans has been rejected not only because of its seemingly oppressive history, but also because it is considered, like Damara, Silozi, Nama etc., to be an ethnically and regionally bound language with supposedly divisive consequences for Namibians. English, on the other hand, has been chosen because "it has a lot going for it—a global language, it is a language in which most of the United Nations' work is carried out; it is a language of many of our neighbors in Africa. Its role is likely only to widen, as most of the global satellite networks use English for their broadcasts" (Hage G. Geingob, 1995:177).

Unlike Namibia, however, South Africa made a linguistically pluralist choice. Nonetheless, we should bear in mind that the end of political apartheid in South Africa represents the triumph of a particular kind of African nationalism—the struggle against legalized and institutionalized racial oppression and cultural imposition. Paradoxically, the struggle sometimes enhanced the status of the English language among the oppressed. English became not just the language of oppression but also, by a strange destiny the language of liberation. As McLean and McCormick indicate:

> The recent restructuring of state and society which has enfranchised African language speakers achieved the recognition of all major languages as official, thereby effectively demoting Afrikaans and English to an equal status with nine others. The evidence from various domains, however, is that this policy thrust towards multilingualism is often

intended and perceived as a symbolic statement, and that for instrumental purposes English remains the dominant language in South African public life. (McLean and McCormick, 1996:329)

And so South Africa has probably been experiencing an expanding role of the English language in spite of its pluralist choice.

As we approach the twenty-first century, therefore, South Africa is still caught between the forces of nationalism and pragmatism, each reinforced by theoretical arguments from relativism and universalism, respectively. And it is to this dichotomy between linguistic relativism and linguistic universalism that we must now turn.

LANGUAGE POLICY: BETWEEN RELATIVISM AND UNIVERSALISM

The nationalist school, as suggested before, is the one that advocates the centering of "African languages" on the premise that only they can adequately encapsulate and transmit knowledge from an Africa-centered perspective. In the words of Peter Mwaura, for example,

> Language influences the way in which we perceive reality, evaluate it and conduct ourselves with respect to it. Speakers of different languages and cultures see the universe differently, evaluate it differently, and behave towards its reality differently. Language controls thought and action and speakers of different languages do not have the same world view or perceive the same reality unless they have the same culture or background. (Mwaura, 1980:27)

In other words, languages of non-African origin are deemed inherently incapable of relaying an African world view. Similar sentiments have been expressed by other members of the African intelligentsia, from Ngugi wa Thiong'o (1986) in East Africa to Chidi Maduka (1980) in West Africa.

In South Africa this nationalist position is perhaps best represented by Mazisi Kunene who sees a direct relationship between African languages and African knowledge systems. In his words, "in dealing with language, people in the African context are not considering the same phenomena as are those who employ western concepts and classifications of meaning" (Kunene, 1992:36). As a result, "they cannot be said to be African cultural representatives who write in another language because, in spirit at least, they speak from the perspective provided for them by the effective apparatus of mental control exercised by the former colonial power" (Kunene, 1992:32).

The pragmatists, on the other hand, seem to be of the view that any language is malleable enough to present and represent the world view of any culture or community, and that the determination of an appropriate language policy, therefore, should only be based on "pragmatic" considerations. Many of the adherents of this position are not necessarily opposed to the centering of African languages, but they would see no need for it if, for example, English proved to be the more pragmatic choice for a country for both local and international reasons. Thinkers associated with this position have included Chinua Achebe (1976:67) of Nigeria, Kofi Awoonor (1975:149) of Ghana, and Ezekiel Mphahlele of South Africa. Responding to the "language of African literature debate" for example, Mphahlele writes:

> The creative instinct runs ahead of social, political, and economic development, and the creative impulse cannot wait for such developments [in African languages] before it expresses itself. So we use English, French and Portuguese, which we know and have mastered. (Mphahlele, 1963:8)

According to Mphahlele then, the insistence upon using African languages in creative writing at this particular historical juncture would only relegate African literature to a state of perpetual underdevelopment.

The nationalist position on the relationship between language and cognition has close affinity with the linguistic relativism associated with Edward Sapir and Benjamin Lee Whorf. According to Edward Sapir for example,

> Human beings are very much at the mercy of a particular language which has become the medium of expression for their society...The fact of the matter is that the 'real world' is to a large extent built up on the language habits of the group. No two languages are ever sufficiently similar to be considered as representing the same social reality. (Sapir, 1929:208)

Whorf (1959) was an even more enthusiastic proponent of linguistic relativism, with a persuasion that is clearly deterministic. He claimed that a person's basic ontology is structured by language and that grammar embodies an outline of a cultural metaphysics. For this reason he concluded that speakers of different languages will map the world in different ways.

We understand, of course, that there is a wide spectrum of relativistic positions, ranging from the strong claim that language actually *controls* thought in a culturally specific manner, to the relatively weak claim that merely posits some correlation between some aspects of language and some aspects of culture. Even Sapir and Whorf themselves vacillated between strong and moderate claims in their conception of relativism. But, as demonstrated in Peter Mwaura's views quoted above, it is the deterministic strand of relativism that seems to have had the greatest impact among African linguistic nationalists.

The pragmatists, on the other hand, would probably seek inspiration from the universalism of Noam Chomsky who stressed the common features of language and played down the 'surface features' that characterized individual languages. As Chomsky declares "it is plausible to suppose that apart from pathology (potentially an important area of inquiry) such variation as there may be is marginal and can be safely ignored across a broad range of linguistic investigation" (Chomsky, 1986:18). Superimposed on this linguistic uniformity is the assumption that the language faculty in itself is an innate human characteristic. Chomsky views it as a genetically predetermined, organized property of the mind and not as an acquisition that is obtained from outside the individual by means of social, psychological or cultural conditioning (Chomsky, 1968:ix–x).

Chomsky thus came to support one of the Enlightenment's most cherished ideals, universal human identity. For, in his account of linguistic phenomena, Chomsky provides what amounts to a general theory of human beings as uniquely defined by their linguistic capacity. This linguistic attribute, in turn, endows all humans, and in equal measure, with the capacity for rational thought and for "free, causally undetermined and creative activity which is nevertheless intelligible to others because all human beings share innate propensities which, under suitable circumstances, induce the development in each individual of standards of intelligibility which are similar to those which develop in other human individuals" (D'Agostino, 1986:207).

From the psycholinguistic point of view, there is little hard evidence to support either of these hypotheses in their extreme forms.

Chomsky's universalism tends to be strongly anti-empiricist, having originated in a speculative intellectual tradition that continues to shape its doctrine. Attempts have been made to adduce evidence from natural language, child language and language acquisition, speech errors, speech pathology, linguistic universals, pidgins and creoles, but none of this evidence can be said to provide concrete proof about the inner workings of Chomsky's 'mental faculty' of language.

As for the relativist hypothesis, its premise that there is a causal relationship between language, culture and cognition has been called into question by several writers. By the mid-1960s so much had been written against the Sapir-Whorf hypothesis that Robbins Burling (1964:26) regarded the entire question of linguistic relativism as having falling into disrepute.

But what about at the more ideological or political level of the debate? Does the African experience lend greater credibility to one hypothesis as opposed to the other? In our opinion, both hypotheses have contributed to the political agenda since the colonial era in ways that clearly reveal their complementarity. Conversely, their mutual reliance on a world view that bases its concept of social progress on an ahistorically defined human nature has resulted, at best, in mixed blessings for Africans.

Colonialism ushered in the use of European languages on the African continent and it usually serves as the political point-of-departure in the debate on the language question in Africa. There is no doubt that one rather uniform feature of colonialism in Africa was its treatment of European languages as ideological institutions whose particular relationship with the African colonial subject could either consolidate or undermine the colonial status quo. But the colonial language policies themselves were not quite uniform. They often varied on the basis of two major considerations: first, that language was a reservoir of culture and a vehicle of cultural transmission. Second, that language was a reservoir of knowledge and a transmitter of ideas, including those that could serve subversive ends through resistance against colonial rule.

In a sense, then, colonial language policies had to deal with a seemingly paradoxical situation: if the colonial language in its role as a cultural transmission belt could numb the consciousness of the colonized to a point of acquiescence to the colonial status quo, would not language as bearer of knowledge imbue the African with a counter-consciousness dangerous to the very survival of colonialism? These two considerations were often in the foreground of colonial language policies in Africa.

The French had great confidence in their language as a transmitter of French cultural values. By implication, therefore, any subversive knowledge that the African could have acquired in the process of education in the French language was expected to be neutralized by the "potency" of French culture. French colonialism, therefore, sought its security in linguistic and cultural assimilationist policies. And, generally speaking, it is in French (and to some extent Portuguese) colonies that we find the clearest evidence supporting the nationalist thesis that the imposition of European languages was an important cultural aid to colonialism. "Francophone" Africa[63], for example, Paulin Djité explains:

> French was imposed at the outset of the colonial era as an instrument of multidimensional domination...Persons who did not speak French were considered barbarians, and the civilized people of France had the divine duty to educate such persons...The imposition and expansion of the language was then seen as the best way to control and "assimilate" the "subjects" of the colonies. (Djité, 1992:166)

Unlike the British who were sometimes wary of the quick and "reckless" spread of their language, the French, then, were linguistically hegemonic to the extreme. Where the British provided some room for the use and development of some African languages, for example, the French officially banned the use of African languages in

---

63. It is, of course odd to characterize African countries as "Anglophone," "Francophone" or "Lusophone" when the proportion of speakers of the imperial languages is so small. Asia too was colonized. And yet nobody refers to "Anglophone Asia" or "Francophone Asia." Perhaps the difference in the two regions of the world—Africa and Asia—lies in the scale of political dependence on the imperial languages. Where legislatives exist in sub Saharan Africa, the overwhelming majority have conducted their debates in European languages. Most legal business in the great majority of sub-Saharan African countries has to be done in the imperial languages. The constitutions or basic laws are still expressed entirely in European languages. When we look at the educational systems of sub-Saharan Africa, almost all are predicated on the supremacy of European languages as media of instruction. Terms like "Anglophone" and "Francophone Africa," therefore can be considered appropriate if we use them to describe the degree of the linguo-cultural dependency in the societies concerned rather than the proportion of speakers of the languages.

education and "ruled that only French was to be used" (Djité, 1992:166). But if language as a transmitter of culture was the source of French confidence in their language, German confidence in their own language was predicated upon its potential to impart German knowledge. Assuming an increasingly aggressive role in European geo-politics which had world ramifications, Germany was in a hurry to outstrip other European nations in technological advancement, with its leading Western philosophical tradition, Germany could only regard its language as a custodian of "German knowledge" which it wanted to monopolize. An exclusivist language policy that would deny colonial subjects access to the German language, therefore, was believed to be in the greater interest of German colonialism. This policy contributed to the consolidation of the Swahili language in German East Africa, later known as Tanganyika, or Tanzania (after Tanganyika's union with Zanzibar).

The British, on the other hand, tried, though inconsistently, to strike a balance between the two considerations. In many instances of British colonialism, the African was allowed a somewhat regulated access to the English language. This meant regulated acculturation, on the one hand, and regulated induction into spheres of western knowledge on the other. Both doses were to be just sufficient to render the African functional in British-introduced administrative institutions, while limiting exposure to the kind of knowledge that had subversive potential.

Whatever the case, it is quite clear that all these colonial language policies, despite their variation, had common ideological foundations. Whether in favor of encouraging the acquisition of the European language by the colonized, or of using African languages, colonial language policies at this macro-level were all intended to consolidate the colonial status quo.

South Africa offers the example of a slightly different intra-European rivalry. Adopting a language policy influenced by the Sapir-Whorf hypothesis and supposedly designed to keep Africans "African" and European power unchallenged, Afrikaner officialdom introduced the so-called "Bantu Education Act" in the mid-1950s. Justifying it as an exercise in separate but equal development,

Afrikaners attempted to preempt the cultural "westernization" of the African by restricting him/her to an African tongue, allowing him/her access to Afrikaans only at a later stage in his/her education. Except at the university level, the English language was accorded a subsidiary role in education. However, partly in response to the coercive manner in which Bantu Education was administered, Africans rebelled during the 1976 Soweto protest against Afrikaans and in favor, not of indigenous languages, but of English, the language that was more widely used among the elites in many parts of Africa.

What is clear from the above discussion, then, is that neither the psycholinguistic evidence nor the African socio-political experience from the colonial era to the present unambiguously supports the positions of the relativists/nationalists or the universalists/pragmatists. At both levels of analysis, the two hypotheses seem to complement each other: in any language we experience the particular and the universal working with each other, making it a potential instrument of either Western epistemological hegemony or Africa-centered knowledge. It does not seem sensible, therefore, for African nations to design language policies based exclusively on one or the other paradigm.

Between universalism and relativism, however, there is a third paradigm which seems to favor policies rooted in African languages. This is the dependency paradigm.

LANGUAGE POLICY: THE DEPENDENCY PERSPECTIVE

As suggested earlier, the dependency perspective essentially accepts the conclusion of the nationalist school without accepting its argument that without African languages there can be no Africa-centered thought. On the other hand, it accepts the reasoning of some of the pragmatists that any language can be transmuted to create a counter-discourse without acceding to the suggestion that, in the present global constellation of political forces, such a language for Africa can, in fact, be one or the other of the imperial languages from across the sea. In other words, the dependency argument is rooted, not in the nationalist assumption of some deterministic relationship between language, culture and cognition, nor in the pragmatist belief that there is an inherent malleability in language which is sufficient to freely cast from it discourses and counter-discourses, but in the reality of power relations on a global scale. While the imperial languages do indeed have the potential of performing a counter-discourse function against imperialism, Africa currently lacks the power to set its own terms of discourse in these inherited languages.

Africa-centered knowledge has become a problem partly because of the foreign origins of the modern educational institutions. The African university, for example, is so uncompromisingly alien in the African context and has been transplanted with few concessions if any to African cultures. Its impact therefore has been more culturally alienating than it might have been. A whole generation of African graduates has grown up despising its own ancestry and scrambling to imitate others. Contrary to colonialist views, it is not the traditional African who resembles the ape; it has been more the westernized one often fascinated by the West's cultural mirror. A disproportionate number of these cultural "apes" continue to be products of universities.

Those African graduates who have later become university teachers have themselves on the whole remained intellectual imitators and disciples of the West. African historians have begun to innovate methodologically as they have grappled with oral tradition and the oral history of Africa. But most of the other disciplines are still condemned to paradigmatic dependency.

An important source of intellectual dependency is the language in which African graduates and scholars are taught. For the time being, it is impossible for an African to be even slightly familiar with the works of Karl Marx or Ricardo without the help of European languages. Marx' premier work *Das Kapital* is not yet available in trans-ethnic languages like Hausa, Silozi or Zulu, let alone in more ethnically bound languages like Kidigo. In short, major intellectual paradigms of the West are likely to remain unavailable even in a single African language unless there is a genuine educational revolution involving widespread adoption of African languages as media of instruction.

As matters now stand, an African who has a good command of a European language has probably assimilated other aspects of western culture as well. This is because the process of acquiring European languages in Africa has tended to be overwhelmingly through a formal system of western-style education. It is because of this that the concept of an African Marxist who is not also westernized is at the present time a sociolinguistic impossibility. This also applies to the modern African surgeon, zoologist or economist.

Nor is this simply a case of the surgeon or economist or Marxist acquiring an additional skill called a European language which he/she is capable of discarding when he/she discusses matters of surgery, economics or Marxism with fellow professionals in his/her own society. Professional Chinese or Japanese social scientists for example can organize a conference or convention and discuss professional matters almost entirely in Chinese and Japanese, respectively. But a conference of African social scientists, devoted to issues of social science, and conducted primarily in African languages is still impossible in the majority of African situations. It is because of these kinds of considerations that intellectual dependency in Africa is perhaps inseparable from linguistic dependency (Mazrui and Mazrui, 1996:209–211).

The linguistic domestication of knowledge from the West and other parts of the world can indeed be the beginning of breaking the cycle of dependency in Africa. This process will, first, expand the capacity of African languages for the type of scientific intellection necessary in higher education. Secondly, scientific knowledge that is more accessible to those who are not culturally westernized is likely to be subjected to a different mode of critical assessment, leading eventually to a more organic adaptation of western knowledge and paradigms to the African cultural milieu.

There have been suggestions of course that European languages too have a potential for African intellectual and cultural liberation. Invoking the Caliban-Prospero analogy, for example, Kofi Awoonor states:

> It is like Caliban in *The Tempest*. When he was taught English he used it against its conquerors. Prospero gloats about the fact that he taught him English. And Caliban said "Yes, you taught me so I learned how to curse and I will curse you for as long as you occupy my Island and deny me my rightful place in it." So it becomes an internalized weapon of our self-assertion because what we are also doing in the same process is, to

liberate ourselves from the stranglehold of western cultural structures. (Awoonor, 1975:149)

Similar sentiments have been expressed by Alastair Pennycook:

> English is not only a structural producer of global inequalities, but also produces inequalities by creating subject positions that contribute to their subjectification. But it is also at this point that possibilities for resistance present themselves in alternative readings of Rudyard Kipling, post-colonial struggle in English, and the formation of counter-discourses (Pennycook, 1995:53).

Against this backdrop of the malleability of English, Pennycook calls on all applied linguists and English teachers around the world to "become political actors engaged in a critical pedagogical project to use English to oppose the dominant discourses of the West, and to help the articulation of counter-discourses in English" (Pennycook, 1995:55).

But as Paulin Hountondji rightly points out, the requirement that one must have proficiency in a European language to have access to the knowledge produced in the West, not only further marginalizes African languages, but actually constitutes a major obstacle to the democratization of knowledge at both the local and global levels (Hountondji, 1988:17). Essentially endorsing Houtondji's position on pro-imperial language policies in Africa, Paulin Djité has argued that "it is hard to believe that there can be, or that one can possibly argue for, a true and lasting development under such policy when so many people do not know their constitutional and legal rights, cannot understand the developmental goals of their governments, and therefore cannot actively exercise their basic democratic right simply because they are written in [foreign languages]" (Djité, 1990:98). For example, there is considerable research which clearly demonstrates that less than 15% of the African population of the "Francophone" countries barely function in French, while 90% of the same population functions very well in the widespread African linguae francae such as Hausa, Djula/Bamanankan, Fulfulde, Kiswahili and Wolof (Djité, 1990:94–98). In a sense, what the pragmatists' position fails to capture is precisely this class dynamics on language choice and language use operating in Africa. In spite of themselves, then, the pragmatists have to contend with the question of how pragmatic the choice of an imperial language can be for Africa when it is not accessible to the majority of Africans at the essential levels of functionality.

Furthermore, counter-discourse is not the same thing as independent discourse. Counter-discourse is often a reactive process to the terms of discourse established by the other. The African quest for intellectual independence must be based on independent terms of reference capable of guiding South Africa and the continent in general toward a more organic path, i.e. a path that is not imposed politically from outside but one that emerges democratically from within in direct response to local needs and conditions. Under the present global configuration of power relations, the English language is not likely to allow Africans the politico-economic space for this kind of intellectual independence. African languages may fare better, for the very act of recentering them sets in motion new dynamics that may provide some room for intellectual manoeuvre.

APPENDIX

Note: The country's national policy on language is articulated in Chapter 1, article 6 of the Constitution of the Republic of South Africa adopted in 1996. It states as follows:

Languages

(1) The official languages of the Republic are Sepedi, Sesotho, Setswana, siSwati, Tshivenda, Xitsonga, Afrikaans, English, isNdebele, isiXhosa, and isiZulu.

(2) Recognising the historically diminished use and status of the indigenous languages of our people, the state must take practical and positive measures to elevate the status and advance the use of these languages.

(3) (a) The national government and provincial governments may use any particular official languages for the purposes of government, taking into account usage, practicality, expense, regional circumstances and the balance of the needs and preferences of the population as a whole or in the province concerned; but the national government and each provincial government must use at least two official languages.

(b) Municipalities must take into account the language usage and preferences of the residents.

(4) The national government and provincial governments, by legislative and other measures, must regulate and monitor their use of official

languages. Without detracting from the provisions of subsection (2), all official languages must enjoy parity of esteem and must be treated equitably.

(5) A Pan South African Language Board established by national legislation must-
    (a) promote, and create conditions for, the development and use of-
        (i) all official languages;
        (ii) the Khoi, Nama, and San languages; and
        (iii) sign language; and
    (b) promote and ensure respect for-
        (i) all languages commonly used by communities in South Africa, including German, Greek, Gujarati, Hindi, Portuguese, Tamil, Telegu and Urdu; and
        (ii) Arabic, Hebrew, Sanskrit and other languages used for religious purposes in South Africa.

REFERENCES

Achebe, Chinua. *Morning Yet on Creation Day*. Garden City, New York: Anchor, 1976.
Adjaye, Joseph K. Time in the Black Experience, Westport Connecticut: Greenwood Publishing Group, 1994.
Awoonor, Kofi. "Tradition and Continuity in African Literature", pp.133–163 in *In Person: Achebe, Awoonor and Soyinka at the University of Washington*. Morell, Karen L. (ed.). Seattle: University of Washington, 1975.
Burling, Robbins. "Cognitive and Componential Analysis: God's Truth or Hocus-Pocus?", *American Anthropologist*, No. 66, 1964:20–28.
Carrol, John B. (ed.). *Language, Mind and Reality. Selected Writings of Benjamin Lee Whorf*. Cambridge: MIT Press, 1959.
Chomsky, Noam. *Language and Mind*. New York: Harcourt, 1968.
Chomsky, Noam. *Knowledge of Language: Its Nature, Origin and Use*. New York: Prager, 1986.
D'Agostino, Fred. *Chomsky's System of Ideas*. Oxford: Clarendon Press, 1986.
Djité, Paulin G. "The Place of African Languages in the Revival of the Francophonie Movement", *International Journal of Sociology of Language*, No. 86, 1990:87–102.
Djité, Paulin G. "The French Revolution and the French Language: A Paradox?", *Language Problems and Language Planning*, Vol. 16, No. 2, 1992:163–175.
Geingob, Hage G. "Our Official Language Shall Be English: The Namibian Prime Minister's Perspective", pp. 175–179 in *Discrimination through Language in Africa: Perspectives on the Namibian Experience*. Pütz, Martin (ed.). New York: Mouton de Gruyter, 1995.

Harlech-Jones, Brian. *You Taught Me English: The Implementation of English as a Medium of Instruction in Namibia*. Cape Town: Oxford University Press, 1990.

Hountondji, Paulin. "L'Appropriation Collective du Savoir: Taches Nouvelles pour une Politique Scientifique", *Genève Afrique* Vol. 26, No. 1, 1988:11–23.

Jansen, Jonathan D. (ed.). *Knowledge and Power in South Africa: Critical Perspectives across the Disciplines*. Johannesburg: Skotaville Publishers, 1991.

Kunene, Mazisi. "Problems in African Literature", *Research in African Literatures*, Vol. 23, No. 1, 1992:27–44.

Maduka, Chidi. "The Concept of Igbo Novel", *Kiabara*, Vol. 3, No. 2, 1980:183–193.

Mazrui, Alamin. "Language and the Quest for Liberation in Africa: The Legacy of Frantz Fanon", *Third World Quarterly*, Vol. 14, No. 2, 1993:351–363.

Mazrui, Alamin. "The World Bank, the Language Question and the Future of African Education", *Committee for Academic Freedom in Africa: Newsletter* No. 11 Fall, 1996:14–22.

Mazrui, Ali and Alamin Mazrui. *The Political Culture of Language: Swahili Society and the State*. Binghamton, New York: Institute of Global Cultural Studies, 1996.

Mazrui, Ali and Alamin Mazrui. *The Power of Babel: Language in the African Experience*. London: James Currey (forthcoming).

Mazrui, Ali A. "Race in the Black Experience", *The Dalhousie Review*, Vol. 68, No. 1+2, 1989:87–110.

McLean, Daryl and McCormick, Kay. "English in South Africa: 1940–1996", pp. 303–337 in *Post Imperial English: Status Change in Former British and American Colonies, 1940–1990*. Fishman, Joshua A., Andrew W. Conrad, and Alma Rubal-Lopez (eds.). Berlin: Mouton de Gruyter, 1996.

Mda, T.V. *The Making of the Language-in-Education Policy in South Africa*. Unpublished paper, 1996.

Mphahlele, Ezekiel. "Polemics: The Dead End of African Literature", *Transition*, Vol. 3, No. 11, 1963:7–9.

Murray, Nancy. "Somewhere over the Rainbow: A Journey to the New South Africa", *Race and Class*, Vol. 38, No. 3, 1997:35–48.

Mwaura, Peter. *Communication Policies in Kenya*. Paris: UNESCO. 1980.

Ngugi wa Thiong'o. *Decolonising the Mind*. London: Heinemann. 1986.

Pennycook, Alastair. "English in the World/the World in English", pp. 34–58 in *Power and Inequality in Language Education*. Tollefson, James W. (ed.). Cambridge: Cambridge University Press, 1995.

Pütz, Martin. *Discrimination through Language in Africa: Perspectives on the Namibian Experience*. New York: Mouton de Gruyter, 1995.

Sapir, Edward. "The Status of Linguistics as a Science", *Language*, No. 5, 1929:207–214.

War and the Negotiation of Gendered Identities in Angola

Horace Campbell

INTRODUCTION

From the period of Queen Nzinga of Matamba to the present, African women have been at the forefront of resisting the militarism and the death tendencies of the colonial economic relations and the social structures that privileged masculinity and violence. Queen Nzinga is remembered all over Africa and beyond as a person whose quest to preserve the humanity of the African person required the development of a flexible gender identity. This precolonial ruler brought a new kind of political and moral leadership to the society. Nzinga's record as a military leader, diplomat, spiritual leader and mother belied any simplistic conception of gender identities in African societies. The flexibility of African gender systems is now the focus of many recent studies.[64] Ifi Amadiume has developed the concept of a flexible gender system to grasp the ways in which gender roles were available to both men and women. Her study underlines how women could occupy positions and roles occupied by men and therefore exercise considerable power and authority over both men and women. African history is replete with women such as Nzinga, Nehanda, Muhumusa, Me Katilili and countless others who rose up to give overt leadership and guidance to their society. In this sense an identity of resistance and struggle has been an important component of the cultural identity of African peoples since the onset of colonial genocide and occupation. The historical and cultural identity of African peoples informed the gender roles in society. Our interest here is to understand the resistance of the peoples of Angola in the multiple wars that have been fought against them.

---

64. Amadiume, 1987.

All over Africa, an identity of personhood and humanity was claimed in the context of reproducing life and the conditions for human survival. The experiences of the slave trade, colonialism and warfare had tremendous implications for the household and family relations in Africa. In the struggle for survival, African women have been targeted as bearers of savagery and uncivilized social practices. Colonial missionaries, representing a masculinized monotheism, demonized the skills and knowledge of African peoples, and African women were especially demonized. European colonialists carried with them the deformed gender perceptions of Europe, (especially the fetishisms of Victorian Britain) in the colonial enterprise. Recent scholarship by Anne McClintock on *Imperial Leather*, brought out the interconnections between race, gender and sexuality and violence in the colonial context. Despite the fact that her work focused on South Africa, emerging scholarship from the CODESRIA gender network is sharpening our understanding of the specificities of how imperialism, violence, patriarchy and class based social structures have become internalized by both those who hold and those who are fighting for power in Africa.[65]

Portugal, as a semi-feudal society, was always sensitive to its economic status with respect to Britain and other European powers. The Portuguese exported a deformed gender and racial idea to their exploited territories. This deformity created subjective concepts of male, female and a civilized 'assimilated' person that shaped the consciousness of colonial officials. Those Africans who became assimilated internalized this deformity. It is this distortion at the intellectual level that allowed African allies of Europe to engage in warfare and violence which dispensed with the lives of literally millions of persons. Angola, a society in West Africa, is one of the places where Portugal attempted to shape the gender and race relations over a period of five hundred years. Whatever the successes or failures were at the level of identity, at the level of violence and warfare Portugal was eminently successful in importing warfare, patriarchy and destruction.

---

65. Mama and Iman, 1996.

The colonial world was shaped by gendered meanings and this affected all areas of social reproduction. Since the colonial enterprise was one of intense economic exploitation, it was necessary to develop intellectual and moral arguments to legitimize the obscene forms of exploitation. Throughout the period of colonial rule, concerned journalists, travelers and educated Africans chronicled the use of force, violence and murder in colonial economic relations. The spiritual, ethnic and assimilated identities of the Angolan peoples have been important terrains of struggle, as the Angolan peoples, since the time of slavery, have struggled to assert the simple fact, that Africans are human beings. Once Africans were constructed as less than human and could only become civilized by internalizing European culture, it was possible to dispense with their lives, since, they were heathens in any case. It was this constructed tradition which cheapened the lives of Africans that ran through the history of the society and, in part, explained the complete lack of concern for the humanity of the people by the militarists who launched the war in Angola after the 1992 elections. The kind of destruction exhibited in the war exposed the violence of monolithic masculine patriarchy. Warfare had become a business enterprise with a professional warrior class. This class, which doubled as warriors, arms and diamond merchants, carried forth the military traditions of those Africans who had become agents of Europe in the Atlantic slave trade.

This paper deals with the multiple wars against the Angolan peoples and the centrality of gendered identities in these wars. Angolan women and men have had to draw on the historic memories and practices of resistance and survival to maintain their dignity as human beings. Cheikh Anta Diop's concept of the historical, linguistic and psychological factors in the creation of the collective personality of a people seems to be an important starting point in seeking to grasp the renegotiation of gendered identities in Angola. The record of the spiritual, military and cultural resistance of the peoples manifest in the social structures, and an accompanying ideological reflection in songs, dance, art, drawings and other areas, continue to inspire large sections of the population. The spirit of resistance has been manifest in numerous ways but nowhere as evident as in the forthright emergence of Angolan women on the center stage of the economic life of the society. Despite the noteworthy presence of the women in all spheres of existence, in the discussions on peace and reconstruction women are still marginalized. When one negotiator was questioned in the context of the Lusaka Peace Accords (of 1994) why women had not been consulted, he retorted that they were present in the discussions, as sexual providers.

One of the more important arguments of this paper is that the war of ideas, which demonized the skills and knowledge of African men and women, was lost in the military struggles of the past ten years. Angolan women, though not holding formal political power, through their knowledge, skills and strategies for self-reliance, created a force in the body politic which undermined the hollow and shallow ideas of peace promised by the militarists and their international humanitarian allies. In this sense, the project of modernization and "community rehabilitation" of the United Nations and various humanitarian agencies seeks to carry forward ideas of the male controlled nuclear family which had been injected into the village communities by the missionaries. The monogamous nuclear family was introduced in Angola by Portugal and remains the foundation of the patriarchal gender system of capitalism.

It will be the argument of the paper that the organized and spontaneous activities of poor African women in the society challenged the militarism and violence of the wars, especially the war launched by the National Union for the Total Independence of Angola (UNITA) after 1992. The activities of the women of Kuito, Bie, in breaking the siege of UNITA stood as one of the most outstanding episodes of the wars in Angola. However, these activities have not affected the fundamental issue of the structural violence of this rich society whose resources are recycled for arms manufacturers. The structural violence of the economic arrangements is reinforced by the cultural violence which continues against the African cultural values. The renegotiation of gender relations is concerned with power relations at all levels of the society. In so far as the liberation movement which came to power at independence in 1975, The Popular Movement for the Liberation of Angola (MPLA), internalized the modernization project of modern capitalism (and what was termed socialism), the language of the women's movement could not find a base in the concrete reality of the lives of men and women of the village community. The contradiction of the class base of the women's movement in the society undermines the immediate possibility of the development of a social force capable of building on the resistance to be able to move from resistance to transforming, in a fundamental sense, the gender and race relations in the society.

How can the renegotiation of gendered identities empower ordinary producers as well as sharpen the transformation of the colonial identities and the masculinized individualism of the European ideation system? These issues present a challenge to those with a project for African independence and freedom on the economic and cultural fronts. The struggles for the rights of women at the level of individual equal status remain an important issue but this struggle must build on the positive aspects of the communalistic values embedded in African beliefs and thinking. When the MPLA party considered itself an anti-imperialist nationalist movement, it embraced the ideas of the liberation of women. At the legal level, it enacted a relatively "progressive" family code. However, the underlying assumption was the protection of women in a context where the norm of the family was the monogamous European nuclear family.

Angolan men and women have been forced to build new family structures. The reality is that there are women who, in the absence of male partners, must develop new family structures in the context of war, displacement and urbanization. It is in this context that the struggles of Angolan women link up with the larger struggles of other women in Africa to think of ways forward beyond the ideas of patriarchy and economic exploitation. In precolonial societies in Africa, these forms of family structures were seen to be genderless. This meant that either a man or woman could be the husband or family head. Real experience of warfare created a school for new forms of gender relations beyond the simplistic masculine/feminine divide of the assimilated culture of the educated Angolan.

The failure of politicians of the nationalist era and the limitations of theories which marginalized the women ensure that the struggling men and women and their allies in the intelligentsia are positioned to make a lasting and valuable contribution in redefining political struggles in the society. The argument that there need to be new economic and power relations which break the centuries of exploitation in the society is a forceful one which is being made by the sacrifices of the ordinary men and women. In the short term, this will involve new sites of struggle, and the household will be one of these. The argument that in this struggle there will be the need for a new educational process which builds on the African cultural experience is a compelling one. This argument stresses the need for a scientific appreciation of African cultural elements and experience to be able to ensure that Africans see science as a means of understanding their cultures and as a tool to serve and advance the quality of their lives.

This paper starts out by examining the relationship between war and the construction of ethnic identities. From this analysis there is a link to how the tussle over spiritual reference points created the intense ideological struggle over the place of African women. European religious reflection and its link to the colonization process is analyzed. These factors are then linked to the creation of the assimilated Africans who could only become civilized by denying their own history and culture. It was in this context of the masculinized personhood that the resistance in the society created a self-definition which was opposed to the colonial identity. The paper argues that the renegotiation of gender identities is a component of the self-definition process which now confronts the humanitarian model of civilization.

WAR AND ETHNIC IDENTITIES IN ANGOLA

Of the battles of the Angolan society, between the colonizers and the colonized, the struggle to construct ethnic identities ranks along with the stealing of the spiritual identity and the assimilado project, as a central theatre of war. All three of these contradictions, (ethnic, spiritual and assimilation) combined to buttress actual military confrontations. During the anti-colonial war ethnic identities were shaped as a component of the counter-insurgency warfare of Portugal. After 1975, the South African military inherited the counter-insurgency tactics and the disinformation infrastructure of the Portuguese. Then, South African think tanks, strategic institutes and the media built upon the myth of ethnic chaos in Angola. Despite the fact that the peoples of

Angola were colonized and had waged a struggle for self-determination, the description of the military confrontations has been that of the clash of ethnic nationalism to delegitimize the liberation process. When UNITA made an alliance with the South African apartheid regime and elements from the Cold War in the USA, the representation of the war by many authors used the language of "civil war" to characterize the war against the people of Angola by UNITA.[66] Even during the period of the South African invasion, the nomenclature of "civil war" was used to underscore the subtext of the importance of ethnic identities in Angola.

From the period of the Berlin Conference, the imperial authorities had paid special attention to the idea of ethnic kingdoms in order to develop relations with "tribal leaders". Constant mobility by the peoples to escape the ravages of the slave trade simultaneously integrated the population while reinforcing the consciousness of resistance. David Birmingham, in his book *Frontline Nationalism in Angola and Mozambique*, pointed out how Queen Nzinga created multi-ethnic alliances in order to oppose external military rule. Birmingham's work also highlighted the regionalisation of the colonial economy and the role of the church in this regionalisation.[67] More recent work on Queen Nzinga which focused on *Ritual, Power and Gender in the Life of a Precolonial African Ruler* brought to the fore the flexibility of Nzinga in confronting the patriarchy of Portugal.[68] This highlighted the levels of cooperation and conflict which were induced by the slave trade and after. One of the more important points which emerged was that people identified themselves politically, especially with respect to those political/military leaders who could protect the society from the ravages of the slave trade.

By 1885, Portugal needed to establish its claim to the territory of Angola in the face of the competing claims by the French and Germans. Catholic missionaries, military personnel and the few administrators sent to Angola perpetrated violence and rape against the peoples of Angola. The pacification projects of Portugal started the first disinformation where warfare and violence against the African

---

66. See for example the extensive bibliography compiled by Beth Strachan, 1994.
67. Birmingham, 1992.
68. Skidmore-Hess, 1995.

people were presented as keeping peace and preventing 'tribal warfare'. This involved a massive pacification campaign between 1840 and 1926. Pélissier studied the more than 180 campaigns and military operations to conquer the whole of Angola. This work, in describing the fierceness and scale of military resistance, detailed the terrorism of Portugal against the African independent societies. Under Portugal, pacification meant, to conquer militarily and force the African population to submit to European sovereignty, as required for effective pacification. The campaigns were extremely bloody and involved wholesale slaughter of entire villages. Success depended on both Portuguese technical superiority in firepower and on African auxiliaries, soldiers from rival tribes who were encouraged in the slaughter by the promise of booty, which was their early form of payment.[69]

The massive violence of the pacification process became intertwined with the very institutions that gave the colonial society its coherence. The perpetrators of violence and their collaborators established pliant political authorities and called them tribal leaders. These ethnic leaders exploited their relationship with the colonial state for political and economic gain. It is in this period of pacification that the importance of warfare and ethnicity became interwoven with the map and the census in the creation of totalizing classifications in Angola. The mapping of Angola did not simply outline the territorial boundaries (though the exact status of Cabinda is still in dispute) but also laid the modern basis for the construction of ethnic classifications. The system of the quantification and classification of ethnic groups in the society for the purposes of taxation, military conscription and forced labor ignored the historical links between African societies over thousands of years and the sharing of intelligence to resist the pacification campaigns.

> Almost all recent studies of 19th century precolonial Africa have emphasized that far from being a single tribal identity, most Africans moved in and out of multiple identities, defining themselves at one moment as subject of this chief, at another moment as a member of this cult, and at yet another moment as an initiate of a professional guild. These overlapping networks of association and exchange extended over wide areas.[70]

---

69. Pélissier, 1975:609.
70. Drayton, 1995:10. See also, Mafeje, 1973.

The relevant point from this quotation is that there was a multiplicity of precolonial identities associated with age sets, secret societies, religion as well as distinctions based on the division of labor and class. Ethnic identities were neither static nor fixed, but were instead amorphous, and, "constantly re-worked and transformed by historical processes of migration, conquest and trade". Angola was a clear example of how these identities were transformed by the slave trade and the pacification campaigns and by the early twentieth century it was necessary to invent sharp ethnic identities in Angola for administrative purposes. Christian missionaries with their Eurocentric conception of family and religious forms were very active in the imperial enterprise. The African societies and their leaders that resisted colonialism were punished with obscene repression and military campaigns. One of the goals of the pacification project was to create pliant chiefs. These political creations of the imperialist partitioning helped to give legitimacy to the newly created ethnic boundaries in the colony.

In many senses, the missionaries were involved in their own census (not only in the number of converts) but in the enumeration of potential converts in order to lobby for more resources from home based missionary societies. In the process, they carried out a mini-partitioning with the different denominations carving out mission stations in areas where they would be immune from competition from other denominations. The mission stations sought to give credence to the arbitrary ethnic boundaries which were used for the purposes of colonial administration. Studies of the church in Angola have pointed to the influence of the Baptists, the Congregationalists, the United Church of Canada, the Methodists and other missionary alliances that confronted a Catholic hierarchy which, after three centuries of work, was weak and largely confined to the towns of Luanda and Benguela.[71]

The missionaries were involved in a spiritual war, and in the process of spreading their ideas they were very active in the invention of 'vernaculars'. African languages, which were in the main gender neutral, were reconstructed with sharp gender divisions with the

---

71. Henderson, 1992. See also Birmingham, 1992, for the role of the church as accomplices of the colonial order.

privileging of the male. The missionaries, who wanted to systematize the languages they were hearing into a written form in order to translate the Bible for evangelization, ended up in the forefront of the development of orthographies and literacy in African languages. Scholars who have pointed to the role of missionaries in the development of orthographies and in the shaping of ethnic identities have focused attention on the negative legacies of the attempts of the missionaries to shape African languages.

The mapping and quantification of the peoples was carried forth in gendered terms which reinforced the mini-partitioning of the society and gave it a legal base via administrative divisions. In the process of classifying the population according to ethnic groups, the colonial authorities were vigorous in the inculcation of sharp ethnic identities, especially through the chiefs who were installed after pacification. The reinforcement of Portuguese as the language of instruction in the educational system after independence marginalised the rural and poor in the educational process. The important point for this analysis is that the construction of ethnic identities went hand in glove with racial and masculinized identities. The crucial point is related to the fact that the sharp female/male distinctions of Europe were exported via the Portuguese language.

In the process of creating a system of inequality, the egalitarian basis of the African village community had to be reconstructed. Gender difference served as one of the most basic sources of inequality. Class and racial inequality were built on this foundation and this was written into the languages constructed by the colonial authorities. Most of the knowledge which was valued was that of males and reflected the narrative of male experiences. Masculinity, knowledge and ethnic identities were transmitted through the Portuguese language. Instead of the multilingualism of the society being seen as the cultural strength of the people, the differences between African languages and Portuguese began to take on the characteristics of the inequalities which were installed by the colonial state. The insecurities of the Portuguese vis a vis other European powers was accompanied by the masculinization of language and introduction of patriarchal reference points. Educated men were the bearers of knowledge and masculinity was privileged in this environment. In this context the meaning of knowledge, the definition of what is known, and can be known, was controlled and owned by men. The gendered and ethnic constructions of the church were built upon and taken a step further in the contribution of John Marcum in *The Angolan Revolution*. By classifying his study as a case study of ethnic nationalism he reinforced the work of the missionaries who studied the social structures of particular societies in Angola in order to reorganize the ethnic identity in the service of colonialism. The educated African males then became the bearers of gender and ethnic identities in their quest for political space.

Missionaries, through their schools, propagated ideas of ethnic rivalries portraying minor differences in order to divert attention from the anti-imperialist identity which had been instilled in the population by the sterling resistance all over the territory. Because African women were most tenacious in the resistance to the spiritual reference points of Europe, the missionary/anthropologists paid special attention to the significance of lineage structures and those ideas which afforded a flexible identity among men and women. Through the pulpit and the school African women were constructed as bearers of the ethnic boundaries of the society. Feminist scholarship has sharpened our understanding of how women were implicated in the construction of ethnic and "tribal" identities:

(a) as biological reproducers of the national/ethnic collectivities
(b) as reproducers of the boundaries of national groups (through restriction on sexual and marital relations)
(c) as sexual transmitters and producers of the national culture
(d) as symbolic signifiers of national difference and as
(e) active participants in national struggles.[72]

Once Angolan women were constructed as the bearers of ethnic consciousness, they were implicated in the custodianship of masculinist cultural constructions. The Angolan society by 1900 had matured far above the stage of having small ethnic groups. Angolan kingdoms, which had become real inter-ethnic entities, were the states which formed the basis of the resistance mentioned above. Walter Rodney

---

72. McClintock, 1996.

had made the distinction between nations and ethnic groups in *How Europe Underdeveloped Africa*. He argued that one of the most important manifestations of historical arrest is the formulation of what is called tribalism in Africa. Even the authors of ethnicity (such as the US area army handbook for Angola) refer to the imprecision in the definition of ethnic groups in Angola and the rest of Africa. Whatever the dispute so far, recently feminist scholars have begun to centralize the role of women as biological reproducers of ethnic boundaries. Patricia McFadden argued that,

> Central to the definition of ethnic difference is a notion of boundaries - those real and imagined parameters which groups of individuals set up as frontiers for entry into a claimed history, about the past, about who they are in the present based on remembered narrations which find expression in a particular language, dress, culture, folklore - all conflated into popular yet ambiguous terms called culture and tradition. And women have been burdened with the task of ensuring that this glorious male past, which is unashamedly partial and chauvinistic, speaking only to male privilege and power as a 'natural endowment of being male - especially in African societies', is preserved and treated as sacrosanct.[73]

Once ethnic identities began to emerge as a tool of gender, class and military contest, they emerged as a force in all of the nationalist parties in the territory. The educated African propagated the ideas of ethnic boundaries and refined these ideas inside and outside of Angola with respect to the sexual and marital relations of kinswomen. Wamba Dia Wamba has recounted how Bakongo nationalists had hoped to develop the archaic aspiration of establishing a Congo Kingdom, until both Frantz Fanon and Kwame Nkrumah advised that this was not feasible in the era of decolonization.[74] Regional differentiation and class formation meant that the educated from those regions more integrated into the colonial economy had greater access to education. In this sense regional identities, class and ethnic identities tended to be self-reinforcing. The very same religious centers which challenged the spiritual identity of the people (missionary centers), were viewed as the principal means of planting the church and promoting its growth, and the pupils of these schools graduated to

---

73. McFadden, 1994:33.
74. Wamba Dia Wamba, 1989:157.

become the ethno-nationalists who mystified ethnic identities to lobby for support and political leverage.[75]

Despite the evidence of external manipulation of the constructed identities, Bakongo nationalists are still at the center of fanning the flames of ethnicity in the context of the no war no peace. Their active manipulation of ethnic consciousness arose in the context of the pogroms against Angolans of Bakongo origin in 1992 and January 1993. The government had broadcast the news that Zaireans were fighting with UNITA in Huambo. In the heightened sense of insecurity generated by the occupation of over 60 per cent of the municipalities by UNITA, passions were inflamed and Angolans from the provinces of Zaire and Uige were attacked as Congolese. The women of the market organized to protect other women (who were being attacked as Congolese) by changing their dress and sheltering them. This act of solidarity by women in the Rocque Sentiero market was built upon by women seeking to develop associations for their protection.

This solidarity by women in the midst of the provocations by both the government and the defenders of Bakongo traditions can be contrasted to the recent spate of activities by elements in Brazzaville, Kinshasa and Paris calling for an independent Bakongo kingdom, incorporating the regions of Uige and Zaire (with the oil deposits of Soyo) and Cabinda. In all societies ethnic consciousness is greater among exile elements than among the ordinary people who have to live with each other on a day to day basis. This class appeal by males calling for separation from Angola was fueled by provocative stories in the government controlled newspapers which suggested that the Angolans of Bakongo descent lived in the area of Palanca (an area of Luanda known for citizens with keen entrepreneurial skills) as if they were in a separate country.

The peoples now called Ovimbundu were a mixture of groups of diverse origins, and the process of national identity was being formed by the ruling classes. The Portuguese had paid special attention to the

---

75. Lawrence Henderson who studied the impact of the missionaries minimized the importance of cultural resistance in halting the spread of western values. The thrust of missionary activities and its link to the pacification project was spelt out at a conference in Belgium in 1926. See Mafeje, 1973.

defeat of the political leaders among this emerging trading nation and the missionaries were most active in inculcating a 'tribal' identity among the sons of the assimilated elements. The literature from missionaries on the tribal customs of the Ovimbundu attests to the intensity of the campaign to create ethnic consciousness among sections of these people.[76] Up to the present the church of Angola has been torn apart by the ways in which sections of the church leadership internalized ethnicity to the point that while UNITA held thousands under siege, there were religious leaders providing spiritual guidance and comfort to UNITA.

UNITA fought its military battles by making explicit ethnic appeals. Through its manipulation of nationalist symbols and language, UNITA had mobilized the rural population on the basis of ethnic exclusiveness. When UNITA had originally broken off from the FNLA in 1966, it accused the leadership of practicing tribalism and nepotism. However, in order to consolidate UNITA, the leadership carried the language and ideas of ethnic rivalry to new heights. The leaders of UNITA sought to mobilize women as mothers, and the concept of the racialised rooster (The Black Cockerel) was a powerful symbol of male sexuality and superiority. Young chicks were fair game for the rooster and the top rooster could have any hen in the coop. There have been numerous episodes and reports in the history of the party where the top rooster took away the hens of other roosters and disposed of the competing roosters.

The traditional reproductive roles of women were seen as an extension of the war effort since women produced the human labor necessary for UNITA to keep on fighting. Their roles as mothers were seen as essential in fostering the "ideals of ethnic solidarity". In the fight for power, it was the women who were expected to socialize and rear the next generation into the privileges which are 'natural' to males, and the burdens which are 'natural' to females. The conservative philosophy that women were simply child bearers was propagated even when UNITA became totally dependent on the South African army for food, supplies and weapons. Though UNITA propagated ethnic nationalism, the medicinal skills of the women

---

76. Heywood, 1988. This thesis provides a coherent bibliography of this missionary work.

were bypassed as UNITA deepened its links with international nongovernmental agencies. The women of Kuito had learnt, from those relatives who had been in Cuando Cubango and in Jamba, of the place of women under UNITA and were not prepared to accept the militarized leadership of UNITA.

The historic significance of the women of Kuito in the war was the way in which they exposed the myth of ethnic solidarity to be a thin veil for the struggle for power by Jonas Savimbi. The political leadership of UNITA paid attention to surviving lineage structures among the peoples called Ovimbundu and sought to exploit these structures for the purposes of warfare and political legitimacy. UNITA continued this tradition by trying to mobilize ethnic identities for warfare but in this, the Kuito struggle expressed the opposition of Angolan women to an identity which justified their oppression.

WOMEN OF KUITO

Bie province is supposed to be the heartland of Ovimbundu ethnic identity. Kuito is the administrative capital of Bie. The peoples of Kuito, whose memory of African military and cultural resistance to colonial pacification campaigns was still fresh, shared a history of resistance to colonialism with the other peoples of Angola. These people had voted for UNITA in the 1992 elections. Jonas Savimbi, the leader of UNITA, claims his lineage from Kuito, and had pinned his hopes on a quick victory in this town to reinforce the military occupation of over 65 per cent of the administrative centers in Angola. After the 55 day siege of Huambo, from January to March 1993, UNITA captured an important town at great cost in lives. The next target after Huambo was Kuito. UNITA had dithered in the "peace talks" in Abidjan in April 1993, hoping to take Kuito in order to boost its bid to seize power by force. The army of UNITA had controlled most of the barrios of this city but there were three barrios which were not taken. The barrio of Katonge struggled to remain free and it was from this community that the women seized the ability to stay alive.

The women of Kuito demonstrated exemplary courage in breaking the siege by going out at nights to forage for food, transiting land mines and using different techniques of dress, language and trading patterns to bypass the men of both armies. UNITA had bombarded the city indiscriminately in the military confrontation and on the radio deployed the ideals of Umbundu identity and family to legitimize the war. The civilian population lived in underground bunkers by day only to seize the night to find ways of living. The indiscriminate bombardment had killed thousands and it was unclear why UNITA wanted that kind of victory at the expense of killing the very people who they claimed they were fighting to defend. So many people died in the sieges of Kuito and Huambo that dogs died from overeating cadavers. Scenes of death and bodies piled on the streets forced the living to draw on their innermost strengths to find ways of survival. This sense of survival and solidarity by the women of Kuito defeated the army of UNITA and reinforced the historical identity of self-reliance and endurance which had been a component of the culture of Angola for over 500 years.

In the process of cementing the identity of survival the women and men of Kuito were at the same time unmasking the myth of ethnic solidarity and ethnic identity, which had been unleashed to demobilize and divide the peoples of Angola by militarists who had internalized their colonial education that Angola was a society of deep "tribal" rivalry. The women of Kuito, as did the women during the siege of Huambo, deepened the matrilineal linkages of the society in order to be able to breach battle lines to break the fetishism of war and masculine power which came to characterize the war of 1992–1994, when UNITA resumed the war after losing the elections. Women in Angola faced social and military violence which deepened in the society in the wake of militarism, war and the politics of the gun.

Oppressed women in Kuito, like women all over Angola, fell back on the knowledge and skills of plants, medicine and empirical sciences to subsist in a country where the governmental apparatus had been forced to deploy the resources of the society in the purchasing of artillery pieces and jets. The knowledge of the African past proved the most important factor in the victory of the women and people of Kuito, which sealed the reversal of UNITA, a party which had placed its military, diplomatic and political strategy on taking the Central Highlands of Angola. The poor registered a spiritual identity which inspired freedom rather than oppression when the organized church was compromised by their political alliances. After the defeat of UNITA at the hands of the women of Kuito, the organization retreated to Bailundo and sought to mobilize traditional authority structures to assist Jonas Savimbi in holding the peoples of Angola hostage. In many ways, the resurrection of a pliant ethnic leader continued the traditions which the Portuguese had begun after the pacification campaigns. It was significant that sections of the church split down the middle over the military campaign of UNITA. As in the spiritual wars, in the military campaigns, the spiritual leaders were divided on their response to warfare and cultural domination.

GENDER AND THE SPIRITUAL IDENTITY OF THE ANGOLAN PEOPLES

African feminists have focused the question of the matricentric production unit as a central aspect of the identity of the African peoples. They have penetrated the limitations of the nationalist discourse to be able to demonstrate the fact that the nationalist agenda incorporated the concept of the Western gender systems and family structures. Even in societies where there were still residues of matriarchy, male nationalist leaders began to refer to themselves as "fathers of the nation". The concept of the father of the nation ran counter to the reality that "female leadership existed at various levels in African society. The leadership existed at varying levels of formal and informal organizations. Most African societies had women's organizations which controlled or organized agricultural work, trade, markets and women's culture and its relevant ideology."

In West Africa, where the intellectual culture is more developed, African women have exposed how the political powers of women were devalued under colonialism. Ifi Amadiume observed that,

> It was Christianity, Western education and the secular European state system in Africa which, in less than a hundred years forced wide ranging radical changes through the colonial system of the male based ruling system. Male bias was reflected in legislation, land rights, naming after the father, monogamous marriage and the moral values of a ruling European-produced elite class. It was therefore the introduction of a

western system which led to the erosion of centuries of political gains which African women had achieved.[77]

The Christian church played a crucial role in undermining the traditional power of African women who had an economic and ideological base. In so far as religion formed an important arsenal of this ideological base, the spiritual battles were some of the fiercest in the shaping of gender identities in Angola.

In the process of legalizing and establishing colonial gender relations there was a constant struggle between the vestiges of African matriarchy and social collectivism on the one side and private property, individualism and male domination on the other side. Colonialism was a terrain of intense gender struggles, where African women sought to resist the gender identity of submission and docility. Colonialism, as a cultural phenomenon to reorganize the ideas and value systems of the African whether concerning life or death, depended on the intellectual base of Western European education. In the process of trying to develop a Christian identity, the missionaries, as Christian soldiers, served to shape concepts of morality, identity and self-worth which were to have a lasting significance in the tussle between the self-expression and self-definition of the African people, and the idea that Africans needed to be saved. Africans were to be converted from their 'tribal' ways without social equality on earth but with the promise of future equality in heaven.

The representation of Africans as heathens, savages and ungodly, which was prevalent in the nineteenth century, is still current and provides for the callous attitude towards African lives. During the nineteenth century, the stereotypes of savages and heathens were necessary for the major popular role of the Western missionary in Africa. In the twentieth century, the image of warfare and chaos is necessary to justify the humanitarian intervention. African art and culture were presented as devil images cut in wood. The rituals and spiritual practices which were initiated from childbirth to death to protect Africans were considered satanic. The protective spiritual strings around the wrists of small African children were simply

---

77. Amadiume, 1997:111.

praising the devil, since only Christian baptism could provide spiritual and physical protection.

African philosophy did not separate the material from the spiritual, and traditional healers then and now are respected in the village communities. In all societies, knowledge is produced through a social process incorporating economic, political, cultural, personal and spiritual elements. The knowledge of plants, herbs and basic skills in healing and looking after the spiritual well-being and health of a person were (and still are) valuable skills in African societies. The survival of these skills in the context of cultural aggression is a manifestation of the depth of knowledge in Africa. Missionaries battled this aspect of African spiritual identity and medical practices with zeal. African knowledge of plants and herbs was frowned upon, while in the missionary literature the idea of the male missionary hero conquering the evil witches became widely reproduced in books, postcards and other iconography of the missionary infrastructure.[78] For the missionaries, what was known and what could be known was controlled and owned by men. This masculinization of knowledge was a central aspect of the spiritual war.

The tussle between matriarchy and patriarchy was expressed in the conceptions and philosophies of the missionary. As in the rest of the Third World, people were separated from nature, and its creativity, involved in the process of regeneration, was denied. Creativity became the monopoly of men, who were considered to be engaged in production. Women were engaged in mere reproduction or recreation which, rather than being treated as renewable production, was looked upon as non-productive.

> Activity, as purely male, was constructed on the separation of the earth from the seed, and on the association of an inert and empty earth with the passivity of the female. The symbols of the seed and the earth, therefore, undergo a metamorphoses when cast in a patriarchal mold; gender relations as well as our perception of nature and its regeneration are also restructured. This nonecological view of nature and culture has formed the basis of patriarchal perceptions of gender roles in reproduction across religions and through the ages.... Central to the patriarchal assumption of men's superiority over women is the social construct of

---

78. Marian Mies linked this witch hunting at an earlier stage in Europe to the deskilling of European women and the phenomenon of housewifisation. Mies, 1986.

passivity/materiality as female and animal, and activity/spirituality as make and distinctly human. This is reflected in dualism like mind/body, with the mind being nonmaterial, male and active, and the body physical, female and passive.[79]

African women were at the forefront of the attempt to retain those spiritual values which provided a base for social, sexual, medical and economic autonomy. African women jealously guarded their knowledge when they were prosecuted as witches. The historic battles between the Capuchins (an Italian Missionary Order) and Dona Beatriz (an African spiritual leader) exposed the political machinations and military campaigns that were launched to deny women their historic role as spiritual intercessors in the African community.[80]

The vicious struggle of the Catholic missionaries against women who were spiritual leaders meant that women had to find other ways to demonstrate ideological leadership in the community. As adult providers for themselves and their families, they guarded their autonomy even when colonial society sought to enact legislation which portrayed them as minors. As in other parts of the world, the contest between patriarchy and matriarchy was most intense, but more so in Africa because of the economic independence of African women. Scholarly studies on the tussle between matriarchy and patriarchy in pre-colonial Africa have pointed to the inordinate influence of women which mitigated the military powers of warrior elements in society. These studies have exposed how the position of women was negotiated, disputed and transformed over time.[81] African women challenged the idea that the female had to be conquered by the aggressive masculine mind.

The history of Christian missionaries and the male centered religious practices of Europe had profound effects on gendered identities in Angola. The mapping and quantification of the peoples were carried out in gendered terms, since hut taxes saw African males as heads of households, when the nature of the family structure meant that there were different forms of leadership in the community and the household. Western Christianity (as distinct from the Orthodox

---

79. Shiva, Biopiracy, 1997:44.
80. Thornton, 1998
81. Amadiume, 1997.

Christianity of Ethiopia) presented itself in Africa in gendered forms in the middle of the 19th century, at the time when Europe wanted to penetrate Africa beyond the coastal plains.[82] The role of the male missionary in Africa in promoting the ideas of patriarchy and sexless family life is now receiving some attention in the study of colonial ideology. In the Christian church the role model for African women was the Virgin Mary, Mary the mother, Mary the powerless, Mary without sexual instincts, the servant of men.

Angola was one such society where the penetration by David Livingstone and subsequent European missionaries reinforced the role model of the sexless passive woman. Christianity presented itself in Angola in a form of religious expression which required male intercessors between humans and the supreme being (who was supposed to be male). The New Testament was invoked to proclaim that women were to be obedient to men as they were to be obedient to Christ.

> Wives, submit to your husbands as to the lord. For the husband is the head of the wife, as also Christ is the head of the Church and he is the savior of the body.
> Therefore just as the church is subject to Christ, so let the wives be to their own husbands in everything.[83]

African spiritual and religious observance did not entail such obedience and passiveness on the part of women, and they were considered fallen, sinful and only saved by Christian marriages. To be saved African women were to be like white women. Studies in many African societies demonstrated the instability of the missionary identity. "Caught between two cultures, the interpreter of the one to the other produced the dream of the third, where blacks and whites lived harmoniously in a regime of truth. Such a dream was based on a fatal flaw, the refusal to recognize an existing Black and African culture."[84]

It was this assault on the cultural outlook of men and women which made the spiritual resistance a bedrock of the identity of the majority of the producers in Africa. African concepts of spiritual reflection, which placed diviners and spirit mediums at the center of

---

82. Nederveen Pieterse, 1992, explored how the metamorphosis of Europeans in Africa from explorers and missionaries to colonizers meant a transition from an attitude of diplomacy to an attitude of domination, essentially male domination.
83. Ephesians, Chapter 5, verses 22–24.
84. See Engendering History, op.cit.:137.

the cultural life of the village community, were deemed to be backward, reflecting the primitive past which must be erased. The missionaries understood how ritual and spirituality were experienced through gendered identities and the importance of women in the spiritual experience of Africans came in for special assault. Missionaries, therefore, struggled to occupy spaces traditionally occupied by women as transmitters of knowledge, as healers, as spirit mediums communicating with gods and with the ancestors and as authority figures.

It was in this sense that the spiritual identity of the African woman stood at the crossroad of the construction of ethnic and assimilated identities. In Angola, a woman could not be a real person until she became Europeanized and was married. The conception of the African woman was one which was focused on monogamous marriage, individual and biological (as opposed to social) motherhood, individualized childrearing and domestic duties. Western concepts of domesticity depended on a denial of the different forms of family which issued from the village community and a denial of the different forms of masculinities and femininities in the African village. Missionaries denied the spiritual importance of African women and demonized their knowledge of agriculture, mathematics and medicine.

Spirituality is at the core of the identity of all peoples. How this spirituality was expressed to maintain social solidarity and social collectivism is one area of research which had been started by scholars of African religion and philosophy. All things material or immaterial which met the social and individual needs of the community had spiritual significance. African art, dances and other forms of cultural representation were tied to a philosophical view of the relationships between humans, their ancestors, the natural environment and nature. Various foodstuffs, tools, utensils, clothing and shelter, art objects and collective monuments were all useful objects, but in the same way were the means of expressing scientific ideas, beliefs, (ritual sacrifices and prayers) and ways of satisfying emotional needs and of solving family and social problems.[85] An African utensil was not simply a utensil, but it was a work of art as well as an expression of religious emotion.

---

85. For an elaboration see Amin, 1977:75.

The male Christian missionary was aghast at the ideas of cooperation and collectivism which were prevalent in Angola. One missionary was explicit in his conviction that the Christian duty was to stamp out community solidarity and promote individualism (i.e. male centered concepts of accumulation and property ownership).[86] A missionary and anthropologist had noted with complacency, "Bantu collectivism is dying out. In its stead Christianity will promote a healthy and progressive individualism.... I see no other way in which it (the race) can escape destruction."[87]

The women of the urban areas in Angola still manifest aspects of community solidarity and the experiences of Huambo and Kuito exposed the fact that men may hold social and military power but women wield influence through children and through relations with other women. The place of maternal aunts and grandmothers in community decision making processes are areas of research and reflection which can shed light on future family forms in Africa. Recent scholarship on the *Invention of Women* in Africa has reinforced the position that men and women have been invented as social categories, and history is presented as being dominated by male actors.[88] The policy of Portugal which sharpened the invention of male actors as the primary force in society was the policy of assimilation.

THE ASSIMILATED IDENTITY IN ANGOLA

> The imposition of a European state system, with its attendant legal and bureaucratic machinery, is the most enduring legacy of European colonial rule in Africa. The international nation-state system as we know it today is a tribute to the expansion of European traditions of governance and economic organization. One tradition that was exported during this period was the exclusion of women from the newly created colonial public sphere. In most colonial societies, formal political power was gender based.[89]

---

86. Childs, 1949:64.
87. Quoted in Childs, 1949:64.
88. Oyewùmí, 1997:123.
89. McClintock, 1995.

Formal political power was in the hands of European functionaries and the education provided by the missionaries was supposed to produce Africans with European minds. Colonial education in Angola was racialized and gendered. The missionaries who educated less than one per cent of the Angolan African women before 1975 stressed "domestic science" to teach women how to be housewives. Agricultural extension schools recruited males when the reality was that the main agricultural producers in the society were women. The education of women was consistent with the admonition that they should be submissive to men, in this case submit to the knowledge that men had over nature.

The assimilation policies of Portugal devalued the knowledge and work of African women and they were superexploited in the forced labor regime of the Portuguese system. The close relationship between forced labor and slavery in Angola has been the subject of numerous reports by the International Labor Organization and need not be repeated here. What is significant is that the major programs for reconstruction and rehabilitation in Angola are still premised on the idea that African women should be housewives and that agricultural production will be revived by foreign consultants and "modern agricultural schemes" based on privatization of the land tenure systems. In this sense, the authors of the schemes for reconstruction continue the policies of the colonialists in marginalising women in the policies for economic recovery.

Portuguese colonialism emanated from an economically backward society in Europe. Hence though all colonial states used forced labor, after the campaigns of the ILO, states such as Britain sought to use dull economic compulsion in the colonies, though force and the threat of force were never far from the surface. In the case of Portugal, forced labor was the basis for Portuguese colonial economic activities, and the only way Africans could escape the burdens of forced labor was to become educated in the Portuguese language and to internalize the cultural values of colonialism which made them eligible for Portuguese citizenship. The missionaries, as accomplices of the policy of assimilation, took on the task of instructing African men and women "how to keep their houses clean, how to eat as families, with sit down meals with the man at the head of the table, with cloth, knives and mines and using different techniques of dress, language and trading patterns to bypass the men of both armies. UNITA had bombarded the city indiscriminately in the military confrontation and on the radio deployed the ideals of Umbundu identity and family to legitimize the war. The civilian population lived in underground bunkers by day only to seize the night to find ways of living. The indiscriminate bombardment had killed thousands and it was unclear why UNITA wanted that kind of victory at the expense of killing the very people who they claimed they were fighting to defend. So many people died in the sieges of Kuito and Huambo that dogs died from overeating cadavers. Scenes of death and bodies piled on the streets forced the living to draw on their innermost strengths to find ways of survival. This sense of survival and solidarity by the women of Kuito defeated the army of UNITA and reinforced the historical identity of self-reliance and endurance which had been a component of the culture of Angola for over 500 years.

In the process of cementing the identity of survival the women and men of Kuito were at the same time unmasking the myth of ethnic solidarity and ethnic identity, which had been unleashed to demobilize and divide the peoples of Angola by militarists who had internalized their colonial education that Angola was a society of deep "tribal" rivalry. The women of Kuito, as did the women during the siege of Huambo, deepened the matrilineal linkages of the society in order to be able to breach battle lines to break the fetishism of war and masculine power which came to characterize the war of 1992–1994, when UNITA resumed the war after losing the elections. Women in Angola faced social and military violence which deepened in the society in the wake of militarism, war and the politics of the gun.

Oppressed women in Kuito, like women all over Angola, fell back on the knowledge and skills of plants, medicine and empirical sciences to subsist in a country where the governmental apparatus had been forced to deploy the resources of the society in the purchasing of artillery pieces and jets. The knowledge of the African past proved the most important factor in the victory of the women and people of Kuito, which sealed the reversal of UNITA, a party which had placed its military, diplomatic and political strategy on taking the Central Highlands of Angola. The poor registered a spiritual identity

Angola today. They form the leadership of the government, the armed opposition and the religious organizations. Many of these assimilated persons who were ambivalent to African cultural values were mestiço. Mestiços in Africa were the products of European and African sexual liaisons. Some societies developed intricate classifications in order to ensure that white identity was claimed by only those with pure European ancestry. This deformity is still dominant in Brazil. The influence of Brazilian racial ideas is communicated most forcefully through the church, education, the media, (especially television and imported soap operas) and through the influence of corporate elements from Brazil who try to reinforce the historic links between Brazil and Angola from the period of slavery.

In the colonial era, the theory of assimilation was confined to the urban enclaves of Benguela and Luanda, but in the period of settler colonialism after World War II these ideas followed the patterns of the concentrations of white settlers. Recent scholarship on race and sexuality under colonialism has underscored the master syndrome and the sexuality of the white male. "Since he is the master and more simply the male, the white man can allow himself the luxury of sleeping with many women."[92] This syndrome is being reproduced by the influx of humanitarian workers in Angola who traffic in female bodies. It is this appropriation of land, labor and the sexuality of the African woman by white males in the colonies which reinforced the hierarchy of race, class and gender in Angola. The offspring of the white-black liaisons internalized the ideas of white supremacy and black inferiority such that the majority of the mestiço accepted the idea of the civilizing mission of Europe. White males had unrestricted sexual access to African women as a right of "whiteness" and the refusal to exercise this privilege was considered strange if not irresponsible. The theory of assimilation sought to establish the superiority of the (European) male productivity over female productivity. One scholar captured this exploitation thus:

> Portuguese racism, like the early racism of South Africa, was intimately linked to sexual exploitation. Few women migrated to Africa in the early colonial years either as convicts or as wives of officials. Black women could sometimes gain long term benefits, even marriage, from the imba-

---

92. Fanon, 1967. See also, McClintock, 1995.

lanced sex ratio; others were the disregarded victims of a combined racial and sexual exploitation. Distinguished politicians of the metropolitan dictatorship were even offered convent novices as virgin "hostesses" on their official visits to the colonies. Soldiers took their opportunities where they could. During the colonial war one uninhibitedly racist officer even expressed the hope that each of his white soldiers would father children among the undefended black female population as part of the process of colonization.[93]

The image of the African woman as lazy, immoral, slothful, savage and uncivilized was promoted by single white males who were the agencies of the slave trade and the military campaigns in Angola. African women had to consciously fight against this racial and sexual exploitation.

Gerald Bender, in his study of *Angola under Portuguese Rule*, brought out the role of the soldiers, traders, administrators and degregados (criminals) in the rape and violation of African women in the society. He noted that, "the sexual activities of European men were rarely inhibited by the fact that the women were of different races and cultures. In fact, there is considerable evidence indicating that these differences stimulated the Europeans' sexual fantasies and drives."[94] Bender failed in his analysis to locate the place of white women in the deformed sexual hierarchy of the colonial society (especially in the period after World War II when Portugal actively supported white settlement).

White women (especially those from the class of big planters and top colonial administrators) were central to the construction of, and defense of, patriarchy. Despite coming from a poor society in Europe, once in Africa where there was an abundance of cheap and coerced labor, "white women were considered unsuited for physical exertion in the tropics as a consequence of their possession of a faint heart and delicate skin. The constructed image of the white female was that of a chaste person, terrified of black male sexuality on account of her chaste, virginal and jet white purity; and devoid of lust, gaiety and passion, having embraced in its fullness the importance of ordered moral discipline and self-denial."[95] This constructed image which had

---

93. Birmingham, 1992:39.
94. Bender, 1978:51–53.
95. Beckles, 1995.

emerged from the period of the slave trade would be a guiding philosophy for white women in the colonies, whether the colony was British, French, German or Portuguese.

The constructed image of European women from Portugal was inconsistent with the identity of poverty and exploitation of women from peasant communities in Portugal but after the outbreak of the war of national liberation in February 1961, these images were molded as part of the war effort in Angola. Glossy books were published by Portugal as part of the war effort, and the war against African nationalists was framed as a war to preserve the position of white women. After the outbreak of the war in 1961, the Information Department of the colony printed a book with the picture of St. Michael's Fortress, reminding the population of the five centuries spent in populating, civilising and developing Angola. There were emotive pictures of the funeral of those who died in the uprising of February 1961. This book, entitled *Luanda 1961*, also carried idyllic pictures of the Luanda European hospital with children being born. There were also pictures of children going to school, interracial parties, bands and the good life. What stood out in this glossy pictorial was the feminine formation course at commercial schools and white women demonstrating against the UN in 1961.[96]

Portuguese anthropologists were deployed in the rural areas to study the 'traditions' of the people in order to better organize the protected villages and the counter-insurgency campaign against the nationalist movement. One constant theme of study by these scholars was the genitalia of African men and women. The books of this period carry photographs which display the breasts of African women. These anthropologists were especially concerned with the invention of the body of the Chokwe women because of the artistic expressions which were evident in body markings. The book on the invention of the African woman brought to our attention how Europeans constructed African women with mindless bodies. The history of the contact with the Chokwe peoples is a prime example of this gendered construction. The Portuguese male scientists could not see and understand the intricate mathematical skills which were present in the Lusona tradi-

---

96. Santos, 1961.

tions. Recent scholarship on *Women and Geometry in Southern Africa* by P. Gerdes is beginning to highlight the mathematical genius of the Chokwe, Lunda, Lwemba Xinge and Minungo peoples. The pictures of half dressed, semi-savage African women became a constant reference of both the Portuguese military and the missionaries. Black women and white women were not equal beings. The myth of the racial harmony of Portuguese colonial settings that has been recounted by scholars minimises this crucial point. Pictures of half naked African women meant that Europeans carried to the villages their sexual fantasies and African women were fair game for any soldier, administrator, merchant or priest. These men were at the same time protective of the 'white woman' in the colony. The conscious protection of the white female had arisen from the real anxiety created by the outbreak of the national liberation struggles. At the same time as extolling the virtuous white woman, the colonial authorities were reminding the Afro-Portuguese of their historic alliance in the slave trade and called on them to join the fight against 'terrorism'.

Commenting on the imbalance between while males and females in Angola throughout the period of Portuguese penetration, Bender noted that, "Mestiços not only made an early identification with whites but performed important roles as middlemen during the slave trade. Following the end of the slave trade, mestiços continued to occupy key positions in commerce, the civil service, journalism, the military and politics."[97] The educational system was the main area for the formation of the mestiço and assimilated person. The perversion of sexual and reproductive roles which emanated from the legacies of the assimilation policy has not yet been the subject of scientific analysis in Angola.

MESTIÇO IDEOLOGY AS GENDERED IDEAS

Racial and sexual alienation as a double process in the creation of colonial identity was most pronounced in the mestiço section of the

---

97. For an analysis of the perversion of marriage and sex in a similar colonial situation see Jeater, 1993.

population. During the 19th and early 20th century, these elements looked down on African women and saw themselves as heirs to the civilizing mission of Portugal. In the period after the partitioning of Africa, energetic intellectuals in Luanda opposed the excesses of the pacification projects of Portugal. Some of these intellectuals were associated with W.E.B. DuBois, in the calling of a Pan-African Congress in Lisbon after World War 1. The rise of an authoritarian movement in Portugal and the rise of fascism eclipsed the aspirations of the mestiço, and the policy of Portugal after 1945 was to export its surplus population to Africa. White settler colonialism after World War II dented the vision of the meztizo who saw themselves inheriting the colonial state. The militant racism of the settlers sought to develop the kind of apartheid conditions of Rhodesia and South Africa. Africans were displaced from the market places and central residential areas of Luanda after 1920. With white settlement the segregation in housing and urban organization became established throughout the urban areas of the country. Poor whites competed with African labor in the *musseques* (shanty towns). The mestiço elements suffered increased discrimination in the 20th century reversing the role they had occupied in the late 19th century.

The more perceptive of the educated meztizo stratum opposed this hierarchy of racialism and cultural identity, and many of these elements were at the forefront of the struggle for independence. Those Africans who revolted against this cultural war have left written records of the impact of this assimilation policy which was very gendered. Amilcar Cabral, who recognized the importance of African culture in the war of ideas in Angola and Guinea, declared that, "the assimilation theory was unacceptable not only in theory but even more in practice. It is based on the racist idea of the incompetence or lack of dignity of African people, and implies that African cultures and civilization have no value."[98]

African religions and cultural values acted as the reservoir to resist this policy of assimilation and for all intents and purposes this policy was a failure. However, the policy created a base in the politics of Angola which provided scope for manipulations compounding the

---

98. Cabral, 1980.

ethnic constructions which served to divide the working poor. During the period of the war of liberation the presence of the meztico elements in the ranks of the MPLA halted the spread and manipulation of ethnic identity. Marxism as the official ideology of the party also acted as a constraint on the development of crude ethnic identification. (One can contrast this period with the current period when ethnic identity is a basis for recruitment for certain areas of the bureaucracy). The assimilated political leadership in Angola is most ambivalent to African languages and cultures.

Despite the spectacular failure of the policy of assimilation, one of the most enduring aspects has been the masculinized version of citizenship and modernity. The assimilation policy was a policy reinforcing racial identities and it was simultaneously a gendered identity. The fact that these "cultured" elements represented an infinitesimal section of the population meant that in all spheres of social intercourse Africans resisted the forced labor, taxation and racism of Portugal. In this sense, African women were at the forefront of the identity of resistance. After the penetration of the missionaries, there was a special attempt to educate and civilize a number of women so that they would be good marriage material for the educated and assimilated men.

GENDER IDENTITY AND NATIONAL IDENTITY IN ANGOLA

The destruction wrought by the war of ideas was to find its practical manifestation in the warfare and violence which plagued the society. Angola is one society where all of the features of cultural violence, structural violence, militarism, warrior traditions and warfare merged to challenge the humanity of the people. The concepts of mobility, embodiment and resistance which formed the core of the historic identity of the African woman from the period of slavery stand at a different remove from the spate of writings on identity which locates African identity within the 'modern' period of the industrial age. Deconstructing masculinity and the warrior traditions along with an understanding of the oppression of women were not major theoretical issues in the period of the national liberation struggle in Africa, but in the past ten years, African women have brought into sharper focus the limits of a project of national identity which diminishes the importance of gender identity.

It is in the context of the challenge by African feminists that one can develop new lenses to understand how war and peace in Angola remain a component of the warrior traditions of a section of the educated Africans. These 'educated' Africans internalized the ideas of militarism and patriarchy and sought to use force and violence to solve political differences. The palaver as a means of conflict resolution in the African community was completely overtaken by the use of the weapon. During the Cold War, the manipulation of sections of this educated unleashed massive destruction. A gendered analysis of the role of UNITA in Angola is essential to be able to advance beyond the 'civil war' label and the concept of 'collapsed state' which is now in vogue with those who supported UNITA during the period of the South African destabilization and invasion of Angola. What is of significance for this analysis was how the war of ideas reinforced the destruction in the society. Throughout the wars, the centrality of women in resisting military domination and death tendencies emerged in full force. In the wars of 1992–1994, the role of women in rupturing the militarism is an aspect of the society which will have to be told in greater detail in the future. An analysis of the struggles of women for peace will underline an identity of resistance which was at the core of the psychological identity of the Angolan peoples for the past five centuries.

Cheikh Anta Diop, who studied the cultural base of African societies stressed the fact that in defining cultural identity, one must analyze the components of the collective personality. The three factors which contribute to the formation of a collective personality were, (a) the historical factor, (b) the linguistic factor and (c) the psychological factor. In defining the elements of the historical factor, Cheikh Anta Diop elaborated on how the material, historical and spiritual factors contributed to transformation and regression in society. It is now possible to place slavery and colonialism in the proper context of regression and understand how this regression had the dialectical effect of unifying the different peoples of Angola into a whole, with a feeling of historical continuity. The current quest for peace is a profound attempt by the peoples to rediscover those values which connect the different peoples so that the society can recover its historical conscience. This conscience forms the core of the national identity of the Angolan peoples.

In the words of Diop,

> The essential thing, for people, is to rediscover the thread that connects them to their remote ancestral past. In the face of cultural aggression of all sorts, in the face of all disintegrating factors of the outside world, the most efficient cultural weapon with which a people can arm itself is this feeling of historical continuity. The erasing, the destruction of the historical conscience also has been since time began part of the technique of colonization, enslavement and the debasement of peoples.[99]

In Angola the feeling of historical unity and continuity was embedded in the consciousness of the people despite the cultural assault by the assimilated to instill sharp ethnic identities. This consciousness played a protective role against cultural aggression and it was the spiritual identity of the people which inspired the kind of confidence to resist in the midst of the most destructive battles in the society.

ANGOLAN WOMEN IN WAR IN SEARCH OF PEACE

The scourges of war in Angola are manifest in all areas of social reproduction. Bombed out buildings, broken sewage mains, schools without roofs, and entire communities gutted by artillery and aerial bombardment are the physical signs of the wars in Angola since 1961. But none of the confrontations were as pan-territorial as the war of 1992–1994. If one visits Huambo or Kuito or the destroyed urban centers one is immediately humbled by the level of destruction. There was the destruction of buildings, the destruction of neighborhoods and the most devastating consequence, the destruction of human lives. The population of Angola has remained stagnant because of the massive bloodletting which took place in the society. The estimates were that more persons died in the two year period 1992–1994 than in the period 1975–1991.[100] In Kuito, the bravery of the men and women of the Kangote barrio is recounted to expose the depth of the opposi-

---

99. Diop, 1991:212.
100. Maier, 1996. For the view of a UN official on the depth of the war see Anstee, 1996.

tion of the people to militarism. The official reason given for the military reversals by UNITA is the engagement of the South African mercenary army, Executive Outcomes, on the side of the government. This version minimized the centrality of the women of Kuito and Huambo in the defeat of UNITA and is consistent with the militaristic vision of the leaders of both sides which discounts the pivotal role of African women in the life of Angola.

Those journalists who documented the rhythm of the recent war in Angola have given some sense of the ways Angolan women fought for peace. Feminist scholars have pointed out the limitations of the available literature on women and the liberation process in Africa. The official history of the MPLA on Deodlina Rodriques and others who fought in the war have painted a picture of one or two women in the midst of armed combat against colonialism, but in the main the literature on the military roles of women in liberation movements is limited. The available literature tends to have essentially two main depictions of women in resistance: as aiders and supporters and as victims. The former refers to women's roles as couriers, providers of protection, resources and food for the guerillas. Women formed a network for caching and transporting supplies. These gendered roles were crucial to the success of the liberation movements; and it is not the intention of this paper to belittle the significance and contributions of women who performed these tasks. However, what is problematic about these roles is the representation of women only in supportive roles—i.e., that women were supporters of the male actors. This picture "structures the participation of women in a constraining and marginalizing manner". The women of Kuito and Huambo demonstrated that they could act independently in their own interest for survival.

African women in Angola are the bearers of the traditions of resistance and this resistance was communicated from one generation to the next. Excluded from access to the basic educational frame which was reserved for the assimilado, African women retained African languages and culture, medicinal practices and rituals which reinforced their sense of dignity and self-worth. At the outset of the period of armed struggles, the MPLA had sought to capture this spirit and channeled its energies into the Organization of Angolan Women (OMA).

Starting from its position where it accepted the European nuclear family form, the MPLA as the government did not interrogate the strength and weaknesses of customary forms which still existed in village communities. From the outset, the MPLA had underscored the importance of women in the military and cultural confrontation between colonialism and self-determination, but it did not seek to deal with the complexity of the position of women, especially in the rural areas, in Angola. In its propaganda documents, the MPLA affirmed that, "The role of women and the need for them to mobilize on their specific questions, was recognized from the start. In 1962, one year after the MPLA launched the armed struggle, the OMA was set up."[101] The leadership of the MPLA sought to bring into historical visibility women's active cultural and political participation in all phases of the resistance to external domination. However, the leadership of the liberation movement coming from the enclave cities did not grasp the complex gender systems of the society, so, while on paper the MPLA enacted liberal legislation with respect to women, its ability to communicate with large sections of the society was constrained by war and the language of the communication system.

The published record of the OMA has attested to the tremendous efforts which were made in the body politic of Angola with respect to the position of women and the legal initiatives on sex discrimination and the family code. By 1985, under the impact of pressures from the OMA the Angolan government enacted one of the most progressive Family Codes in Africa. The code granted equal rights to women in matters of employment, the household, inheritance and in all aspects of public life. During the 1970's the OMA had embarked on literacy campaigns and set up day care centers, especially in the urban areas. There was for a short time a notable campaign against domestic violence.

The important point of the position of the MPLA was the belief that women's entry into the labor force would bring gender equality and break the patriarchal values of the urban educated. Experience in

---

101. Organization of Angolan Women, 1984:14.

socialist Cuba pointed to the fact that legislation alone was insufficient to overcome patriarchal practices of centuries.[102] The difficulties of a "socialist" party coming to terms with questions of gender were compounded in Angola where there was clearly a complex and flexible gender system. The upheavals in the countryside and the dislocations created by the besieged towns increased the visibility of women in the context of war and destruction. War and the economic hardships of scarcity, lack of fuel, water supply and health systems changed the range of possibilities for women. African women of all classes, but especially the poor expended a disproportionate amount of labor time carrying the double burden of unpaid work in the reproduction and maintenance of human resources. By 1996, 60 per cent of the population lived in urban areas and in the overcrowded *musseques*, the search for food and the provision of daily subsistence was a major undertaking.

On top of the massive loss of life and limb experienced in this society, the living conditions of the Angolan people have deteriorated by every index of the quality of life, health care, delivery of water, infant mortality, access to primary education, nutrition and food security, basic food, shelter, pre- and post-natal care and household food intake. The levels of violence in the wars of the past thirty years have meant that women were the subject of structural and direct violence. It is in this situation that the resilience and the resistance of African women laid the basis for the renegotiation of gendered identities.

> The negotiation of gender relations incorporates several dimensions. First, is the idea that the negotiations are never static, but are always ongoing. Given that these negotiations are about gender relations and the construction of gender identity, they invariably start from the basic premises about masculine and feminine roles in the specific class and culture, and from knowledge of a system of gender relations, which in general is familiar to all parties concerned. Thus one can theorize that negotiations in gender relations involve collusion, between men and women, between individuals and institutions. We must see collusion compromise and accommodation as part of the construction of gender identities, retaining many of the features from a gender system with which people are comfortable and familiar.[103]

---

102. Smith and Padula, 1996:179.
103. Mohammed, 1995:28.

The military confrontation in the society sharpened the divide between those who could repair to South Africa or Portugal and the mass of men and women who had to withstand the privations of militarism and masculinity. One study on the conditions of women in war opined that:

> On the one hand, the war opened more opportunities for women because they had to take on the responsibilities of men. On the other hand, war has been very destructive for rural life, where women have traditionally had a strong and independent position. The economic crisis has given rise to problems in many of the public services, that worked reasonably well before, but that are now more expensive, ineffective or not working at all. This affects women in a negative way since they are the ones responsible for maintaining the household, especially in terms of nutrition and health.[104]

The economic survival of family units depended on the mobility of women and this had a detrimental effect on the schooling of girls. Despite the fact that the government education stressed gender equality between 1975 and 1990, and the fact that there were genuine attempts to expand educational opportunities for women, the reality was that as the crisis deepened young girls were called upon to shoulder burdens of trading, household chores and other labor intensive activities. By law, women and men had equal access to education with the first four years of schooling being compulsory. However, by the fourth class, the number of girls in school declined as young girls were kept at home to do domestic work. In the period from 1992 to 1994 there were twice as many boys as girls enrolled in school, and from that point on, women in education decreased in inverse relation to their years of schooling.

The costs of schooling in the society became a luxury for the poor during the wars, and all of the figures from the country gender analysis pointed to the detrimental effects of the war on the 'formal' education of women. School buildings were not spared the artillery bombardment nor the aerial bombs and school buildings were bombed out in the areas of war. Supplies, books and equipment for education were never procured so that teachers and students had to devise creative strategies to carry on learning in the formal context.

---

104. Country Gender Analysis, Development Workshop.

Enrollment in the University grew from 1,400 in 1975 to 5,700 at the end of 1996. At the University one third of the students enrolled were women, though in the faculty of medicine women constituted 56 per cent of the students.[105] By the middle of the nineties women dominated the teaching and medical professions in Angola. This did not affect the reality that the warriors attempted at all times to disempower women.

Millions of dollars are spent on the quartering and demobilization of soldiers and the displacement of women and civilians takes second place to the incessant meetings of soldiers and the reconciliation with warrior elements who have made warfare a business. Angolan women are not seen as partners in the reconstruction process, instead they are depicted as ignorant obstacles to modernization and privatization, by clinging to 'traditions'. Since 1994 the UN has orchestrated a series of meetings and agreements that are portrayed optimistically as steps towards peace. These meetings then serve as the basis for more humanitarian appeals. In reality, the meetings and the promises are hollow accords and one writer properly termed this peace process, *Angola: Promises and Lies*. The 'peace' process has strengthened the military leaders in the same proportion as the disempowerment of the ordinary men and women in the society.

One can see the disempowerment of women in the dependence on food aid in one of the most fertile societies in Africa. The tragedy of Angola is reinforced by the present high importation of food which acts as a disincentive for the recovery of agriculture. Between 1992 and 1995 the budget of the World Food Program in Angola increased from US $10 million to US $106 million. Less than one per cent of this money could be spent on stimulating the recovery of agriculture and the resettlement of women with research into developing higher yields for locally produced food. To compound the consequences of the dependency, land mines and displacement, the policies of liberalization and privatization have led to the erosion of those services which existed prior to 1989 in areas of health, education and food subsidies. Structural adjustment and "humanitarianism" in the society have increased the number of international workers in the society

---

105. For the figures of women educated in Angola see Angola: Country Gender Analysis, Development Workshop, October 1991.

who see themselves as the modern missionaries, dispensing food aid and setting up emergency programs for rehabilitation. Prostitution in both the literal and figurative senses has deepened in the society in the wake of the humanitarian invasion. Fourteen year old sex workers have become familiar sights in Angola as the traffic in women's bodies follows the traffic of diamonds, imported food and disaster relief.

The peace process in Angola since 1991 has been characterized by an effort to continue the "modernization" process which had been halted when the MPLA came to power in 1975. Millions and possibly billions of dollars have been expended to conciliate warring parties, and the base of the UN mission in Angola has been to silence guns only. The emphasis on soldiers and their "rehabilitation" has meant compromises with UNITA to satisfy the Western view that any political settlement in Angola should reward UNITA for destroying the society.

The humanitarian efforts which have exploded in the society have carried with them the in-built patriarchal conceptions of family structures. Many of these international workers came from societies where there is intense racial discrimination against Africans and many carried these ideas of white superiority to Angola. In this sense the humanitarian workers continue the traditions of the Christian missionaries in devaluing the skills and knowledge of the Africans, especially women.

One can see this from the planned expenditures for the Social and Economic Rehabilitation Program of the UNDP, which was presented at the "donor" meeting for Angola in Brussels in September 1995. This was at the time when the dislocations created by the war had left many women on their own. Many were separated from families, others were widows and many were abandoned because of military conscription. Demobilization and reintegration in the society is presented in gendered terms and as far as the UN is concerned it is only the men of the society who need reintegration. The World Bank and the multilateral agencies present major programs for "reforms" and modernization of the administration without taking into account the centrality of women in the administration of the needs of life on a day to day basis. The humanitarian activities of the United Nations and the Department of Humanitarian Affairs in the main ignore the fact that women's work of feeding, rearing, healing humans and building and rebuilding households and communities under conditions of constant change has produced skills and resources that have been critical to survival and human development.

THE RENEGOTIATION OF GENDER IDENTITIES

Since the Lusaka Accords in November 1994, there have been further attempts to create a balance of "power" to be able to integrate the armies of UNITA into the Angolan army and to integrate the political leadership into the circuit of accumulation and control of the state. Angolan women at leadership levels are noticeably absent from the negotiations for the reintegration of UNITA into the political process. During the 1992 elections, when women had the opportunity to vote for or against UNITA throughout the country, they rallied to express their opposition to the militarism of Savimbi. The example of the woman who gave birth to a child in the voting line and named her child "Vote" was a testament to how strongly women felt about the need for peace.[106] The explicit rejection of the politics and gender ideology of UNITA which was manifest in the 1992 elections has been overlooked by the peacemakers in Angola.[107] International nongovernmental organizations with their transnational (but clearly imperial) identity now seek to become central to the reproduction of ideas in the society.

The active participation of women in the search for peace at the grassroots level can be contrasted to the activities of the church organizations which want to reproduce the 19th century image of the helpless, docile woman in a society where the independence and self-reliance techniques of women are most developed. Fundamentalist Christian churches from the USA and Brazil are very active in the poor urban areas, where more than 60 per cent of the population now struggle for survival. The Catholic church has sought to reclaim the old confidence of being a state religion after its years of opposition.

---

106. Campbell, 1993:23–63.
107. Campbell, 1993:23–63. For another version of the election process see Anstee, 1996.

The visit of the Pontiff to Angola in 1992 was a fillip to this institution which now has plans for radio stations and institutions of higher education to promote its version of patriarchy and the docile African woman.

In terms of an organization which combined the war of ideas, the military war and the construction of male dominance, UNITA stood out in the history of the society. From its male symbol of a rooster, to the actual representation of the place of women in the community, the social relations between men and women in UNITA camps reflected the position of male superiority. Like all of the leaders of political parties, the leaders of UNITA were missionary educated, but they sought to promote ideas of "tradition" to promote a concept of the African personality, which did not include independent decision making by women. The tradition of the political party having a women's wing was carried forth by UNITA through the organization, the Independent League of Angolan Women (LIMA).

Urbanization and war, then, not only created disruption but challenged the "traditional" values which conservative ideas on family and family structures tried to impose. Rural dwellers coming to the city have had to develop new strategies for survival and this has affected gender relations in profound ways. One of the more profound ways has been the ethnic unity fostered by living and surviving in urban areas and the development of new social sanctions among the people.

The survival techniques of Angolan women could be seen not only in the bravery of the women of Kuito and Huambo, but in the daily struggles for existence, processing food, preparing meals, caring for the ill, children, the elderly, the wounded, cooking and consoling the bereaved. Death and funerals created new tests for the fortitude of Angolan women during the last phase of the war 1992-1994. Land mines in the rural areas ensured that women were confined to the urban hustle and bustle where women in trade are the most visible sign of the women in the urban areas. In this area of economic activity, one can see the clear negotiation of gendered identities and the attempt to reclaim the solidarity, mobility and self-reliance of women. This was most evident in January 1993 when there was the attempt to deepen the politicization of ethnicity in the society. While the exile leaders were calling for an independent republic of the Congo to defend Congolese identity, the women in the urban areas were demonstrating that culture is not static but is learnt, shared and is dynamic. The women who struggle on a day to day basis were giving up the tradition of kneeling before men.

Women are very visible as traders and operators in the so-called "informal sector". These women have been solving with their wits problems of trade routes and foreign exchange which still bewilder those who set exchange rates. The expansion of this sector subsequent to the deregulation of the economy in 1989 has brought changes in the lives of many women. Rural women who fled the rural areas have entered the market place in large numbers. Not only has this sector acted as a unifying force or healing factor (symbolized by the sheltering of Congolese women), but women of different regions are building an independence around functions of supply, transport, marketing intelligence, to name some of the areas of interdependence. The "informal sector", responding to need and without pre-philosophy, has established commercial and inter-ethnic relationships of trust which are not easy within the sector dominated by World Bank philosophy of privatization and devaluation.

Those who speak of the establishment of market forces overlook the activities of the working poor and the long record of the centrality of women in trading and commercial activities in Angola. The centrality of women in the markets is bypassed since the "real market" involves financial institutions dominated by men, especially from foreign firms. It is in this society where there is a practical example of the need to reconceptualize economics away from the narrow conceptions of work and production which devalue the fundamental nature of gender, care and economics. Such an analysis would refocus economics away from the idea that the commanding heights of the economy lay in the production of petroleum products and diamonds. In fact, it would be understood that the very processes of mineral extraction and militarism formed part of the same process. The rapid growth of the oil industry in the midst of the war contrasted with the devastation and destruction suffered by the rest of the economy. The diamond industry is also dominated by men and most of the diamonds produced in Angola are exported illegally so that the revenues for diamonds do not pass through the official accounting system of the Angolan government.

CONCLUSION

The history of Angola since the slave trade has been one of continuous struggle between oppressors and the oppressed. The construction of gender relations has gone through many phases but in all phases the dominant issue has been that of women seeking ways to develop economic and sexual autonomy. From the period of Queen Nzinga in the 17th century, Angolan women were involved in military, ideological, economic and psychological warfare. The military domination of the society was to be complimented by the economic and political forms of colonial rule. After the partitioning of Africa, the missionaries were at the forefront of the civilizing mission and a war of tremendous implication for both gendered and ethnic identities in Angola. Resistance from the people ensured that it was a small stratum of educated assimilado which internalized the Christian admonition that women should be obedient to men.

In the present situation of the real legacies of war and destruction male peasants, wage earners, traders and even low level salaried employees are increasingly unable to reproduce themselves as well as their women and children. Recent surveys in the urban areas of Angola have commented on the high percentage of female headed households. "Donors" have termed this phenomenon the feminization of poverty without drawing the important lessons for gender relations. There are millions of women in Angola who have no men to depend on as well as a significant class of men who cannot afford to become heads of households. Rudo Gaidzanwa has argued that this development in Angola and Southern Africa points to the need to reconceptualise the alternative models of social and economic organization given the magnitude of the social crisis prevailing in Angola and Southern Africa.[108]

Pointing to the need for an alternative theory of society rooted in the historical identity of the African people, African feminists are at

---

108. Gaidzanwa, 1992:121.

the forefront of thinking of ways forward beyond the ideas of superiority (both racial and gender) which places African women at the mercy of local and international exploiters. The experience of the economic, military and political wars as well as the war of ideas against Africans reinforces the argument that there is the need to develop theories and models of accumulation and production that are not premised on exploitation and do not accept the subordination of women.

The failure of politicians of the left and right has been spectacular in Angola. This failure has been reinforced by the numerous efforts to conciliate the macho policies of UNITA when women sought to find ways to live outside the boundaries imposed by the call to "traditional" Ovimbundu structures. The women of Kuito, as did the women of Rocque Sentiero, demonstrated concretely that they were seeking new ways to conceptualize gender, society, religion and politics. The major limitation in the society has been the ambivalence of the assimilated women who are in the leadership of the 'official' women's movement in Angola. This ambivalence is deepened by the thrust of western donors who want to finance the more articulate women so that they are concerned with small 'economic' projects instead of the question of political power. Men and women in Angola will have to find ways to relate in the private sphere which forces men to rethink the modes of economics and politics which require war and subordination. Unfortunately, those in the leadership of the women's movement are still linked to ideas of assimilation which do not engage the complexities of the interface between individualized rights for women and the communalistic forms and values which are embedded in generational thinking and beliefs in ancestral spirits.

The task to realize the emancipation of human beings in harmony with their spiritual and emotional identities is a major task which requires a new mode of politics and a break with the forms of exploitation bequeathed by Portugal. Angola is a rich society and far more research needs to be done to ascertain the extent of the destruction of war damaged lineage structures and those forms of family relations which could form the basis for transforming the inherited patriarchal and violent state structures of the society. The concepts of peace which have been presented since 1975 all devalue the knowledge of women. A project of peace in Angola that is going to break the cycle of militarism must embody respect for the interests of workers and peoples and must inevitably start with the reinforcement, through their struggles, of their power in the society. It is on this basis of respect for women, youth, workers and peoples that concepts of national identity can be built. It will be based on a concept of democracy which respects differences in languages and other heritages from the past.

A program of national identity can be built on the cultural and historical unity of the peoples of the society. The women of Kuito and the women of Rocque Sentiero sent a clear message, that they did not want to be manipulated to serve as biological agents of ethnic differences. Their actions demand that progressive elements develop political strategies which focus on ending economic exploitation and extend democracy in all dimensions of life. In this sense the renegotiation of gendered identity involves the extension of political participation by all sectors of the population, but especially by women. One step in this process may involve cultural critical education which recognizes the positive elements of African matriarchy, religion and culture.

The present technological revolution forces serious scholars in Africa to seek alternatives to war and destruction in the capacities of the people, especially women. This would imply the development of the skills and knowledge of the producers ending the dependence on the hoe.

How can women be expected to play an effective role in the reconstruction of society and in the wider movements needing their talents and energies when they are hemmed in by life itself? Angolan women are constrained by multiple social oppressions which are not the concerns of peacemakers and politicians. Angola is potentially a very prosperous country which should be able to provide electricity to women at the flick of a switch or water with the turning of a tap. Instead the various programs of the international financial institutions are to place these amenities out of the reach of the majority of the population. The schemes of the World Bank for the privatization of water supply systems expose the gendered nature of the ideas of market forces in Angola.

It is not now inconceivable to conceptualize the development of village communities using the most advanced technology and harnessing the natural resources for an autocentric economy. "In the material world the Third World has access to modern technologies. Given judicious management, it could put them to use without having to go through all the previous stages of technological development."[109]

In areas of health, education, water supply systems, hygiene and food production the material culture of the African was challenged by colonial capitalism. However, regardless of the military and economic power of the external forces, the spiritual identity of the peoples provided the basis for self-worth and self-respect. This spiritual identity reinforced the historic and cultural identity of the people. In Kuito and Luanda, during the height of the fighting, women demonstrated that their solidarity as human beings was more important than ethnic manipulation. The multiple wars exposed the complexity of the gender relations in Angola. African men and women want peace and an end to violence so that the society can begin to develop healthy social and gender relations outside of the trauma of warfare and displacement.

REFERENCES

Amadiume, Ifi, 1987, *Male Daughters, Female Husbands: Gender and Sex in an African Society*, London: Zed Books.

Amadiume, Ifi, 1997, *Re-inventing Africa: Matriarchy, Religion and Culture*, London: Zed Books.

Amin, Samir, 1977, "In Praise of Socialism", in *Imperialism and Underdevelopment*, Sussex: Harvester Press.

Amin, Samir, 1987, "Development and the Cultural Issue: Reflections on Arabo-Islamic Thought", *Bulletin of the Third World Forum*, Dakar, Senegal.

Angola: Country Gender Analysis, Development Workshop, October 1991, Luanda.

Anstee, Margaret J., 1996, *Orphan of the Cold War: The Inside Story of the Collapse of the Angolan Peace Process, 1992–93*, New York: St. Martin's Press.

Beckles, 1995, "Sex and Gender in the Historiography of Caribbean Slavery", pp. 20–43 in Shepherd, Verene et al., eds., *Engendering History: Caribbean Women in Historical Perspective*, London: James Currey.

---

109. Amin, 1987.

Bender, Gerald J., 1978, *Angola under the Portuguese: The Myth and the Reality*, Berkeley: University of California Press.
Birmingham, David, 1992, *Frontline Nationalism in Angola and Mozambique*, Trenton, N.J.: Africa World Press.
Cabral, Amilcar, 1980, "The Facts about Portuguese Colonialism", in *Unity and Struggle: Speeches and Writings*, London: Heinemann.
Campbell, Horace, 1993, "Angolan Woman and the Electoral Process in Angola, 1992", *Africa Development*, Vol. XVIII, No. 2.
Childs, Gladwyn Murray, 1949, *Umbundu Kinship and Character*, Oxford: Oxford University Press.
Diop, Cheikh Anta, 1991, *Civilization or Barbarism: An Authentic Anthropology*, Brooklyn, New York: Lawrence Hill Books.
Drayton, Shelley, 1995, "De-Mystifying 'Tribalism': Identity, Politics and Conflict in Modern Africa", *CODESRIA Bulletin* No. 1.
Fanon, Frantz, 1967, *Black Skin, White Masks*, New York: Grove Press.
Gaidzanwa, Rudo, 1992, "Bourgeois Theories of Gender and Feminism", in Meena, Ruth, ed., *Gender in Southern Africa: Conceptual and Theoretical Issues*, Harare: SAPES Books.
Hall, Catherine, "Gender Politics and Imperial Politics", in Shepherd, Verene et al., eds., *Engendering History: Caribbean Women in Historical Perspective*, London: James Currey.
Henderson, Lawrence W., 1992, *The Church in Angola: A River of Many Currents*, Cleveland, Ohio: The Pilgrim Press.
Heywood, Linda, 1988, *The Dynamics of Ethnic Nationalism in Angola: The Case of UNITA, 1964–1987*, PhD Dissertation, Washington D.C.: Howard University.
Jeater, Diana, 1993, *Marriage, Perversion, and Power: The Construction of Moral Discourse in Southern Rhodesia, 1894–1930*, Oxford: Clarendon Press.
Mafeje, Archie, 1973, "The Ideology of Tribalism", *The Journal of Modern African Studies*, Cambridge: Cambridge U.P.
Maier, Karl, 1996, *Angola: Promises and Lies*, London: Serif Books.
Mama, Amina and Ayesha Iman, 1996, *Engendering Social Science*, Dakar: CODESRIA.
McClintock, Anne, 1995, *Imperial Leather: Race, Gender and Sexuality in the Colonial Contest*, New York: Routledge.
McClintock, Anne, 1996, "No Longer in a Future Heaven: Nationalism, Gender and Race", in Eley, Geoff and Ronald Grigor Suny, eds., *Becoming National, a Reader*, New York: Oxford University Press.
McFadden, Patricia, 1994, "Ethnicity in Africa and African Female Authenticity", *Southern Africa Political and Economic Monthly*, Harare: SAPEM Publications project, Vol. 8, No. 1.
Mies, Maria, 1986, *Patriarchy and Accumulation on a World Scale: Women in the International Division of Labour*, London: Zed Books.

Mohammed, Patricia, 1995, "Writing Gender into History", in Shepherd, Verene et al., eds., *Engendering History: Caribbean Women in Historical Perspective*, London: James Currey.

Nederveen Pieterse, Jan, 1992, *White on Black: Images of Africa and Blacks in Western Popular Culture*, New Haven: Yale University Press.

Organization of Angolan Women, 1984, *Angolan Women Building the Future: From National Liberation to Women's Emancipation*, translated by Marga, Holness, London: Zed Books.

Oyewùmí, Oyèrónké, 1997, *The Invention of Women: Making an African Sense of Western Gender Discourses*, Minneapolis: University of Minnesota Press.

Pélissier, René, 1975, *Les Guerres Grises: Résistance et Revoltes en Angola (1845–1941)*, Montaments: Published by the author.

Santos, Almeida, 1961, *Luanda 61, Angola*, Luanda: Repartição Municipal de Cultura e Turismo.

Shiva, Vandana, 1997, *Biopiracy: The Plunder of Nature and Knowledge*, Boston, MA: South End Press.

Skidmore-Hess, Cathy, 1995, *Queen Njinja, 1582–1663: Ritual, Power and Gender in the Life of a Precolonial African Ruler*, PhD, University of Wisconsin.

Smith, Lois M. and Alfred Padula, 1996, *Sex and Revolution: Women in Socialist Cuba*, New York: Oxford University Press.

Strachan, Beth, 1994, *Angola, the Struggle for Power: The Political, Social and Economic Context, 1980–1993*, Bibliographical Series, No. 28, Johannesburg: South African Institute of International Affairs.

Thornton, John K., 1998, *The Kongolese Saint Anthony: Dona Beatriz Kimpa Vita and the Antonian Movement 1684–1705*, Cambridge: Cambridge University Press.

Wamba Dia Wamba, 1989, "Some Aspects of the Historical Background to National Liberation Struggles in Southern Africa: The Case of Angola", in Mlahagwa, J.R. et al., eds., *Landmarks in Southern African History*, Historical Association of Tanzania.

Wheeler, Douglas L. and René Pélissier, 1971, *Angola*, London: Pall Mall.

Conceptualising Coloured Identities in the Western Cape Province of South Africa[110]

Zimitri Erasmus and Edgar Pieterse

> Everything that can be spoken is on the ground of the enormous voices that have not, or cannot yet be heard
> (Stuart Hall, 1991:48)

INTRODUCTION

The majority (56 per cent) of the voting population of the Western Cape is coloured (Eldridge and Seekings, 1996:520). Most of these people (68,7 per cent) (*Cape Times*, 19 December 1996) voted for the National Party (NP) in the April 1994 democratic elections. This has precipitated a range of political and scholarly interpretations of 'the coloured vote'. Consequently we have heard that coloured people voted the way they did because they are white-identified sharing language and religious affiliation with white voters; because they are racist towards africans and hence voted against the African National Congress (ANC); because they suffer from 'slave-mentality' (Legassick, 1996; Holiday, 1995), and that this voting behaviour can be explained in terms of NP propaganda and the 'psychological damage' this has caused in coloured communities who are yet to free themselves 'from the stranglehold of psychological enslavement' (Williams, 1996:22, 26). We find these interpretations unsatisfactory, often decontextualised and uncritical of the discursive roles they fulfill in re-inscribing racist frameworks of interpretation.

---

[110] We would like to thank Professor Robin Cohen for discussions and comments on particular views on coloured identities and Dr Andries du Toit for reading and commenting on several drafts of this work. Thanks also to Cecilia van Staden, financed by the J.O.B. programme at UCT, for her invaluable assistance with collecting information.

What do these particular political developments mean for processes of coloured identity formation? What do they mean for the place of coloured people in our new nation-building project? The answers to these questions are not simple. We do not attempt to provide solutions in this paper. Furthermore, one cannot examine coloured identities simply in terms of party-political support. For us, the consequences of voting patterns in the Western Cape are significant in that they provide one of the contexts in which coloured identities are contested. We are concerned with some of the more common responses to these contestations and re-assertions of coloured identities.

This paper critically explores the underlying assumptions which dominate the current debate on coloured identities in South Africa. Our concern with these questions stems from our political and personal concerns as coloured scholars in the new South Africa. For Zimitri, it has been a long journey trying to figure out the relation between being black, african and coloured and whether these parts of her identity matter at all. For Edgar, such interest stems from his commitment to contribute to social tolerance and to explore the multiple dimensions of difference. This is with a view to identifying contingent moments and spaces to articulate alternative ways of living and fostering community through new political discourses and practices. Despite a lengthy spell of activism he has not yet experienced this and current trends seem to suggest a move away from finding such political (and epistemic) communities.

These personal politics are linked to four more general concerns. One is an anxiety about regressive trends toward an essentialist coloured nationalism. The second is a worry about responses to such essentialism which deny that 'being coloured' means anything beyond a racist apartheid classification. Our third concern is with the seeming inability of the ANC to acknowledge the need for some fundamental debate and contestation about 'the coloured issue' and particularly the way in which the party has dealt with this issue. Finally, we are concerned with the terms in which South African identity is considered and about the anti-democratic implications of essentialist and exclusionary conceptions of 'nation-building'.

The paper begins with a sketch of the historical and socio-political context. This is followed by an overview and critique of some of the more common views on coloured identities. We then proceed with an outline of a more useful conceptualisation of coloured identities.

For the purposes of this work, we use 'black' to refer to all people oppressed under white domination. 'Coloured' refers to those South Africans loosely bound together for historical reasons such as slavery and a combination of oppressive and preferential treatment during apartheid, rather than by common ethnic identity. For us, the identity 'coloured' is sometimes seen as overlapping with 'black' and always with 'african'. In this paper, however, we use 'african' in the official South African sense that denotes people who speak indigenous languages with the exception of Afrikaans. The lower case indicates an anti-essentialist view of these identities.

THE HISTORICAL AND SOCIO-POLITICAL CONTEXT

This section provides some notes on the broader historical, discursive and social context in which debates about coloured identities are taking place in the Western Cape.

Brief History of the Terms 'Coloured' and 'Black'

Since the days of colonialism and slavery very distinctive racial hierarchies of organisation and power have always underpinned South African society. Contrary to the notion that the term 'coloured' is a creation of the apartheid era, Bickford-Smith (1994:289) notes that the idea of being 'coloured' had emerged among freed slaves and their descendants between 1875 and 1910. Coloured identities had emerged from those social and political identities created in the era of slavery.

Bickford-Smith notes that

> [b]y the early 1890s, overtly coloured political organisations began to emerge to fight white discrimination and were active among communities of slave descendants in Cape Town.... 'Coloured' became an acceptable self description for many slave descendants in Cape Town to distinguish themselves from 'Natives' for pragmatic reasons. But also [and significantly] because such distinction made sense at the time in

terms of existing kinship, occupational and communal ties, the culture these supported, and because new divisions of labour were tending to confirm a tri-partite division of Cape Town's social formation into 'white', 'coloured' and 'native' as migration of the latter into the city increased. (Bickford-Smith, 1994:308, 309)

Apartheid South Africa was a racially-defined democracy for white citizens. People classified as 'African' were subjects relegated to ethnically defined 'independent states' referred to as the 'bantustans'. People classified as 'coloured' and seen as 'of mixed-race', along with those classified as 'Indian' occupied an ambiguous position within the South African polity. The latter groups were neither full citizens (in terms of access to rights before the law), nor complete subjects. The dominant articulation of 'African' identity was in terms of 'tribal' identities while at the same time there was an overarching black/white division of the population. Mamdani aptly conceptualises the apartheid state as 'the generic form of the colonial state in Africa' in which racial domination was 'mediated through a variety of ethnically organised powers' (1996:8). This state form shaped resistance movements. Following the non-racial strategy of the Congress Alliance during the 1950s and 1960s, an important shift happened in the 1970s in the wake of the Black Consciousness Movement. It emphasised black unity rejecting the racial labelling of apartheid ideology. During this period a general unease and rejection of the notion 'coloured' entered the progressive political movement which emerged from a history shaped by both ANC non-racialism and the Black Consciousness tradition, and coloured people were referred to as 'so-called coloured'.

Despite this discomfort the term 'coloured' was seen as necessary, although always qualified, for mass politics amongst all South Africans opposed to the apartheid state. When the ANC was unbanned and eclipsed the UDF important shifts emerged. These became apparent in the early post-apartheid period when coloured activists within the ANC 'rediscovered' their specificity and that of their communities. In the context of an emerging africanist lobby within the ANC nationally and the resulting marginalisation of coloured people within the party, new contestations arose about the place of coloured activists within the ANC, about who is 'black' and what it means to be 'black' - 'black' here conflated with 'african'. Coloured activists identified this africanist resurgence as the main cause of their marginalisation within the party. Today, the meanings of african, black and coloured are more ambiguous than they had ever been in the 1980s or for that matter the 1950s.

Politics of Post-Apartheid

In this post-apartheid era there is no longer a single white supremacist enemy against which to unite in struggle. The absence of such an enemy, however, does not mean that post-apartheid South Africa is completely unmarked by its history of slavery, colonialism and apartheid. It is important to acknowledge both continuities and changes in this period of transition. Such acknowledgement would mean a move away from dominant conceptions in liberation circles that ethnic and racialised identities are 'purely a creation of the apartheid state' (Wilmsen et al., 1994:347) with no place in the new South Africa and its priority of building national unity.

Among the continuities and changes in the new South Africa are that we have black politicians and black people in power in some spheres while white dominance persists in others. This substantially weakens a Black Consciousness strategy, which tends to perceive of struggle in binary black-against-white terms. Furthermore, in the context of a negotiated settlement a concerted political assault on white privilege is strategically very difficult or nearly impossible. This settlement has meant some accommodation of white privilege. These political realities in South Africa today remove the incentives and context which make possible an alliance between coloured and african people. The terrain of struggle has thus shifted considerably.

The Rainbow Nation discourse operates in many different and complex ways. Politically, it forges hegemony and control for the dominant political party and a broader circle of elites because it has managed to appropriate it as a quintessential value of the new South Africa. Economically and socially its evasion of power soothes the racially based inequalities that persist but were established through the racially skewed processes of colonialism and apartheid. Culturally it operates as a new metanarrative which could effectively marginalise other voices or discourses that counter the superficiality of the rainbow nation discourse. Thus, there is a fundamental question about how social spaces will be created for racialised (as opposed to rainbow inseparability) political and cultural struggles that are not about essentialist self-interest.[111] In other words, this discourse forecloses political struggles against various manifestations of white dominance which are not based on constructions of a 'pure' black identity, yet recognising the particularism of black experiences in a general sense. In addition, the priority of building a Rainbow Nation in the context of the New South Africa raises all sorts of questions about belonging. What colour is 'coloured' in the Rainbow Nation? Where is 'black'? And where is 'white'? Furthermore, the nation-building project raises questions about what unity means in a highly heterogeneous society. This is especially the case where the construction of a singular, homogeneous national identity would deny the diversity of experiences in South Africa.

The problem with the Rainbow Nation discourse is that it forecloses on critical questions of contestation which need to be recognised and explored. This foreclosure manifests itself in the notion that despite history and its consequences, suddenly 'we are all one nation' and *equal* in our positions in this nation. Any matter that may divide or create conflict among us needs to be avoided to ensure that the aesthetic of the rainbow kaleidoscope remains intact. This discourse ignores the fact that such co-existence is premised on highly unequal power relations systematically shaped over centuries. The nation that will be constructed through this framework will be extremely precarious and unstable and necessarily mediated through an overly optimistic and 'happy-go-lucky' sentimentalism so as to compensate for its frailties.

To illustrate the inappropriateness of such premature invocations of 'oneness' it is critical to contextualise the emergence of this discourse in the political processes of the early 1990s. The price of a relatively peaceful and negotiated transition has been the absence of any chance of effecting any significant redistribution of power and resources between those who benefited from colonialism and apartheid and those who were exploited. To add insult to injury those

---

111. Projects in line with the ideas of: Young, 1993; Hall, 1991; Gilroy, 1993 and Rattansi, 1995.

who benefited are legally and constitutionally protected to the extent that they are allowed to siphon off vast amounts of resources in the post-1994 period through pension systems and other forms of 'compensation'. These resources could have been used for developmental purposes.

These banalities of a negotiated transition clearly serve to further protect the institutionalised and embedded nature of racialised class power and cannot simply be erased or displaced through vague political insistence that we need to leave the past behind us and march into a glorious future of equality and nationhood. These socio-political absurdities need to be interrogated. Such interrogation cannot be accommodated in the patronising platitudes of the Rainbow Nation discourse.

The experiences and positions of survivors of apartheid as articulated through the process of the Truth and Reconciliation Commission are a clear reminder of just how cruel and painful the formal transitional arrangement/agreements are from the perspective of those who suffered under the system. These processes directly counterpoint the hollow ring of being 'one' in citizenship of a 'rainbow nation'. These brief examples clearly illustrate the primary function of the rainbow nation as that of legitimisation. It attempts to be the glue that keeps the brittle pieces together.

The way in which these historical, political and social contexts are being negotiated is intricately linked to the changing social economies of the Western Cape. Historically, poorer coloured people, mainly in urban areas, were privileged in relation to africans with regard to certain categories of work; the provision of higher levels of access to education and health services; the provision of unemployment benefits that emanated from being part of the recognised/'legal' labour force; the provision of housing infrastructure (both buildings and services) and the extension of a range of welfare services such as disability grants, (higher) state pensions, maintenance grants, amongst others. In the current context of democratic transition equity measures in social development strategies are likely to leave these coloured communities hard hit.

DISCOURSES ON COLOURED IDENTITIES

White Nationalist Discourse

There are three key discourses on coloured culture and identity in South Africa. The one is a white Nationalist discourse which constructs coloureds as 'left over people' (Marieke de Klerk cf. Adhikari, 1992:9). This construction is accompanied with patronising and racist depictions of coloured culture. For example, coloured culture is represented as involving 'coon' carnivals and speaking 'capey' Afrikaans while coloured people are represented as drunken, happy-go-lucky clowns (die *jollie hotnot*/ 'happy Hottentot') who often/always become violent when drunk (Gerwel, 1983). The stereotype of drunkenness is explicit in the common saying: *So dronk soos 'n kleurling onderwyser* ['As drunk as a coloured teacher']. Recently, none other than Mr Percy Sonn, vice-president of the Western Province Cricket Association and deputy attorney general of the Western Cape, reinforced this notion by publicly justifying his drunkenness stating that 'drinking is so much part of the culture of my people' (*Mail and Guardian*, Feb. 14–20, 1997:2).

A Discourse of Blackness: 1970s and 1980s

An alternative to this patronising discourse emerged in the 1970s and 1980s among radical activists in the Black Consciousness Movement and in the non-racial United Democratic Front (UDF) and ANC. This discourse denies that colouredness is possible and different/specific in favour of an all encompassing black identity. Ineke van Kessel has dealt with this extensively. She argues that coloured activists were

> acutely aware of the price that had to be paid for becoming part of mainstream resistance. In this political home, there was no place for 'Coloureds' as such, but only for 'Blacks'. In order to be accepted as 'Black', Coloured identity had to be foresworn. (van Kessel, 1994:8–9)

She continues to capture this position aptly through a statement made by Jonathan de Vries, who served as the Publicity Secretary of the UDF Regional Executive Committee, 1982–85:

> ...the liberation culture was an African culture; the songs were either military songs or church hymns. There was no incorporation of Colou-

red identity in the UDF. That [coloured identity] could not even be discussed. (quoted in van Kessel, 1994:9)

This approach was seen as necessary in a context of resistance to white supremacy. Reflecting on the 1980s in the current context, Eugene Paramoer of the Community Youth Movement (CYM) expresses this singular notion of being black as follows: *'ek het in organisasies ingekom met die belief dat ek swart is en nie kleurling nie. Die verskille tussen kamerade is nooit regtig geaksentueer nie'* ['I entered organisations with the belief that I was black and not coloured. The differences between comrades were never really accentuated.'] (interviewed in Burgess and Dikeni, 1995:16).

This discourse does not acknowledge the specificity of coloured experiences nor the heterogeneity and situatedness of blackness. It tends towards a totalising and single notion of being black.

Ethnonationalist Discourse

Contrary to expectations, most coloured people did not vote as 'black' (Eldridge and Seekings, 1996). In other words, the majority did not vote for any of the political parties that represented the 'liberation of black people', e.g. the ANC, the Pan-Africanist Congress, etc. Instead, more recently a third discourse has emerged among 'Brown Nationalist' movements in the Western Cape. These grope desperately after a mythical ethnic purity based in selectively reconstructed mythical pasts in attempts to 'show us what coloured culture and identity is'. Among these movements are the *Kleurling Weerstands Beweging* (Coloured Resistance Movement, KWB), the Brown Nationalist Movement, the National Liberation Front and the Coloured Forum among others.

Mervyn Ross of the KWB represents the voice of ethnonationalism:

> We are proud that we are ethnic. And once we are ethnic and being recognised by various other people, we can also go further and say, 'Look, we are ethnic. We have our own language, our own culture, our own land and we want to govern ourselves'. We are not prepared to be governed by the white man anymore—he has made a mess of it for 300 years. We are not prepared to be governed by black people. (cf. Caliguire, 1996:10)

This ethnonationalism falls back on racist and cultural essentialism and so becomes a bedfellow with apartheid discourse and right-wing movements such as the *Afrikaner Weerstandsbeweging* (Afrikaner Resistance Movement, AWB) despite Ross's claims that this movement is 'an extension of his fight against apartheid, rather than a call for apartheid anew' (cf. Brummer, 1995).

Stefaans Brummer notes the similarities in the discourses of the AWB and KWB:

> In both, there is a sense of consolidation of a *volk* on a hostile continent, where recognition of that *volk*'s ethnically distinct nature, with their own culture, language and land is the only guarantee against the rapacious hordes without and the traitors within. For both, the affirmative action which they see as a government-dictated strategy to advance others at the expense of their own people, and the loss of the land which is their birthright, are the strongest rallying points. (Brummer, 1995)

A Discourse of Denial

In response to this essentialist nationalism left-wing academics have not been able to formulate any convincing arguments. Instead, they keep falling back on the decade-old assertion of the unreality of coloured identity. In 1987 Gavin Lewis noted that talking about coloured people 'as a separate and identifiable group [with a separate identity] apart from the black majority' (Lewis, 1987:1) was extremely controversial. In the same vein as Goldin (1987) he also suggested that 'Coloured identity is a white-imposed categorisation' (ibid.:4). These ideas persist in various responses to the outcome of the April 1994 elections in the Western Cape and to subsequent attempts at and discussions about mobilising coloured people 'as coloureds'. This is so despite new developments in conceptualising identities in the context of the ever-changing political terrain in South Africa (see Field, 1990; 1996 and Wilmsen and McAllister, 1996). In this section we focus on the arguments of two local intellectuals on the left, Neville Alexander and Norman Duncan. These academics have in the media most clearly and publicly articulated what we call the discourse of denial. Alexander's views have been and continue to be particularly influential because of his historical role in opposition politics. We provide a short introduction to each of these scholars before proceeding with our critique of their views on coloured identities.

Neville Alexander, historically classified coloured, is a well known intellectual of the socialist left in South Africa. He was involved in the structures of the Non-European Unity Movement. His ideas regarding the need for guerilla warfare precipitated his suspension from this movement. He was subsequently involved in the formation of the National Liberation Front (NLF) to mobilise people committed to the violent overthrow of the state. Alexander's involvement in the NLF eventually led to his imprisonment on Robben Island for ten years (1964–1974). After his release from prison and his years under house arrest, he helped launch the Cape Action League in 1983 and played an instrumental role in the formation of the National Forum. In 1990 he was elected head of the Workers Organisation for Socialist Action (WOSA), a new political organisation committed to promoting working class interests. Alexander has been employed as a lecturer in the Faculty of Education at the University of Cape Town since the early 1980s and is currently based in this faculty (Villa-Vicencio, 1993:9–17).

Norman Duncan, also historically classified coloured, is of a much younger generation and has been an active member of the UDF in Cape Town. He is trained as a psychologist and has a key interest in anti-racism. Duncan is currently Head of the Psychology Department at the University of Venda.

In the late 1990s intellectuals such as Neville Alexander and Norman Duncan continue to articulate the view that coloured identity is (a) white-imposed, racist and reactionary; (b) an apartheid relic best left behind us in this post-apartheid era and (c) a basis for ethnic nationalism and thus possible Rwanda/Burundi and Bosnian type genocide. (Alexander, 1996; cf. Fakier, 1996a and 1996b).

These views are illustrated in a debate about coloured identities in the Cape Times, one of the local newspapers in the Western Cape. This particular debate occurred in the context of the municipal elections in the region during 1996. In the course of this debate Alexander challenged Chris Nissen, former ANC leader in the Western Cape, for asserting his coloured identity. Alexander writes:

> Comrade Chris Nissen (Cape Times, March 18) shows a singular lack of historical and political understanding when he proclaims...that he is first of all a coloured person. (Alexander, 1996)

In our view Alexander's implicit denial of historical formations of coloured identities begs a more complex understanding of South African history and politics. In addition, although he correctly describes Peter Marais' (National Party Member of Parliament from the Western Cape) response to Nissen's assertion as 'racist and tribalistic drivel' (ibid.), he fails to recognise that not all assertions of coloured identity are racist.

Alexander further argues that

> identities are usually prescribed or described in the ideology of the ruling or dominant groups in any unequal society ... [b]ecause they are defenceless, *slaves generally accept the identities their masters impose on them* [and that South Africans now need to] lay to rest the *slave mentality* we were forced to inherit from the colonial and apartheid past. (ibid., our emphasis)

Part of the view that coloured identity is white-imposed is the commonly held notion that coloured people have no culture. Norman Duncan argues that claiming coloured identity points to 'a new form of racism'. He says:

> [i]t's incorrect to speak of 'coloured'. It cannot bring us anywhere [but lead to bloodshed] because there's no such thing as a coloured culture, coloured identity. Someone has to show me what it is... (Fakier in *Cape Times*, 4 December 1996)

Returning to Alexander (1996), he further notes that South Africans 'live in a period in which it is eminently possible to *promote and consolidate a South African consciousness and a South African identity*' (our emphasis). For Alexander our national identity should be primary with all other identities subsumed under this nationality:

> [I]f the nation does not become the primary identity of the people of South Africa, they will willy-nilly imbibe all manner of ethnic and racial allegiances or sub-identities as their ideological life-blood. (Idasa Conference, Panel Speech, Aug. 1995)

In his conceptualisation of 'the nation', he ignores the gendered and racialised content of the concept of nationhood. He also reduces all aspects of our subjectivity to nationhood. In our everyday lives, however, we are never simply 'South Africans' and our South African identity cannot always be and is not always our primary identity as Alexander wishes. Instead, all our lives are gendered, racialised and classed.

In our view these academics deny processes of coloured identity formation. This forces coloured people to choose between being either 'black', 'white' or 'South African'. The former falls into a binary perception of our complex racialised world. The latter denies difference and racialised relations of social power. Besides, processes of identity formation are hardly this clear cut. Finally, no identity is inherently progressive or reactionary.

There is some basis in fact to the link between the term coloured and apartheid racial classification. However, this one-sided way of thinking is not helpful in understanding the construction of any identity, including various constructions of coloured identities. It loses sight of the reality that as subjects we do not simply internalise what dominant ideologies say about us. Instead, in our struggles against various forms of domination including racism we define and redefine our own senses of self. It is this subjective aspect of the construction of coloured identities that makes it valid and worthy of exploration and examination. As Field (1990:11) argues: 'it is incorrect to define any people as the product of state action and ideology'. Such thinking reduces human subjects to passive victims of domination and oppression. Significantly, Field (1990:11) notes that the important unasked question is: 'what are the implications of denying coloured people's role in the process of their definition of themselves and of their identity as based on their everyday life experiences?'

The danger of Duncan's argument, however, that coloured people lack their 'own' culture, is that he may be falling into the trap of reifying culture 'show me what it is' he says. Underlying the notion that there is no such thing as coloured culture and identity is the assumption that because coloured identity does not have an 'essence' in the sense that african ethnic identities are assumed to have, it is in this sense not a 'real' identity. Ironically, such arguments fall into the same trap of apartheid discourse, which attempted to divide black South Africans into distinct ethnic groups with distinct and conflicting cultures. For such views culture is only culture if it is pure and internally unified.

In contrast to the view of coloured people as helpless and hopeless remains of Afrikaner and racist apartheid manipulation we attempt to conceptualise the making and remaking of coloured identities as a fluid process involving agency and shaped by time and place. We challenge singular notions of blackness which are open to repressive sameness as well as essentialist notions of colouredness which hark back to the Verwoerdian era. Finally, we point to the validity of coloured identity formation on the basis of the following conceptual foundation.

CONCEPTUALISING COLOURED IDENTITIES

> [I]dentities are not found but made; they are not just there, waiting to be discovered...but they have to be culturally and politically constructed through political antagonisms and cultural struggle. (Mercer, 1994:292)

In this section we draw on relevant works of Kobena Mercer, Stuart Hall, Amina Mama, Craig Calhoun and Ali Rattansi in an attempt to outline a non-essentialist theory of identities.

All Identities Are Constructed, Unstable, and Heterogeneous

All identities, including coloured identities, are constructed and given meaning in particular social contexts. It is important to see the content of this meaning in its historical, socio-political, cultural and spatial contexts. This meaning is always contested, hence unstable.

Amina Mama (1995:2) develops and applies a conceptualisation of subjectivity as a discursive process during which subjects take on multiple positions. For her, subjectivity is not an easy, nor effortless process. It is a dynamic process of continuous conscious and unconscious self-reflection on our relation to the 'us-ses' and 'them's' in our particular worlds. Furthermore, it is a process with a multiplicity of possibilities.

Conceptualising formations of identity as processes involving active subjects/agents helps challenge the notion that coloured identities are simply white-imposed by slave-owners and/or apartheid politicians and passively accepted by coloured people. Instead, it facilitates a conceptualisation that accounts for the fact that coloured people played and continue to play an important role in giving meaning to their identities.

Furthermore, we "assume different identities at different times, identities which are not unified around a coherent 'self'. Within us are contradictory identities, pulling in different directions, so that our identifications are continuously being shifted about... No single identity... [can] align all [our] different identities into one, overarching 'master [or primary] identity'" (Hall, 1993:277, 280). Thus all South Africans have multiple and often contradictory identities based on race, class, gender, sexuality, ethnicity among other factors. Nation-building in the new South Africa and the consequent pressure to see ourselves primarily as South Africans can fall into the trap of denying difference and shifting identities among South Africans.

A Historicised Approach

Processes of identity formation are embedded in specific historical contexts. An approach towards coloured identities as historically constructed and re-constructed in particular social contexts allows one to acknowledge that processes of coloured identity formation can be defined in terms of what they 'are', namely valid processes of identity formation which shift with time, place and space. These processes are rooted in historical processes of dislocation in the context of slavery, and of cultural dispossession in the case of genocide and of subordination of indigenous peoples. This points us to the importance of an examination of the role of slavery in the collective history and partial 'origin' of coloured communities. Drawing on the literature from Latin America (Taussig, 1990), Africa (Mbembe, 1991) and South East Asia (Tsing, 1993) we know that practices and social relations during slavery engrave themselves deeply into the fabric and tissue of enslaved and non-enslaved communities in various ways, with complex aftermaths. Although much historical work has been done on the history of slavery at the Cape (Shell, 1994; Worden and Crais, 1994; Eldridge and Morton, 1994) we remain unclear about what exactly this history might mean for processes of coloured identity formation today. At a minimum there needs to be an acknowledgement of that period in the history of 'a people' before processes of re-writing and re-claiming colonially defined histories and interpretations can begin to be understood.

In the context of colonialism, dislocation and cultural dispossession a key survival mechanism for the subaltern peoples was to appropriate the dominant culture and in so doing, to create their own 'new' cultures. In this sense coloured identities and cultures are less about what was lost culturally along the Middle Passage and as a result of genocide and more about the articulation of these diverse identities and fragments of cultural formations with the colonial culture. Creolisation of the Dutch language is one manifestation of this process of cultural and identity formation among slave communities in the Western Cape. This is one place to which our attention should be turned when thinking about coloured identities to the dialogue between subaltern and dominant cultural forms in the colonial context.

Racialised Identities, Identities as Relational

Processes of creolisation and racialisation occur within the context of very particular and multiple sources of power relations leaving them politically open-ended. In the context of a history of colonialism, slavery and apartheid all processes of identity formation in South Africa, including the formation of white identities, have historically been shaped by racialised relations of social power. Multiple, shifting meanings of race give rise to multiple discourses of race and multiple racisms. Not only do ideologies of racism/discourses of race change over time, they also vary within one broad context at one time. These variations are shaped by very particular relationships of social power between specific white people and specific black people.

Writing on black experiences in England, Mama argues that

> [ra]cial oppression itself is inadequately conceptualised as monolithic, total and homogeneous in its effects. The nuances and intricate sets of social etiquette and behaviour, of betrayal and collusion, of inversion and resistance that constitute racism as a social process are barely touched upon. (Mama, 1995:48)

In similar vein, Anthias and Yuval-Davis (1992) point us to the importance of understanding racism not as a uniform phenomenon, and racialised identities not as abstract, homogeneous categories, but in relation to specific sets of social relations. An understanding of racialised identities based on the particularity of experiences challenges the common perception that 'black' and 'white' are homogeneous binary opposites.

Calhoun (1994:26) echoes this conceptualisation. He argues that seeing identities in terms of categories of individuals 'allows a kind of abstraction from the concrete interactions and social relationships within which identities are constantly renegotiated, in which individuals present one identity as more salient that another, and within which individuals achieve some personal sense of continuity and balance among their various sorts of identities'.

Like elsewhere in the world, racism in South Africa before, during and after apartheid was and is not a uniform, immutable phenomenon. Instead, racism has, and continues to take on, different forms in relation to different groups of black people. Any non-racial or anti-racist project has to take this variation into account if it is at all aiming at some success over the long term. Even though we talk of the apartheid system as a singular force, we need to look more closely and realise that different forms of racism were and are applied to different groups of black people in different contexts. Without necessarily reducing black experiences to people's responses to racism, this approach leads one to an acknowledgement of multiplicity and diversity within black experiences.

Coloured identities have been shaped by very particular racist discourses. It is important to conceptualise coloured identities as relational identities shaped by complex networks of concrete social relations rather than seeing 'coloured' as a particular category of individuals and/or as simply an imposed name from a racist past. The value of this approach is its challenge to any notions of colouredness as homogeneous and/or an essentialist ethnic identity with fixed cultural boundaries as well as its acknowledgement of the particularity of identities.

This means that coloured politics can unfold in a number of different directions. Rattansi (1995:256) insightfully reminds us that if we are to make sense of all identities, including racialised identities, as relational, created and recreated through struggle, situational, contradictory, and multiple, it is important to acknowledge that identities have 'no necessary political belonging'. Instead, people mobilise around reconfigured articulations of identity for various purposes, whether reactionary or for resistance. Coloured identities are neither inherently progressive nor inherently reactionary. Instead, articulations of coloured identity are resources available for use by both progressive and reactionary social movements. These identities are more likely to articulate to reactionary movements under some circumstances.

CONCLUSION

This paper has pointed to some problems with the ways in which coloured identities have been understood both before and after the 1994 democratic elections. These problems are indicative of the critical need for a thorough debate about the national project that has been spurned by the particularity of the South African transition as constructed by the main political players. It is our view that this national project is very far removed from the everyday realities and politics of ordinary South Africans. It is also counterposed to the emergence of a critical public sphere in which issues of differential power are voiced and critiqued.

We need to ask penetrating questions about the precarious business of (re)constructing a nation. How can a national project be kept open-ended and critical? How can we ensure that it refrains from prescribing processes of identification and establishing itself as the policing agent of various boundaries between people and their various communities? This paper has been an effort to demonstrate that more open-ended and empowering conceptualisations of coloured identities are possible. These, we believe, are instructive for a broader debate about national identities and their 'fit' with deep democracy. An inclusive democracy cannot be built on a notion of 'the Nation' (those who 'have' a national identity as 'primary') and 'its Others' (those who do not 'have' this 'primary' identity but who, instead, 'willy-nilly imbibe only sub-identities'). Nor can it be built on a blinded normalising notion of *simunye* (oneness—a slogan used by the South African Broadcasting Corporation, SABC, Channel 1 in the post-1994 period). Instead, our attention should be turned to the ways in which South Africans from diverse experiences (gendered, racialised, class, cultural, sexual orientation) interpret and appropriate the meaning of a New South African national identity in making sense of their lived experiences.

REFERENCES

Adhikari, M. 1992. "God, Jan van Riebeeck and 'the Coloured People': The Anatomy of a South African Joke", in *Southern African Discourse*, Vol. 4: 4–10.
Alexander, N. 1996. "Sow the wind, reap the whirlwind", in *Cape Times*, 28 March.
Anthias, Floya and Yuval-Davis, Nira. 1992. "Racism and the colour 'Black'", Ch 5 in *Racialised Boundaries*. London & New York: Routledge.
Bickford-Smith, Vivian. 1994. "Meanings of Freedom: Social Position and Identity Among Ex-Slaves and Their Descendants in Cape Town, 1875–1910" in Worden, N. and Crais, C. (eds.) *Breaking the Chains*, Johannesburg: Witwatersrand University Press.
Botha, T. 1992. "Civic Associations as Autonomous Organs of Grassroots' Participation", in *Theoria*, No. 79: 57–74.
Brümmer, S. 1995. "New struggle for coloureds", in *Mail and Guardian*. March 24–30.
Burgess, A. and Dikeni, S. 1995. "Kleurling Jeug Toyi-Toyi uit die ANC", in *Die Suid Afrikaan*, No. 53: 16–17.
Calhoun, Craig. 1994. "Social Theory and the Politics of Identity", Ch 1 in Calhoun, Craig (ed.) *Social Theory and the Politics of Identity*, Oxford UK & Cambridge USA: Blackwell.
Caliguire, Daria. 1996. "Voices from the Communities", Ch 2 in James, Wilmot Godfrey, Caliguire, Daria, and Cullinan, Kerry (eds.) *Now That We Are Free: Coloured Communities in a Democratic South Africa*, Cape Town: Idasa.
Cape Times. Cape Town.
Du Toit, P. & Gagiano, J. 1993. "Strongmen on the Cape Flats", in *Africa Insight*, Vol. 23(2): 103–111.
Eldredge, Elizabeth A. and Morton, Fred (eds.) 1994. *Slavery in South Africa*. Pietermaritzburg: University of Natal Press.

Eldridge, M. and Seekings, J. 1996. "Mandela's Lost Province: The African National Congress and the Western Cape Electorate in the 1994 South African Elections", in *Journal of Southern African Studies*, Vol. 22 (4): 517–541.
Fakier, Y. 1996a. "A debate coloured by race", in *Cape Times*, 4 December.
Fakier, Y 1996b. "Identity question 'creation of apartheid", in *Cape Times*, 11 December.
Field, S. 1990. *The Politics of Exclusion: A Case Study of the Factreton Area*. M. Soc. Sci. Dissertation, UCT Sociology Department.
Field, S. 1996. *The Power of Exclusion: Moving Memories from Windermere to the Cape Flats, 1920s–1990s*, PhD Dissertation, University of Essex, Sociology.
Gerwel, G.J. 1983. *Literatuur en Apartheid*. Kasselsvlei: Kampen Uitgewers.
Gilroy, Paul. 1993. *Small Acts*. London: Serpent's Tail.
Goldin, Ian. 1987. *Making Race*. London: Maskew Miller Longman.
Hall, S. 1991. "Old and New Identities. Old and New Ethnicities", in King, Anthony D. (ed.) *Culture, Globalization and the World System*. London: Macmillan.
Hall, Stuart. 1993. "The Question of Cultural Identity", Ch 6 in Hall, Stuart, Held, David and McGrew, Tony (eds.) *Modernity and its Futures*. Cambridge: Polity Press.
Holiday, A. 1995. "Mastering Slave Politics", in *Cape Times*, 25 August.
Legassick, M. 1996. "Slave Mentality", Debate on Nuafrica internet discussion group between Legassick, M. and Du Toit, A., June/July.
Lewis, Gavin. 1987. *Between the Wire and the Wall*. Cape Town: David Philip.
Mail and Guardian. Johannesburg.
Mama, Amina. 1995. *Beyond the Masks*. London: Routledge.
Mamdani, Mahmood. 1996. *Citizen and Subject: Contemporary Africa and the Legacy of Late Colonialism*. London: James Currey.
Mbembe, A. 1991. "Power and Obscenity in the Post-Colonial Period", in Manor, James (ed.) *Rethinking Third World Politics*. London & New York: Longman.
Mercer, Kobena. 1994. "1968: Periodising Politics and Identity", Ch 10 in Mercer, Kobena. *Welcome to the Jungle*. New York & London: Routledge.
Rattansi, A. 1995. "Just Framing: Ethnicities and racisms in a 'postmodern' framework", Ch 9 in Nicholson, Linda J. and Seidman, Steven (eds.) *Social Postmodernism: Beyond Identity Politics*. Cambridge: Cambridge University Press.
Shell, Robert. 1994. *Children of Bondage*. Johannesburg: Witwatersrand University Press.
Taussig, M. 1990. "Violence and Resistance in the Americas: The Legacy of Conquest", in *Journal of Historical Sociology*, Vol. 3(3): 209–224.
Tsing, Anna Lowenhaupt. 1993. *In the realm of the Diamond Queen. Marginality in an out-of-the-way place*. Princeton: Princeton University Press.

Van Kessel, I. 1994. *Grassroots: From Community Paper to Activist Playground* Paper presented at Journal of Southern African Studies Conference on Identities 9–11 September 1994, York.

Villa-Vicencio, Charles. 1993. "Neville Alexander" in *The Spirit of Hope*. Johannesburg: Skotaville. pp. 3–19.

Williams, B. 1996. "The power of propaganda", Ch 4 in James, Wilmot Godfrey, Caliguire, Daria, and Cullinan, Kerry (eds.), *Now That We Are Free: Coloured Communities in a Democratic South Africa*. Cape Town: Idasa.

Wilmsen, Edwin N. and McAllister, Patrick A. (eds.) 1996. *The Politics of Difference*. Chicago & London: University of Chicago Press.

Wilmsen, E., Dubow, S. and Sharp, J. 1994. "Introduction: Ethnicity, Identity and Nationalism in Southern Africa", in *Journal of Southern African Studies*, Vol. 20 (3): 347–353.

Worden, N. and Crais, C. (eds.) 1994. *Breaking the Chains: Slavery and Emancipation in the Nineteenth Century Cape Colony*. Johannesburg: Witwatersrand University Press.

Young, M.I. 1993. "Social Movements and the Politics of Difference", in Fisk, Milton (ed.) *Justice*. New Jersey: Humanities Press.

Intimate Transformations: Romance, Gender and Nation

Maria Olaussen

In this paper I wish to discuss two novels written in South Africa at crucial times; Bessie Head's *The Cardinals*, which was written in 1960–1962, although first published posthumously in 1993; and Nadine Gordimer's *None to Accompany Me*, which is set in post-apartheid South Africa and was published in 1994. Both novels evolve around rather complicated romance themes intertwined with issues of place, belonging and the shifting ground of political reorientation.

Despite the differences between these authors they have both been given representative functions by the Western academic establishment. Gordimer is often read as "spokesperson" for white South Africa and Bessie Head as "African Woman Writer" by readers and critics abroad. An understandable reaction here is that local readers question the legitimacy of "the spokesperson" and question the text from this perspective.[112] This is already an important question of place and involves much larger issues than simply that of determining who speaks "for" a certain place. The fact that certain texts are written into a national and an African continental canon from abroad shows us that any question of representative texts should be discussed within the context of the global centre-periphery discrepancy we live with today. In *Edge of Empire,* Jane M. Jacobs defines the "spatial

---

112. See, for instance, Michael Wood's review of Kathrin Wagner's *Rereading Nadine Gordimer*. Wagner's main focus is on the differences between domestic and foreign audiences' perception of Gordimer. The "insights" which the foreign audience find in her texts are, according to Wagner, rather banal for the domestic audience. According to Wood, Wagner needs to focus more precisely on the source of the unease among South African readers and critics. Wood does not touch upon the importance of questions concerning the relationship between representation and realist narratives and the function of realism in this context. Wood, 1994:12–13.

struggles" of post-colonial texts as "formed out of the cohabitation of variously empowered people and the meanings they ascribed to localities and places." These spatial struggles are also "constituted from the way in which the global and the local always already inhabit one another."[113] The texts by Gordimer and Head are informed by these struggles and constitute in themselves different manifestations of the struggle over the meaning of place. The power relations involved are not determined only by the situatedness of the authors but also by the global critical establishment.

The representative function given to certain texts in certain periods of time is therefore part of a much larger process of cultural fabrication than the individual choices of authors and critics. Bessie Head wanted to escape this function altogether. During her visits to African universities she found herself in situations where she had to defend her way of writing and her seemingly apolitical approach to apartheid South Africa. In a letter describing her visit to Nigeria, Head writes:

> One student questioned me very aggressively. He said: "When we read Achebe and Ngugi and Armah, we find things there we can identify with, but with you we are disoriented and flung into Western literature." [114]

Head displays a rather dismissive attitude towards this question as well as towards another recurrent theme in her discussions with audiences in African countries, that of her political involvement. On this particular occasion Head simply answers that she sees herself as being "above an environment".[115]

In "The Essential Gesture" Nadine Gordimer addresses this question of the writer's commitment and specifically as regards writing in apartheid South Africa. The wish to be a story-teller free of responsibilities and the idea of writing somehow existing "above" an environment Gordimer describes as a fantasy which sooner or later comes to an end. "The writer loses Eden, writes to be read, and comes to realise that he is answerable."[116] Gordimer draws on Roland

---

113. Jacobs, 1996:5.
114. Head, 3.9. 1982.
115. Head, 3.9. 1982.
116. Gordimer, 1988:286.

Barthes' idea of language as a common prescription and habit creating the work which is the writer's essential gesture as a social being.

Bessie Head's refusal to take up the specific commitment as a South African writer is closely tied up with her ideal of universality. This ideal is in turn a result of the awareness that her writing could never aspire to the representational function that Gordimer seems to take as self-evident. In *The Cardinals*, Head's aspirations for universality enable her to create a world of exclusion and disintegration. Gordimer's novel, on the other hand, never quite lets go of its aspirations for specific validity which paradoxically leads to a tale evolving around a strong central voice even when what it is describing is how the centre cannot hold.

My focus here is on how the cultural construction of womanhood within a romance theme changes within the changing circumstances of nation-building. My concern is to link nationalism and sexuality and, like the authors of a volume with that very name, look at "two of the most powerful global discourses shaping contemporary notions of identity."[117] In their introduction, the editors of *Nationalisms and Sexualities* problematize Benedict Anderson's *Imagined Communities*[118] because of the inherent masculine bias of his analysis and the underdeveloped comparison with gender identities as relationally constituted. Anderson himself shows how nationality gains its meaning only within a system of differences in the same way as "men" and "women" are defined in opposition to each other. The nation will thus be defined through what it excludes and hence will be involved in a constant process of monitoring that exclusion.

This process is not only comparable to that of constituting gender difference but, more importantly, it is in itself gendered. The meaning of the nation, i.e. the style in which the community is imagined, is determined within a "distinctly homosocial form of male bonding."[119] This takes the form of representing the nation as female as in the common trope of homeland as female body with its ideological links to an idealization of motherhood, heterosexuality, the family and the idea of the nation as a fraternity. According to the editors of *Nationa-*

---

117. Parker et al., 1992.
118. Anderson, 1983.
119. Parker et al., 1992:6.

lisms and Sexualities, this idea of the nation as imagined from a male perspective is implied in Anderson's work but never analysed further. The nation as a fraternity also excludes women's political movements from the nationalist agenda. According to Gisela Kaplan, nationalism in western Europe has been highly adaptable to a great variety of different ideologies but "[t]here is at least one ideology with which nationalism has been incompatible in most western European countries, and that is feminism."[120] In anti-colonial struggles, women's movements have constantly negotiated the struggle for women's rights within various nationalist agendas. At independence these struggles have often been removed from the nation's agenda or subsumed within a centralized state structure no longer controlled by the movements themselves. As Lois A. West points out in her introduction to *Feminist Nationalism*, it is a matter of working out contradictions in "women's struggling for women's rights within contexts that have denied them rights as citizens at the same time as they are working on various nationalist struggles rooted in their kin, ethnic, religious, or regional group."[121] The presence of these struggles within the gendered national narrative opens up the possibilities of a differently imagined community.

The Making of a Good-Time Girl

In an article on "Bessie Head's Southern Spaces", Rob Nixon points to the fact that Bessie Head's literary development followed a different trajectory from that of her South African male contemporaries.[122] Whereas writers such as Peter Abrahams, Bloke Modisane, Es'kia Mphahlele and Lewis Nkosi, all celebrated the urban life style or at least developed the "Jim Comes to Jo'burg" theme of rural-urban migration, Bessie Head depicted urban South Africa only in her first novel *The Cardinals*. After leaving South Africa on an exit visa in 1964, Bessie Head turned to descriptions of rural Southern Africa in all her writings. According to Nixon, Head "anticipated the need to counterbalance South African literature's fixation with male, urban space and

---

120. Kaplan, 1997:8.
121. West, 1997:xxx.
122. Nixon, 1996:243–254.

with realms of spectacular conflict rather than the 'small' pressures of daily survival."[123]

Bessie Head's writing also goes against the grain of the literary development in South Africa in the sense that she, through her exile, leaves South Africa also in the literary sense. Whereas other refugees, for instance Alex La Guma, continued to use South Africa as the basis for their literary imagination, Head depicts Botswanan village life. In this respect, her writing both implicitly and explicitly constitutes a critique of the "grand narratives of national politics".[124] Head's writing is profoundly informed by her surroundings and by the history and politics of Southern Africa but she refuses to fit it into a nationalist paradigm.

Despite her alliance with Panafricanism in the early sixties, Head later developed an aversion to political activities. With the publication of *The Cardinals*, this aversion can be traced back to the very roots of her experience of the beginnings of black urban political and cultural activities in South Africa. *The Cardinals* is a novel about the necessity and the difficulties of writing, "a passionate exploration of the craft and the calling", as M.J. Daymond puts it in her introduction.[125] It brings writing into close juxtaposition with the shaping of a self in a situation of oppression and disadvantage. By choosing a female protagonist and focusing on sexual vulnerability, Head thematizes a gender-specific form of oppression. Head's novel also shows that the formation of female subjectivity is closely tied up with heterosexual power relations.

The Cardinals is set in the year 1959 but written in the early sixties. It is therefore a retrospect on the year before the turn to a more violent anti-apartheid resistance, mass detentions and exile. The novel depicts two aspects of the apartheid legislation: the Immorality Act and the Group Areas Act and analyses how the introduction of these boundaries in the most intimate personal areas of place and sexuality translates itself into a particular subjectivity.

The protagonist, Miriam, is an orphan brought up in a slum: "Until the age of sixteen she was placed and replaced in ten homes"

---

123. Nixon, 1996:250.
124. Nixon, 1996:244.
125. Daymond, 1993:viii.

(*The Cardinals*, 10). Here she learns to read and write from an old man who writes letters for the entire community and therefore is looked upon as someone special. Through the ability to read and write and to serve the community with these skills he earns the right to an otherwise unacceptable individualism. The old man is allowed to sing for hours on end when drunk. "Usually such a display of individualism would have been violently repressed but the valuable service he performed for the community set him apart and protected him."[126] After the death of the old man. Miriam is forced to flee her home into "a new way of life" because of the drunken advances of her foster father. This is how Miriam eventually starts working as a journalist for *The African Beat*, a reference to Drum publications where Head herself worked.

The two men who created the basis for her literary career in the slum now come together in one person, Johnny. He gives her the nickname Mouse and their relationship develops along the lines of a romance between strong, forceful man and insignificant but spiritually superior woman. In Head's story, this theme is further underlined by the brutal and degrading treatment that Mouse receives both as a woman at the hands of Johnny but also as a journalist at the paper. In a review of *The Cardinals* in *Southern African Review of Books*, Dorothy Driver sees the significance of the novel exactly in its treatment of the Drum-decade from a female point of view. Driver writes:

> The standard critical view today is that *Drum* provided an enabling context for writers, and that its ebullient style marked an important lifeforce in black South African writing. *The Cardinals* asserts otherwise. The editorial demand for sensationalism, along with political constraint, damaged rather than promoted writing. Besides this, the patronising and insulting atmosphere towards women inhibited Mouse's self-expression, whether as writer or as woman. [127]

In a recent article "*Drum* Magazine and the Spatial Configurations of Gender", Dorothy Driver goes into this in more detail. She argues that the black urban presence which was being created through *Drum* also involved a "process of psychic resettlement" where gender differences were being recreated. According to Driver, "*Drum* gives invaluable

---

126. Head, 1993:4.
127. Driver, 1993:17.

insight into the ways in which rural patriarchal structures were giving way to urban forms, as well as into the ways in which women's voices were silenced and a set of 'feminine' voices constructed in their place."[128] Driver sees this reconstruction of femininity as due to the fact that gender was in a state of flux because of the rapid urbanization. *Drum* magazine thus served as one of the instances through which sexual difference was enacted in a new way.

> In the face of this social confusion, *Drum* magazine blandly reproduced European and American constructions of gender as part of an overall ideology of romantic love. This was not romantic love in the courtly tradition, but a modern form of romantic love within an ideology of domesticity, aiming for the establishment of a consumer-oriented nuclear family, headed by the husband and father and hospitable to female authority in only its most carefully controlled domestic forms. [129]

The Cardinals gives a keen insight into this process and places the sexual politics squarely within the overall and intensifying racial politics of the times. The first thing that is reported in the novel as being written for *The African Beat* is Johnny writing: "Recently, 80,000 people were moved out of the slums of the Cape into new homes. Another government township was established. ... Dominating the scene is a large police station and barracks. ... The houses are like those square boxes you see at a loading-zone, empty of imagination or style" (p. 19–20). Johnny's and Mouse's personal relationship also develops in conjunction with what Mouse reveals about her own upbringing. When Johnny and Mouse visit the slum where Mouse spent her childhood, Johnny admits to having encountered something unusual: "I think nothing can surprise me, and then life turns up something like you. You have a beautiful soul that was nurtured on a dung heap" (p. 24).

When the reader is convinced that the relationship between Johnny and Mouse is moving in a romantic direction it is revealed to the reader that Johnny is in fact Mouse's biological father, a fact that remains unknown to both of them. Here Head complicates a relationship which because of its abusive character is already quite complicated. Furthermore the chapter about Johnny and Mouse's mother

---

128. Driver, 1996:232.
129. Driver, 1996:233.

introduces a rather different aspect of the romantic love relationship. Here it is seen as highly desirable, almost transcendent in its disregard of the difference in status between the two lovers. They are both totally detached from their surroundings, individualists who care only for the perfection of their love. This happy love story is abruptly interrupted when Mouse's mother becomes pregnant. She is locked in the house and after having given up her baby, kills herself.

The love story between Johnny and Mouse now abruptly changes in character. It is viewed against the background of the relationship Johnny had with Mouse's mother, and as a direct consequence of that failed love story. The reasons for the imminent father-daughter incest are thus contained in the curtailed possibilities of a traditional heterosexual relationship. Johnny tells Mouse:

> You are young and might prefer to believe that love is moonlight and rosy sunsets. It is not. It is brutal, violent, ugly, possessive and dictatorial. It makes no allowance for the freedom and individuality of the loved one (p. 103).

Although both Johnny and Mouse remain unaware of their biological connection, the issue of incest is brought up when Johnny describes his childhood and the incestuous relations he had to his sister, a young girl forced to support the family as a prostitute. Here Johnny describes that relationship as the closest that the sister could come to a sane and loving relationship. Mouse is not shocked by Johnny's reference to incest: "That's because you are not aware of family relationships" (p. 78).

Another issue brought up in juxtaposition with the theme of incest is the court cases against persons contravening the Immorality Act. Johnny and Mouse together try to write reports on the Immorality Cases and the editor, PK gets arrested under the Immorality Act. Bessie Head's choice of this particular aspect of the apartheid legislation can be understood against the backdrop of what she knew of her own personal history. Like the protagonist of her novel, Head herself grew up with a foster-mother and was only rather late in life in a brutal manner told about her white mother and her black father. The racial classification that ensued with the Population Registration Act entailed a rejection of her very existence. Head's writing further shows how the very protest against this rejection also entailed a problematical position for women. She illustrates that "the period of the most rigid state enforcement of racial and ethnic difference (1960–90) was also the period of gender relations marked by an increasing economic, political and ideological subordination of women."[130]

Interestingly enough, it is in conjunction with the description of the writing up of a Immorality Act case that Johnny makes a pass at Mouse. He tells her that she needs to move in with him and to give him total control of her life in order to develop as a writer. This is further connected to the need of a country.

> We need a country the way we need food and clothes. A human life is limited so it has to identify itself with a small corner of this earth. Only then is it able to shape its destiny and present its contribution. This need of a country is basic and instinctive in every living being. ... You cannot feel like the underdog and at the same time feel you belong to a country (p. 71–72).

Head's view of national identity can be considered a "primordialist" one, where a nation is seen as natural and universal.[131] On the other hand, this view is expressed within the context of a total lack of self-determination. What Head most crucially stresses is the extreme sense of dislocation and the disintegration of family patterns due to apartheid policies. Head works within a nationalist agenda in the sense that she describes the lack of a nation and thus reveals the "contradictions between the ideal image of the nation state" and the actual lived reality of black people in South Africa in the late fifties.[132] Most importantly, Head shows how the ideal notion of the family interacts with the ideal situation of national belonging and how the disintegration of these systems creates alternative patterns.

These patterns are, however, primarily negative ones. They are born out of necessity to compensate for something which is unattainable. Despite the fact that Head idealizes belonging she writes as one of the dispossessed. Head's writing can thus be seen as exemplifying the necessary excluding of the interlinked constructs of nation and family.

---

130. Unterhalter, 1995:236.
131. See Anthias and Yuval-Davis, 1992:23.
132. Stausiulis and Yuval-Davis, 1995:17.

Nation and Family

In Nadine Gordimer's novel *None to Accompany Me* (1994), the process of political change in South Africa is described through the central issue of land reallocation and housing problems. In this sense the novel is located at the opposite point to *The Cardinals* where black urban life is being claimed in the face of new restrictive apartheid legislation. Whereas *The Cardinals* is located at the beginning of exile, both personal for the author Bessie Head and collective for many of her intellectual contemporaries, *None to Accompany Me* describes the problems of a return from exile.

The house takes on a metaphysical significance in the novel. While the protagonist Vera Stark struggles with the legal complications of land redistribution and involves herself with personal problems of housing shortages among friends, she is also involved in a highly personal development away from the restrictions of a traditional heterosexual female identity. In Western literature by women, the house has often come to represent that which imprisons and represents the female self.[133] And as Leslie Kanes Weisman points out, "in many modern works of art by women, images of the house, woman's body, and the role of house/wife merge symbiotically in a vivid social commentary on the house as woman's prison."[134]

In this novel, the explorations for a new female self are directly related to the political process through which white South Africans will have to give up power and privilege. That these two processes do not both lead towards a disintegration of the self, but rather in opposite directions makes the novel an illustration of how "the cultural constructions of womanhood inscribed in many nationalist and ethnic identities and ideologies of nationalism demand women's submission."[135] In this case it is the old crumbling nationalist construction of white South Africa which leaves the protagonist free to find her self.

The nuclear family and the romantic heterosexual relationship is questioned right from the very beginning of the novel. The opening pages describe Vera Stark contemplating a group photograph which

---

133. Berglund, 1993.
134. Weisman, 1994.
135. Stausiulis and Yuval-Davis, 1995:27

she sent to her husband during the war. On this photograph, she marked the picture of her lover, thus pointing him out to her husband. This first marriage is dismissed as a war time marriage, its meaning and duration circumscribed by the need for security and respectability. The second marriage is contained within the ideology of romantic love, it is a "pure" relationship in the sense that it is seen as totally self-contained, not serving any ulterior purpose. Throughout the novel the basis for this relationship is seen as falling apart, a process parallelled with the construction of a new political order, a new nation. The important thing to note here is that Gordimer describes the disintegration of the heterosexual romantic relationship not in terms of a sense of alienation, the wrong choice, but in terms of the necessity for shedding an existence. When Vera Stark's marriage to her one-time lover comes to an end she moves out of the house she acquired together with her first husband and becomes a tenant on the property of a friend, a black man. In this way she sheds her identity as wife, mother, grandmother and—in the final scene of the novel where she by accident encounters the mistress of her friend—as a sexual being. The giving up of the house while totally devoting her life to housing problems is not only a political gesture. It contains an awareness of the fact that new political constellations do not come about independently of the redefinition of subjectivity. The novel shows how forging of new identities acts as a starting point for larger political changes and that the social relations implicated in this process are shaped through the powerful forces of desire.

While the novel is written with the white heterosexual couple at centre stage, it sets off this couple through descriptions of other couples. The process of political transformation brings the activists in exile back home and the land reforms finally make it possible for families to become reunited. In the description of this process, Gordimer on the one hand, sees the creation of new structures of land ownership as a possibility for the creation of a different national identity, on the other hand, she expresses some doubts about the function of the women when their households will once again be headed by a man. In an article on "Women and Land Reform", Cheryl Walker discusses the notion of "tradition" in rural societies and the gendered power structures inherent in this concept:

> Policy-makers need to acknowledge both the dynamism and the gendered nature of the popular discourse on 'tradition' in rural society. Too often it is official, male definitions of 'culture' that are accepted uncritically as those of 'the community', a cultural hegemony that the proponents of this view readily promote. Given their subordinate position, many rural women find it difficult to challenge the dominant view of 'tradition' head-on and their views are likely to display a degree of ambivalence, even contradiction, as a result. [136]

Gordimer's protagonist risks her life in this work for land reform. She deals exclusively with men, both black men representing different squatter communities and white farmers who show great hostility towards the imminent change. The only black rural woman whose point of view is considered here, through the consciousness of Vera Stark, is the wife of Oupa who has been head of the household for a long time with Oupa working as a clerk for the Legal Foundation. She is here primarily seen as a woman living without a man, self-sufficient and strong but not as a figure for an alternative female self. White rural women are not even described, only hinted at as farmers' wives whose vulnerability lies exactly in this relation.[137]

For both the central white couple, Vera and Ben Stark, and the black couple, Sibongile and Didymus Maqoma, work for the bringing about of the new nation implies a reversal of gender roles. Ben is the one who has given up his artistic ambitions in order to provide for the family. He is also the one whose attractions are mainly sexual and who has to give way for another man despite the fact that he himself already was "the other man" (p. 61). In this way Vera takes up the role of the subject who is shaped through infinite displacements of desire, whereas Ben is contained and shaped by the house to which she returns. Sibongile and Didymus have lived the extreme of the housebound wife and the absent husband while in exile. With their return this is reversed with Sibongile becoming the active politician and her husband staying mostly at home, whereas "[h]ome for her was the politics of home" (p. 78).

---

136. Walker, 1996:150.
137. Coetzee's *In The Heart of the Country* describes life on a farm from a female perspective which challenges the implicit unity of the farm suggested by Gordimer and advances a view of a different consciousness.

Vera's lesbian daughter is described as one of those who can now claim their rightful place. When Vera gives up her house and her marriage and her function as wife, mother and grandmother, she is also shown the possibility of "making home of a new kind entirely" (p. 314). The lesbian couple have adopted a girl and Vera is invited to play the role of the grandmother. Curiously enough, the antagonism between mother and daughter is here played out over the issue of Vera's inability to function as a proper wife. It is the mother's sexuality which destroys the foundation of heterosexual relationships. The lesbian daughter is depicted from the mother's point of view. Vera discusses the matter with Didymus who replies: "Of course, it'll be part of our constitution that there'll be no discrimination against any sex...but that doesn't cover about your own child becoming—d'you have any idea what made her?—" (p. 177). In the novel it is, however, the mother who gives up the right to a house and the daughter who carries on with her family.

The right to a house can be read metaphorically in terms of a politics of identity where Vera as the war time bride is qualified through her "rosy feminine submissions" (p. 10). Even when the husband is replaced by a lover she keeps her right to the house. It is only when she moves away from the heterosexual relationship altogether and sends her husband into exile that she also moves out of the house. This is depicted as a process of replacements where different groups now take over the house, the black couple, the African squatters in the rural areas and the lesbian couple. It is as with the drafting of the constitution: "Everyone wants their own future arranged around them, everyone has plans for a structure of laws to contain their ideal existence. It is the nearest humans will ever get to the myth of being God on creation day" (p. 315). There are no new subjectivities involved here as in the theories of for instance Monique Wittig[138], the lesbians simply take over the place of the heterosexual couples. The new self that is created is not a radically different self, it is not situated in a different place and it is dependent on a God-like creator.

The white woman as outsider can therefore be depicted as involved in a process of finding her personal freedom when she moves out

---

138. Wittig, 1992.

of the house. As in the literature of nineteenth century European women writers, Gordimer's house imprisons the female self within a construct of heterosexual romance. It is also significant that the novel ends with the old white woman living as a tenant on the property of a prominent black man. What this new self outside the main house implies is therefore never entered into. Head's novel deals with a different form of placelessness, an awareness of the vulnerability of those who have never lived in the house. It expresses a wish for belonging but it also questions the simplistic vision of Gordimer's tale of replacements. Both novels are involved in nationalist narratives which build on specific subjugated roles for women.

REFERENCES

Anderson, Benedict (1983), *Imagined Communities: Reflections on the Origin and Spread of Nationalism*. London: Verso.

Anthias, Floya and Nira Yuval-Davis (1992), *Racialized Boundaries: Race, Nation, Gender, Colour and Class and the Anti-Racist Struggle*. London: Routledge.

Berglund, Birgitta (1993), *Woman's Whole Existence: The House as Image in the Novels of Ann Radcliffe, Mary Wollstonecraft and Jane Austen*. Lund: Lund University Press.

Coetzee, J.M. (1977), *In The Heart of the Country*. London: Penguin.

Daymond, M.J. (1993), "Introduction." In Bessie Head, *The Cardinals with Meditations and Short Stories*. Cape Town: David Philip.

Driver, Dorothy (1993), "Gestures of Belonging and Expatriation." *Southern African Review of Books*. September/October, 16–18.

Driver, Dorothy (1996), "*Drum Magazine* (1951–9) and the Spatial Configurations of Gender." In *Text, Theory, Space: Land, Literature and History in South Africa and Australia*, eds. Kate Darian-Smith et al. London: Routledge, 231–242.

Gordimer, Nadine (1988), *The Essential Gesture: Writing, Politics and Places*. New York: Knopf.

Head, Bessie (3.9.1982), *Letter, Bessie Head Archives*, KMM, file 71.

Head, Bessie (1993), *The Cardinals with Meditations and Short Stories*. Cape Town: David Philip.

Jacobs, Jane M. (1996), *Edge of Empire: Postcolonialism and the City*. London: Routledge.

Kaplan, Gisela (1997), "Feminism and Nationalism: The European Case." In *Feminist Nationalism*, ed. Lois A. West. London: Routledge.

Nixon, Rob (1996), "Rural Transnationalism. Bessie Head's Southern Spaces." In *Text, Theory, Space: Land, Literature and History in South Africa and Australia*, eds. Kate Darian-Smith et al. London: Routledge, 243–254.

Parker, Andrew et al. (1992), "Introduction." In *Nationalisms and Sexualities*, eds. Andrew Parker et al. London: Routledge.

Stausiulis, Daiva and Nira Yuval-Davis (1995), *Unsettling Settler Societies: Articulations of Gender, Race, Ethnicity and Class*. London: Sage.

Unterhalter, Elaine (1995), "Constructing Race, Class, Gender and Ethnicity: State and Opposition Strategies in South Africa." In Daiva Stausiulis and Nira Yuval-Davis (1995), *Unsettling Settler Societies: Articulations of Gender, Race, Ethnicity and Class*. London: Sage, 207–240.

Walker, Cheryl (1996), "Reconstructing Tradition: Women and Land Reform." In *Reaction and Renewal in South Africa*, ed. Paul B. Rich. London: MacMillan, 144–169.

Weisman, Leslie Kanes (1994), *Discrimination by Design: A Feminist Critique of the Man-Made Environment*. Urbana and Chicago: University of Illinois Press.

West, Lois A. (1997), "Introduction" In *Feminist Nationalism*, ed. Lois A. West. London: Routledge.

Wittig, Monique (1992), *The Straight Mind and Other Essays*. London. Harvester.

Wood, Michael (1994), "Free of the Bad Old World", *The New York Review of Books*, December, pp. 12–13.

From Masters to Minorities:
The Swedish-speaking Finns and the Afrikaans-speaking Whites

Mai Palmberg

INTRODUCTION

National identity cannot build on the romantic idea of European 18th century nationalism of the nation state as a culturally homogenous unit. The adjustment process of once dominant elites built on ethnic mobilisation becomes a special and urgent issue in the democratic process of a multi-cultural society.

This paper is a comparison of two such groups, the Swedish-speaking Finns in Finland and the white Afrikaans-speakers of South Africa.[139] They were able to dominate only as long as access to the political system was restricted. When universal suffrage was introduced in Finland in 1906 (under Russian tutelage since 1809 until Finnish independence in 1917) the Swedish-speaking Finns became for ever and ever a minority. The Afrikaners achieved dominance in competition with the English-speaking whites through their election victory in 1948 and became a minority on the political arena only with the 1994 majority elections in South Africa.

In the South African transition there are lessons to be learnt from a comparison of these two groups. The white Afrikaners cannot be looked upon as merely the past masters and oppressors who have now been defeated, but also as a minority with legitimate minority concerns. This significantly calls for a new thinking among the white Afrikaners themselves, a "Reconstruction and Development" of Afrikaner identity.

---

139. If not qualified I use the term "Afrikaner" for this group, but will return to the issue of other Afrikaans-speakers.

The parallels

The Afrikaners[140] and the Swedish-speaking Finns[141] represent about the same share of the population in their respective countries, one twentieth.

Besides the minority share the two groups have enough substantial features in common to make a comparison interesting:

- Both trace their origin to migration many centuries ago at a time when their home country took over rule in the new land.
- Despite the fact that they originally came mainly from one country, they do not see themselves as belonging to this country, but have a strong attachment to the country where the majority of them were born and live.
- The majority of these two minorities were farmers and the folk culture as it developed in the countryside is in fact quite similar (having Northern European peasant cultural roots in common). The traditional "folk music" is a case in point. For the same reason the languages are not so distant cousins. Protestantism is the dominant religion in both groups.
- Although a minority they managed to dominate for many decades before majority rule was introduced.
- Geographically they are spread across the land, which makes separatist projects quite difficult.
- The construction of their ethnic identity is a fairly recent phenomenon, and is in both cases part of a political project.
- The states were constituted in connection with a civil war, the Anglo-Boer War 1899–1902 in South Africa, and the Civil War in Finland in 1918.

---

140. I will use the term "Afrikaners" or "white Afrikaans-speaking South Africans", not the roughly synonymous "Boers", which during the apartheid years became associated with racist policies and attitudes.
141. The term "Swedish-speaking Finns" is officially established, and recommended by the non-partisan Swedish People's Assembly in Finland. Like most ethnic labels its clarity can be questioned. "Finnish-speaking Swedes" would denote something different, Swedish citizens with recent Finnish origin, who have migrated to Sweden and stayed. The self-description of "Swedish-speaking Finns" is "Finland's Swedes", which again brings with it the misunderstanding that they are somehow part of Sweden. In Finland it is used to denote a separate cultural identity of a category of the Finnish people.

Similarities and common features do not mean identical development. One cannot mechanically transpose the two groups over the matrix of their societies. For example, while the Swedish-speaking Finns in early capitalism in 19th century Finland did constitute an overwhelming majority of the industrialists and the large land-owners, the Boers were in an inferior position in relation to English-speaking capital in South Africa. Nor do we find in Finland any equivalent to the black population, alienated from economic and social progress by an almost coinciding colour and class line. But there are enough similarities and parallels in the political process of minority dominance, the opening up of the political arena to majority rule, and the necessity to adjust to a minority status in the political system to make a comparison meaningful.

To understand in depth the specific case of either one we would need to examine the specific historical conjectures, and power relations. This paper's aim is different: to stimulate rethinking of received myths and concepts such as "Volk", language, culture and minority.

This paper is based on the assumption that ethnicity, and in particular ethnicity as a political project, is *not* an expression of age-old primitive bonds of the members of a group, but rather a historically constituted and constructed project, whose content, moreover, changes with changing conditions.[142] This needs stressing since the view is still influential in social science[143], that "primordial identities" although sometimes 'dormant' are more powerful than other social sentiments. It is almost unquestioned in popular thinking, for example, in self-descriptions, tourist pamphlets, school books and mass media. With the collapse of the socialist world system, and thereby the cold war conflicts, the ideas of primordial ethnic identities have become an easy blanket explanation for today's conflicts of all sorts and in all places.

This paper discusses three stages of the political process which the two ethnic groups have gone through: construction of their ethnic identity, consolidating minority dominance, and reacting to majority rule. The point is that since ethnic identities are constructed, they can also be reconstructed. Radical changes in the political arena make

---

142. See Anderson 1991, and a summary of the perspectives in Eriksen, 1993:92 ff.
143. The nestor in social science thinking on this is Clifford Geertz.

such reconstruction both possible and necessary. That golden opportunity is now at hand in South Africa.

CONSTRUCTING IDENTITIES

In the early 19th century there were neither Afrikaners nor Swedish-speaking Finns. There were ancestors to those who later expressed an Afrikaner or "Finland-Swedish" identity, but that is a different matter. The social identity of both Afrikaner and the Swedish-speaking Finns was constructed when nationalism swept over Europe, set in motion by the Napoleonic wars, inspired by Rousseau's ideas of "people" as a metaphysical category, and Hegel's idea of every nation having a soul, and the language being its "unison resonant sound", and nurtured by romanticism in the letters and the arts.

Nationalism, Ernest Gellner writes, "is the doctrine that the legitimate political unit is also the ethnic one. Or to put it more simply still: it is about the marriage of State and Culture."[144]

Micro-nationalism and the state

While Gellner gives us an elegant definition of the idea of the nation state, he here overlooks the cases of "micro-nationalism" of the kind dealt with here. In these cases the attitude towards the state is not given and is often complex and conflicting. By simplifying one can distinguish between three basic strategic aims:

- *Hegemonic claim* by the group ruling the state to be the sole representative and custodian of the interests of the whole nation.
- *Hyphenated nationalism* — where the nationalism of one group of two or several is combined with patriotism in relation to the state. The loyalties are on two levels, to the group and to the nation. This two-level nationalism can be the strategy both in an inclusive democracy and in exclusive elite based rule. It makes a distinction between nationality/ethnic identity and citizenship.
- *Separatism* — demands by one group for varying degrees of autonomy up to setting up a separate state.

---

144. Gellner, 1994:7.

Since micro-nationalism does not just arise like a sleeping animal we must look at how it comes into being. Four cornerstones are needed in the construction of ethnic identity as a political project:

a) Ideas about the need for a common front against threats to the interests and the very existence of the group;
b) Conceptions about a shared history, including ideas about a common past;
c) Bonds of language and religion;
d) Creation of structures to protect and advance the interests of the group as an ethnic minority.

Ideas about the need for a common front

Finland had been part of Sweden since the 13th and 14th centuries, and became an autonomous grand-duchy under the Russian Czar empire 1809 when Sweden lost its war against Russia. In South Africa the Cape colony was conquered in 1806 by the British. The only Russians in Finland were the administrative representatives of the Czar and Russian soldiers, and a few merchants who often settled for good. In South Africa, the imperial British element was represented both by administrators, investors and workers from overseas, and by people who came to settle or were born to settlers. Micro-nationalism in both cases was developed not in reaction to the foreign power, but against the competing domestic elite.

Finland—whose nationalism?

In the latter part of the 19th century the growth of Finnish capital and a self-conscious Finnish nationalism clashed with increasingly authoritarian tendencies of the Czar's rule, whose Pan-Slavic expansionism was seen as a severe threat to Finnish independence, Under these circumstances, the elites of both Finnish and Swedish language speakers were engaged in the patriotic project of asserting Finnish autonomy and identity (not yet political independence), and political links were created between the elites and the masses. Swedish was the language of the educated elite, a heritage from the time when Finland was part of Sweden (from the 12th century until 1809).

We find a large number of Swedish-language speakers among those who took part in this nationalist movement and are still placed among its founding fathers, among them *Johan Ludvig Runeberg*, who created the national anthem in 1849.[145]

In the mid-19th century *J.V. Snellman* argued (in Swedish) in Hegelian fashion that there could be only one language in a nation, and that it had to be that of the Finnish majority. The educated elite generally agreed, but some differed on the pace at which Swedish could be replaced. This "Fennomanic movement" resulted in the formation of a "Finnish party" in the Diet (the four-estate legislative assembly) which had been convened from 1863 onwards.

The construction of the identity of the Swedish-speaking Finns at the end of the century was a reaction to the idea that the Swedish language had no place in the new Finland. A "Swedish party" was formed in the 1870s in the Diet, and held a majority in the estates of the nobility and the bourgeois. A bitter language strife raged for several decades.

Axel Olof Freudenthal expressed sentiments for radical solutions and active struggle against threats from the Finnish majority, even *separatism* [146], but Axel Lille's more moderate line, emphasising equal rights for both language groups won with the slogan "fatherland and Swedishness".[147] The need to unite against Russian threats to the autonomy, intensified after 1899, favoured this *hyphenated nationalism*.[148]

South Africa — Afrikaners vs. British, both against blacks

In Finland the nationalist sagas were comprised of romantic tales about the modest, enduring and persevering soul of the Finnish

---

145. Elias Lönnrot who assembled the national epos *Kalevala*, an edited collection of Finnish oral literature, was one of the few constructors of Finnish nationalism who had Finnish as mother tongue.
146. von Bonsdorff, 1950:19.
147. Ibid.:21.
148. An expression of the efforts to gain acceptance for the equal status of the languages was the attempt to change the meaning of the word 'Finnish' to only denote language, and introduce the word *finländsk* ("Finlandish") to cover both Finnish- and Swedish-speaking citizens. After a century it has not yet been widely accepted or understood by the Finnish-speaking majority, but is still high on the agenda of Swedish-speaking Finns. See Colliander, 1945.

people, set in the wars where Finns were fighting as part of the Swedish empire, mostly against Russia. Although based on real events this literature is regarded more as tales than as true stories. In South Africa "Afrikanerdom" has created its own "sacred history", which clouds the vision of what really happened. This sacred saga, or Afrikaner "civil religion" is made up of "two cycles of suffering and death — the Great Trek and the Anglo-Boer War".[149]

In reality it was not Afrikaner ethnicity that moved those Dutch-speaking whites who left the Cape colony in 1835–38 in disgust over British policies to *trek* first to Natal, then after British attacks to the interior. Those who trekked considered themselves 'emigrants' and 'expatriates'.[150] Nor is there any reliable proof that the Voortrekkers really considered themselves a uniquely chosen people with a Covenant with God.[151] But this was later to become part of the Afrikaner nationalist myths.

The view of the Afrikaner ideology as being from the start a racist ideology is equally misleading. The Boers reacted not so much against abolition of slavery, although this did disturb them and hamper their access to cheap labour, as they reacted against the broken promises of fair compensation. British interests were just as eager to exploit the black labour, although on a free labour market, and just as unwilling to accept franchise for the black people of South Africa.

The Great Trek resulted in the mid-19th century in the *separatism* of the two Boer republics of Orange Free State and Transvaal[152], but not as a result of ethnic mobilisation. There was an absence of Afrikaner ethnic consciousness before 1870, due to acquiescence in British cultural and political dominance, not only in the Cape but even in the Boer republics.[153] In 1857 the mouthpiece of the Dutch-Afrikaner farmers in the Western Cape, the *Zuid-Afrikan*, wrote of a "gradual amalgamation of the Dutch and English nationality", and advised that "the less we speak of nationality the better".[154]

---

149. Moodie, 1975:12 ff.
150. Giliomee, 1995:22.
151. Giliomee, 1995:22., ref. to A.B. du Toit.
152. In 1853 renamed the South African Republic.
153. Giliomee, 1995:22–27.
154. Giliomee, 1995:27.

The ideological battle between Boer and British was sparked off with liberal British policies, the secularisation of the colony, and an Anglicisation drive of the educational institutions. The British annexation of Basutoland in 1868 and of the Diamond Fields in the Orange Free State in 1871 "made the burghers feel that they had been wronged as an ethnic group".[155] The ethnic project took the form of defence for the independent Boer republics. *Separatism* became ethnic.

The Anglo-Boer war 1899–1901 was a consequence of this. The Boers lost, but their leaders were invited to write the constitution with the British for a Union of South Africa. It was founded in 1910, the former Boer republics plus Natal and the Cape became provinces, although with little autonomy. The two groups agreed that the blacks should be treated only as labour, and that their land could be used for better purposes while they could be moved into reserves.

The bitterness of war and the sordid consequence of more than 20,000 dying in British prison camps coloured the Afrikaner ethnic project. Key expressions were 'real' Afrikaners, 'traitors' and 'martyrs'. Traitors were those Afrikaners who cooperated too closely with the British, as when generals Smuts and Botha mobilised the Afrikaner citizen force for the British campaign against Germany in South West Africa in the first world war.[156]

It seemed as if *hyphenated nationalism* was on the agenda when in the early days of Union general Hertzog in opposition to Botha's 'reconciliation with imperialism' talked of the "two-stream (Afrikaner and English) nationalism". A nationalism which only includes two minority elites is, of course, a strange albeit not totally uncommon type of "patriotism". Democracy is not a twin of nationalism. The hyphenated nationalism in South Africa at this time was a hegemonic project shared between two white elites.

For decades after the Anglo-Boer war the Afrikaner movement was fiercely arguing what line to take in regard to the British: continued reconciliation or bitter struggle. The latter line won only at the end of the 1930s. It was now that the idea of divine destiny became

---

155. Giliomee, 1995:28.
156. Jopie Fourie who rebelled and was executed became one of the martyrs.

central.[157] It was also only now, when the limited franchise of the Coloureds was abolished, that racism became part of the Afrikaner ideology.[158] With the growth of industry in the cities Africans were seen as a threat to Afrikaner economic interests, and the English were suspected of welcoming their cheap labour.

The Afrikaners could fight for *hegemony* because the whites of both ethnic groups had agreed to keep the majority out of the political arena. Hegemony was achieved with the National Party election victory in 1948, and broken only with the transition to majority rule in 1994.

Ideas about a common past

The legitimacy of the ethnic project is enhanced by references to a common past, and to claims that the group has been in the country for ages and thus possesses birthright.

The established truth today about the origin of the Swedish-speaking Finns is that the migration from Sweden resulting in the present habitation of Swedish-speaking Finns dates back to the 12th and 13th centuries. We are also told that the coastal land they occupied for some reason was empty, and that there are no documented violent conflicts between Swedes and Finns.[159]

The slightly ironical thing about it is that only part of the Swedish-speaking upper class, which dominated public life and therefore also the ethnic mobilisation of the Swedish-speaking Finns in the late 19th and early 20th centuries, was descended from the coastal population. Other ancestors were: (1) officials, merchants, military officers and nobles who had moved at some point from Sweden; (2) the Finnish-speaking peasantry, whose sons (and daughters) had to adopt

---

157. This was expressed in the Ossewa Gedenkboek (1940), called 'the New Testament of Afrikanerdom' where Henning Klopper writes: "We believe that the Afrikaner will do it again under the guidance of God. He will arise from the debris and ashes of his defeats, shake them off, overcome them and finally become a powerful and victorious people." See Moodie, 1975:14.
158. See Giliomee, 1995.
159. *Svenskt i Finland. En informationsbroschyr om finlandssvenskarna*, 1996:7. The question of origin and age of the Swedish-speaking population in Finland is today presented as a matter of fact, but was a crucial question for the pioneers of the Swedishness movement. According to the Finnish-speaking historian Puntila (p.171) it was a matter of proving that Swedish nationality had been there for ages.

Swedish when being educated; and, (3) merchants, artisans, and bourgeoisie from different Baltic countries. [160]

In South Africa the origin of the Afrikaner in South Africa was at least as mixed in composition. Those who later called themselves 'the Afrikaners' were descended from many different groups, particularly people from Dutch, German and French background in the 17th and 18th centuries.[161]

The importance given to a common ethnic descent is a reflection of the tenacity of the basic tenets of the nation state ideology. It is as if the ethnic group could be recognised only if it proved to be a historic nationality of its own. The fact that the Swedish-speaking Finns genetically are closer to the Finns than to Swedes in Sweden, and the fact that genealogists estimate a six–seven per cent contribution from non-Europeans to the Afrikaners[162] must be disturbing to the ethnic purists.

Bonds of language and religion

The linguistic development of the two minorities was not given. Giving primacy to language evolved with the need to create a strong sense of unity. This in turn made language the most important bond of cohesion and marker of identity.

Finland

Swedish had been the administrative and elite language in the areas which later became Finland ever since these lands became part of Sweden.[163] But the administrators from Sweden often learnt Finnish, and the clergymen preached in the language of the local community. It should be noted that while Swedish is an Indo-European language, incidentally a not too distant cousin of Afrikaans, Finnish is a Finno-

---

160. Allardt, 1977:8,
161. Giliomee, 1989:22.
162. Loc.cit.
163. There really was no Finland before 1809 or possibly before the mid-18th century, when an elite wanted to break away Finland from the rest of Sweden. It is part of nationalist ideology to write history as if the origin of the modern territorial unit was as far back as possible. Both historians in Sweden and Finland have committed this non-scientific mistake (see Klinge, 1990).

Ugrian language with a completely different grammar and vocabulary. The rural Swedish-speakers on the coast spoke many local dialects. But up to the late 19th century ethnic mobilisation "language was not an issue or a basis for social bonds", as sociologist Erik Allardt writes. He summarises that "there was no particular connection between the Swedish-speaking rural population, and the Swedish-speaking upper class. Nor were there any particular ties between the Swedish populations living in Ostrobothnia[164] in the West, the south western archipelago and the southern coast".[165] A sign of the intervention of the ethnic project even in the geography was the creation at about the time of Finnish independence 1917 of the concept "Åboland" for that part of the south-western archipelago, where the majority of the population on the islands spoke Swedish.[166] Previously the whole south-western archipelago, including islands with a Finnish-speaking population, had been called the Åbo archipelago after the closest city on the mainland.

As much of Finland was Lutheran religion played little part as a particularist marker in the formation of the identity of the Swedish-speaking Finns. On the other hand, the church was one of the institutions, where the importance of being able to use one's mother tongue, was stressed.

South Africa

The established language movement for Afrikaans was a rather late phenomenon, formed as a reaction to the successes of the Anglicisation drive, first in Transvaal and the Free State, later in the Cape Colony in the late 1800s.[167] 1906 was the year that the first novel was published in Afrikaans. In 1908 the *Suidafrikaanse Akademie vir Tal*,

---

164. Ostrobothnia, the largest, and mainly farming, area with a Swedish-speaking population in Finland, is jokingly but a little disparagingly called "Pampas" "plattlandet" (cf. "Plattenland") by the Swedish-speaking Finns in the cities on the southern coast.
165. Allardt, 1977:8.
166. Nikander, 1922:144.
167. Giliomee, 1989:22–30. Among the Coloured population in the Cape, especially among the Muslims, another Afrikaans movement developed, centred on the Moslem community near Genaadental, but this strand of the language movement has been neglected in Afrikaner officialdom.

Letter en Kuns was founded in Pretoria. The first secondary schools with Afrikaans as the language of instruction were opened in 1917. In 1925 the South African parliament recognised Afrikaans as one of the official languages of the country, co-equal with Dutch and English.[168] The entire bible was available in Afrikaans in 1933. [169]

In South Africa the Calvinist religion was an important attribute of the Afrikaners. But the church was not united, and the religious schisms compounded political divisions. The dominant church was the NHK, the Dutch Reformed (*Hervormde*) Church, established in 1853 as a state church. In opposition to it, a fundamentalist Reformed (*Gereformeerde*) Church was founded (called the Doppers), which in the 1870s developed a strongly anti-British consciousness. The smallest but growing Nederduits Gereformeerde Church favoured close ties with the English in the Cape Colony.[170]

Structures for unity

The National Party (NP) was founded in 1914, and signalled the entry of Afrikaner nationalism into the political arena. After 34 years of opposition to Afrikaner cooperation with the English-speaking whites, and increasingly fearful of African urbanisation and advancement, it reached the pinnacles of power.

South Africa—Afrikaner advancement

When in 1948 the National Party came to power it did so "as the political organisation of an unruly Afrikaner nationalist social alliance...held together by the ideological glue of a classless *volk*" united to struggle for breaking the ties with British imperialism by declaring South Africa a republic.[171]

The ethnic mission was eroded with the proclamation of the Republic in 1961 and the class differentiation resulting from the successful policy of Afrikaner favouritism in employment in the

---

168. Only in the 1961 constitution was Dutch no longer mentioned.
169. Kloss, 1978:17.
170. Giliomee, 1989:25.
171. An excellent analytic account of the National Party is Dan O'Meara's book *Forty lost years* 1996. The quote is from p. 164.

growing civil service and Afrikaner-dominated state capitalism.[172] Some *verkrampfte* founded the *Herstigte Nasionale Parti* (HNP) in 1969 having been expelled for opposing NP Premier Vorster's idea to enlarge the party to include English-speakers.[173]

NP's position as champion of all Afrikaners was put to an even more severe test in the early 1980s, with increasing subjective and objective difficulties in containing the revolt against apartheid especially in the black suburban areas and crushing the support for the African National Congress. The Conservative Party (CP) was founded in 1982 by a section of the NP expelled for opposing Prime Minister Botha's willingness to give in to pressure from big business for reforms (although far short of franchise to Africans).[174] In the 1980s the NP also started to change its ethnic composition. A larger share than before of the voters came from the English-speaking South Africans.[175] From this time NP started wavering between being a purely ideological party and one clinging to its claim to be the spokesman for all Afrikaners. From 1982 the NP no longer commanded the support of the majority of Afrikaners voting.[176]

Besides the National Party, which after 1948 was married to the state, the most important structure of influence for the Afrikaner movement was the Broederbond. Founded in 1918, and turned into a secret society (for men only) in 1921, it became a very influential secret organiser of Afrikaner civil society, seeking key members in education, business, the civil service, the churches and government.[177]

The Broederbond founded the *Federasie van Afrikaanse Kultuurvereniging* (FAK), a federation for cultural organisations in 1929 as its open wing. Under FAK tutelage a whole array of parallel organisations were created, by 1980 four hundred of them. There were among others the *Noodhulpliga*, an Afrikaner alternative to the Red Cross (considered too English); the *Voortrekkers* , an Afrikaner alternative to the scout movement founded by the British general in the Anglo-Boer

---

172. See O'Meara, 1983 and O'Meara, 1996:136–148.
173. O'Meara, 1996:163.
174. Ibid.:290–303.
175. In 1977 one out of seven, in 1982 a third of the voters declaring themselves for NP were English-speakers. O'Meara, 1996:308.
176. Ibid.:308.
177. O'Meara, 1996:43–48, Harrison, 1993:84–102.

War, Lord Baden-Powell; the *Jukskeibond* for the playing of a supposedly Voortrekker game with a wooden pin from the ox-yoke; a women's organisation, a student organisations etc.[178] Some organisations were set up explicitly to help uplift the poor white Afrikaners, a group the Afrikaner establishment became increasingly uninterested in when the exclusive ethnic basis weakened.[179]

The Broederbond's relationship to the state-ruling National Party was sometimes uneasy. General Barry Hertzog gave publicity to a Broederbond circular from 1925 which stated that "the Afrikaner Broederbond shall rule South Africa". This has been used to support the contention that they actually did. Hertzog's criticism of the Broederbond is an interesting expression of a hyphenated nationalism of the exclusive type, and an interesting definition of 'Afrikaner', here expressed in a speech at Smithfield in November 1935:

> ...in this way they stand in direct racial conflict with our English fellow Afrikaners, striving by means of Afrikaans-speaking domination to place the foot on the neck of the English-speaking South African.
>
> It is being forgotten... that there are also English-speaking Afrikaners in South Africa who are also entitled to a place in the South African sun. When will this foolish, fatal idea cease that some people are chosen of the gods to rule over others?[180]

The forging of unity on ethnic loyalties demands symbols and festivities. The Broederbond in 1938 coordinated the most effective celebration of Afrikanerdom ever with the Commemorative Trek to celebrate the centenary of the battle at Blood River, and the laying of the foundation stone of the Voortrekker Monument outside Pretoria (opened in 1949). It was now that the Great Trek rose to prominence as the key event in the historiography of Afrikanerdom. It also gave the movement a symbol, the ox-wagon.[181]

The other sacred monument of Afrikanerdom was the *Vrouemonument* (Women's Monument) in Bloemfontein, inaugurated in 1913 in dedication to the memory of women and children during the Anglo Boer War. The Afrikaner woman was lauded as the sacrificing

---

178. Harrison, 1993:95–96.
179. This is one of the main propositions in O'Meara, 1996.
180. Quoted in Harrison, 1993:100–101.
181. See Harrison, 1993:103–113; Moodie, 1975:18–21.

volksmoeder. Elsie Cloete reminds us that they had also had to sacrifice the hope of franchise for the *Volksraad*, promised to them in the 1840s.[182] The architects of Afrikanerdom were men.[183] In the ethnic mobilisation of the Swedish-speaking Finns, similarly, the image of the leader, called a "chieftain" (*hövding*) is always a, preferably tall , man. The universal franchise achieved in 1906 had almost no support in the Swedish party.

Finland — rallying the Swedish together

There had been both elitist and populist concerns behind the mobilisation of "Swedishness". These tendencies became known as *kultursvenskhet* (culture Swedishness), and *bygdesvenskhet* (rural community Swedishness).[184]

The elitists argued that the loss of Swedish would mean the loss of cherished Western values, even of 'civilisation'.[185] The populists worried that the interests of the Swedish-speaking population in the countryside would be abandoned. In the 1880s societies were founded to establish schools and libraries, and to promote Swedish-language culture generally.[186] A student-based movement emerged to go out and educate the Swedish peasants and foster unity.

The Swedish-speaking countryside became dramatically important to the elite with the extension of the franchise. When universal suffrage was introduced in 1906 the Swedish-speaking minority also became for ever and ever a political minority. "Traditions, intelligence, and capital", which had been the catchwords for the defence of Swedishness for the elitists could no longer guarantee a secure and influential position. Part of these assets was now used to bolster the ethnic mobilisation so essential to secure as large a constituency as possible for the Swedish-speaking People's Party (SFP) which was

---

182. Cloete, 1992:48.
183. See Butler, 1989 for a contrary perspective. Based on research in Craddock he claims that "women were crucially important in the creation of Afrikaner ethnic consciousness" (p. 62).
184. See von Bonsdorff, 1950:18–19.
185. This was the line taken by R.A. Wrede among others.
186. *Svenska folkskolans vänner* and *Svenska Litteratursällskapet*. The former supported basic schooling and literacy in a broad sense. The latter association for Swedish-language literature in Finland was founded in 1885 as a reaction to the Finnish Literature Society becoming a tool for the Fennomans.

formed in 1906. The Swedish peasantry had been "a hitherto untapped reserve"[187] to quote an unusually candid schoolbook.

SFP did succeed. Up to the 1970s it commanded about 75 per cent of the votes of the Swedish-speaking Finns, after the 1970s 60–70 per cent.[188]

The cultural movement intensified with collection of folk songs, song festivals, the performance of rituals such as lavish peasant weddings[189] and the revival or invention of old folk costumes. A special red-yellow banner was chosen as the symbol for Swedish-speaking Finns.[190]

Another marker of "Swedishness" in Finland was introduced with the "Swedish Day", instituted in 1908, and still celebrated in almost all corners of Finland where there are Swedish-speaking Finns. The day chosen was 6th November, the day that in 1632 the Swedish king Gustavus Adolphus II died at the battle of Lützen in the great European religious wars. The choice of this day indicates that the celebration of the Swedish Day was not to be a demonstration against the Finns, but rather a manifestation against the Russian masters (who with their Greek Orthodox religion were considered all but heathen, while Gustavus Adolphus II was the closest you could come to a Protestant hero and saint). But it can, on the other hand be interpreted as a statement that the Swedish-speaking Finns are the bearers of western civilisation, although this ideological undertext is lost today.

Many new institutions supported the ethnic project. The SFP founded the Swedish Cultural Foundation (Svenska Kulturfonden) in Finland in 1907. The Foundation for the Arts (Konstsamfundet) among other things finances newspapers. The Swedish-language university of Åbo Akademi (Åbo Akademi University) was founded in 1920.

The influence of the Swedish-speaking People's Party on these and a large number of other Swedish-language institutions has sometimes been indirect but in all cases quite powerful. On the mass media scene

---

187. From an established school book for Swedish-speaking Finns, *Boken om Svenskfinland*, 1982:38.
188. Markku Joas in Ståhlberg, ed., 1995:161.
189. See Lönnqvist, 1981:146–147.
190. It can be seen especially in the summer cottages in the archipelago in the summer. For ceremonial purposes, however, the Finnish blue and white flag is always used.

the major papers are all dominated by the SFP, and increasingly directly owned by the Foundation for the Arts. Only the radio and television, up to now state monopoly public service institutions, have accorded any significant space in the Swedish transmissions for alternative political perspectives. The small Swedish-language left does have its own weekly newspapers.[191] In "Swedish-Finland" (*Svenskfinland*)) there has been no need for a secret Broederbond.

BECOMING A MINORITY

In Finnish and especially Swedish-speaking Finnish historiography the Swedish-speaking Finns graciously left their position of dominance, and willingly accepted their position as a minority. The National Party, as we all know, refused during a long and bitter struggle to bow down to the pressure of the various popular forces demanding an end to minority rule. It seems like a stark contrast. Yet the peacefulness of the process in Finland is much dependent on how one interprets the cruel civil war in Finland which followed the December 1917 independence.

Stepping down graciously?

The civil war in the spring of 1918 is usually treated as a tragic episode in Finnish history, a parenthesis, although deeply influential both on personal and political levels. Language policies and the elite position of Swedish-speaking Finns is never seen as having anything at all to do with this civil war between, as they were called, "the Reds" and "the Whites".

The issues were related to class not ethnicity. It was a war between 'the reds', mainly workers supported (by words and some weapons) by the Russians, since the revolution in October 1917 under the revolutionary leadership of the Bolsheviks, and 'the whites', supported by the bourgeois parties, the majority of the farmers and the companies. The Whites won with German assistance. As in South Africa, prison

---

191. Both Social Democrats (*Arbetet*) and the Leftist Party (*Ny tid*).

camps took a heavier toll after the war than the fighting itself, and created bitter scars in people's memories.

The question is why the Swedish language and 'white' class position almost totally coincided. Was it simply a result of a successful ethnic mobilisation for the ideals of the Swedish People's Party, which was not only Swedish but bourgeois? Was the war seen as an attempt to regain influence for the Swedish "traditions, intelligence, and capital" using the "hitherto untapped reserve" of the Swedish-language peasants?[192] These are still heretical questions in Finland. [193]

What did they hope for from halting the advance of the uneducated masses? The universal suffrage was retained, but the communist party was outlawed in the 1920s and only allowed again after the second world war.

So perhaps the relinquishing of minority privileges for the Swedish-speaking minority in Finland was not all that peaceful. But for the future what was important was that they did relinquish them. There will be much discussion and research on the clinging to power of the National Party through manoeuvres and oppression, before giving up and sitting down with the ANC to work out a transition to majority rule. Yet for the future what is important is that they did it.

Lapsing into dreams of separatism

After the civil war in Finland the Swedish People's Party took a decision to work for autonomy. Certain issues during the civil war had contributed to this decision: the disappointment in non-intervention on the white side from Sweden strengthened the conviction that the Swedish-speaking Finns had to go it alone; the eagerness with which Sweden supported the secession of the Åland islands from Finland

---

192. All through the period of autonomy under Russia (1809–1917) Finland did not possess any army and weaponry so the arms had to come from outside. Most of the arms used by the whites derived from arms caches accumulated by the small group of so-called activists in the coast area of Ostrobothnia, the major area for Swedish-speaking farmers. The arms had been smuggled into Finland to be used in an envisaged uprising against the Russian Czar.
193. The victors' history was that this was a war for independence, and the Russians were the real enemy. Even thoroughly researched works on the civil war still arouse heated debate. *Tie Tampereelle* by historian Heikki Ylikangas in 1993 is the latest example.

was seen as a deplorable splitting of the Swedish-speaking forces in Finland; and there had been some skirmishes and accusations of discrimination in the field, especially in Ostrobothnia.[194]
The autonomy movement of the Swedish-speaking Finns, was fraught with difficulties from the start. The Swedish-speaking population was spread out along a long coastal area, and a growing number lived in the cities where both languages were spoken. The project was finally abandoned in the mid-1920s.

In South Africa, the Volkstaat idea appeared in the 1960s[195], and was sidelined in the 1970s[196] and 1980s to be placed seriously on the agenda with the negotiations on the transition to majority rule.

In 1994 the Freedom Front (FF) was created among right-wing Afrikaners under the leadership of general Viljoen to take part in the election with the explicit aim of furthering the *Volkstaat* idea of Afrikaner autonomy. ANC leader Nelson Mandela invited suggestions for a Volkstaat. To realise separatist dreams was even more difficult than in Finland, as much of the labour force in any conceivable Afrikaner enclave of any size would be black. Not long after the 1994 elections, where FF received 7 per cent of the vote it was reported to have abandoned the Volkstaat idea as a separate geographical entity.

The government set up a Volkstaat Council to explore the idea further, but its report in 1996 did not clearly advocate territorial autonomy. In the new constitution provisions are made for a statutory body on cultural and language matters, equivalent to the Human Rights Commission, but as yet (January 1998) it has not been established. We can safely say that Afrikaner *separatism* is dead or at least dying.

Language as the basis of minority rights

The ethnic myths once created might have long since been discarded or forgotten. But the sense of common identity on which the ethnic

---
194. von Bonsdorff, 1950:72–73.
195. Jung, 1996:14.
196. The journalist Paul Moorcraft suggested in 1980 in his book *A Short Thousand Years* that a victory by Zimbabwe could spill over to South Africa, and that Pretoria might opt for partition along the so-called Eiselen line, making the Cape a 'white homeland'.

project has been able to mobilise is likely to have been enhanced in the process, and a social organisation of interaction within the group and outside the group is there as a reality that one cannot just think away. [197] This paper has stressed the acts of invention, but it does not mean that the idea of the existence of an ethnic group is a bluff (although the fluidity of the boundaries can be more the rule than the exception). We do have people in South Africa who feel like Afrikaners and people in Finland who feel like Swedish-speaking Finns even though they might be very critical of the ideology of their group's ethnic mobilisation. What effects if any should the group identity have at the political level of the state?

As yet, there is no UN convention on minority rights. The 1966 International Convention on Civil and Political Rights of the UN Economic and Social Council speaks not of minorities as groups, but of minority group members. These should not, the convention says, be denied their right to enjoy their own cultural life together with other members of their group, nor should they be denied rights to practise their own religion or language.

The respect for the members of minority groups is an important part of democratic rights. Giving ethnically defined groups political rights, however, invites non-democratic development. It means giving whatever entrenched establishment that dominates the group the power to decide, and takes away the broad citizens' rights of the members. Whatever beautifying term one gives to this, like "consociational democracy", it rarely means democracy but rather authoritarian rule. In cases of *territorial autonomy* you also usually find that the territory includes people who have no wish to identify with the group given the ethnically defined special rights.

To safeguard minority rights one can start by looking at what rights need protection. Religious freedom is best guaranteed by simply prohibiting discrimination on religious grounds. What needs legal protection, and even official investment, is the language. In South Africa, what is required on the language scene is a massive

---

197. According to Allardt this is the point stressed by social anthropologists like Fredrik Barth as necessary among the criteria defining an ethnic group, while sociolinguists are satisfied with the criteria of self-categorisation, descent, and specific cultural traits, like language. See Allardt & Starck, 1981:43 ff.

development of the African (so-called black) languages, with a reduction in the relative linguistic privileges that NP rule and Broederbond influence have entrenched. Even so, and perhaps the more so, the Afrikaans language also needs protection.

If territorial autonomy for ethnic groups is mostly ill-conceived[198], *functional autonomy* on the other hand can be a useful means for minority policies. By functional autonomy I mean institutions catering to a minority in a certain sector but not territorially defined or restricted. Examples of such functional autonomy in Finland are a parallel education system in Swedish, a special diocese in the Lutheran church for the Swedish-language congregations with its bishop in the town of Borgå, a special brigade in Dragsvik for Swedish-language recruits to the army (with Swedish-language training but a Finnish commando system to enable war-time integration into the main body of the army), allotted national public radio and television time in Swedish, a Swedish-language university (Åbo Academy University) etc. There are also parallel NGOs, Swedish-language scout and girl guide organisations, a Swedish section of the Red Cross with its own branches etc. There are more than a dozen daily papers in the Swedish language in Finland, more than 200 Swedish-language periodicals, a handful of publishing houses etc.

There are, as we have seen, many Afrikaner equivalents to these parallel institutions. In new South Africa, Afrikaans must relinquish the privileged position achieved during NP rule. With eleven official languages, matters are of course complicated. The idea to standardise the varieties of Nguni and Sotho is an interesting proposal which could strengthen the position of African languages. Many argue that South Africa should go all out for English. (see Alidou & Mazrui in this volume). For democracy the appropriate question is how to replace "two-stream" development with many streams, if not in all walks of life, then at least in education and the mass media.[199] The principle of mother-tongue education is tainted by apartheid oppression, which is unfortunate because growing evidence from socio-

---

198. In Finland there is a case of rather clear-cut territorial autonomy, the Åland islands. Probably only islands or clearly separate geographical entities are suitable for territorial autonomy.
199. Neville Alexander, 1990

linguistic study shows that this is best for children's intellectual development.

Language strife and language peace in Finland

The Swedish-speaking Finns are not legally a minority, since both Finnish and Swedish according to the constitution from 1919 are national languages.[200] A language law (1922) and a law on language requirements for civil servants implemented the principles.[201]

The constitutional foundation did not prevent a second language strife from breaking out in the 1920s and 1930s centring on demands to make the University of Helsinki entirely Finnish. This gave a new impetus to Swedish mobilisation, and a petition with 154,000 signatures.[202] A law was enacted guaranteeing a specified minority role for Swedish-education and professors. The wars against the Soviet Union 1939–40 and 1941–44 put a heavy lid on the language strife and it has not reached such temperature levels since.

A Swedish People's Assembly was first convened on the initiative of the Swedish People's Party as a grass-roots lobby in 1919. It was revived in a less partisan form after the war, and now acts as a consultative assembly for the Swedish-speaking Finns of all party persuasions (under the name *Svenska Finlands folkting*).

In post-war Finland the decrease in the number and proportion of the Swedish-speaking Finns was long the greatest perceived threat to Swedishness. Many migrated to Sweden, the birth-rate was low, and the language change to Finnish increased with a growing number of bilingual families in the cities.

A third language strife is under way in Finland, with voices demanding that compulsory Swedish be totally eradicated from the school curriculum, often coupled with a call for a reorientation away from the Nordic community, and towards continental Europe and the English and German languages. Yet the respect for minority rights was strong enough to make Martti Ahtisaari, the current president of

---

200. Allardt & Starck, 1981:87.
201. The key stipulation is that every local community with at least 3,000 persons or 8 per cent of the minority language represented is bilingual.
202. Ibid.:209.

Finland, flatly refuse support for today's Fennomans[203] against the candidate of the Swedish People's Party in the presidential campaign of 1994. In the beginning of 1997 Prime Minister Paavo Lipponen in an unprecedented circular letter to all authorities reminded them that they have to fulfil the language legislation and offer service in Swedish when demanded. The attitude on a grass-root level is perhaps best exemplified by the Finnish school pupils who said that the Swedish-speaking Finns were "just like us", but for some strange reason spoke Swedish. [204]

The Finnish experience shows that it is possible for a once dominant minority to be accepted and welcomed as a minority, even though the minority makes a visible and sometimes even ostentatious display of its distinct identity, including a political party successfully mobilising on ethnicity.[205]

The Afrikaner identity crisis

The transition to new South Africa has predictably meant a crisis in Afrikaner identity. In an ill-fated televised speech the National Party leader F.W. de Klerk declared after the 1994 election that NP is "no longer a white party", and as if by providence all the lights instantly went out.[206] During the election campaign the NP leadership had embraced a non-racial definition of the term 'Afrikaner' and branded as racists the Conservative Party (CP) which clung to the racial definition that NP had used for 40 years. The Coloureds were now, when they were in the same political race, "an untapped reserve". This redefinition of 'Afrikaner' is too calculated to appear genuine, and also contradicts the ambition of the NP to win electoral majority on a general conservative and family values platform. The Coloureds in Western Cape seem to have been won over more with the old "black

---

203. Suomalaisuden Liitto (The League for Finnishness). See Herberts, 1994.
204. Herberts, 1996.
205. A seminar in Tampere in 1991 asked whether Finland was a model for minority policies. The general reply of the invited specialists was: yes, when it comes to the Swedish-speaking Finns, but not when it comes to the smaller minorities of the Sami people of the North ("the Lapps"), nor the Romany people (the gypsies), who have suffered much discrimination.
206. Dan O'Meara (1996:417) ends his analysis of NP's 40 years in power with this symbolic anecdote.

danger" gut message than with a generous redefinition of "Afrikaner".

The CP and other far-right forces cling to an even more narrow laager-type definition. They are the real 'boere' and claim they alone descend from the Voortrekkers, whereas the liberal 'Afrikaners' descend from the Cape burghers.[207]

The Freedom Front sticks to the old NP definition of Afrikaner, and is perhaps the most likely candidate for an ethnically based Afrikaner party, if they can decide to accept fully parliamentary politics. Whether they can accept the logical extension of their base to all Afrikaans-speaking is a different matter.

Choosing your image projection

The history of a self-defined group is written to serve particular interests. The history of the Swedish-speaking Finns, therefore, is a history full of tolerance, patriotism, internationalism, peaceful life and work, industry and contributions to the cultural life of Finland. The heroes are those that fit this image: Runeberg and Mannerheim, to mention two of those whose statues can be gazed at in central Helsinki. Runeberg was mentioned above. Mannerheim was a former general in the Czarist army, but in the civil war in 1918 the commander of the white troops, and again the commander of the whole Finnish army in the so-called Winter War against the Soviet Union in 1939–40, and in the World War against the Soviet Union (in alliance with Germany). From his involvement in the 1918 civil war the Reds gave Mannerheim the name "the Butcher". But it is his patriotism that the Swedish-speaking Finns refer to when they talk about this hero.

In South Africa the Afrikaners have had other needs: cohesion, struggle against the British cultural and economic dominance, and a need to legitimise the racist order. Therefore the heroes have been the victors or martyrs in battle: The victors Andries Pretorius, Paul Kruger, and the martyr Piet Retief. The cultural self-image has rather been one of exclusion and seclusion than one emphasising the contributions to a larger whole.

---

207. Jung, 1996.

In South Africa a new past is needed. And a new past is available. All constructions of the past are based on omissions, distortions, aggrandisement of the good and blessed neglect of the evil. A new Afrikaner history could emphasise the African roots, the contributions to South Africa's common culture by Afrikaner literature, the capacity for conciliation when needed: in the construction of the Union of South Africa, in Smuts' contributions to the United Nations, in the negotiated settlement with ANC and the willingness, in the end, to be party to the dismantlement of apartheid. New heroes can be sought among those Afrikaner dissidents, not a negligible number, who contributed to making the new South Africa (at the time, of course, treated as the most despicable traitors by the apartheid establishment).

A new past needs a new monument. Formidable among the monuments of the constructed white Afrikaner past is the Voortrekker Monument on the hills outside Pretoria, still cherished by the Afrikaners cum Boers. In contrast, there is no trek of any ideological import to the monument celebrating the historical feats of the English-speakers of South Africa, the Rhodes Memorial on the Table Mountain slopes of Cape Town, which is visited simply for its beautiful view.

Much better than simply forgetting and abandoning the Voortrekker Monument would be to give it a new role. A wonderful and powerful proposal has been put forward, inspired by the Lincoln Memorial in Washington, which has become the site for a memorial of the Vietnam war, with the name of all who died inscribed on a surrounding wall. At the Voortrekker Monument one could honour all those who died for the new non-racist South Africa, regardless of which side they were on. This could be a positive and dramatic step towards constructing a new past for a new future, and redefining Afrikaner identity in the new South Africa.

REFERENCES

Note: Where the meaning of the titles of books in Swedish and Finnish is difficult to guess, the author's translations into English are given in brackets.

Adam, Heribert & Kogila Moodley (1993) *The Negotiated Revolution: Society and Politics in Post-Apartheid South Africa*. Berkeley and Los Angeles: University of California Press.

Ahlskog-Sandberg et al. (1983) *Boken om Svenskfinland* ["The book about Swedo-Finland"]. Vasa: Svenska Läromedel.

Alapuro, Risto (1994) "Nineteenth-Century Nationalism in Finland. Comparative Remarks", pp. 65–74 in Ø. Sørensen, ed. *Nordic Paths to National Identity in the Nineteenth Century*, Nasjonal Identitet Vol. 1/1994. Oslo: The Research Council of Norway.

Alexander, Neville (1990) "The Language Question in South Africa", pp. 126–146 in *Critical Choices for South Africa: An agenda for the 1990s*. Cape Town: Oxford University Press.

Allardt, Erik & Christian Starck (1981) *Språkgränser och samhällsstruktur. Finlandssvenskarna i ett jämförande perspektiv* ["Language boundaries and social structure. The Swedish-speaking Finns in a comparative perspective"]. Lund: Studentlitteratur.

Allardt, Erik (1977) *Finland's Swedish-speaking minority*. Helsinki: The Research Group for Comparative Sociology at the University of Helsinki.

Allardt, Erik (1985) *Samhället Finland. Omvandlingar och Traditioner* ["Finnish society. Transformations and traditions"]. Helsingfors: Holger Schildts förlag.

Anderson, Benedict (1991) *Imagined Communities. Reflections on the Origins and Spread of Nationalism* (first edition 1983). London: Verso.

Bagerstam, Erik (1986) *Finlands svenskar—ett livskraftigt folk i Norden* ["Finland's Swedes—a vigorous Nordic people"]. Stockholm: Sveriges Radios förlag.

Butler, Jeffrey (1989) "Afrikaner women and the creation of ethnicity" pp. 55–81 in Leroy Vail, ed. *The creation of tribalism in southern Africa*. London: James Currey.

Cloete, Elsie (1992) "Afrikaner Identity: Culture, Tradition and Gender", *Agenda. A journal about women and gender* (No. 13):42–55.

Colliander, Börje (1945) *"Finländsk". Ordet och begreppet* ["Finlandish". The word and the concept]. Helsingfors: Söderströms & Co.

Davenport, T.R.H. (1963) "Nationalism and conciliation: The Bourassa and Hertzog posture", *Canadian Historical Review*, Vol. 44 (Summer) pp. 193–212.

de Klerk, W.A. (1975) *The Puritans in Africa*. London: Penguin.

de Villiers, Marq (1987) *White Tribe Dreaming*. New York: Viking (Penguin Books).

Eriksen, Thomas Hylland (1993) *Ethnicity and Nationalism. Anthropological Perspectives*. London & Boulder: Pluto Press.

Geldenhuys, Deon 1995 "International perspectives on Afrikaner self-determination", *Strategic Review for Southern Africa* XVII (No. 1), pp. 26–45.

Gellner, Ernest (1994) "Nations and Nationalism: General Perspectives" pp. 7–16 in Ø. Sørensen, ed. *Nordic Paths to National Identity in the Nineteenth Century*, Nasjonal Identitet Vol. 1/1994. Oslo: The Research Council of Norway.

Giliomee, Hermann (1989) "The Beginnings of Afrikaner Ethnic Consciousness 1850–1915" pp. 21–54 in Leroy Vail, ed. *The Creation of Tribalism in Southern Africa*. London: James Currey.

Giliomee, Hermann (1995) "The non-racial franchise and Afrikaner and coloured identities, 1910–1994", *African Affairs* 94 (375), pp. 199–225.

Harrison, David (1993, © 1987) *The white tribe of Africa*. Halfway House, South Africa: Southern Book Publishers.

Herberts, Kjell (1994) *Mara eller Lillan? Presidentvalets språkpolitiska dimension i finsk dagspress*. ["Mara or Lillan? The language policy dimension in the presidential election in the Finnish daily press"]. Vasa: Institutet för finlandssvensk samhällsforskning.

Herberts, Kjell (1996) *Sex procent — en finlandssvensk halvtimme. Hurri eller kaveri? Elevreaktioner på tre skolpjäser om finlandssvenskarna*. ["Six per cent— a Swedofinnish half hour. Pupils' reactions to three school plays about the Swedish-speaking Finns"]. Vasa: Institutet för finlandssvensk samhällsforskning.

Jung, Courtney (1996) "After apartheid. Shaping a new Afrikaner 'Volk'", *Indicator South Africa*, Vol. 13, No. 4, pp. 12–16.

Klinge, Matti (1990) *A Brief History of Finland*. Helsinki: Otava.

Kloss, Heinz (1978) *Problems of language policy in South Africa*. Wien: Wilhelm Braumüller, Universitäts-Verlagsbuchhandlung GES.

Lille, Axel (1921) *Den svenska nationalitetens i Finland samlingsrörelse*. Helsingfors: Holger Schildts förlagsaktiebolag.

Lindman, Sven (1954) "C.G. Estlander och svenskhetsrörelsen i Finland", *Finsk Tidskrift* CLVI (5–6).

Lönnqvist, Bo (1981) *Suomenruotsalaiset*. ["The Swedish-speaking Finns"]. Jyväskylä: Gummerus.

Macmillan, W. M. (1963) *Bantu, Boer, and Briton. The making of the South African native problem*. Oxford: Clarendon Press.

Moodie, T.D. (1975) *The rise of Afrikanerdom. Power, apartheid and the Afrikaner civil religion*. Berkeley: University of California Press.

Moorcratt, Paul L. (1980) *A short thousand years*. Salisbury: Galaxie Press.

Munger, Edwin S. (1974) *The Afrikaner as seen abroad*. Pasadena, Cal.: California Institute of Technology.

Nikander, Gabriel, ed. (1922) *Det svenska Finland*. ["Swedo-Finland"] Volume 2. Helsingfors: Holger Schildts förlag.

Nikander, Gabriel, ed. (1923) *Det svenska Finland*. Volume 3. Helsingfors: Holger Schildts förlag.

Nyberg, Paul (1949) *Zachris Topelius. En biografisk skildring*. Helsingfors: Söderström & Co.

O'Meara, Dan (1983) *Volkskapitalisme. Class, capital and ideology in the development of Afrikaner nationalism 1934–1948*. Cambridge: Cambridge University Press.
O'Meara, Dan (1996) *Forty lost years. The apartheid state and the politics of the National Party 1948–1994*. Randburg: Ravan Press.
Omar-Cooper, J.D. (1994) *History of Southern Africa*. London: James Currey, Heinemann.
Puntila, L.A. (1944) *Suomen ruotsalaisuuden liikkeen synty. Aatehistoriallinen tutkimus* ["The origin of the Swedish movement in Finland. An analysis of the history of ideas"]. Helsinki: Otava.
Salminen, Johannes, (1963) *Levande och död tradition* ["Living and dead tradition"]. Helsingfors: Söderströms.
Salminen, Johannes (1984) *Gränsland* ["Border country"]. Borgå: Alba.
Schrire, Robert (1991) *Adapt or Die: The End of White Politics in South Africa*. Ford Foundation and the Foreign Policy Association.
Smith, Anthony D. (1981) *The Ethnic Revival*. Cambridge: Cambridge University Press.
Smith, Anthony D. (1983) *State and nation in the Third World*. Brighton: Wheatsheaf Books.
Snellman, J.V. (1904) *J.V. Snellman*. Helsingfors: Otava.
Ståhlberg, Krister, ed. (1995) *Finlandssvensk identitet och kultur* ["Identity and culture of the Swedish-speaking Finns"]. Åbo: Åbo Akademi.
Svenskt i Finland. En informationsbroschyr om finlandssvenskarna (1996). ["Swedish in Finland. An information booklet on the Swedish-speaking Finns"]. Helsingfors: Svenska Finlands folkting.
Templin, J. Alton (1984) *Ideology on a frontier. The theological foundation of Afrikaner nationalism 1652–1910*. Westport, Connecticut: Greenwood Press.
Troup, Freda (1972) *South Africa: An Historical Introduction*. Harmondsworth, Middlesex: Penguin.
van den Berghe, Pierre L. (1966) "Albinocracy in South Africa - a case study in tyranny", *Journal of African and Asian Studies* 1, pp. 43–49.
Vad säger lagarna om språkliga rättigheter? (1996) ["What does the law say about language rights?"]. Helsingfors: Svenska Finlands folkting.
von Bonsdorff, Göran (1950) *Självstyrelsetanken i finlandssvensk politik åren 1917–1923* ["Self-rule ideas in Swedo-Finnish politics 1917–1923"]. H. 94, No. 1. Helsingfors: Finska vetenskaps-societeten.
Wikman, K. Rob & Lindman, Sven (1941) *Svenska Finlands folkting 1919–1920. En orientering*. Åbo: Förlaget Bro.
Willner, Sven (1979) *Söner av nederlaget* ["Sons of the defeat"]. Helsingfors: Söderströms.
Wrede, Johan (1988) *Jag såg ett folk...Runeberg, Fänrik Stål och nationen*. ["I saw a people...Runeberg, Second Lieutenant Stål and the nation"]. Helsingfors: Söderströms.

Nation-Building Discourse in a Democracy

Brendan P. Boyce

This article considers the highly contentious issue of nation-building and national identity in the new South African dispensation. While reference is made to existing conceptual frameworks, the thrust here is to examine and challenge some of the problematic assumptions associated with this notion. Conventional wisdom would seem to suggest that in the wake of the political transition, and in view of the most recent constitutional developments, the new political imperative should be "nation-building".

It should be noted from the outset that the building of a new political and social identity in a polarized and deeply divided society is indeed an ambitious experiment.

It is often felt that any movement towards unity in a plural society is not only moral but necessary and desirable. This essay takes a decidedly different stance. The main view propounded here is that of constitutional patriotism rather than state nationalism. The aim is to point out that although identity can be redefined, this may only be done within certain limits.

Therefore while I am in full agreement with critics, that the nation is a myth, a constructed and invented phenomenon, I think it is important that the role of history and how it is interpreted is carefully analysed. Thus a major task of this essay is to reconcile the issue of identity redefinition in a democracy given South Africa's unique historical limitations and opportunities.

Further, this paper questions the implied argument that unity necessarily means uniformity. In arguing against the repressive homogeneity, which nationalism necessarily implies, and for a more open situation where individuals are able to choose between a multiplicity of identities.

NATION-BUILDING DISCOURSE IN A PLURAL SOCIETY

The concept of national identity has always been the subject of intense political and philosophical debate in South Africa. For decades before national liberation, and more recently since the transition to democracy, the one issue which stirred up the most debate and controversy both in the liberation movement and within the apartheid regime was the national question.

In summary the national question may be defined as the rubric of issues that arise from the project of cultivating a sense of nationhood out of the diverse ethnic, racial, regional, class and gender identities that pervade the country.

This contestation was evidenced by a myriad of diverse approaches to the subject. Within the liberation movement some scholars and activists favoured a class based analysis,[208] others favoured Africanist philosophies,[209] still others preferred the nonracial approach.[210] In sum there were as many views on the topic as there were commentators.

The transition to democracy has led to a renewed interest in this debate. Since the successful completion of the multiparty talks, the 1994 elections and the finalisation of the 1996 constitution, South Africa has been dubbed the 'political miracle'. These events have removed the spectre of racial and ethnic civil war and have given way to unbridled optimism for the future. In this light it has become increasingly clear that the new political elites are intent on *engineering* a new homogenous South African society. Therefore while this situation has engendered much academic interest around the subject (of nation-building) it has also highlighted the numerous inconsistencies inherent in and the complex nature of this project.

---

208. Neville Alexander emphasized this approach in much of his earlier work. See Alexander, 1985 and 1989.
209. See Mzala whose approach has a definite Africanist emphasis. Also See Thabo Mbeki's recent speech delivered on the adoption of the new constitution: "I am Africa", although it should be noted that he does take an inclusive approach (*Daily News*, 9/5/1996).
210. See Pallo Jordan's comments in an interview by I. Filatova. In her paper: *One, Two or Many? Aspect of South African Debate on the Concept of Nation*.

It is against the historical background sketched above and in the light of the recent political developments, that this paper undertakes to examine the debate on national identity.

Firstly, it is necessary to critically view the terms of the debate in order to have conceptual clarity. The term *nation-state* is largely a misnomer.[211] Very few states, if any, are able to lay legitimate claim to being nations, if by nations we mean ethnically homogenous political entities. In most cases "the state is larger than the nation" (Ra'anan, 1989:6). It is indeed very seldom that a state's national boundaries coincide with or totally encompass any one ethnic group. Therefore the vast majority of polities and states throughout history have been multi-ethnic in composition.

Advocates of the nation-state thesis (racial nationalism) have conceded that the so-called developing world does not fit their neat conceptual framework. For these the prescribed solution has been— "nation-building", the implementation of policies to achieve rapid and effective integration and assimilation of peoples especially national minorities and ethnic groups. The consequences of these actions have often been disastrous. Therefore to state that nation-building was unproblematic would be false.

Anthony D. Smith (1981:1), M.O. Heisler (1989:21) and R. Nicholson (1994:49) point out that liberals as well as marxists severely underestimated the durability of ethnicity. Modernisation, far from being the wonderful antidote for ethnic division and conflict in modern societies, has often played the role of catalysing agent for ethnic conflict. On the other hand are we to uncritically accept the hypothesis that the modern world is at present experiencing an ethnic revival? I think not.

Upon closer analysis even the classical examples of the Western nation-state model, Britain, France and their North American counterparts have had continual problems with national minorities and racial issues.

---

[211]. This point made by Walker Connor is referred by A. Smith in his *The Ethnic Revival*, 1981:58.

REVISITING NATION-BUILDING IN THE SOUTH AFRICA CONTEXT

Nevertheless nation-building, the redefinition of South Africa's national identity and the development of a new national character are the new imperatives. Yet if the policies put in place to achieve these mean assimilating other ethnic groups into a homogeneous whole we are sure to be lighting a powder keg beneath our fledgling democracy.

The definitive question to the national identity /nation-building debate is: 'What should the post-apartheid South African nation look like?'

Should the emphasis fall on multiracialism, cultural rights and ethno-politics echoing the apartheid discourse and thereby rendering it immutable. Or should the goal of the post-apartheid constitutional dispensation be to draw the sting out of ethnicity by advocating the transcendence of differences including race, class, gender, ethnic, religious differences and realize their essential 'unity' and negate the balkanization of the South African state into separate ethnic and racial enclaves.

What is clear is that the building of our new nation must overcome the legacy of apartheid, with its gross and inhumane effects of large scale forced removals, inferior education systems and the racial division of labour. It is fundamental that the new nationhood, therefore needs to overcome the social inequalities and the discrimination of the past system. The more successful and coherent this process is the more stable and resilient the nation will ultimately be.

Percy More in a thoughtful paper entitled *Universalism and Particularism in South Africa* considers the thorny issue of national unity. Here he characterizes the problem primarily as one between 'particularity' (i.e. ethnicity or cultural identity) and 'universalism' (i.e. non-racialism or assimilationism) or what may be termed 'the politics of sameness' versus 'the politics of difference' (More, 1995:35–36).

In this paper he suggests that there is a necessary tension between universalism and particularism, as the choice of one constitutes a denial of the other. More proposes that the tension between the two radical positions may be irreconcilable. The synthesis he puts forward to sustain a democratic, united South Africa is moderate universalism with the recognition of ethnic and cultural difference (More, 1995:47–

48). This put simply is the "unity and diversity" theme prevalent in ANC documents and speeches.

Since the elections and the ANC's securing of power, the political implications which have flowed from these principles have been the establishment amongst other measures of the Commission for the Promotion and Protection of the Rights of Cultural, Religious and Linguistic Communities. The commission was agreed on in the final stages of the constitutional negotiations as a last attempt by the ANC to accommodate the desire of some Afrikaners for self-determination. Already one of the foremost commentators and activists on the topic of nation-building, Neville Alexander, has warned that this could actually entrench ethnic differences rather than encourage nation-building. On the other hand, Blade Nzimande has argued that the commission provides "the institutional framework within which to mediate and negotiate issues of cultural diversity and nation-building, instead of leaving them to be contested by brute force" (*Natal Witness*, p. 6, 16 July 1996). Nzimande sees common values as the superglue to nation-building. This is a useful starting point but the more vexed question is *who* identifies the common values and *how* do they become the common property of citizens at large.

Similarly Schreiner notes, "Nationhood does not imply uniformity and lack of difference ...nor should it imply a static and unchanging nation." (Schreiner, 1994:309). Thus the central question remains how does one engender the evolutionary nation.

In beginning to answer these questions it is essential that we consider another theme which has grown out of the "unity and diversity"/moderate universalism approach.

This approach is embodied in the Rainbow Nation thesis. The central idea espoused here is an essentially pluralist notion which emphasises ethnicity as the defining experience of all South Africans. A dangerous implication that may be drawn here and practised is the classification of all South Africans according to ethnic and racial criteria, again rendering these criteria to a certain extent permanent. The flaw of this ethnic interpretation of South African history is the fact that a transformative notion of the South African nation is undermined.[212] What is even more interesting is the evident contradiction between this typology and the ANC's longstanding commitment to a nonracial nation. It is in the context of this shift that we are introduced to the defensive idea of managing our diversity rather that engaging in a much more radical and transformative debate. I would even venture to suggest that we can not look with complacency at this notion of a Rainbowism which has the danger of glorifying the distinct and immutable ethnic and racial communities each taught to cherish their own apartness from the rest.

While the imagery of the rainbow is indeed a powerful and beautiful metaphor. It is important that we recognise that often the logical extreme of pluralism is ethnic separatism. I would like to concur with Said when he states that we should be vigilant to the development of a gloating and uncritical idea of the nation (Said, 1994:337).

Therefore we can formulate the problem as follows: How do we move away from the divisive dogma of Apartheid which was premised on the formal policy of "separate development" and ethnic fragmentation, this ideology which cultivated the ideas of ethnic pluralism, cultural pluralism and ethno-nationalism without falling into the trap of fleeing to an abstract universalism?

In the end, therefore, nationhood is achieved within a state when the citizens of that particular country perceive themselves as belonging to a specific territory, actively identify themselves with the state institutions, and feel a sense of shared values (having a shared identity). Schreiner notes that in South Africa, nation-building cannot be premised on "narrow nationalism" (Schreiner, 1994:294).

One of the goals of nation-building in South Africa should be to achieve individual, group, or communal identification within an independent state. Nation-building as it has transpired in other post colonial nations, as the assimilation of other ethnic groups to a dominant one, will fail in South Africa because "there is no single contender for the role" (Simpson, 1996:473). This is in my opinion South Africa's greatest advantage.

As noted by Schreiner (1994:294), Wallerstein (1983:84) and others the development of Nationhood is a historical process. Nation-build-

---

212. Arthur M. Schlesinger Jr. makes a similar observation in analysing American Society in *The Disuniting of America* (1993:16).

ing as conceived and practised in many of the former colonial states was seen as a means to speeding up this historical process. In the end though all that these states ended up doing was short-circuiting the process. Therefore in my view nation-building in the present South African dispensation should seek first to consolidate the new democracy by promoting a new democratic culture.[213] Therefore I would agree with Degenaar's emphasis on the creation of a civic culture and his strong advocacy of citizenship. What I am proposing is that national cohesion should centre on the idea of shared values and ideals.

This should not be seen as a flight to abstract universalism. What I am proposing here is that the various cultures engage in meaningful debate. The various cultures and languages have never been totally unitary or homogeneous. Cultural differences whether they be language, religious practices, manners, dress etc. do exist. What is required (as already occurs), is a higher degree of cross-over and dialogue. Furthermore this needs to be contextualised within the framework of the nation-building/ national identity debate. It would be a great pity if we did not take full advantage of the cultural variety present in our nation. As Peter Caws puts it, "consider the abundant opportunities when we turn to the genuinely multicultural." Nation-building in the new South Africa need not become "an exercise of repressive correctness rather than an expansive celebration" (Caws, 1995:381). It is my view that we need to engender a genuine curiosity in other cultural forms. It is useful to note Hughes adage that, "mixture is greatness" (Hughes, 1993:98). At this point we should be emphasizing the shared aspects of our cultures and thereby developing a new national identity unconstrained by cultural particularity or prejudice.

MAKING CITIZENSHIP THE GOAL

Inherent in a process of nation-building is the danger that it can become an elite process. The construction of enduring social, and

---

[213]. According to a survey conducted by the Institute for Democratic Alternatives for South Africa (IDASA), democratic culture is not yet entrenched in South African Society and this is especially true in Kwazulu-Natal (*Natal Witness*, Echo, 25 June 1996).

political entities requires the organization of state as well as societal organizations' input at grassroots level. The task of nation-building is affected by and should grow out of the nature of the constitutional system the country has embraced. The constitution, the bill of rights and the laws are documents that need to become the possession of each and every citizen. These have to be put into practice.

Furthermore nation-building in South Africa will most certainly have to overcome the narrow and sectional interests that have for decades been the mobilizing principle and one of the most fundamental principles of the Apartheid system, ethnicity.

The single most unifying project has been the struggle to gain full citizenship. As Schreiner succinctly points out, "the birth of citizenship in South Africa was not an inclusive process". Initially white women were excluded until the suffrage movement in 1930 won the vote for them. In the Cape, African people were deprived of the vote on the basis of property and education criteria. In the 1950's coloureds were stripped of the vote and when it was given back to coloured and Indian people via the 1983 Tricameral Parliament, it was not full citizenship. Further the formulation of TBVC states[214] created the illusion of citizenship for peoples like the Tswana, Vendas, and others but this was flatly rejected by these people. The issue of citizenship has been the rallying call of all the democratic forces since the 1920's and was fundamental to the collapse and ultimate reincorporation of the TBVC states.

According to Simpson,

> ...while the record of nation-building is far from an unqualified success, one should not then fall into the easy trap of treating ethnicity as would a primordialist or ethnicist, as being in the blood and according it the role of primary determinant of a person's identity and outlook on life. (Simpson, 1994:472)

As Wallerstein observes "race" as well as one's cultural orientation are not the only social identities individuals use (Wallerstein, 1983:80).

Simpson postulates the issue of the competing identities thus...

> ...loyalty to one's ethnic group is not necessarily incompatible with loyalty to the state one finds oneself in, nor does it preclude the possibility

---

214. The so called TBVC states were the "independent" bantustans Transkei, Botswana, Venda, and Ciskei.

of identification with one's fellow citizens even if they are not of the same ethnic origin. What is important for the stability of the state is that the latter set of allegiances overrides the former. (Simpson, 1994:472)

Therefore, *state loyalty*, the securing of citizens' loyalty to an independent state and their identification with the political institutions of the day is a key element of nation-building. The fostering of obedience to the state, ensuring compliance with its rules, regulations, customs and invented traditions are an important element of nation-building and national identity. The utilisation of national symbols, the institution of state traditions and ceremonies are important to the development of *state loyalty*.[215] Hobsbawm notes that often the effect of officially invented traditions is unifying if defined in terms of citizenship within a defined territorial space. My view is that state loyalty is only the framework, the exoskeleton, which needs to be nourished from grassroots level.

Although the involvement of elites in the manipulation of identity narratives is undeniable[216], one has to give due consideration to the masses. It is essential that coupled with this there are initiatives set in motion at grassroots level which will provide the emerging national mosaic with its colour. We should not be working towards a situation where the state mechanically cultivates a loyalty to the state which forms the basis of nationhood as this would be a monopolistic imposition by the state.

Tocqueville in analysing American society noted that what held society together was ordinary Americans' commitment to democracy and self-government. He observed that "civic participation ...was the great educator and unifier" (quoted in Schlesinger, 1993:24).

Therefore the solution I propose is that when considering the vexed question of nation-building and national identity we analyse it on three levels. Firstly on the political level one needs to look at the role of elites and political processes (i.e. the cultivation of state loyalty towards political institutions, constitution making, and the *masakhane* campaign etc.). Secondly one needs to be cognescent of the roles of

---

215. Hobsbawm distinguishes between officially invented traditions and unofficially invented traditions. For a useful summary see Prinsloo, 1996.
216. D. Martin's observations in the essay, *Narratives of Power: The Choices of Identity* (1993), are instructive here.

social groups (i.e. the role of cultural groups, religious communities, and non-governmental organisations etc.). Lastly one needs to consider the individual.

MOVING BEYOND MECHANICAL PROCESSES: POLITICAL PSYCHOLOGICAL ASPECTS OF THE IDENTITY DEBATE

Identity whether social, cultural or political meets a very basic psychological need for recognition and belonging. Furthermore it contributes to an individual's self-esteem.

It has been argued that ethnicity meets a very important ontological need for personal identity and recognition in a larger and impersonal mass society (Nicholson, 1994:51).

This is indeed arguable. Nevertheless individuals and groups require a feeling of continuity and the maintenance of a strong sense of self. Related to the human needs for affection and belonging are the needs for self-respect or self-esteem and the respect and esteem of others. What is important to note here is that the esteem of others is often reflected in recognition, attention and dialogue. Shotter observes that "we cannot just position ourselves as we please: we face differential invitations and barriers to all 'movements' (actions and utterances) we try to make in relation to the others around us." (Shotter, 1993:192).

In developing this point, Charles Taylor argues, correctly in my view, that "identity is developed in *dialogue* with, sometimes in struggle against, the things our significant others want to see in us" (Taylor, 1993:75, emphasis added).

The glaring gap in the nation-building debate in South Africa is the role of groups and individuals in the process. In order to prevent a situation where nation-building is exclusively a top-down process one must include the masses.

The writings of Shotter are instructive in this regard. In considering the politics of identity and belonging, he suggests that what is required is continuous debate on certain topics. It is this creative debate that will generate a tradition of argumentation which is essential for us to understand how we as individuals make sense of our lives. Therefore it is crucial that we become more than just routine producers of ways of life, of thinking, but that we in a real sense also play a part in creative living tradition. Shotter's view is that, "it is possible for dialogue, for argumentation to produce the very object which the talk in the argument is supposed to be about" (Shotter, 1993:3).

Therefore the task of the new politics of citizenship is to articulate a new critical descriptive vocabulary of terms, a new frame of reference that all the old and new diverse groups in civil society can use in expressing their ontological needs.

Martin quoting Manoni, 1969, notes as far as identity is concerned, human beings require the existence of the other. Further, psychoanalysis demonstrates the case that the other reveals the self and the reality of a multifaceted self (Martin, 1993:37).

Given South Africa's history, cultural pluralism exists. Nevertheless people are in constant dialogue, expressing opinions, exchanging ideas, sharing and developing a new mosaic, a cultural tapestry by highlighting the areas of cross-over and commonality. The sharing of universal values contributes not only to personal development but to healthy societal relations as these activities dispel ethnic taboos and silence racial epithets. This window of opportunity enables individuals and groups to develop and preserve a set of new and ever evolving shared values and universal principles.

This does not imply the flight to an abstract universalism, nor does it imply the homogenization of cultures to form a new alternative (single) culture. We should not fall into the multiculturalist trap of uncritically adopting an alternative culture based on our rejection of the dominant one. What it does imply is the affirmation of a new ever evolving hybrid culture. This mosaic generated by argumentation, dialogue and intercommunal sharing is what is needed to be fed into the framework constructed by the state.

Identity, whether social, cultural or political meets a very basic psychological need for recognition and belonging, furthermore it contributes to an individual's self-esteem. In this regard group identity is often an integral element of an individual's self concept.

Therefore a subsidiary aim is to attempt to broaden the debate and bridge the void in traditional theoretical analysis by drawing on the much neglected field of political psychology. It is in this light that I want to focus much of the debate on psychological and sociological aspects of the identity debate.

REFERENCES

Alexander, Neville, 1985, *Sow the Wind*, Johannesburg: Skotaville.
Alexander, Neville, 1989, *Language Policy and National Unity in South Africa/Azania*, Buchu Books, Cape Town.
Alexander, Neville, 1994, "Comment on Liebenberg" in Rhoodie, Nic and Ian Liebenberg (eds.) *Democratic Nation-Building in South Africa*, Human Sciences Research Council, Pretoria.
Degenaar, Johan, 1993, "No Sizwe: The Myth of the Nation", *Indicator South Africa*, Vol. 10, No. 3
Degenaar, Johan, 1994, "Beware of Nation-Building Discourse" in Rhoodie, Nic and Ian Liebenberg (eds.) *Democratic Nation-Building in South Africa*, Human Sciences Research Council, Pretoria.
Filatova, Irene, 1994, *One Two or Many? Aspects of the South African Debate on the Concept of Nation*, South Africa Institute of International Affairs.
Heisler, Martin O., 1989, "Ethnicity and Ethnic Relations in the Modern West" in Montville (ed.) 1989.
Hughes, Robert, 1993, *Culture of Complaint*, Oxford University Press, Oxford.
Martin, C. Denis, 1993, "Narratives of Power: The Choices of Identity", *Indicator South Africa*, Vol. 10, No. 3.
Montville, Joseph V. (ed.), 1989, *Conflict and Peacemaking in Multiethnic Societies*, Lexington Books, Massachusetts/Toronto.
Montville, Joseph V., 1989, "Epilogue the Human Factor Revisited" in Montville (ed.) 1989.
More, Percy, 1995, "Universalism and Particularism in South Africa", *Dialogue and Universalism*, Centre of Universalism, Warsaw University of Poland Vol. 5, No. 4.
Mzala, 1988, *Gatsha Buthelezi: Chief with a double agenda*. London: Zed.
Nicholson, B. Ronald, 1994, "Ethnic Nationalism and Religious Exclusivism", *Politikon; The South African Journal of Political Studies*, Vol. 21, No. 2.
Prinsloo, Rachel, 1996, "Studying the cleavaged society: The contributions of Eric Hobsbawm", *South African Journal of Sociology*, Vol. 27, No. 1.
Ra'anan, Uri, 1989, "The Nation-State Fallacy in Conflict and Peacemaking" in Montville (ed.) 1989.
Said, Edward, 1994, *Orientalism*, Vintage Books, Random House, New York.
Schlesinger, M. Arthur, 1993, *The Disuniting of America*, W.W. Norton Company, New York.

Schreiner, Jenny, 1994, "Reconstruction: The path to non-sexist nation-building" in Rhoodie, Nic and Ian Liebenberg (eds.) *Democratic Nation-Building in South Africa*, Human Sciences Research Council, Pretoria.

Shotter, John, 1993, *Cultural Politics of Everyday Life*, Open University Press.

Simpson, Mark, 1994, "The Experience of Nation-Building: Some Lessons for South Africa", *Journal of Southern African Studies*, p. 463–474, Sept. Vol. 20, No. 3.

Smith, Anthony D., 1981, *The Ethnic Revival*, Cambridge University Press, Cambridge.

Taylor, Charles, 1993, "The Politics of Recognition" in Gutmann, Amy, Steven C. Rockerfeller, Micheal Walzer and Susan Wolf (eds.) *Multiculturalism and "The Politics of Recognition"*, Princeton University Press, Princeton, New Jersey.

Wallerstein, Immanuel, 1983, *Historical Capitalism*, Verso, London.

The Notion of 'Nation' and the Practice of 'Nation-Building' in Post-Apartheid South Africa

Gerhard Maré

In order to achieve the stated aim of 'building a nation' (creating the desired congruence between a political, economic and geographic unit, and a citizenry with a single over-riding loyalty) in South Africa, a tremendous legacy of fragmentation—pre-colonial, colonial, segregational and apartheid—would have to be overcome. This would have to occur under contemporary global circumstances where the world has largely moved beyond what seemed to be an unproblematic association of 'nation' with 'state'; and where the 'nation state', in many cases, operates in circumstances of extensive population movements and demands for recognition of sub-populations. In other words, the contemporary world is characterised by the conflicting, if related, pressures of globalisation and fragmentation, while South Africa has to deal with those same issues overlaid onto the apartheid social contours and erosions.

In this paper I address three issues: first, that South Africa is an incredibly fragmented society, demanding some form of integration or cohesion; second, that there is no ideological organising principle nor organisational or institutional centre that can pull the society together (the ANC, otherwise apparently ideally placed, carries with it its own 'millstone of the past'); third, I do, however, argue that there is a way out, neither easy nor quick, but of which several elements are already in place—I argue that the appropriate cohesion can be found in a notion of democracy. Essentially I question the viability of the present project of 'nation-building' in South Africa, without necessarily doubting the sincerity of its advocates. In addition, I will question whether such a task is even desirable, in the form that it has been implicitly envisaged, but hardly ever explicitly theorised, since 1994. The argument in this paper is informed by thoughts, tentatively presented, on how identities are formed, giving weight to the local (the 'minutiae of everyday life' (Comaroff, 1996:166); to the 'intersubjectivity of everyday life [within which] human self-reproduction is welded to the wider process of social reproduction' (Wright, 1985:6–7); to pre-existing memories (Connerton, 1989); and also to existing material conditions and responses to, and explanations for, those conditions—in other words to the 'availability' (Saul's term, 1979:397) of a population for the 'nation-building' project. These memories, stories and explanations are all gendered and shaped by class and age, by ethnicity and religion. Attempts at deliberate construction or social identities from above often generate their own unintended consequences and resistances, otherwise apartheid, otherwise apartheid, a massive attempt at identity formation and social engineering, would have been a successful policy. 'Construction' is clearly not something simply imposed through socialisation from the top (see, for example, Calhoun, 1995:201). In addition, while *social* identities are what concern us in a discussion of nation-building, individuals are bearers of these identities (Appiah, 1994:151)

I argue that there has not been a conceptualisation or theoretical formulation of the struggle against apartheid, nor a history of that struggle, adequate to allow the task of creating a unified commitment to a central political authority in post-apartheid South Africa, as well as a 'deep, horizontal comradeship' (Anderson, 1983:16) that is located on the political level among all citizens. To state it boldly, the 'nation' is unimaginable in the local context, unless it be constructed on the basis of an exclusive rider, such as 'race' (the approach explicitly adopted by *The Sowetan*'s Aggrey Klaaste in his nation-building initiative launched and promoted through his newspaper, where his essentialist idea of 'the Black Thing' features prominently). I will, however, argue for another articulating principle towards a 'deep, horizontal comradeship', namely that of an extended notion of democracy within a responsible society. I will argue that this approach, while no less difficult and probably always elusive, is probably the more feasible alternative to nation-building in creating social cohesion in a society riven by racism and 'race' thinking.

It is only since 1994 that a juridically-equal citizenry was created. Even the modern centralised state-form was slow in coming to South Africa and when it was created, through British imperialist reconstruction after the Anglo-Boer war to facilitate effective labour exploitation in the gold mines, that form excluded certain racialised citizens and was built on the confirmation of territorial division (Christopher, 1994:chapter 1). In addition, the decades of struggle within the country and against the state-form that had been created in 1910 and the various governments that imposed a racist society, led to the formation of an opposition to central authority and a racialised construct to mirror the racialised state. Despite an earlier commitment to 'four nations' and later 'non-racialism', in effect one pole in this conflict was essentially perceived to be black african—the *reflection* of the hierarchy of ideological and political denial and discrimination through racism and of material exploitation through wage labour and social neglect.

When oppositional attempts were being made to theorise the position of social groups as it related to nation-building, debates around 'the national question' as well as 'colonialism of a special type' (or 'internal colonialism'), built on these same foundations—foundations whose strength lay precisely in the *obviousness* of 'race' conflict, or in mobilising an ethnic population through reference to pre-capitalist polities (such as was the case with Inkatha). While admirable efforts were made over the years to introduce a strong class (and much more recently gender) analysis into political organisations and social research, such interests were placed in a chronologically subordinate position within the practice of the envisaged two stages of revolution. Since the achievement of democratisation as form of government, signalled in 1994 through general enfranchisement, deliberate attempts are being made to aid dominant-class formation, justified on the basis of previous 'race' oppression (such as through the policy of 'black economic empowerment').

'UNBREAKABLE THREAD'?

The past does indeed lie heavily on the South African physical, emotional, political, economic and ideological landscape. The obviousness of the apartheid legacy is there not only in the vast separations between people, in the horror of racist oppression (revealed or, rather, confirmed in part through the Truth and Reconciliation Commission—sittings), but also in the mind-sets, the racialised thinking that informs probably all South Africa's citizens in their daily social interaction.

From 1910, building on prior settler and colonial conquest, the 'racial' patterns of the specific national form of exploitation were established. 'Race' was central, if not to the essentials of capitalist accumulation, then to maintaining the *forms* of labour exploitation and political exclusion. This story is too familiar to recount again, even in broad strokes, except to say that there will no doubt be value in re-examining the past from the new vantage point of the turn of the century and a formally democratic South Africa. 'Racial' allocation (to space, political opportunities, social and economic benefits, as well as ideological discourses of the oppressor and the oppressed) were ever more 'refined' and crudely and brutally imposed during the twentieth century. The exposures revealed in the sessions of the Truth and Reconciliation Commission, for all their effectiveness, have hardly mentioned the deliberate cruelty of forced removals and the pass laws, for example.

It is, therefore, not surprising, if less often acknowledged, that segregation and apartheid left their mark not only at the level of material discrimination but deeply in the racialised identities of the self and of others that were created. Julie Frederikse set out to trace 'the development of the theory and practice of non-racialism in South Africa through the words and writings of its people' (1990:4). Published in 1990, just when the walls of apartheid finally crumbled, it is remarkable not for its intention, but for the inability of author and interviewees to break out of the mould of 'race' thinking. Most frequently the 'non-racialism' under discussion explicitly or implicitly accepts that there are indeed four 'races' (at best four 'race-nations'), and that 'non-racialism' will merely mean that such 'racial' categories will not form the basis of discrimination (for earlier criticism of this position, see, for example, No Sizwe [Alexander], 1979; Alexander, 1996). In a slightly earlier work, with contributions written largely by prominent ANC members (several of whom became cabinet ministers in 1994), the same unproblematic mix of 'race' terminology with the claim of 'non-racialism' is made (Van Diepen, 1988). It could not be otherwise when the notion of 'race' is never consistently questioned. Oliver Tambo, president of the ANC while it operated from an exile base, said in a rambling reply in 1985 when questioned on the use of the term 'non-racial' rather than 'multi-racial':

> There must be a difference. That is why we say non-racial. We could have said multi-racial if we had wanted to. There is a difference. We mean non-racial, rather than multi-racial. We mean non-racial—there is no racism. Multi-racial does not address the question of racism. Non-racial does. There will be no racism of any kind and therefore no discrimination that proceeds *from the fact that people happen to be members of different races*. That is what we understand by non-racial (Tambo, emphasis added).

Under such conditions 'racialism', Appiah's term (1992:13) for accepting 'that there are heritable characteristics, possessed by members of our species, which allow us to divide them into small sets of races ...', remains prevalent (also see Miles, 1989:chapter 3, for his discussion of the processes of the similar processes of signification and racialisation).

The frequency with which 'mirror-responses' to that against which is being struggled occur (as well as instances of deliberate use of such mirror-responses, such as by Frantz Fanon, 1970), is to be found in several contexts. Appiah (1992), Paul Gilroy (1993), Jan Nederveen Pieterse (1996), Bhiku Parekh (1997), and Ernesto Laclau (1996:52) for example, all draw attention to the manner in which rejection of European or American domination or racism falls into an alternate essentialism (that of an 'African' or 'race' essentialism). Pieterse (1996:32), for example, notes that '(a)s long as anti-racism follows the logic of binary opposition, the current is the same; only the polarity changes'. It is obviously an inaccurate generalisation to attribute such positions to all who responded to racism in South Africa, and I certainly make no such claims, but it is remarkable how little discussion of the theoretical/analytical standing of racism, 'race' and racialism has taken place within political or academic circles—such a comment would apply to the post-1994 situation as well. Racialism within political discourse has been noted, often with concern, but little analysis occurs.

UNITY OF THE OPPRESSED

The theory of 'colonialism of a special type' (CST) or 'internal colonialism' was the theoretical answer found by the Communist Party in South Africa to meet the demands of trying to marry an alliance of communists with a black nationalist movement (see, for example, most of the contributions in Van Diepen, 1988, such as those by Mzala and Wolpe). The unity it proposed was of the colonised—all black african people were colonised. Such an approach was, of course, not unique to South Africa. It had also been employed, for example, to *analyse* the relationship between England and the rest of Britain, rather than for mobilisatory purposes.

What CST did do was largely to close the door on alternatives to ANC-led opposition to apartheid. Those who did not support the obvious correct position of opposition to 'colonial' rule (albeit of a special type), the policy of apartheid, were in the service of their colonial masters—in many cases quite correctly labelled as stooges or puppets, but in others a situation dangerously over-simplified for short-term political gain. The notion of democratic pluralism was difficult to maintain under such conditions. What I have not explored here is the manner in which, for the Communist Party, notions of democracy were also linked to the ultimate 'dictatorship of the proletariat', and what effect this may have had on democratic practice and theory.

The poles of the 'centre-periphery contradiction', applied by John Saul (1979:400) to analyse ethnic and nationalist mobilisation in colonial societies, was played out in South Africa as a 'racial' polarisation to match the 'racially' oppressive *and colonial* system. As Saul comments on imperialism's duality in its penetration of the world:

> There is, on the one hand, the tendency to create globally the production relations and class structures characteristic of the capitalist mode of production *per se*. On the other hand, this process of penetration also tends to polarize 'center' and 'periphery' within the global system, to create

colonial and neocolonial relationships ... (T)he point to be made here is that, for actors in this drama, *both* of these realities spawn realms of 'ideological discourse' which can begin to make sense of the world.

Following Laclau, Saul adapts the former's 'people' and 'power bloc' polarisation to a centre-periphery contradiction within which an 'ethnic interpellation is at least as likely a possibility as a "new nation" interpellation' (1979:401). Saul, in addition, accepts Laclau's argument that such an interpellation (call or appeal) is as possible as a class interpellation.

I would suggest that within a situation characterised as *'internal* colonialism' or 'colonialism of a special type', a racialised interpellation of 'race nations' was inevitable and much more plausible than a class account. Jordan (1988:111), to take one of many possible examples, noted that 'the people of South Africa today constitute two antagonistic blocs (one being the colonizer, the other the colonized)'. Those two 'blocs' are defined repeatedly in the contributions to the volume edited by Van Diepen (1988) as 'race' blocs—confirming that 'non-racialism' is most often seen as non-antagonistic relations between 'races' or the absence of racism. Jordan does continue to say that the resolution of the 'antagonism is through democracy', but I argue that because the organising principle of the CST approach is 'race', democracy has also been inadequately theorised and hence remains racialised. It is difficult to see how the 'colonisers' can become fellow citizens with more than formal equality, in their own eyes, but especially in the eyes of the 'colonised'. The temptation, even if not yet the consistent practice, will be to see democracy as a victory of a 'race' majority. In addition, democracy is narrowly perceived as 'government of the people' (Jordan 1988:117)—in other words, the restricted definition of democracy.

My argument certainly does not deny the validity of such an interpretation of the extreme discrimination and exploitation of a race-based capitalist system such as was to be found in South Africa— that would be absurd. What it does do, however, is to question the over-reliance on racialism, both during the years of struggle and since formal democratisation. What it also notes is a further fragmentation, reflecting the racialisation of the society, into four nations and not just oppressed and oppressor (see, for example, Singh and Vawda, 1988; James et al. (eds.), 1996).

Of course, there was 'class' within the alliance during resistance, but placed within the lonely moment of the second phase of the bourgeois democratic revolution (see Mzala, 1988). Since 1994, in language remarkably similar to that employed by Inkatha leaders in the 1970s, the ANC now also justifies the enrichment of a few as the advancement of the (black) nation. The National African Federated Chambers of Commerce (NAFCOC), not publicly known for a close affiliation to the ANC, has been quick to seize upon this justification in its claim for tax exemption for all its members to compensate for their suffering because of their participation in 'the struggle' (TV news, February 9, 1997; also *Daily News*, February 10, 1997), a request rejected by president Mandela a week later. Within the governing element of the alliance, rather than within the support structures (COSATU and the SACP), even the next stage is being openly questioned.

NATION-BUILDING IN A POST-APARTHEID SOUTH AFRICA

In the previous section I argue that both apartheid and opposition to 'race' rule were racialised (interpreting social relations essentially as based on the existence of distinct 'races'), and that this has introduced a serious obstacle to the process of nation-building. I will now take issue with the centrality of the African National Congress within that process. It is generally accepted that the ANC served as the most powerful symbolic centre in the struggle against white minority rule in South Africa. From its formation in 1912 until the first democratic elections in 1994 the ANC had provided not only a political home for its members, but also a rallying point through its leadership and ideology of resistance for many more who rejected racism and political exclusion and, from 1948, objected to and fought against the policy of apartheid. Such pre-eminence was part of the ANC's self-perception (see, for example, quotation in Maré, 1996:323), and was confirmed by the support gained in the 1994 elections.

While the movement never achieved consistency or clarity in its own policies (as evidenced in the debates around the meaning of the Freedom Charter, a document whose vagueness allowed free scope to the exegetes), it always represented rejection—of racism, of exclusion, of apartheid, of gross inequality. There lay its strength (it could call on support far wider than any specific position would have allowed), but also its weakness (in the unproblematic nature of support based largely on the basis of rejection of what the movement was not). Opposition was mobilised through popular slogans (of which the Freedom Charter provided many), but much more infrequently through detailed alternatives.

The moral and organisational high ground occupied by the ANC translated quite easily into claims for the representation of various notions of 'the nation(s)'. The movement stood for all except those who fell outside its moral ambit. We need not look much further than the vehemence of the ANC's attacks on some of the other groupings and individuals who defined themselves in opposition to apartheid, Inkatha being the most obvious.

However, this position that was so important to maintain in the quest to preserve a broad alliance and enormous sympathy during the struggle years, has had implications in the few years since the collapse of apartheid. As a *movement* the ANC claims a continuation of the previous stance, whereas it has to operate effectively as a *party* within the domain of pluralist 'democracy as type of government'. No longer is it shielded from public scrutiny through, ironically, apartheid's extensive censorship legislation, nor through taken-for-granted political and ideological loyalty. Nor is the monstrous system, against which it defined its position, in existence except as a legacy (the abolition of which had in any case always been accepted by the ANC as its goal and responsibility). The contradictions of its present position (neither movement nor party) will undoubtedly continue to erode either its nation-building project (claimed within its guise as an overarching movement), or (much less likely) its operation as a governing party attempting to win elections and please and extend its voting support.

It is important to note that during 1996 (for example), internal conflict and criticism, as well as falling membership and collapse of party structures, as well as several regional 'border' disputes, had increased to such an extent that Eastern Province ANC secretary, Bongani Gxilishe, wrote in his annual report of a 'state of complete lawlessness and anarchy as manifested by the complete breakdown of discipline, unity and cohesion'. He argued that '(t)hese negative tendencies pose a threat to destroy the very moral fibre ... of our liberation movement' (quoted in *Sunday Times*, December 8, 1996). The Eastern Cape, while it might be one of the extreme cases, is not alone in this predicament: the ANC in KwaZulu-Natal (KZN) and in the Eastern Cape have been divided over the incorporation of Griqualand East into one of the provinces; the Western Cape ANC has had to deal with the difficulty of finding the Western Cape ANC has had to deal with the difficulty of finding provincial leadership that can appeal to coloured voters in that province, with national leadership demanding at one stage that they display racialised preferences and elect a coloured person to provincial leadership; the Free State and Northern Province and Gauteng have had intense leadership struggles, as has KZN (although not to the same degree).

The ANC is faced with a challenge that offers its own rewards, but then only after a change that would involve redirection from claims to being a liberation movement to being a party that offered a moral vision for the country as a whole, and that acted on that basis in its everyday role as government in power, a role consisting of policies, agents whom it controlled, and social institutions and apparatuses which it aided and supervised. Not only does it have to maintain an image of moral certitude in a country where the monster of apartheid is increasingly becoming, at least in perception, the ogre of the past, but it also has to ride the storms of revelations and public criticism within the democracy that it fought for. If the ANC can no longer function as the oppositional pole to apartheid and, hence, not as the core of the nation-building project as at present expressed, it can meet the demands of its principles, rather than of its organisational centrality, and commit itself to safeguarding and extending democracy.

Ron Aronson, in a contribution written soon after the transition to majority rule started, noted that the fall of apartheid would, ironically, itself be one of the dangers to be faced by the internal democratic movement, shaped as it was by its role within 'anti-colonial resistance':

> Creating itself literally under siege, the internal democratic movement has never had the opportunity to develop an internal democratic culture—this is virtually prohibited by definition to an anti-colonial resistance—although it has developed a variety of forms for rooting itself in, and remaining responsible to, the masses who created it.

Aronson perceptively noted then that the movement would have to guard against continuing to perceive anything outside of its fold as 'a mortal enemy threatening to undermine the movement', and that the 'danger, and perhaps the historical logic, is that this particular legacy of apartheid will continue to poison South African political life into the future' (1991:14).

Although a fairly obvious point, it has to be noted here that the parliamentary 'democracy' enjoyed by white South Africans was also circumscribed in the extreme (even within the limitations of democracy perceived solely as type of government), through the same plethora of repressive laws and the obvious exclusion of the majority of the population from participation in the political rights of citizenship. Democracy, even in its limited sense, has to be established, nurtured and protected for all in South Africa.

The second major obstacle in the way of the ANC's nation-building project lies in a hurdle placed in the way of any smooth transition to a common citizenship, in which rights and also responsibilities towards a central authority are shared. The racialised spatial demographics of apartheid left a chequer-board of 'race' communities, with differential access to central authority, to services, to employment opportunities, etc. The present is not, however, just an apartheid-imposed pattern of inequality; it is also a mix of responses within 'the struggle', where participation and acquiescence carried its own relative reward. These two aspects of inequality, together with the specific policies of redress, whether it be affirmative action or black economic empowerment (or at the very least then the experience and perceptions, and not only of whites, of these policies, even if not their intention), has left a volatile climate for popular and manipulated mobilisation.

There are countless examples of the way in which the tensions associated with social inequality, and resentment at measures to redress inequality, have flared up or resulted in the expression of racialised perceptions (Maré, 1996). Two examples are the protest by coloured people in Gauteng at the flat rate system for african urban residents (see, for example, *Mail and Guardian*, February 7, 1997); and the anger expressed by coloured fishermen at the opening of parliament at what they perceive to be the allocation of quotas to 'blacks' who had never previously had anything to do with the industry. In the television coverage verbal attacks were levelled at the policy of 'black economic empowerment' (perceived to be a mix of favouring africans, outsiders, and aimed at individual enrichment at the cost of fishing communities) (TV News, 08:00, February 7, 1997). At this level nation-building competes against impossibly deep and complex identity formations and racialised material interests.

DEMOCRACY AND NATIONAL COHESION

My argument has been that any attempt to create a single political identity, with 'its parameters ... set by individual acts of voluntary adherence, which adherence requires the submergence of other loyalties to this larger unit; ... a commitment to the country, its people and its future' in South Africa (Jordan 1988:118), is doomed to failure for a very long time. Furthermore, such attempts carry the danger of intense conflictual fragmentation as the field of 'construction' of the nation in this form is also the field of intense contestation between both formal and informal political groupings. In addition, by placing nation-building in this terrain (that of power politics), those marginalised in society remain peripheralised (women, rural-dwelling people, the large illiterate population, the unemployed).

Instead, I contend that a wide notion of democracy offers many of the elements that are argued to accompany the 'nation-building' project: political stability (but not through the imposition of a single centre, but through recognition of diversity of ideas and identities and interests); economic growth (but not at the cost of the working class—those in employment and especially those outside of formal employment, largely women); and the possibility of a united effort towards social justice. This wider notion follows on what Tom Bottomore (1993:15) described as the area within which 'all citizens are encouraged to participate, as fully as possible in the organization and regulation of their whole social life'. This would obviously include the basics of democracy 'as type of government', that rests on accepting the 'rules of the game' of political contestation (Bobbio, 1987:24–26; 63–67, also 1988).

For example, an illiterate woman, living in rural KwaZulu-Natal is certainly excluded from being in full control of decisions taken that affect her everyday life, occupied as she is with survival under harsh conditions with often an inferior position within power relations, and is also deprived of much of the knowledge that is necessary for her to make an informed and independent decision during local and national elections. No society can call itself democratic while children remain out of school until such time as their grandmothers receive their pensions to be able to pay their school fees. The expectation of submergence of 'other loyalties' under these conditions of gross inequality between racialised groups, between sexes, between urban and rural as applies in South Africa (see for example TURP 1994), is so much wishful thinking. Instead, the points made by John Comaroff (1996:166) and by several other contributors in the same collection (Wilmsen and McAllister (eds.), 1996) in relation to that other powerful loyalty, ethnicity, is appropriate:

> ... ethnicity typically has its origins in relations of inequality: ... Ethnic identities, — are always caught up in equations of power at once material, political, symbolic.

It is becoming increasingly common for theorists to advance the quest for democracy as a reply to the collapse of universalist perspectives, and as a response to the shortcomings of the relativism of postmodernity as an answer to the (present) death of totalising theories. Laclau calls for the 'modification' of the 'historical link' between the interests of dominant groups and a universal such as democracy, in order to deepen and expand 'the democratic process in present-day societies' (1996:56); Nederveen Pieterse (1996:27) argues that '(e)thnic politics *may* represent a deepening of democracy' (my emphasis); Aronson issues a stirring call for '*maximum possible democracy*—this is a goal worth pursuing for its own sake' (1991:17, original emphasis); while Miliband brings together several of the strands argued for in this paper:

> I understand (socialism) to involve two fundamental and intertwined objectives—democratization beyond anything capitalist democracy can afford; and egalitarianism, that is to say the radical attenuation of the immense inequalities of every kind ... (1994:3).

It might be stating the obvious to say that the creation of common perceptions, imaginings or stories that make sense of the social world, is the result of an interaction of social agents and their ideological perceptions, and the structural conditions they are shaped by and shape. It is no different with 'democracy', both as type of government and as type of society. In the former it is essential that the 'rules of the game' of democracy should have been internalised and accepted as valid and constantly reinforced and maintained, but also that the structures of democratic practice are seen to be available and functioning (regular elections or other opportunities meaningfully to participate in decision-making; public bodies where elected representatives openly and accountably debate and make decisions etc.). In the latter it is essential that citizens not only accept that they can, and have the right to be meaningful agents in shaping their own individual or collective destinies, but that the material conditions of life are being addressed to enhance the quality of life and meet basic needs. Such an approach will build a horizontal comradeship from the societal and not from the political realm; it will focus debate and measures to address the gender inequalities, class inequalities, etc., that are so easily lost sight of in the sloganeering (and sporting symbols of national unity) that is nation-building from above; it will take peace-making away from the gestures of politicians shaking hands and take it to the level of stories of everyday life that have to (once more, often) become shared; it would challenge the validity of differences that are based on prejudice (such as 'race') and demand the construction of a politics of diversity and be allowed to aid in that construction, a politics that openly addresses the inevitable racialisation of much of social interaction in a society such as ours.

The scourge of racism, but also the implications of 'race thinking' ('racialism' as Appiah calls it), will have to be addressed vigorously to build the wider democracy that is essential to a society that has the support of all the overwhelming majority of its citizens in a common quest towards greater material equality and tolerance. It is proving to be virtually impossible to address the past without also using the same terminology, classifications, stereotypes and also (albeit with different intentions) policies—often situations of conflict are racialised and fixed through the dangerous essentialisms that signification of colour allows, instead of being resolved within a climate of debate and acceptance of difference. How is it possible to respond to the attribution of the most diverse of actions to a 'race' motive; how can calls to a 'racial' solidarity allow democratic practice?

My argument is that the measurable notion of social (not class specific) disadvantage, is sufficient to address the immense demands for redress within this society; that it is not necessary to turn to the admittedly warped reflection of 'race capitalism' simply to create another type of rampant capitalism, even if it should, at best, be 'non-racial'.

Where symbols do unite, great care should be taken to distance them from any political party links—the new South African flag has most certainly come to stand, for most of the population, for the moment of democracy and not for the moment of an ANC electoral victory. For that reason it soon came to indicate pride in a new South Africanism. It is for this reason that it has attained near-exclusive display at public events. However, even this unifying symbol, that now largely excludes the politically-sectional old flag, can serve to indicate a racialised or cultural divide as at recent cricket matches. The fragility of new symbols can undo whatever good intentions may reside in the notion of the 'rainbow nation'.

A political movement can never live up to the ideals implied in a shared commitment to a process of democratisation—even without the extremes of corruption and power seeking politicians operate within a context of competition and vote seeking. However, political parties can share in and contribute to that process. For example, the ANC government's *Masakhane* campaign, an attempt to instil a sense of civic duty to the new state, had (and maybe still has) the potential to move beyond the party political policy domain through its stress on responsibility towards the common good. The new constitution similarly serves to stress a common loyalty and some of the values of democracy as type of government. The task of the state, demanding a common commitment from whichever government is in power, is to foster and maintain the conditions that are necessary for citizens and the many organs of civil society to create democracy, a desirable alternative to the project of nation-building as at present envisaged.

REFERENCES

Alexander, Neville (1996) 'The rainbow nation: South Africa between unity and diversity', talk delivered at Haus der Kulturen der Welt Symposium 'Sud-Afrika: zwischen einheit und vierfalt', Berlin, June 14, 1996.

Anderson, Benedict (1983) *Imagined Communities: Reflections on the origin and spread of nationalism*, London: Verso.

Appiah, Kwame Anthony (1992) *In My Father's House: Africa in the philosophy of culture*, Oxford: Oxford University Press.

Appiah, Kwame Anthony (1994) 'Identity, authenticity, survival: Multicultural societies and social reproduction', in Amy Gutman (ed.) *Multiculturalism: examining the politics of recognition*, Princeton: Princeton University Press.

Aronson, Ron (1991) 'Is socialism on the agenda? a letter to the South African left', in *Transformation* 14.

Bobbio, Norberto (1987) *The Future of Democracy*, Cambridge: Polity.

Bobbio, Norberto (1988) *Which Socialism: Marxism, socialism and democracy*, Cambridge: Polity.

Bottomore, Tom (1993) *Political Sociology*, Johannesburg: Ravan.

Christopher, A.J. (1994) *The Atlas of Apartheid*, Johannesburg: Witwatersrand University Press.

Comaroff, John (1996) 'Ethnicity, nationalism, and the politics of difference in an age of revolution', in Ed Wilmsen and Patrick McAllister (eds.) *The Politics of Difference: Ethnic premises in a world of power*, Chicago: the University of Chicago Press.

Connerton, Paul (1989) *How Societies Remember*, Cambridge: Cambridge University Press.

Fanon, Frantz (1970) *The Wretched of the Earth*, Harmondsworth: Penguin.

Frederikse, Julie (1990) *The Unbreakable Thread: Non-racialism in South Africa*, Johannesburg: Ravan.

Gilroy, Paul (1993) *The Black Atlantic: Modernity and double consciousness*, London: Verso.

James, Wilmot, Daria Caliguire and Kerry Cullinan (eds.) (1996) *Now That We Are Free: Coloured communities in a democratic South Africa*, Cape Town: IDASA.

Jordan, Pallo (1988) 'The South African liberation movement and the making of a new nation', in Van Diepen (ed.) *The National Question in South Africa*, London: Zed.

Laclau, Ernesto (1996) 'Universalism, particularism, and the question of identity', in Wilmsen and McAllister (eds.) *The Politics of Difference: Ethnic premises in a world of power*, Chicago: the University of Chicago Press.

Maré, Gerhard (1996) 'Swimming against many currents: Nation-building in South Africa', in Louise de la Gorgendière, Kenneth King and Sarah Vaughan (eds.) *Ethnicity in Africa: Roots, meanings and implications*, Edinburgh: Centre of African Studies, University of Edinburgh.

Miles, Robert (1989) *Racism*, London: Routledge.

Miliband, Ralph (1994) *Socialism for a Sceptical Age*, Cambridge: Polity.

Mzala (1988) 'Revolutionary theory on the national question in South Africa', in Van Diepen (ed.) *The National Question in South Africa*, London: Zed.

No Sizwe [Neville Alexander] (1979) *One Azania, One Nation: The national question in South Africa*, London: Zed.

Parekh, Bhiku (1997) 'Shattering some arrogant Eurocentric and parasitic Afrocentric myths', in *Sunday Independent*, February 9.

Pieterse, Jan Nederveen (1996) 'Varieties of ethnic politics and ethnic discourses', in Wilmsen and McAllister (eds.) *The Politics of Difference: Ethnic premises in a world of power*, Chicago: the University of Chicago Press.

Saul, John (1979) *The State and Revolution in Eastern Africa*, New York: Monthly Review Press.

Singh, Ratnamala and Shahid Vawda (1988) 'What's in a name?: Some reflections on the Natal Indian Congress', in *Transformation*, 6.

Tambo, Oliver (1985) Interview with Oliver Tambo on the occasion of the Second National Consultative Conference of the African National Congress, *Mayibuye*, 5/6.

TURP (Trade Union Research Project) (1994) *A User's Guide to the South African Economy*, Durban: Y Press.

Van Diepen, Maria (ed.) (1988) *The National Question in South Africa*, London: Zed.

Wilmsen, Edwin N. and Patrick McAllister (eds.) (1996) *The Politics of Difference: Ethnic premises in a world of power*, Chicago: the University of Chicago Press.

Wolpe, Harold (1988) 'Race and class in the national struggle', in Van Diepen (ed.) *The National Question in South Africa*, London: Zed.

Wright, Patrick (1985) *On Living in an Old Country: The national past in contemporary Britain*, London: Verso.

Do Diverse Social Identities Inhibit Nationhood and Democracy? Initial Considerations from South Africa

Robert Mattes

Understanding the link between social identity and democracy has become increasingly important since the advent of what has been called "the global resurgence of democracy" or democracy's "third wave".[217] While modern democracy allows people to govern their own affairs through regular elections, political parties, and representative legislatures and executives, democracy cannot tell us which people should be included or excluded from the process of ruling themselves within a given political unit.[218] Democracy presumes widespread agreement on the identity of "the nation" or "the people" that are supposed to govern themselves as a political unit. Agreement on "the national question" has been seen to be the irreducible prerequisite necessary to have a democratic state. Dankwart Rustow has called national unity "the single background condition" that must be present before democratisation can proceed. "[T]he vast majority of citizens in a democracy-to-be must have no doubt or mental reservations as to which political community they belong to."[219]

During the first and second "waves" of democratisation, the nations that were to govern themselves within their respective states seemed to be more self-evident. Over the past three decades, however, the identification of self-governing nations and respective states has proven to be extraordinarily difficult. In many former colonies or formerly authoritarian and totalitarian states, the identity of the polit-

---

[217]. These phrases are taken from Diamond and Plattner, 1993; and Huntington, 1993.
[218]. For variations on this question, see Connor, 1981:180–200; Gellner, 1983; Smith, 1993:48–62; du Toit, 1994; and Manent, 1997:92–102.
[219]. Rustow, 1973:120–122. Also see Rustow, 1990:84.

ical community had often been artificially imposed from above upon a diverse range of social groups, rather than naturally emergent as a reflection of people's own chosen identities.

Scholars have been widely sceptical of the prospects of establishing a common national identity and stable democracy under conditions of social diversity.[220] Arend Lijphart has expressed this scepticism in what he called a "well established proposition in political science" that "[s]ocial homogeneity and political consensus are regarded as prerequisites for, or factors strongly conducive to, stable democracy. Conversely, the deep social divisions and political differences within plural societies are held responsible for instability and breakdown in democracies."[221] At its most extreme, a lack of agreement on national identity may enable aggrieved groups to portray themselves as an autonomous, sovereign nation and lay claim to the powerful international principle of "national self-determination."[222] According to a group of influential American behavioral political scientists, calling on the U.S. National Science Foundation to launch a new funding initiative on democratisation:

> theorists have argued that the existence of distinctive subcultures makes the development of democratic institutions and processes more difficult...[F]ew argue that cultural homogeneity is a necessary condition for democracy. However, the fact that bargaining and compromise are key elements of democracy causes many political scientists to fear that the existence of strong and distinctive subcultural minorities in a society will weigh heavily against democratisation.[223]

Thus, Lijphart had has put forth a widely accepted idea that democracy in diverse societies is possible only through "special" arrangements such as consociationalism.[224]

Social diversity seems to become even more problematic for democracy when the key social cleavages are based on ascriptive or nearly ascriptive characteristics such as race, language, or religion. As far back as the early 19th century, John Stuart Mill proposed that

---
[220]. Rabushka and Shepsle, 1972; Lijphart, 1977; and Horowitz, 1985.
[221]. Lijphart, 1977:1.
[222]. Kolodziej, 1995:4.
[223]. Working Group on Democratisation Workshop Report, Democratisation: A Strategic Plan for Global Research on the Transformation and Consolidation of Democracies (National Science Foundation: Washington DC), 1995:13.
[224]. See Lijphart, 1977.

"Free institutions are next to impossible in a country made up of different nationalities."[225]

Indeed, democratic consolidation has proven particularly elusive in states characterised by racial, ethnic or religious diversity. Writing in the mid-1960s, Robert Dahl found that only 15 per cent of those countries characterised by extreme social pluralism had democratic or semi-democratic government (what he called "polyarchies" or "near polyarchies") compared to 58 per cent of those countries with low pluralism. By 1994, the height of the third wave of democracy, David Welsh could report only eighteen to twenty ethnically diverse states sustaining democratic practices. And according to the Carnegie Commission for Preventing Deadly Conflict, nearly all of the world's thirty-five armed conflicts raging in 1995 occurred in multi-ethnic states.[226]

DIVERSITY AND DEMOCRACY: THE PROBLEM OF POLITICAL COMMUNITY

While it has not usually been expressed in such terms, the obstacles to democracy presented by social diversity are problems of political culture. In their 1963 classic, *The Civic Culture*, Gabriel Almond and Sydney Verba defined a political culture as that set of popular dispositions or orientations (in the form of norms, knowledge and beliefs) toward political objects at four different levels: (1) the political community; (2) the constitutional regime; (3) incumbent governments, leaders and their policies; and (4) the individuals and their role as citizens.[227] Thus, social diversity could inhibit democracy in at least four different ways. At each level, however, the linkages between the two are different and their analysis requires different types of data.[228]

Most scholarly arguments about the effects of social diversity on democracy can be located at the level of political community. At its core, the problem of diversity is seen as a problem of "social identity" and "nation". Henri Tajfel has defined social identity as "that part of

---

225. Mill quoted in Lijphart, 1977:18.
226. Dahl, 1971:110–111; Welsh, 1994; and Stremlau, 1997:3–4.
227. Almond and Verba, 1989.
228. Mattes, forthcoming.

an individual's self-concept which derives from his knowledge of his membership in a social group (or groups) together with the value and emotional significance attached to that membership".[229] The principle question has usually been seen to be whether people in diverse societies identify primarily with one of the plurality of social groups, or with the overarching political community?

Answers to this question, however, have been shaped by analysts' definition of "nation." Most have traditionally used an ethnically based definition of a nation as a group of people united by a belief in common descent or birth. Thus, Walker Connor distinguished patriotism (loyalty to the state) from nationalism (loyalty to the nation—a people defined by ethnicity).[230] The conventional wisdom has held that socially diverse societies lack a common agreement on social identity and thus (given the ethnic view of nationalism) lack a common national identity.

This has been seen to be especially true for a class of countries, including South Africa, called "deeply divided societies". In such societies, the plurality of well-defined social groups or "segments" are structured along religious, linguistic, cultural, religious, or racial cleavages. The political divisions tend to follow social differences, so that each segment generally has its own media, educational, civil, and political institutions. Economic and political interaction occurs far more within defined groups than among them. Political conflict, however, is largely structured between and among these groups. In divided societies, people are said to tend to define themselves in terms of the groups to which they belong, rather than the larger political community in which they live.[231] Nobody sees themselves as Soviets, Czechoslovaks, Yugoslavs, Bosnia-Herzegovinians, Zairois or

---

229. Tajfel, 1978:63 (quoted in Taylor and Moghaddam, 1994:60).
230. Connor, 1981:201–203; Connor, 1987; and Connor, 1990.
231. This definition is based largely upon the definition of "plural societies" found in Lijphart, 1977:3–4, though Lijphart also includes non-cultural/ascriptive factors such as ideology and region as possible lines of cleavage. Hermann Giliomee places ethnicity into the very definition: a divided society is one where conflict takes place among ascriptively defined groups, not classes. Such groups are the basic political unit, and people vote overwhelmingly for political parties representing their group. See Giliomee, 1990:299. For a nuanced discussion of the differential and complex nature of the divisions present in these types of societies, see Brewer 1990:84.

Burundians. This brings about a crisis not of regime or government legitimacy, but of national legitimacy.[232]

The act of self-definition is generally assumed to involve a mutually exclusive choice between membership in and loyalty to the ethnic group or membership in and loyalty to the state. While affective ties to the state can coexist with ethno-national consciousness, Connor argues that the two things tend to be in tension and conflict with one another. "Questions of accumulating ethno-national heterogeneity within a single state revolve around two loyalties, loyalty to the nation and loyalty to the state, and the relative strength of the two."[233] Those groups seeing themselves as dominant often see the state and nation as the same and "thus the two loyalties become an indistinguishable reinforcing blur". It is national minorities, he argues, who are much more likely to experience tension between these loyalties. He cites comparative survey evidence showing that ethnonational minorities express substantially less affection toward the state, although minorities within the same state may differ.[234]

In this contest, the group usually wins out over the secular political community. "The great number of bloody ethno-national movements that have occurred in the past two decades within the First, Second and Third Worlds bear ample testimony that when the two loyalties are seen as being in irrevocable conflict, loyalty to the state loses out." This happens because the transcendent identities offered by most states are seen to be much less powerful and appealing than those offered by kinship or ethnic groups.[235]

According to Pierre du Toit, ethnic groups are "powerful units of social control. Because of the emphasis on perceived bonds of descent, as expressed in family and kinship ties, the reciprocal obligations, duties and prescriptions which bind family members are also projected onto the more extensive ethnic groups".[236] Ethnic groups are also said to provide psychological security and self-esteem to members.[237] Finally, ethnic identities, attitudes and value commitments are

---

232. Connor, 1981:205.
233. Connor, 1990:25.
234. Connor, 1990:25–26.
235. Connor, 1990:25–26.
236. du Toit, 1995:39.
237. Horowitz, 1985; and 1991.

presumed to be less resistant to change than identities based on other criteria. "These are primordial values and commitments that seem to be almost indestructible" argues Almond, and are maintained across generations through the socialisation process. This is seen to be a major reason why the USSR was ultimately unable to change the political culture of Eastern Europe.[238]

ARE GROUP IDENTITIES AND NATIONAL IDENTITY MUTUALLY EXCLUSIVE?

Many new democracies in Africa and Eastern Europe have embarked upon explicit programs of "nation-building" in order to counteract what Lijphart called the "centrifugal tendencies inherent in a plural society"[239] and establish a single political community—or nation— that claims common loyalties from all juridical citizens. In South Africa, the necessity of some form of nation-building has been widely taken for granted. According to President Nelson Mandela:

> a common allegiance is what helps to define a nation. You either have divided loyalties on fundamental questions or an overwhelming sense of pride and belonging. A nation state without this attribute exists only in name. It survives by coercion and subterfuge. It is a time bomb waiting to implode upon itself.[240]

Yet many analysts, premised on the notion of a mutually exclusive choice of loyalties, warn against nation-building. Connor goes to great length to describe the difficulties faced by attempts to "supplant group ties with loyalty to a state structure". Horowitz warns against attempts to affect a "massive transfer" of loyalties from the group to the state.[241] Indeed, South Africa's prospects appear dim if we operate within a paradigm consisting of a mutually exclusive choice of loyalties and a distinction between nationalism and patriotism.

However, our understandings of the linkages between social diversity, national unity, and democracy may be limited by this narrow, ethnic definition of nation. The very real existence of some-

---

238. Almond, 1990:151–152.
239. Lijphart, 1977:2.
240. Cited in Johnson, 1995.
241. Connor, 1978:389; and Horowitz, 1985:599–600.

thing called the "American nation" testifies to the fact that the term cannot be limited to beliefs about common descent or birth. Such forms of national loyalty can only be understood through a different conceptual framework. A first step forward comes from Anthony Smith's distinction between "state nationalism" and "ethnic nationalism".[242] A second contribution comes from Rupert Emerson who defines "nation" as the broadest collectivity to which an individual owes his or her ultimate loyalties and allegiances.[243] A third can be found in Benedict Anderson's conception of a nation as an "imagined community".[244]

Putting these together, a nation is a product of common inter-subjunctive agreement, or imagination. It refers to the broadest imagined community which people are willing to obey voluntarily and give valued resources such as taxes and national service. Thus, everyone has a nation. The key question is whether people's nations are equivalent to the state in which they live. This nation can be based on perceived ethnic traits, or it can be based on powerful secular symbols.

But we should not simply reject Connor's distinction. Our conceptual framework needs to retain a category for a non-nationalist patriotism, yet also admit of the possibility of the development of non-ethnic forms of state nationalism. A more adequate framework for categorising different configurations of loyalties to overarching communities and sub-groups should include the following three possibilities.

Ethnic Nationalism. Here, citizens of a state actually think of themselves as a member of some group based on perceived common descent or origin. They believe that the group ought to be a self-determining political unit with its own state. "Ethnic nationalism" is not simply identification with a sub-national group, but includes a withdrawal or withholding of allegiance from the state in favour of that group. They may recognise the existence of a larger political community, but disagree with its existence. They may realise that they are legal members, but feel antipathy toward that membership.

---

242. Smith, 1993.
243. Emerson, 1960.
244. Anderson, 1983.

Secession from or extreme autonomy within the larger community may be desired policy goals.

Non-Nationalist Patriotism. In this situation, citizens identify with and give primary allegiance to a national group within the larger state. They believe that they should have a large amount of autonomy and self-determination within the larger political community. Yet they accept their membership in the larger community and are proud of the state representing that community. However, this allegiance is premised conditionally upon that state's respect of their group's claims to sovereignty and national rights such as culture and language. One example might be the way that many Quebecois feel about Canada, or Catalans feel about Spain.[245]

State Nationalism. Here, people accept the legitimacy of the territorially demarcated political community represented by the state, accept that they are members in it, and are proud of that membership. The state is seen to represent a people, an imagined community that should govern itself as a people, not as a collection of peoples. This feeling need not be based on a belief in common origin or descent.

ARGUMENTS ABOUT THE SOUTH AFRICAN "NATION"

Assessments of the prospects for developing widespread patriotism or state nationalism to support democracy in South Africa depend a great deal on your view about the nature of the groups in that country and the divisions among them. These questions have been at the centre of a long intellectual debate, what Donald Horowitz called the "conflict about the conflict".[246]

There have been at least four identifiable major elements to this debate. First, on what I call the "hard right", were the leaders and intellectuals of white Afrikaner nationalism who, rooted in German romanticism, attempted to develop a theoretical justification for apartheid. Based on primordial, organic racial and ethnic understandings of nation, these National Party-supporting intellectuals and

---

245. I would like to thank Will Klymlicka for this point.
246. Horowitz, 1991:ch. 2. For other excellent analyses of these. debates, see Dubow, 1993; and Sisk, 1994:ch. 2.

bureaucrats took the diversity of groups living in South Africa, imposed upon them their own categorisation, and subsequently attempted to separate and preserve these "peoples", "nations" or "volk" with a repressive hand.

In reaction to apartheid ideology a group of scholars arose on the "hard left", based in marxian analysis, who simply dismissed racial or ethnic cleavages as mere manifestations of state/ruling class attempts to impose false consciousness and mask the true nature of class conflict and capitalist oppression of workers.[247] Subsequently, analysts on the "soft left" conceded the reality of some social cleavages, yet maintained that they did not preclude the creation of a common society in a post-apartheid South Africa. Because people were much more concerned about issues of class than ethnicity, the artificial identities imposed by a despised state would likely be rejected in favour of a common, national identity.[248]

Finally, there has been a vigorous argument from the "soft right", consisting of students of ethnic conflict and divided societies. These scholars ostensibly reject the purely primordial notion of race or ethnicity, yet emphasise the deep, enduring, emotional, non-materialist need for group identity. Racial divides in South Africa were not just artificial legal barriers, nor proxies for class lines, but had come to delineate enduring ethno-national conflict between white and African communal power blocs.[249] Moreover, the end to white domination (which had produced incentives toward black solidarity) would introduce new incentives leading to the rise of ethnic divisions among black South Africans in the post-apartheid era.[250]

"NATION-BUILDING IN SOUTH AFRICA"

Throughout all of this literature, however, one thing is striking. It is almost impossible to find anyone who would concede the existence of something called the "South African nation". Thus, there has been a separate, though related and equally intense debate about how to

---

247. For a discussion of this school of thought, see Wright, 1977.
248. Adam, 1990; and 1994; Adam and Moodley, 1993.
249. Giliomee, 1989a and b; Giliomee and Schlemmer, 1989; and Giliomee, 1995.
250. Horowitz, 1991:ch. 2 (quote on p. 85); and du Toit, 1995.

promote or build a common national identity. The most visible approach to this question can be found in the popular rhetoric of Archbishop Desmond Tutu and the "Simunye" ("we are one") campaign of the South African Broadcasting Corporation. Both portray the emerging South African nation as a "rainbow nation" whose unity emanates from the its very racial and ethnic diversity.

Prominent critics such as Neville Alexander have rejected the rainbow approach, arguing that the metaphor accepts constructs such as race and ethnicity. Offering a second approach, Alexander speaks of the Gariep nation (Gariep is the Nama word for the Orange River that flows from the heart of the country into the Atlantic Ocean). The Gariep symbolises the blending of many colours, languages and cultures into one common stream.[251] Alexander sees a trilingual language policy as the key to constructing this new imagined community, not because everyone should speak the same language, but because they all should be able to understand one another.[252]

A third prominent approach to nation-building consists of a group of analysts who loudly proclaim, "don't do it!". They warn of the dangers of nation-building, though for a variety of differing reasons. Some analysts reject nation-building because of their suspicion of a "Jacobinist" project imposing the culture of the politically dominant group disguised as some new common culture.[253] Rather than nation-building, some recommend a project aimed at building a civic, democratic culture held together by patriotism based on the opportunities provided by the new society.[254] For others, the development of a South African nationalism is impossible almost by definition since they operate along a largely ethnic notion of nation. Rather than nation-building, they have called for political and constitutional systems specifically engineered to accommodate ethnic and national differences: some have argued for "centrifugal", decentralised forms of consociationalism and even confederalism; others have argued for a

---

251. Davis, 1995:26.
252. Alexander, 1997.
253. See Degenaar, 1991:2; and 1994.
254. Degenaar, 1994:25, and Adam, 1990:231-232.

system with very strong centripetal incentives emanating from specific electoral, executive and federal systems.[255]

Finally, fears of Jacobinism have certainly been fuelled by a fourth position consisting of the "Africanist" wing of the liberation movement. Their solutions to "the national question" consist of a "National Democratic Revolution" and the "Africanisation" of political, educational, social and cultural institutions.[256]

SOCIAL IDENTITY AND NATION

Thus, the social identity of citizens is assumed to be a critical piece of information for analysts of divided societies as well as of political culture. The measurement of social identity becomes necessary: (1) to determine the extent of heterogeneity of identity; (2) to determine the important lines of cleavage; (3) to determine the extent and salience of those divisions; and (4) to assess the relative balance between sectarian (racial, ethnic, religious or regional) and secular (national South African) identities.

I have identified five separate efforts to measure social identity between 1994 and 1997. These projects consist of: (1) two national surveys (1994 and 1995) conducted by the Institute for Democracy in South Africa (Idasa); (2) one provincial (Gauteng, 1994) and one nationally representative omnibus survey (February 1995) conducted by the Human Sciences Research Council (HSRC); (3) a series of national surveys being conducted by a joint team of researchers from the Free University in Amsterdam and the HSRC; (4) one national survey (1996) conducted by the Centre for International and Comparative Politics (CICP) at the University of Stellenbosch; and (5) a national survey (1995) conducted jointly by the CICP, Stellenbosch's

---

255. Lijphart, 1985; Van Zyl Slabbert and Welsh 1979; and Horowitz, 1991. The terms "centripetal" and "centrifugal" are taken from Sisk, 1994.
256. For interpretations of the liberation movement and the African National Congress as an exclusionist, black nationalist movement, see Neuberger, 1990:57–64; Gagiano, 1990; and Hanf, 1989. For more positive interpretations of the ANC as promoting an individualistic, inclusive, territorially-defined form of patriotism and identity, see Jordan, 1988; Adam, 1990:232, 234; and James, 1996:3. For the most recent articulation of this view, see Deputy President Thabo Mbeki's "I Am an African" speech to the Constitutional Assembly.

Centre for Interdisciplinary Studies, Markinor, and Idasa that served as the South African version of the international World Values Study project.[257]

Based on the presumed mutual exclusiveness of group and national identity, these surveys asked people, in differing ways, what they called themselves or to which group they belonged: respondents could either call themselves a "South African" or something else. Some also attempted to measure the salience of these identities.

While space does not permit a detailed discussion of these surveys,[258] there are a few clear findings that flow from these initial studies. First of all, wide majorities of South Africans do actively use constructs such as race and ethnicity, and to a lesser extent, language to define themselves. Second, it is evident that, regardless of the measurement method, there are not four racial groups, or two communities, but a wide diversity of identities in South Africa. Third, a variety of different measures seem to indicate that the salience or perceived importance of ethnicity and culture is increasing.

Finally, and most importantly from the perspective of this chapter, either when people are able to offer it on its own in open-ended questions, or where they have the chance to select the option from closed-ended questions, clear minorities of South Africans take the opportunity to call themselves "South African" (anywhere between one-tenth and one-quarter, though it appears that these numbers may have increased significantly between 1994 and 1995).

These findings have been interpreted as dire messages to the long-term future of democracy in South Africa. Broadly speaking, they have been seen to indicate the reality, resilience and strength of ethnicity, the increasing likelihood of ethnic tensions in terms of demands for scarce resources, and as evidence of a lack of national identity and the limited success of the nation-building project thus far.[259]

Elirea Bornman concluded that:

---

257. See Mattes, 1995; Kotze, 1997; Bornman, 1995; Klandermans, Roefs and Olivier, 1995; Olivier and Ngwane, 1995:9–16.
258. See Mattes, 1997:12–23.
259. Kotze, 1997:15–16; and Bornman, :15.

In contrast to an increase in ethnic awareness, no indications were found that nation building has as yet succeeded in establishing a strong South African identity among the majority of blacks... as most groups gave preference for their ethnic group over a South African identity, it seems unlikely that strategies towards nation building can erase the strong ethnic identities illustrated in both studies.[260]

In Kotze's view:

[A] very low level of national identity exists at present. This has the potential to undermine the nation building process, currently under way. If nation building is in any way forced upon reluctant communities, it may result in ethnic protest and conflict. A low level of national identity may also pose problems for the process of national reconciliation.[261]

CITIZENSHIP AND NATION

Does, however, the relative lack of "South African" responses to questions on social identity mean what it appears to mean? The various items reviewed above that have been designed to measure social identity probably capture a good deal about the whole cultural sense of self, which may be much more than we are interested in. Courtney Jung notes that:

Cultural diversity exists all over the world and is not relevant to politics except where it has been politicised. Political and cultural identity are separate conceptual frameworks. Cultural identity is only relevant to politics where cultural symbols are used politically. Therefore standard measures of degrees of division or pluralism, such as social distance scales, are not useful in the study of potentially divided societies. Levels of intermarriage will not determine whether ethnicity is or is not politicised. [We should not be] interested in whole identities, all the levels of cognition that make up a person's or a group's conception of self and other. [We should be] interested in political identities, those that become relevant in the political arena (narrowly understood as the sphere of government or conflict over resources).[262]

Social or collective identity gives meaning to people's personal identity as a reference group of people with similar history, practices, and values, against which they can compare and distinguish them-

---

260. Bornman, 1995:14.
261. Kotze, 1997:28.
262. Jung, (undated paper).

selves.[263] It is not necessarily a statement of political loyalty. As Evan Lieberman puts it, nationhood does not depend on people seeing their state identity as a source of primary identity in everyday life. It is only necessary that they accept and take pride in membership in the territory represented by the states.[264] Thus, it is not at all clear that the legitimacy and stability of the democratic political community depends on collective social identities being coterminous with the identity of that community. Under certain circumstances, social identity might not be crucial to questions of national political community. It is possible to have consensual agreement on "the nation" and one's place in it amidst a plurality of social identities.

Rather, it would seem that the legitimacy of a democratic political community would depend much more on people's values about citizenship. According to Will Kymlicka and Wayne Norman, "Citizenship is not just a certain status. It is also an identity, an expression of one's membership in a political community."[265] In this sense, citizenship becomes a key measure of nation-building. Jannie Gagiano defines nation-building as:

> the integration of communally diverse and/or territorially discreet units into the institutional framework of a single state and the concomitant transfer of a sense of common political identity and loyalty to the symbolic community defined by the founding ideology of such a state.[266]

Thus the legitimacy of the democratic political community depends on people's answers to at least three questions: (1) do people accept the appropriateness of the territorially defined community? (2) Are they willing to be a member in that community? And (3) are they proud of that membership?

For initial evidence concerning these questions in South Africa, we turn to the responses to a simple question included in the 1995 Idasa survey. The item asked respondents how proud they were "to be called a South African citizen". Just over nine-in-ten (92 per cent) said they were either proud or very proud. A similar question asked in the

---

263. Tajfel, 1978; and Taylor, 1997:ch. 3.
264. Lieberman, 1998.
265. Kymlicka and Norman, 1994:352–381. Also see Krasner, 1988; and du Toit, 1995:23–37.
266. Gagiano, 1990:32.

1995 World Values Survey found just under 96 per cent who said they were either "very" or "quite proud" to be South African. Thus, in contrast to the consistent findings of about one-fifth to one-third who carry "South African" as a collective social identity, and in contrast to nearly everyone's expectations, it appears that the legitimacy of the South African political community may be nearly consensual in the body politic.

Table 1.

Idasa (September–November 1995)*	Per cent	WVS (October–November 1995)**	Per cent
Very proud	60.3	Very proud	80.4
Proud	31.3	Quite proud	15.4
Not very proud	5.1	Not very proud	2.7
Not at all proud	2.1	Not at all proud	0.5
		I am not South African	0.8
Don't know	1.2	Don't know	0.2
Total	100.0	Total	100.0
N	2674	N	2935

* Are you very proud, proud, not very proud or not at all proud to be called a South African citizen?
** "How proud are you to be South African?"

Given the huge discrepancy in the responses of a "South African social identity" and pride in "South African citizenship", they seem to be quite different mental concepts. But just how distinct are they? Are those who spontaneously call themselves "South African" even more likely than the overall public to express pride in citizenship? A crosstabulation of the Idasa item measuring social identity with the item measuring civic pride reveals that the distinction between having a secular (i.e. South African) social identity versus a sectarian one does not account for much variation in civic pride (the crosstabulation is not displayed here due to the large number of categories). 71 per cent of those who call themselves "South Africans" are "very proud" to be a South African citizen. But so are 80 per cent of those who identity themselves as "Tswana", 69 per cent of "Blacks" and

"Coloureds", 65 per cent of "Xhosas" and 63 per cent of "Africans".[267] Yet, different types of sectarian social identity do have important impacts on pride in citizenship. For example, only 31 per cent of "English-speakers", 33 per cent of "Indians" are very proud, 41 per cent of self-identified "Zulus", 46 per cent of "Vendas", 48 per cent of "Whites", and 58 per cent of "Afrikaners" and "English".

These conclusions are supported by a crosstabulation of the WVS items on civic pride and identity. As with the Idasa survey, people who choose the "South African" label are not appreciably more proud of their "South Africanness" than people who chose sectarian identities.[268] At the same time, pride in national identity does vary considerably among different types of sectarian identities.

This suggests there is little direct relationship between having a secular versus sectarian social identity on one hand and a national identity on the other. People's propensity to select group versus national identities is hardly related to their pride in citizenship. The question then arises as to which item is a more relevant predictor of the things we are ultimately interested in, people's loyalties and their willingness to be good citizens. The following tables display crosstabulations of the two World Values Survey items on social and national identity with a third item that measures willingness to fight in a war (undoubtedly one of the most severe claims a state can lay on citizens' loyalty).

The tables demonstrate that pride in national identity has a greater impact on whether or not people are willing to fight in a war for South Africa than does their social identity (at least in terms of a secular versus a sectarian identity). Those who spontaneously call themselves "South African" are no more likely to be willing to serve

---

267. An analysis of variance reveals an extremely small, though statistically significant difference between the pride in citizenship of those who call themselves "South African" (2.67 on a four point scale), those who give themselves a "hyphenated" South African identity (2.57) and those with a sectarian group identity (2.47). This distinction accounts for only 1 per cent of the variance in national pride (Eta = .09, significant at the .001 level; Eta Squared = .01).
268. Those with a "South African" identity have a mean pride rating of 2.83 on a four-point scale, "hyphenated" South Africans are at 2.69, but those with sectarian identities are actually higher than the hyphenated group (2.78). This distinction accounts for 1 per cent of the variance in national pride (Eta = .09, significant at the .001 level; Eta Squared = .01).

Table 2. Civic Pride by Social Identity (World Values Study)

	Very Proud	Quite Proud	Not Proud	Not at All Proud	Not a South African	Total
Black	86.4	9.3	3.7	0.3	0.3	21.0
White	66.3	25.5	2.7	2.2	3.3	6.3
Coloured	83.0	15.9		1.1		6.0
Indian	88.5	10.6	1.0			3.5
Zulu	80.1	14.0	5.4			6.3
Xhosa	80.2	14.2	3.7	1.2		5.5
Sotho	79.5	15.9	2.3	2.3		1.5
Tswana	83.3	12.8	1.3			2.7
Sepedi	97.7	2.3				1.5
Venda	87.5		12.5			0.3
English-speaking-SAs	63.5	31.5	2.0	0.5	2.0	6.3
Afrikaans-speaking SAs	73.5	25.0	1.2			11.0
Afrikaner	78.2	9.1	10.9	1.8		1.9
South African	86.1	11.4	2.2	0.3	0.1	23.7
Muslim	83.3	16.7				.2
Swazi	62.5	12.5	12.5		12.5	0.3
African		50.0			50.0	0.1
Other	54.8	21.4	2.4	2.4	19.0	1.4
None		100.0				.0
Total	80.4	15.4	2.7	0.5	0.8	100.0

(Table presents row percentages for ease of presentation.)

in wartime (64 per cent) than are people who choose other labels, such as "Blacks" (71 per cent), "Indians" (69 per cent), "Afrikaans-speaking South Africans" (64 per cent), or "English-speaking South African" (62 per cent). Furthermore, they are only slightly more willing than are people who chose the "Afrikaner" (60 per cent), or "white" (60 per cent) label.[269] As with our previous finding, willingness to fight does vary considerably according to the type of sectarian identity. People who chose African ethnic labels were significantly less likely to fight than those who chose the "black" description.

---

269. There were no statistically significant differences in willingness to fight between "South Africans", "hyphenated" South Africans, and those with a sectarian identity (at the .05 level).

Table 3. Willingness to Fight by Social Identity

	Yes	No	Don't Know	Total
Black	70.5	18.8	10.7	21.0
White	59.8	31.5	8.7	6.3
Coloured	58.5	27.8	13.6	6.0
Indian	69.2	25.0	5.8	3.5
Zulu	50.5	30.1	19.4	6.3
Xhosa	54.3	40.7	4.9	5.5
Sotho	34.1	36.4	29.5	1.5
Tswana	52.6	23.1	24.4	2.7
Sepedi	53.5	34.9	11.6	1.5
Venda	50.0	37.5	12.5	0.3
English-speaking SAs	62.0	29.5	8.5	6.8
Afrikaans-speaking SAs	64.8	24.4	10.5	11.0
Afrikaner	60.0	32.7	7.3	1.9
South African	64.2	4.2	12.2	23.7
Muslim	100.0			0.2
Swazi	25.0	50.0	25.0	0.3
African	50.0		50.0	0.1
Other	42.9	45.2	11.9	1.4
None	100.0			
Total	62.2	26.1	11.7	100.0

"Of course, we all hope that there will not be another war, but if it were to come to that, would you be willing to fight for your country?" (World Values Study) (Table presents row percentages for ease of presentation.)

In contrast, pride in national identity has a stronger impact on willingness to fight in a war for South Africa. Those who say they are most proud of their South Africanness are considerably more likely to be willing to serve in wartime (65 per cent) than those who are least proud (44 per cent).

Table 4. Willingness to Fight by Civic Pride

	Very Proud 80.4%	Quite Proud 15.4%	Not Proud 2.7%	Not at All Proud 0.5%	Not a South African 0.8%	Total
Yes	64.7	53.2	50.6	43.8	43.5	62.2
No	23.7	33.3	41.8	56.3	47.8	26.1
Don't know	11.5	13.5	7.6		8.7	11.7
Total	100.0	100.0	100.0	100.0	100.0	100.0

(Spearman's r = .09, significant at the .001 level.)

We have found widespread pride in membership in the South African political community. The simple question wording testifies to a high amount of face validity (that is, the extent to which it really measures national pride). Furthermore, we have demonstrated a significant degree of construct validity because answers to that question are associated with other citizen behaviour (willingness to fight in a war) in a predictable manner and do so much more consistently than the social identity measure, at least in terms of the secular vs. sectarian distinction.

The responses to the questions on national identity mean that over 90 per cent of the legal citizens of South Africa: (1) accept the appropriateness of the demarcated territory known as South Africa; (2) see themselves as members of that community; and (3) are proud of that membership. A wide range of people with diverse communal identities, vastly different historic experiences, and flung out over a vast territory, have apparently been able to, in Gagiano's words, "transfer a sense of common political identity and loyalty to the symbolic community", the imagined community of South Africa. This seems to indicate, at least, the existence of widespread "patriotism" in South Africa. It may also suggest a bolder proposition: that there is already a widespread degree of "state nationalism".

Focusing on the two most likely sources of ethnonational sentiment, there is little evidence that people's pride in South African identity is premised on the state's respect for a claimed right of self-government of sub-groups, or national self-determination, within a larger South African community. It is true that in the Idasa 1994 post-election survey 44 per cent of white Afrikaans-speakers "agreed" with securing a "homeland for the Afrikaners". Yet a clear minority of Afrikaners vote for or identify with the Freedom Front, the party whose sole goal was the creation of such a homeland. Whatever support they had diminished considerably in the 1995 local government elections as well as in subsequent surveys. In the 1995 Idasa survey, only 13 per cent of Zulu-speakers living in the province of KwaZulu-Natal favoured special constitutional powers for the province.

CONCLUSIONS

In his 1994 review of the prospects for successful democratisation in South Africa, Hermann Giliomee closed with the observation that: "No country that has become democratic since the mid-1970s laboured under the same ethnic and racial divisions and lack of broad-based economic development as South Africa."[270]

Yet South Africans seem to have developed rather quickly, a common civic state nationalism. Why? How can we explain such high levels of political community and national identity in a supposedly divided society? Why have multiethnic or multinational states like the Soviet Union, Yugoslavia, Czechoslovakia fallen apart so easily with the onset of democracy, while South Africa exhibits extremely high levels of national identity? Is there any reason for a people so thoroughly oppressed and repressed by a minority group, and the government and regime representing that group, to so easily and enthusiastically identify with the name of the political society ("South Africa") traditionally associated with the oppressive regime? Why was there no real attempt, as part of transformation, to immediately set about changing the name, the very identity, of that society? And why have the formerly dominant, now a numerical minority, remained committed to an entity dominated by a historical rival? In South Africa, in contrast to those societies mentioned above, no serious politician wants to change the name of the country, or demands partition. The only political parties entertaining such possibilities have been relegated to the dustbin of electoral history. Both "Azania" and "Oranjia" remain a glint in the eye of a handful of activists and intellectuals.

One answer could be that while South Africa is a divided society, it differs in important ways form other such states. As Heribert Adam has pointed out, in contrast to countries with distinct nationalities located in distinct territories (such as Czechoslovakia), the imposed group memberships of apartheid spanned common languages and religions. Social groups were geographically interspersed, and there

---

270. Giliomee, 1995:104.

was a significant degree of economic interdependence among groups.[271]

Another difference is that in former communist and other authoritarian states, a non-democratic regime attempted to suppress ethnicity and impose an artificial transcendent identity. People threw off this identity as soon as they were able to do so. In South Africa, in contrast, the apartheid state tried to impose ethnic and racial identities and deny the "South Africanness" of the majority of its citizens. "By the 1980s, it became quite clear that a South African nation bounded by skin colour was no longer viable and a new political dispensation was inevitable. The form of resistance that reigned hegemonic in the final years of the struggle helped 'imagine' a multiracial South African nation, a newly defined terminal political community with people of varied colours and creed."[272] That South Africans may be claiming their South African identity only because it was previously denied them may be a very negative, limited basis for building a common democracy, but it is certainly something absent in the vast majority of other divided societies.

A final potential factor is something that may differentiate South Africa from other divided societies, yet render it comparable—at least in a limited sense—to another diverse society, the United States. Social diversity might pose less of an obstacle to national unity and democracy when a state is able to offer its citizens an ideational basis for community independent of culture and descent. The ideas contained in the United States' founding documents, liberty, equality, democracy, limited government and private enterprise (what Gunnar Myrdal called the "American Creed") have provided the basis for a popular consensus that has enabled a polyglot of immigrants to become one nation.[273] Is it possible that in South Africa, the symbols of Mandela and the Constitution, the images of the rainbow nation and Simunye ("we are one"), and the ideas of democracy, non-racialism and reconciliation, may be providing a similar basis for a new

---

271. Adam, 1994:38, 41. Irina Filatova admonishes Adam on his geography, noting that the Soviet Union's nation-building project failed despite a widely shared common language and a pervasive ideology, with significant interspersal and intermarriage, and extreme economic interdependence. See Filatova, 1994.
272. Lieberman, 1998:8.
273. Huntington, 1997:29.

national consensus that can enable this country to maintain and consolidate democracy, and leave behind the horrors of racial and ethnic civil conflict that have plagued the 20th century?

Satisfactory answers to these questions will come only with repeated measurement. The survey responses reported here might be "time-bound", coming as they did only months after South Africa's victory in the Rugby World Cup and the palpable wave of patriotic flag-waving that swept the country. Yet even if this were the case, the potential for black and white South Africans to find common pride through victory in such a historically controversial sport as rugby (indeed with a nearly all-white team with only one coloured player and no Africans) would itself be an impressive feat. Nevertheless, the point remains that over-time analysis is clearly needed.

Answers to our questions will also require better conceptualisation and improved measurement of group and national identities. Our finding that social identity and identification with the state are distinct, though related phenomena means that group identity and national identity need to be measured separately. If respondents do see the two in conflict, the survey instrument should enable them to tell us so, rather than having the choice imposed upon them. National and social identities also need to be measured by more reliable multi-item scales that tap different dimensions of each concept.

Lastly, we need to develop an integrated model that enables us to test the effect of identity by looking for hypothesised effects not only at the level of political community, but also at the levels of regime, government, and citizen. None of the arguments in this chapter should be seen to underestimate the challenges to democracy presented by social cleavage, difference and diversity. Rather, the initial data presented in this chapter suggest that the problems presented by diversity and identity, at least in South Africa, may not lie—as is widely assumed—at the level of political community. Diversity may, however, constitute a significant problem with regard to attitudes toward the constitutional regime, toward the incumbent government and government policy, and toward other groups and duties to the state.

REFERENCES

Adam, Heribert, 1990, "Cohesion and Coercion", *The Elusive Search for Peace: South Africa, Israel and Northern Ireland*, Gagiano, Jannie and Hermann Giliomee (eds.), Cape Town: Oxford University Press.

Adam, Heribert, 1994, "Nationalism, Nation-Building and Non-Racialism", *Democratic Nation-Building in South Africa*, Rhoodie, Nic and Ian Liebenberg (eds.) Pretoria: Human Sciences Research Council.

Adam, Heribert and Kogila Moodley, 1993, *The Opening of the Apartheid Mind: Options for the New South Africa*, Berkeley: University of California Press.

Alexander, 1997, "Language and the National Question". Paper Presented to the Inaugural Conference of the Harold Wolpe Trust on "The Political Economy of Change". Bellville: University of the Western Cape, 1-2 August.

Almond, Gabriel A., 1990, *A Discipline Divided: Schools and Sects in Political Science*, London: Sage.

Almond, Gabriel A. and Sidney Verba, 1989, *The Civic Culture: Political Attitudes and Democracy in Five Nations*, Newbury Park: Sage Publications.

Anderson, Benedict, 1983, *Imagined Communities: Reflections on the Origin and Spread of Nationalism*, London: Verso.

Bornman, Elirea, 1995, "Patterns of Group Identification". Paper Presented to the International Political Science Association Research Group on Race and Ethnicity, Witwatersrand University, Johannesburg: 13-15 July.

Brewer, John, 1990, "Policing", *The Elusive Search for Peace: South Africa, Israel and Northern Ireland*, Gagiano, Jannie and Hermann Giliomee (eds.), Cape Town: Oxford University Press.

Connor, 1978, "A Nation is a Nation", *Ethnic and Racial Studies*, 1.

Connor, Walker, 1981, "National and Political Illegitimacy", *Canadian Review of Studies in Nationalism*, 8/3.

Connor, Walker, 1987, "Ethnonationalism", *Understanding Political Development*, Weiner, Myron and Samuel P. Huntington (eds.) New York: HarperCollins.

Connor, Walker, 1990, "Ethnonationalism and Instability", *The Elusive Search for Peace: South Africa, Israel and Northern Ireland*, Gagiano, Jannie and Hermann Giliomee (eds.), Cape Town: Oxford University Press.

Dahl, Robert A., 1971, *Polyarchy: Participation and Opposition*, New Haven: Yale University Press.

Davis, Gaye, 1995, "In Search of the Great Gariep", *Weekly Mail and Guardian*, 25-31 August.

Diamond, Larry and Marc F. Plattner, (eds.), 1993, *The Global Resurgence of Democracy*, Baltimore: Johns Hopkins University Press.

Degenaar, Johan, 1991, *The Myth of the South African Nation*, Institute for a Democratic Alternative in South Africa Occasional Paper, No. 40, Cape Town: Idasa.

Degenaar, Johan, 1994, "Beware of Nation-Building Discourse", *Democratic Nation-Building in South Africa*, Rhoodie, Nic and Ian Liebenberg (eds.) Pretoria: Human Sciences Research Council.

du Toit, André, 1993, "The Meaning of Democracy", *Die Suid Afrikaan*. Feb./March 1993, pp. 3–6.

du Toit, Pierre, 1995, *State Building and Democracy in Southern Africa: Botswana, Zimbabwe, and South Africa*, Washington DC: United States Institute of Peace Press.

Dubow, Saul, 1993, "Ethnic Euphemism and Racial Echoes". Paper Presented to Conference on "Ethnicity, Identity and Nationalism in South Africa: Comparative Perspectives" Rhodes University, Grahamstown: April.

Emerson, Rupert, 1960, *From empire to nation; the rise to self-assertion of Asian and African peoples*, Cambridge: Harvard University Press.

Filatova, Irina, 1994, "The Awkward Issue: Some Comments on the South African Debate on Nation-Building and Ethnicity", *Democratic Nation-Building in South Africa*, Rhoodie, Nic and Ian Liebenberg (eds.) Pretoria: Human Sciences Research Council.

Gagiano, Jannie, 1990, "The Contenders", in *The Myth Makers: The Elusive Bargain for South Africa's Future*, Esterhuyse, W. and P. Du Toit (eds.) Halfway House: Southern Books.

Gellner, Ernest, 1983, *Nations and Nationalism*, Ithaca, N.Y.: Cornell University Press.

Giliomee, Hermann and Lawrence Schlemmer, 1989, *From Apartheid to Nation-Building*, Cape Town: Oxford University Press.

Giliomee, Hermann, 1989a, "The Communal Nature of the South African Conflict", in *Negotiating South Africa's Future*, Giliomee, Hermann and Lawrence Schlemmer (eds.) Halfway House: Southern Books.

Giliomee, Hermann, 1989b, "The Third Way", in *Negotiating South Africa's Future*, Giliomee, Hermann and Lawrence Schlemmer (eds.) Halfway House: Southern Books.

Giliomee, Hermann, 1990, "The Elusive Search for Peace", in *The Elusive Search for Peace: South Africa, Israel and Northern Ireland*, Gagiano, Jannie and Hermann Giliomee (eds.), Cape Town: Oxford University Press.

Giliomee, 1995, "Democratization in South Africa", *Political Science Quarterly* 110/1.

Hanf, Theodore, 1989, "The Prospects of Accommodation in Communal Conflicts: A Comparative Analysis", in *Negotiating South Africa's Future*, Giliomee, Hermann and Lawrence Schlemmer (eds.) Halfway House: Southern Books.

Horowitz, Donald L., 1985, *Ethnic Groups in Conflict*, Berkeley: University of California Press.

Horowitz, Donald L., 1991, *A Democratic South Africa?: Constitutional Engineering in a Divided Society*, Cape Town: Oxford University Press.

Huntington, Samuel P., 1993, *The Third Wave: Democratization in the Late Twentieth Century*, Norman: University of Oklahoma Press.

Huntington, Samuel, 1997, "The Erosion of American National Interests", *Foreign Affairs*, September/October.

James, Wilmot, 1996, "Not Many Jacobins in the Box", *Democracy in Action: Journal of the Institute for Democracy in South Africa*, 10/2 15 April.

Johnson, Anthony, 1995, "IFP Boycott 'Bound To Fail'", *Cape Times* 25 April.

Jordan, Pallo, 1988, "The South African Liberation Movement and the Making of a New Nation", *The National Question in South Africa*, van Diepen, Maria (ed.) London: Zed Books.

Jung, Courtney, "Dissertation Outline," (undated paper).

Klandermans, Bert, Marlene Roefs and Johan Olivier, 1995, *Political Protest and Political Transition in South Africa, 1994–1995*. Paper Presented to Annual Meetings of American Sociological Association, Washington DC: 18–23 August.

Kotze, Hennie, 1997, *Culture, Ethnicity and Religion: South African Perceptions of Social Identity*, Occasional Papers, Johannesburg: Konrad Adenauer Stiftung, April.

Kolodziej, Edward, 1995, "Dilemmas of Self-Determination", *Swords and Ploughshares* 9/2.

Krasner, Stephen, 1988, "Sovereignty, an Institutional Perspective", *Comparative Political Studies*, 21/7.

Kymlicka, Will and Wayne Norman, 1994, "Rethinking the Citizen: A Survey of Recent Work", *Ethics* 104.

Lieberman, Evan, 1998, "Paying for 'Us' versus 'Them': Income Tax Compliance in the New South Africa". Unpublished Paper: Cape Town: Institute for Democracy in South Africa.

Lijphart, Arend, 1977, *Democracy in Plural Societies: A Comparative Exploration*, New Haven: Yale University Press.

Lijphart, Arend, 1985, *Power-Sharing in South Africa*, Berkeley: University of California.

Manent, Pierre, 1997, "Democracy Without Nations", *Journal of Democracy*, 8/2.

Mattes, Robert, 1995, *The Election Book: Judgement and Choice in South Africa's 1994 Election*, Idasa: Cape Town.

Mattes, Robert, 1999, "Hypotheses On Identity and Democracy: Community, Regime, Institutions and Citizenship" *Identity? Theory, Politics and History*. Simon Bekker and Rachel Prinsloo (eds.), Pretoria: HSRC.

Neuberger, Benjamin, 1990, "Nationalisms Compared: ANC, IRA and PLO", in *The Elusive Search for Peace: South Africa, Israel and Northern Ireland*, Gagiano, Jannie and Hermann Giliomee (eds.), Cape Town: Oxford University Press.

Olivier, Johan and Rose Ngwane, 1995, "Marching to a Different Tune," *Crime and Conflict*, 4 (Summer).

Rabushka, Alvin and Kenneth A. Shepsle, 1972, *Politics in Plural Societies: A Theory of Political Instability*, Columbus, Oh.: Charles Merrill.

Rustow, Dankwart, 1973, "How Does a Democracy Come into Existence?", in *The Practice of Comparative Politics: A Reader*, Lewis, Paul and David Potter (eds.) London: Open University Press. Reprinted from "Transition to Democracy: Toward a Dynamic Model", *Comparative Politics* 2 (1970).

Rustow, Dankwart, 1990, "Democracy: A Global Revolution?", *Foreign Affairs*.

Sisk, Timothy, 1994, *Democratisation in South Africa*, Princeton: Princeton University Press.

Smith, Anthony, 1993, "The Ethnic Sources of Nationalism", *Survival*, 35/1.

Stremlau, John J., 1997, *A House No Longer Divided: Progress and Prospects for Democratic Peace in South Africa*, New York: Carnegie Corporation of New York.

Tajfel, Henri, 1978, "Social Categorisation, Social Identity, and Social Comparison", in *Differentiation Between Social Groups: Studies in the Social Psychology of Inter-Group Relations*, Tajfel, Henri (ed.) London: Academic Press.

Taylor, Donald M. and Fathali M. Moghaddam, 1994, *Theories of Intergroup Relations: International Social-Psychological Perspectives*, 2d. Ed., Westport, Conn.: Praeger.

Taylor, Donald, 1997, *The Quest for Identity: The Plight of Aboriginal People, Ethnic Minorities, and Generation X*, Montreal: PS Presse.

Van Zyl Slabbert, Frederik and David Welsh, 1979, *South Africa's Options: Strategies for Sharing Power*, Cape Town: David Philip.

Welsh, David, 1994, *Report to the Constitutional Development Services Workshop on "Democratisation as a Prerequisite for Nation-Building"*, 30 August.

Working Group on Democratisation Workshop Report, Democratisation: A Strategic Plan for Global Research on the Transformation and Consolidation of Democracies, 1995, National Science Foundation: Washington DC.

Wright, Harrison, 1977, *The Burden of the Present: Liberal-Radical Controversy over Southern African History*, Cape Town: David Philip.

Strangers at the Cattle Post: State Nationalism and Migrant Identity in Post-Apartheid South Africa

Michael Neocosmos

INTRODUCTION

Migrant labourers from Southern Africa find themselves in a contradictory situation in the emerging socio-political relations of post-apartheid South Africa. Having been celebrated in cultural and academic discourse during the eighties as the most exploited among the oppressed majority, as the bearers of the cross of *the migrant labour system*, the mainstay of apartheid itself, they are now considered by the new state at best as 'foreigners' and at worst as 'illegal immigrants'. Having been, as workers on the mines, at the forefront of the struggles for unionisation and national liberation, their position in the matrix of policies and ideologies developed by the new state on the one hand and by their employers on the other, seems more and more insecure. While the contribution of migrant labour to the building of South African industry especially in the mining sector and the making of a popular South African history, was celebrated as a unique endeavour, now the pressures emanating from the apparently more 'progressive' social democratic ideologues in the state (as opposed to the frankly 'reactionary' utterances of the 'free marketeers'), are pushing in the direction of the abolition of migrant labour itself. Thus Guy Mhone, the Labour Department's Chief Director of Market Policy recently declared:

> More generally, the suggestion is that the migrant labour system needs to be phased out because of its negative economic and social consequences. (*Business Day*, Dec. 24, 1996)

At the same time it can be observed that there seems to be a congruence of views or at least an implicit agreement, between the policy of 'internalisation' by mine management on the one hand, whereby a dramatic shift has been taking place since 1987 towards the recruitment of South African nationals as opposed to foreigners, and that of the abolition of the migrant labour system advocated by the social democrats (such as Guy Mhone) ensconced in Tito Mboweni's labour ministry and in the unions on the other. The 'Southafricanisation' of recruitment is surreptitiously being equated with the popular interest, or put another way, narrow national interest is being equated with democratisation. Clearly this conception of national interest emanates from the state, from above. Migrant labourers are rarely consulted on what they think. It is generally taken for granted that the abolition of the 'migrant labour system' is in their interests as it is so obviously exploitative and socially demeaning. It seems indeed 'obvious to all' that workers, irrespective of their origins, would wish to settle in urban areas with their families and thereby have access to the social, health and housing services available in the new South Africa, rather than perpetuate the appalling conditions of single sex hostels, divided families and cheap and compliant labour from unproductive rural areas.

Yet the apparent obviousness of social relations is often only skin deep, and usually indicates misunderstanding as illustrated by the following account. As part of the imputed process of 'democratisation' of the labour market, mineworkers from the Southern African Customs Union (SACU)[274] countries have been offered the opportunity to acquire a permanent South African residence permit leading to full citizenship. This benefit is so attractive to the region's unemployed (as well as to many among the middle class) that they are often prepared to brave razor wire fencing, the wild animals of the Kruger Park and the South African police, to enter the country! It is most surprising therefore to discover that in Lesotho, the single most important provider of 'foreign' migrant labourers to South Africa, between 70 and 80 per cent of miners interviewed in a number of recent surveys, asserted that they refused this offer of settling in South

---

274. The Southern African Customs Union includes South Africa, Botswana, Lesotho, Swaziland and Namibia.

Africa. Only a small minority of Basotho miners were concerned to take up the offer, even after the deadline was extended. Is this to be seen as an effect of a romantic attachment to Sesotho culture by alienated miners—i.e. an aspect of a miner's national identity—as some assert? Or is it simply to be put down to 'false consciousness' of a class still linked to rural areas? Or is this reaction objectively founded on a rational conception of miners' own material interests? If the latter, what could such material interests consist of in an 'unviable labour reserve economy' like that of Lesotho?

This paper is intended as a discussion of this apparent paradox. I shall be concerned with bringing out some of the contradictions between South African state nationalism on the one hand, and popular concerns on the other, and thus with problematizing some aspects of what is currently meant by democracy in the new South Africa. In order to do this, it is important first to situate the currently dominant practices of 'nation-building' in their historical context of the past twenty years in South Africa. This context is both ideological and political.

THE IDEOLOGICAL CONTEXT: NATIONALIST DISCOURSE IN
RECENT SOUTH AFRICAN HISTORY

The dominant conception of national oppression in recent South African history was one which saw the racial oppression of the majority as intimately linked with the interests of capital. This view was underpinned by a sophisticated political economy for which the link between apartheid (national oppression) on the one hand and capitalism on the other was the existence of a working class.

Basically, the dominant political economic discourse in Southern Africa had stressed the industrialisation of South Africa and the corresponding formation of a working class through a process of the proletarianisation of the peasantry from the rural peripheries from the late nineteenth century to the present (a similar process on a smaller scale was deemed to have occurred in Zimbabwe). Simply put, this approach visualised the character of the region from both an urban and an economic perspective. The urban perspective maintained that rural-urban migration was a sign not only of temporary but of soon to be permanent proletarian status for a majority of the region's peasants. The economic perspective stressed that only in the urban industrial areas of South Africa were production relations to be found. Rural areas were simply seen as 'dormitory areas', bereft of production relations, classes or any contradictions (other than 'tribal' ones). The politics of these regions and countries in southern Africa were therefore simply seen as reflections of events in the South African metropolitan centres.[275]

At the same time, 'apartheid' was explained as a form of labour control, the apogee of so many forms of labour control historically present in South Africa (from slavery to indentured labour to labour tenancy). It was a mechanism for providing super-exploited cheap labour for white capital in the interests of an expansive industrialisation process under pressure from popular struggles (Wolpe, 1972). The main component of this mechanism was the 'migrant labour system' in which the gradual impoverishment of the rural hinterland provided the conditions for a compliant 'reserve army of labour'.

A number of consequences followed from this perspective. Given the absence of contradictions at the rural periphery the population of those countries and regions was seen as homogeneous while a simple reason was provided for migration, namely the impoverishment of the peasantry and labour reserve nature of the rural economies. In addition, no ways were found to explain the state and politics in these areas other than in simple technical or conspiratorial terms (Neocosmos, 1987, 1993a, 1993b). This was the necessary result of the imputed absence of production relations in those areas. The state ended up being seen as an external imposition (from South Africa). Local people were given no role to play in their own histories. At the same time in South Africa itself, apartheid was simply accounted for in economic terms, as a system of labour control based primarily on migrant labour, instituted simply because it was 'in the interests of South African capital' (Wolpe, 1972) or so intertwined with capitalism itself that the demise of the one could only mean the collapse of the

---

[275]. The writings which expressed this perspective are numerous, they include the works of Bundy, Legassick, Arrighi, Saul, Wolpe *inter alia*. I have evaluated this perspective elsewhere; Neocosmos (1993a).

other (Saul and Gelb, 1986). Thus, because the region was seen as composed overwhelmingly of proletarians or proletarians to be, socialism was visualised as inevitable and 'just around the corner'. For example:

> In our country—more than in any other part of the oppressed world—it is inconceivable for liberation to have meaning without a return of the wealth of the land to the people as a whole. It is therefore a fundamental feature of our strategy that victory must embrace more than formal political democracy. To allow the existing economic forces to retain their interests intact is to feed the root of racial supremacy and does not represent even the shadow of liberation. (ANC, 1969:32-3; see also Slovo, 1976:139ff)

Under these circumstances, a host of crucial processes for the region were ignored and/or left unexplained. These included the differentiation of the oppressed South African population along class and gender ethnic lines *inter alia*, the differentiation of rural dwellers (including worker-peasants) and possibilities of accumulation among the people, the reproduction of petty-commodity production (rural or urban), the fact that labour migration might be a source of accumulation for peasants, the specificity of (popular) politics and state form in the countries of the periphery as well as the form of state rule during the apartheid and post-apartheid periods (Neocosmos, 1993a; Mamdani, 1996). Discussions of the state in South Africa (much as in the immediate post-independence period in Zimbabwe) have been reduced to assessments of policy questions (Neocosmos, 1996a). Finally, it has not always been recognised that the people of the region could show extreme inventiveness in struggle, in the making of their own histories. This has now given use to assertions that even the character of the struggles of the 1980s simply resulted from decisions taken at the leadership level of the ANC (e.g. Mbeki, 1996).

The effect of this discourse which was the central ideological pillar of the nationalist perspective in the region, was thus to place a major obstacle in the way of the understanding of politics in general and democratic politics in particular. Only very gradually is this obstacle starting to be contested. On the other hand, the positive side of this economistic nationalist perspective was that, as the emphasis was on the proletarianisation of labour in general, no distinction was ever drawn between the ethnic or nationality origins of that labour.

Migrant labour was migrant labour, irrespective of where it came from. Thus it was often asserted that labour from throughout the region had "contributed to building South African industry". At the same time the process of regional migration was viewed exclusively in negative terms, as the 'migrant labour system' was seen as the *sine qua non* of apartheid. This followed because apartheid as we have noted, was understood primarily as a form of labour control and not as a form of state. As we shall see below, this means that for this perspective, the demise of apartheid must entail the demise of the migrant labour system.

At the same time, this was combined in nationalist discourse with a view which tended to see ethnicity in a blanket way as reactionary, backward-looking, atavistic, and generally as a conspiracy by White employers (e.g. on the mines) and by the apartheid 'regime' more broadly, to divide and control the oppressed in general and the working-class in particular.[276] It was seen as somehow 'visited from the outside' on an unsuspecting population, as 'invented' to use Ranger's expression, and not produced from within rural production relations and rural political relations of domination (Neocosmos, 1995). In broad terms therefore, the basic theory provided little in terms of a perspective to understand questions of ethnicity, nationality and citizenship. This was to be developed in practice only by the mass movement of the 1980s in so far as the struggle for a 'new nation' in South Africa was concerned as we shall see below. In addition, no way was devised at the level of theory to politically unify the various national or ethnic components of a working class which was assumed to be already given as a unity.[277] The only arena in which it was seen as important to overcome ethnic and nationality divisions was at the workplace itself, through trade union organisation to confront employers. Outside the workplace, the issue of ethnicity or nationality differences was simply seen as resolved by ANC membership/support (which was itself supposedly sufficiently unifying).

---

276. This position is still adhered to by the National Union of Mineworkers, NUM, for example, an organisation which organises mineworkers—i.e. overwhelmingly migrant labour—and which has to confront periodic 'ethnic clashes' on the mines.
277. Constant references to *the* (Black) South African working-class testify to this, see for example, Neocosmos, 1996b.

As I have noted, the basic argument of this nationalist political economy on which everything else hinged was a conception of the linear proletarianisation of the peasantry. This is supposed to have taken place initially from the 1890s to the 1930s so that rural urban migration today is understood as taking place exclusively for the purposes of reproduction. Amounting body of evidence from the rural peripheries of the region, however, points to the fact that rural producers are differentiated and that even in extreme cases of 'labour reserve economies' such as Lesotho, simple as well as expanded reproduction (accumulation) among petty-commodity producers is possible and has been taking place for some time (Phimister, 1986; Hermele, 1988; Neocosmos, 1987, 1993a, 1993b; Johnston, 1996; Pae, 1992).

However, the evidence of differentiation among petty producers in the rural peripheries from which migration originates has largely been ignored by nationalist discourse as it had been in the 1980s. The parameters of this nationalist political economy have had consequences in the post-apartheid period as the 'migrant labour system' has come to be re-examined. Some of these can be seen in a recent article by Davies and Head (1995), but are also replicated in statements by various government commissions and by officials of various ministries.

Taking a policy perspective, Davies and Head are concerned to tackle the twin issues of the South African "democratic government" showing commitment to "reconstructing regional relations on new lines" on the one hand, and the threat apparently posed by escalating clandestine migration to such restructuring along "equitable and mutually beneficial" lines on the other. The perspective taken by long time ANC members which informs the analysis, is exclusively one of state policy concerns regarding regional international relations between states/countries (*not peoples*). No indication is given that the orientation of states on the one hand and migrants on the other, regarding these issues may differ; rather, the perspective is one which seeks to outline background trends and emphasises the concerns of the states of the region which are "bound to recur as an item in bilateral or multilateral negotiations" (Davies and Head, 1995:439).

Apparently, in terms of numbers, legal migration to the mines is no longer the main form of migration to South Africa and is currently being overtaken by the numbers involved in clandestine migration. Although Davies and Head are careful to note that there are no reliable figures on clandestine migration (figures are being bandied about in the South African state and press for propagandistic purposes, as we shall see below), they note that the only reliable figures are those for numbers of deportations which only assess the tip of the iceberg in so far as 'illegal immigrants' are concerned. These indicate that "half as many people were deported from South Africa in 1992 as there were citizens of neighbouring countries working legally in the mining industry" (Davies and Head, 1995:440).

Where legally recruited mine labour is concerned, Davies and Head stress that the decline—especially since 1987—in recruitment of 'foreign' mineworkers continues to accelerate. Thus:

> the average number of SADC citizens employed on gold and coal mines owned by members of the South African Chamber of Mines was 71,224 less in 1993 than it was in 1986—a figure equivalent to almost a third of the total number of SADC citizens employed in 1986...The number of men employed from Lesotho on the gold mines reached an all-time high of 105,506 in 1987. In 1993 the figure stood at 79,530. The reduction of Basotho labour on Chamber-affiliated coal mines is even more dramatic. Whereas in 1981 on average 12,314 men were employed in 1993 only one quarter of that number, 3,186 were employed. (Davies and Head, 1995:442)[*]

The main reasons for this trend are the cheaper cost of local labour, the decline in employment due to mechanisation in the mines, and presumably the substantial nationalist pressures emanating from the post-apartheid state (which the authors ignore). On the other hand this is slightly tempered by the industry's unwillingness to be dependent on one source of supply in case of strikes (Davies and Head, 1995:441). In so far as 'illegal immigrants' to South Africa are concerned, the authors summarise the existing information as follows:

---

[*] SADC, the Southern African Development Community, in 1995 included Angola, Botswana, Lesotho, Malawi, Mozambique, Namibia, South Africa, Swaziland, Tanzania, Zambia, and Zimbabwe. Mauritius joined in August 1995.

> More than one citizen of a SADC member country was deported in 1993 as an 'illegal immigrant' for every two employed legally in the mining industry.
> The number of legal migrants employed in the mining industry in 1993 was equivalent to just over 5 per cent of the three million 'illegal immigrants' estimated to be living in South Africa.
> In the case of Mozambicans, the number of deportations was equivalent to more than one and a half times the number of workers legally employed in the mining industry, who made up less than 2 per cent of the total number of the 2.2 million Mozambicans thought to be in South Africa. (Davies and Head, 1995:445)

For the authors, 'the migrant labour system' is simply an aspect of apartheid and is consequently viewed negatively as a historical way of providing (super-)exploited labour, so it follows that it must be discontinued. At the same time, they argue that the decline in employment of foreign labour in South Africa is a long term trend which has been taking place "irrespective of the [post-apartheid] government's wishes" and that this restructuring of the labour force has resulted "from the breakdown of apartheid and [the] beginnings of a transition to democracy" (Davies and Head, 1995:448).[278] As a result of this 'democratisation' of economic forces:

> a permanent labour force—hired at the gates of the mine irrespective of where it actually comes from—seems likely to emerge in South Africa's mines as a result of a combination of economic and political factors related to the dismantlement of apartheid and independent of the new government's thinking on the question. These processes were already underway by the mid-1980s. There is every reason to believe that they will now be accelerated. (Davies and Head, 1995:449)

The authors note that according to estimates by the Chamber of Mines itself, its half a million employees support 3.1 million family members so that each retrenchment of a legally employed miner "potentially affects the livelihood of anything up to sixteen people" (Davies and Head, 1995:450). Thus, given the lack of employment opportunities in

---

278. As from the perspective of the authors, apartheid is a form of labour control, and a mechanism for the provision of cheap labour for South African capital, the gradually increasing cost of migrant labour for this same capital is seen as an indication of democratisation. The interests of capital rather than those of the working people are what ultimately seem to determine whether apartheid or democracy exists. For a detailed critique of this and allied conceptions, see Neocosmos, 1996b. The most useful recommendation Davies and Head make for reducing the employment of cheap labour, is the enactment of minimum wage legislation in the mining industry.

the 'rural peripheries', the likely outcome will be increased pressure for families to migrate clandestinely to South Africa. "In other words, there could be a multiplier relationship between loss of mine employment and clandestine migration". The conclusion the authors arrive at is that "mine management should be pressured to take on its historic responsibility towards the supplier states and invest significantly in large job creation schemes" (Davies and Head, 1995:450).

First, it is worth noting the extent to which nationalist discourse in South Africa dovetails nicely with economic liberalism (an abstractly 'free' labour market is seen as democratic, while the recruitment of migrant labour is not) and how labour recruitment from 'home' (South Africa) is equated with a democratic practice, while recruitment of foreign labour through 'the migrant labour system' is visualised as reactionary, thus unconsciously feeding the prejudices of South African petty-chauvinism.[279] Recent statements from ANC liberals/social democrats make it plain that human rights are largely inapplicable to foreigners in general and illegal immigrants in particular:

> "There are very few countries in the world which would extend human rights to non-citizens" [said Lockey]...Lockey also accepts the law—considered unconstitutional by many lawyers—which permits suspected illegal aliens to be detained without trial for 30 days. "What else can we do?, he asks. (ANC MP Desmond Lockey, Chairman, Parliamentary Portfolio Committee on Home Affairs, cited in *Mail and Guardian* Vol. 12 No. 23, June 7–13, 1996)

Second, it is also worthwhile considering the fact that Davies and Head throughout their article absolve the new state in South Africa from any responsibility regarding the democratisation of migrancy or the people who helped it defeat apartheid in the first place. Rather, the objective seems to be to divert all responsibility towards mining

---

279. For Davies and Head, "the migrant labour system has long been criticised as both exploitative and an impediment to growth and development in 'labour reserve' areas" (op.cit.: 448). While the first assertion is arguably true (although the original formulation from the 1970s that migrant labour was 'super-exploited' was more accurate as it was paid below value), the latter is certainly not so. The wages which peasants earn from migrating enable them not only to survive but also to reproduce themselves as petty-commodity producers as well as to accumulate (see First, 1983; Neocosmos, 1987, 1993a, 1993b; Johnston, 1996). It seems sad to have to repeat what was established over ten years ago, but the migrant peasantry in the 'labour reserve areas' is not uniformly impoverished but rather differentiated.

capital and to call for it to invest in job-creation schemes irrespective of their profitability (it is generally agreed that the returns on productive investment are low in the rural areas of the region). Presumably the fact, constantly repeated by this nationalist discourse in the 1980s, that migrant labour from the whole region built South African industry is now of little consequence. At the same time, the authors fail to consider the reasons for migration from rural areas other than their apparent economic stagnation. These objectively include the need to reproduce household production at home as well as endeavours to make possible accumulation (although not necessarily in arable agriculture). Davies and Head's urbanist and economistic assumptions, make them unable to visualise migration from the perspective of the rural people. Finally, the change in recruitment patterns from a reliance on migrant labour to a concentration on urbanised local labour has not been unique to mining. It is arguably part of the same trend which had affected other sectors such as the manufacturing industry in the early 1980s, and to which the unions failed to respond adequately (Mamdani, 1996:243–55). In that earlier case migrants were marginalised from the unions which became dominated by the fully urbanised; it seems that the same trend is being replicated in the mining industry today.

For Davies and Head, although the 'internalisation' of migrant labour is an inevitable process as it is an aspect of the 'democratisation' of economic relations which predates the new South Africa, the speed of this process should be slowed down in order to cushion its effects on the peripheral economies of the region, and reduce the pressures for clandestine migration. They stress that retrenchments will have multiplier effects on illegal migrancy to South Africa and argue that improving point-of-origin conditions will reduce migrancy. However, it must be stressed that it is the reinvestment of migrant labour earnings which has provided in the past one of the main conditions for rural economic reproduction as well as the possibilities for accumulation from below; this has been the case especially as there has been no state investment in petty-agriculture throughout the region. There is no reason to suppose that its effects have changed so that in the present post-apartheid period, migrant remittances are not simply necessities for survival but also investments for accumulation from below, for popular development. There is little evidence that business investments in such areas—even if they were profitable—would provide any substitute for petty-commodity production. The Lesotho Highlands water project is an evident testament to that.

Davies and Head's concerns seem primarily to be those of politicians removed from their constituents; the social realities of life of the working people do not seem to be elucidated through analysing those conditions themselves. Yet this was not always the case in South Africa. In the 1980s there was a much closer relationship between the oppressed people and their political representatives which also gave rise to a different conception of 'the nation'. The nature of this conception and its transformation into a different state nationalism in the 1990s will now be briefly assessed.

THE POLITICAL CONTEXT: FROM POPULAR NATIONALISM TO STATE NATIONALISM IN RECENT SOUTH AFRICAN HISTORY

As in the rest of Africa where a clear distinction could be witnessed during the independence process between a popular form of nationalism and state nationalism, South Africa has, over the past two decades, experienced a transition from the dominance of popular politics and popular nationalism in the eighties, to that of state politics and its attendant state-based and state-propagated nationalism in the nineties (Neocosmos, 1996a).

Within the popular-nationalist politics of the 1980s one could see at least two ideological-political trends which ebbed and flowed as the struggle progressed. One was basically economistic, statist and often typified by the substituting of organisational imperatives for popular self-activity, another was popular and democratic. These two trends were not always clearly demarcated from each other and their contra dictions and struggle were not always apparent.

Central to the latter trend which gave rise to the demand for 'people's power', was a specific conception of citizenship and nationhood which exhibited two main components. The first was an actively participatory conception of citizenship in which politics became the day to day business of ordinary people, in which civil society organisations were politicised, and *thereby inaugurated a popular realm of political society outside the state*. The second aspect was a specific inclusiveness in which citizenship was to have a non-racial and not simply a multi-racial character. Both these components were to be found to a greater or lesser degree within the discourse and practices of township and trade union organisations. They never existed in isolation, however, and had to struggle to assert themselves against authoritarian and generally undemocratic practices within the same organisations—as noted above. The fact that they failed to consistently dominate within the popular movement does not decrease their importance from the perspective of understanding the struggles over citizenship and nationhood in South Africa and the region.

The participatory form of citizenship developed in the 1980s was particularly apparent in the 'people's power' movement which attempted, successfully for a period, to develop popular control of local government, of schooling and of popular justice in urban townships. Marx (1992:167) notes that in 1987, 43 per cent of the inhabitants of Soweto, for example, reported the existence of street and area committees in their neighbourhoods. These committees took up grassroots issues as well as organised the resistance to, and direct confrontation with the apartheid state. According to Murphy Morobe, one of the leaders of the movement writing at the time:

> The key to a democratic system lies in being able to say that the people in our country can not only vote for a representative of their choice, but also feel that they have some direct control over where and how they live, eat, sleep, work, how they get to work, how they and their children are educated, what the content of that education is, and that these things are not done for them by the government of the day, but [by] the people themselves. (Morobe, 1987:82)

The manner in which this popular movement demarcated its members ('the people' or 'the nation') from the oppressive state, is also worthy of note. The notion of 'non-racialism' was a way of characterising the ideology of the movement as well as the nature of the state which was being fought for. Originally inherited from Black Consciousness discourse which used the term 'Black' to refer to all oppressed racial groups in South Africa, 'non-racialism' was adapted by the UDF to include Whites who supported the struggle. This struggle was visualised as uniting into a national opposition the disparate groups which the apartheid state divided, hence the main slogan of the UDF: "UDF Unites, Apartheid Divides!". One important aspect of non-racialism was the fact that rather than distinguishing 'the people' or 'the oppressors' on racial grounds, it did so by demarcating on political grounds: popular-democrats from anti-democrats. The former were those who supported change 'from below', the latter those who proposed some form of 'tinkering from above' and who had by this period, lost the confidence of the majority. Democrats were all those who opposed 'minority rule' and supported 'majority rule' through popular democracy. In the words of a UDF discussion document from 1986:

> The essential *dividing* line that we should promote is between supporters of *minority rule and majority rule*. The common ground between the Botha (sic), the PFP [Popular Federal Party, the main White, big business-backed liberal opposition at the time] leadership and big business is that they all seek solutions within the framework of adapting minority rule. Although they differ fundamentally on who to involve in negotiation and how much adaptation is necessary, these elements all agree that the system must be changed from the top down, with the solutions being decided over the heads of the people. All those who accept the right of the people to determine the process of change are allies of the people and part of the NDS [National Democratic Struggle]. (UDF Cape Town Area Committee, 1986:10)

This meant that the conducting of the popular struggle should also be 'non-racial'. Such a position was possible precisely because the social movement was not an elite movement and because White 'progressives' (to use the jargon of the time) contributed invaluable work both in the trade unions as well as the UDF, thus becoming known and appreciated by the people of the townships. It served to divide a minority of White democrats from White racists (while forcing the uncommitted to commit themselves), in the same way as affiliation to popular organisations divided Blacks between collaborators with the state (so-called 'sell-outs') and the majority of the oppressed.[280]

---

280. A similar process was debated at length in relation to the 'Indian community' and the formation of the Transvaal Indian Congress, but interestingly enough not in relation to 'Coloureds', although the UDF's non-racialism was criticised as phoney by vari-

Similar democratic aspects also characterise the "Call for National Unity against Apartheid and the Emergency" by the UDF in August 1986, for example. The discussion documents surrounding this call stress emphatically: "it is essential that the call is not simply for unity at the top. We must ensure a way to ensure contact and planning on the ground, so that membership of different organisations may grow closer together". At the same time they noted that the timing of the call was "delayed to give COSATU affiliates time for thorough discussion—this is crucial, as the leadership of the call must reflect the people's unity right from the start".[281] The contrast between such sentiments and the operations of the post-apartheid government are striking. When is it thought appropriate today to engage in mass popular debate before stating policy? If such debate takes place, it does so at the level of leadership alone and within the confines of state apparatuses.

Thus, these attempts to create the unity of a 'new nation' during a period when struggles were undertaken as much to define the character of popular politics as they were to oppose the apartheid state, can be contrasted with the attempts in the 1990s to do so 'from above' via 'nation-building' and its components of 'reconciliation', the Reconstruction and Development Programme and 'affirmative action'. In actual fact, the much maligned populist character of nationalist discourse in the 1980s allowed for the development of genuine forms of popular democracy; unfortunately, such popular initiatives were to be systematically precluded by the statism of nationalist discourse in the 1990s, as the state gradually arrogated to itself the monopoly of the nationalist project—'liberation'.

As noted above, both township and trade union struggles in the South Africa of the 1980s developed a popular conception of the nation which had two components: first a notion of citizenship founded on the active participation in politics of ordinary people, and second a concept of unity based on non-racialism. What was missing from this conception however was a notion of citizenship founded on

---

ous coloured organisations such as the Unity Movement and the Cape Action League for example.
281. See United Democratic Front Cape Town Area Committee, 1986b:1; United Democratic Front National Office, 1986.

place of work rather than descent. Such a conception was not developed systematically in South Africa in particular and this showed, as Mamdani (1996: chapter 7) has pointed out in the exclusion of migrant workers in particular and the countryside in general, from the concept of community which the urban movement adhered to.

This point is important and should be expanded. As both the township and union movements faced the wrath of the state towards the end of the 1980s, they gradually lost the characteristics associated with popular control, and came to respond more and more to directives from above. The loss of powers of local shop-steward committees for example was accompanied by a dominant trend towards corporatism in the 1990s, while civics dropped their political role in favour of the ANC on the latter's unbanning. The women's and youth organisations were incorporated into the ANC (Neocosmos, 1996a). Concurrently, the dominant political discourse became more and more defined by a leadership not always closely linked to the rank and file and informed by popular experience. At the same time, neither the popular urban movement nor the ANC in exile had developed a link between the rural and urban sectors of the country in their political programmes.

The result of all these factors was the uncritical adherence to an ideological perspective in which migrants were seen simply as workers, and migrant labour was seen solely as a 'system' devised by apartheid to acquire cheap labour for White capitalists. While there was some truth in this nationalist perspective, it remained partial and dominated by the economistic paradigm discussed above. Its one-sided emphasis on proletarianisation and capitalism meant that it could not understand the fact that migrant labourers were only half workers and that as peasants, they might draw some benefits from the migrant labour system.

This can be understood clearly if we realise that not all who migrate for employment in South Africa (mines etc.) do so for their subsistence or survival. A significant proportion migrate in order to acquire funds for their reproduction as middle peasants (First, 1983), and also for purposes of accumulation in agricultural, merchant, transport or other economic activities (Neocosmos, 1987, 1993a, 1993b; Johnston, 1996). It follows from this that not all migrants wish to be settled in urban areas nor do they wish to see the 'migrant labour system' abolished, male hostels destroyed and family housing being put up in their place. In fact Mamdani shows clearly that this policy which the ANC and COSATU pursued vigorously in the early 1990s was instrumental in driving migrants from Kwazulu-Natal into the arms of a political organisation based on mobilising ethnic nationalism—Inkatha (Mamdani, 1996: chapter 7).

The National Union of Mineworkers (NUM) (as well as the recent Presidential Commission on a Labour Market) is currently following a similar form of reasoning in raising the issue of an offer of permanent residence followed by full rights of South African citizenship to Basotho miners with many years of labour in South Africa. While seemingly 'progressive' and democratic, such an offer does not take the wishes of migrants themselves into account, and fails to look at the issue as one of providing rights for all workers, native and foreign, and not only to citizens. Basotho miners would have to lose access to their Lesotho citizenship as well as to their resources in Lesotho in order to acquire South African citizenship.

Nationalist politics in so far as it has affected popular organisations in the post-1990 period in South Africa has had two fundamental characteristics: i) the depoliticisation of popular organisations and the corresponding loss of democratic control by rank and file members within them, so that they no longer reflect popular concerns and culture (politics is now the monopoly of the party of nationalism, the ANC) and, ii) their repoliticisation as they gradually became part of a state corporatist project. The former process was finally completed by 1992 as civic organisations and trade unions withdrew from the political arena in favour of the ANC. The latter is finally being consolidated as either unrepresentative (the National Women's Coalition) or politically emasculated organisations (SANCO and COSATU) have tied themselves to a formal 'alliance' with the ANC and to bargaining structures such as NEDLAC (National Economic and Development Labour Council, the successor to the National Economic Forum) along with the state and employers organisations (Neocosmos, 1996a, 1996b).

This move towards (social democratic) corporatism was accompanied by a top down conception of development (with an admittedly populist gloss) which found expression in the RDP (Reconstruction and Development Programme) (Neocosmos, 1996b). This corporatism, state-induced development, along with state controlled 'reconciliation' and 'affirmative action' programmes, form the main pillars of the post-apartheid state process of 'nation-building'. As in the rest of Africa after independence, the overall process has been one where the popular forces which exploded in the 1980s have been systematically defeated, and replaced by a *statist* process of development and nation-building albeit within a multiparty system (Neocosmos, 1996a). The main economic debate in South Africa (there is no real political debate) is being conducted between orthodox statist (social democratic) developmentalism and neo-classical liberalism (the third popular democratic alternative no longer exists). The former is by far the weaker partner in the debate. A brief example concerning the RDP should illustrate this.

Following the experience of other African countries, 'development' in South Africa was understood by the ANC in particular in a top-down way, along with what can be best described as a 'participatory component'. It is this contradictory combination of bureaucratic-statist (public or private sector) 'leadership' and populist 'participation', finding expression in corporatism, which provides the parameters of the 'debate' on the Reconstruction and Development Programme. This debate now concerns the relative role of the state and that of the market in the process. As the people were never considered as independently active components of the process, the choice ends up being between two forms of statist development: state-led or market-led (usually with some participation by so-called NGOs which are not usually elected by the people and are, in any case, substitutes for state institutions).

While the arguments of neo-classical economics, especially as institutionalised in the international financial institutions, have stressed the 'freedom' of the market in the process of development, those of the opposing position, that of 'social democratic statist developmentalism' which is now clearly on the retreat and in a subordinate position within state and business structures, stressed the centrality of state intervention in redressing historical grievances and in the general equalisation of access to resources and incomes as a prelude to, or concomitant of, economic growth. The two main documents in which this latter position was elaborated were the MERG (Macro-Economic Research Group) document of 1993 and the Reconstruction and Development (RDP) 'base document' of 1994. In the RDP document in particular, which is largely written along the lines of 'Five Year Development Plan' documents of the post-independence period in Africa (i.e. full of abstract state-directed 'good intentions' but short on concrete programmes, the main effect of which was largely propagandistic) the combination of statism and populism characteristic of the ANC is amply evident. Thus the document rightly notes that:

> Our history has been a bitter one dominated by colonialism, racism, apartheid, sexism and repressive labour policies. The result is that poverty and degradation exist side by side with modern cities and a developed mining, industrial and commercial infrastructure. Our income distribution is racially distorted and ranks as one of the most unequal in the world—lavish wealth and abject poverty characterise our society. (ANC, 1994:2)

It continues to warn that: "without thoroughgoing democratisation, the whole effort to reconstruct and develop will lose momentum", and that the state itself must foster "representative, participatory and direct democracy" (ANC, 1994:120). This "fostering" we are told, should be undertaken "in partnership with civil society on the basis of informed and empowered citizens (e.g. the various sectoral forums like the National Economic Forum)" (ANC, 1994:121). So in brief, the idea is for the state to develop the democracy necessary for 'popular' development through the (state-controlled) corporatist institutions already referred to. Needless to say such 'popular participation' has been up to now non-existent while the accent has been on 'delivery' (usually of infrastructure) to a passive populace.[282]

Recently, the arguments of neo-classical economics have acquired so much dominance within the state, that advocates of the social democratic 'developmentalist statist' (orthodox statist) position have been complaining that popular concerns have been all but left out of

---

[282]. A recent article which reviews the progress of corporatism with reference to NEDLAC in particular, argues correctly that: "There is a strong danger that the incorporation of 'community groups' into Nedlac or other forums will serve not to empower civil society but to bureaucratise it" (Friedman and Reitzes, 1996:66).

the equation. Thus, Adelzadeh and Padayachee (1994) have outlined the distance between the original *RDP 'base document'* and the state legislative *RDP White paper*, pointing out the lack of continuity between the two, the latter being uniformly governed by the 'logic of the market' so that:

> while some of the individual principles, policies and commitments are sound, reconstruction, development, growth and redistribution (along the lines set out in the Base Document Vision) has been significantly changed. The current White Paper is incoherent and fragmented. The possibility of retrieving the earlier vision is eroded daily in the cut and thrust of 'reconciliation' and of compromise-making politics within the GNU. This is evident too in the irresolute style characterising negotiations with international financial agencies and representatives of organised domestic (mainly white) capital, and by the dramatic decline in the significance which top policy-makers appear to be according to the trade unions, civics and the tripartite developmental forums, as partners in economic-policy making (Adelzadeh and Padayachee, 1994:15).

Thus bemoaning the gradual defeat of the Left-statist project associated with the original RDP "vision", the authors fail to analyse the reasons for such a defeat and merely restrict themselves to measuring the distance between the two "visions" of growth. Evidently, the rapidity of the replacement of the initial 'state-developmentalist vision' of the ANC and its supporters on the Left, by a kind of 'structural adjustment' package clearly expressed in the recent (1996) "Growth Employment and Redistribution (GEAR)" document which has finally supplanted the RDP, requires some explanation. Such an explanation would surely need to provide *inter alia* an examination of the fundamental *similarities* and *continuities* between the two sides of the 'state versus market debate' which Adelzadeh and Padayachee ignore. A number of central points which are regularly overlooked in the debate can profitably be stressed of which the most important is perhaps that in the debate between state and market, between 'state developmentalism' and 'market-led growth', the most important factor, namely 'the people', is left out. For neither position in whatever variant are the working people—who are deemed by both positions to be the main beneficiaries of growth and development—given an *independent* role to play either in development or indeed in the wider political process which makes it possible. For 'economic liberalism' the market *is* the people so that the expression 'people-driven' for example, is simply used as a synonym for 'market-driven'. For 'statist developmentalism', the state and/or party itself is substituted for the people as not only does it know what is best for them, it also acts on their behalf. This position which until recently had been dominant in the state in Africa, is clearly captured in the identification of the *nation* with the *state* as in the notion of the "nation-state"; in such a perspective, it is the state and not the people which constitutes "the nation" (Olukoshi and Laakso, 1996).

In the case of South Africa, the statism of 'radical' development thinking has been apparent in the setting up of a complex corporatist structure whereby erstwhile people's organisations have either been systematically collapsed into the party and unrepresentative state organisations set up in their place (as with women and youth organisations), or incorporated into state structures at both national and local level (e.g. civics and trade unions). It is noteworthy that Adelzadeh and Padayachee actually bemoan in the above quotation, the fact that the state is showing a tendency to ignore its own corporatist structures, and suggest this as a sign of defeat for the Left. It is indeed sad, and, more importantly, a major reason for its defeat, that the 'vision' of the South African Left has been so limited by statism.

Interestingly for both 'development visions', it is accumulation among ordinary working people (accumulation 'from below'), which is ostensibly the principal concern of 'development'. Yet the people only feature in so far as we are told that 'communities' should 'identify their needs' to government through their representatives in local state structures ('development forums', local councils, 'traditional' authorities, civics, or unelected NGOs), and the government and/or the private sector will then 'deliver' roads, electricity, water or whatever other infrastructure is deemed necessary. Therefore the issue is not one of investment in popular initiative, nor for that matter is it about creating the conditions for the people themselves to mobilise openly and freely around development issues. Whether therefore it is the government or the market which is supposed to 'deliver', the common approach is ultimately 'top-down'; it is an approach which demobilises and disempowers the people as it ultimately treats them as passive recipients of state or White *largesse*.

This example of the construction of the RDP in South Africa provides a picture of the context to the 'debates' surrounding citizenship and nationhood in this country. These have overwhelmingly taken place within the confines of state institutions and have so far taken the perspective of 'illegal immigrants' being a 'problem' for the state. In June 1996 it was reported that in the South African Parliament:

> politicians from all parties lashed out at illegal immigrants...calling them a threat to the Reconstruction and Development Programme, a drain on South Africa's resources, and branding them potential criminals, drug smugglers and murderers. (*Mail and Guardian*, June 7–13, 1996)

While the crassness of politicians can always be blamed for raising chauvinistic hysteria, the fact that these outbursts were not confined to politicians from any one party, along with the evidence of petty chauvinism on the streets of major South African cities (mainly directed at the informal sector), and the utterances of not very serious newspapers, leads one to the conclusion that there is a strong latent chauvinistic trend in South Africa at the moment which could easily be activated at will by unscrupulous politicians. Unreliable figures concerning 'illegal migration' have been shamelessly bandied around in parliament, various sources mentioning figures between 2.5 and 8.5 million people (*Mail and Guardian*, June 7–13, 1996). More sober minds, however, note that it is not known "whether it is the immigrants themselves who are a drain on resources or whether it is the implementation of bad policy which is costing the taxpayer" (*Mail and Guardian*, June 7–13, 1996). What is perhaps more worrying is the attitude of ANC spokespersons such as Desmond Lockey who stress that there is nothing exceptional about denying non-citizens their rights including detaining them without trial for 80 days. At the same time this process is in contradiction to the constitution which only denies voting and trading rights to foreigners and not other rights.

The government attempted to reduce the 'problem' by giving citizenship rights to immigrants from the Southern African Development Community (SADC) countries who can prove that they have lived in South Africa for longer than five years, have jobs or are married to a South African and have no criminal record. The closing date for this one-off "indemnity" was September 1996 and the offer seems to have been directly determined by the perceived need to 'gradually' scrap the 'migrant labour system'. It is important to note this episode because it shows the context within which the recent offer of permanent residence to migrant miners has been made. In fact the first time this idea was made public was just before the local elections of October 1995, when all mineworkers who had entered the country before 13 June 1986 and who had been issued with temporary voting cards to vote during the April 1994 elections, were allowed to apply for permanent residence in South Africa. In other words the normal stipulations of the Aliens Control Act were waived in their case (Department of Home Affairs Circular number 9 of 1995). By March 1997, 26,440 miners had applied for exemptions and a further 20,924 were being processed, a total of 47,364 from an estimated eligible population of around 130,000. The breakdown by nationality included: 8,608 from Mozambique, 31,481 from Lesotho, 3,228 from Swaziland, 3,538 from Botswana and 449 from Malawi (Crush, 1997a). More recent figures suggest that the total number of miners finally granted permanent residence amounted to 50,692 (James, 1997:16), with Lesotho having more than twice the total number of applicants from elsewhere.

A further notice from the Department of Home Affairs recently provided for exemption from the permanent residence conditions for those SADC citizens who can prove continuous residence in RSA from July 1 1991 (and can prove marriage to a South African citizen, engaged in productive activity in the country or have dependent children resident there). The closing date for applications was extended to November 30 1996 but requests by the NUM for further extensions have been turned down (Crush, 1997a:6). By May 1997, 199,596 SADC citizens had applied of whom 100,218 had been granted permanent residence (James, 1997). These offers of permanent residence clearly affect miners primarily and it was under pressure from the NUM that the South African government acceded to them. In Lesotho, the NUM is not only spearheading the campaign to give Basotho miners permanent South African residence and citizenship, but it is also the main force behind the campaign to integrate Lesotho as a whole into South Africa.

The influence of the NUM and its opposition to the 'migrant labour system' also comes across in the *Report of the Presidential Com-*

mission to Investigate Labour Market Policy (or Labour Market Commission in short) published in June 1996. In the chapter dealing with labour migration, it is noted that the NUM, in its submission, wished to end the discriminatory practice which denied miners from foreign countries the right to South African citizenship. "In particular, it is proposed that migrant workers should have the right to permanent residence status and to acquire citizenship after five years of work in South Africa" (section 544). Permanent residence rights will allow miners to qualify for various housing schemes and other social benefits. The NUM also demanded the abolition of the compulsory deferred pay scheme which undermines the basic right of workers to receive their full pay (section 548). In both these instances the Commission concurred with the NUM's submissions. At the same time, the Commission recommends preferential access to the South African labour market for Southern African Customs Union (SACU) countries and Mozambique (section 560) while arguing for the phasing out of the migrant labour system contrary to the wishes of the Chamber of Mines in its submission (sections 583, 584).

Finally it is relevant to note the position taken by the Labour Market Commission on the SADC *Draft Protocol on the Free Movement of Persons in the SADC Region of June 1995*. The objective of this agreement is the progressive abolition of border controls on citizens of member states. The Draft Protocol calls on member states *inter alia* to confer, promote and protect in relation to every citizen of a member state:

> the right to enter freely and without a visa the territory of another Member State for a short visit;
>
> the right to reside in the territory of another Member State;
>
> the right to establish oneself and work in the territory of another Member State (section 566).

The protocol suggests the introduction of progressively freer movement for all people, including work-seekers within SADC and the eventual elimination of all border controls within a period of ten years. While identifying "itself with the ultimate objectives underlying the Draft Protocol", the Labour Market Commission distances itself from its recommendations "in the current circumstances of highly uneven development in the SADC region" (section 568). What this means, of course, is that despite its asserted willingness to support the integration of the regional labour market, the Commission simply backs the South African chauvinist fear of being 'swamped by foreign immigrants' rather than seriously addressing the issue of how such integration is to be achieved.[283]

At the same time, the Labour Market Commission sees the abolition of the 'migrant labour system' as an injunction to 'liberalise' the regional labour market. This process, it says, should only operate along with increasing the free flow of capital and trade in the region (section 562). It ultimately ends up agreeing with the neoclassical economics of the International Financial Institutions that the democratisation of the relations of migrancy in practice means 'freeing' the market. At the same time though, such 'freedom' is seen as limited by the geo-political boundaries of existing states which these guard with the utmost jealousy, so that the free movement of citizens within SADC is seen as a "threat to national sovereignty" (James, 1997:11).

Both the Commission Report and the social democratic arguments of Davies and Head (1995) among others, suggest that even for the most 'progressively minded' South African intellectuals and politicians concerned with democratisation, the wishes of those most affected by the migration process and a change in citizenship have not been addressed. Rather, while paying lip-service to the democratisation of regional relations including the migratory labour system, their perspective is one of 'democratisation from above' and they seem to prefer to adhere to a short term narrow conception of 'national interest' where Southern African regional relations are concerned. This amounts to a 'national interest' defined by the (new) state and its apparatuses. With the sole exception of the abolition of the compulsory deferred pay scheme, the recommendations of the Labour Market Commission on the issue of regional migration simply confirm ANC and NUM prejudices, and offer few openings to democracy. Strangely (and sadly), it is the interests of the Chamber of Mines

---

[283]. Perhaps more surprisingly, *The Draft Green Paper on International Migration* (James, 1997:11) also endorses this short term chauvinistic position. The arguments for and against the Draft Protocol are reviewed by the Centre for Socio-Political Analysis, 1995 and Crush, 1996. The South African Government is fundamentally against the 'open borders' idea behind the Protocol (see also Crush, 1997b:13).

that wishes to have access to migrant labour from the region to keep its price and militancy down, which seem more in tune with those of the peasant-migrants, as at least these argue for the retention of migrancy. A danger therefore exists that peasant-migrants from the region could easily abandon their erstwhile allegiances for an alliance with capital and its representatives, at least on certain issues.

POPULAR MIGRANT-LABOUR IDENTITY

In actual fact, from the perspective of the peasant migrants, the 'migrant labour system' should continue (and arguably be expanded as a way of improving their conditions of life). In the words of Coplan and Thoahlane (1995:149): "a very large majority of migrants and ex-migrants...prefer to carry on or resume migrating". For such migrants, it is the corrupt practices of Lesotho state officials and the lack of democracy which have been responsible for the absence of development, not their own absence from the country through migration or economic dependency or environmental degradation. Witness statements from Basotho Miners recently interviewed by Sechaba Consultants in Welkom, South Africa:

> Lesotho has economic problems which will be worsened if migrants take up South African citizenship but still, there is free land which could balance the situation if well utilised.
> Lesotho is unable to provide for her peoples because of poor governance, and this would ensure that many miners would seek permanent residence...Lesotho will face disastrous economic problems as she will lose all her earnings from migrant labour.
> Migrant workers like everybody else are disgruntled by the fact that their expectations to improve economically have been shattered. Our voices to the government to use the deferred pay money to improve and make education accessible to all, and pensions for the aged and disabled, have not been heard. Government officials use our hard earned money to enrich themselves...
> Many miners who applied for [South African] IDs did so because they feared that they would lose their jobs unless they voted for the ANC. The move to provide permanent residence, some say, was taken without consulting them. (Sechaba Consultants, 1996)

The states of the peripheral rural countries of the region (especially the Lesotho state), have since independence systematically neglected investment in rural areas or 'social upliftment', using the miners' forced savings for unproductive enterprises (speculation, real estate or trading) justified as 'national development'; in addition it is clear that a proportion of these funds has been used for private accumulation through more or less corrupt practices. This availability of funds for financial institutions has apparently led to a situation where 'excess liquidity' is faced by banks in Lesotho, an 'excess' which is finding no profitable outlets in the country and is consequently being gambled on the Johannesburg stock exchange. It may be time to let Basotho migrants invest their own funds as they see fit.

In addition it is abundantly clear that the Lesotho state's opposition to migrants taking up South African residence and citizenship is founded on its fear of losing access to deferred pay and the effects of the loss of remittances on the economy.[284] The Basotho miners on the other hand are opposed to the compulsory deferred pay scheme and have expressed their opposition on a number of occasions. The following comments are taken from interviews with miners in 1996:

> The deferred pay savings scheme is benefiting the banks and government officials who take loans because interests received by the mine workers is not only insignificant but an insult to those who contribute: mine workers have for years complained about this...it would have been better if the interest was improved to benefit old people and pensions. It would have still been far better if miners had been asked to pay twenty rand (R20) monthly to make education free for all.
> The money from the fund cannot be withdrawn more than once a month. The most disgusting thing about the deferred money is that interest that accrue is meagre to can think of doing anything with it: it would have been far better to have one's money and bank it himself. (sic) (Sechaba Consultants, 1996)

In a recent survey by John Gay, 63 percent of a sample of 500 miners preferred the deferred pay scheme to be optional (Gay, 1997:30). From a democratic perspective therefore, the significant factors must be those which influence the perception of migration or national identity

---

[284]. The available evidence regarding the investments made with deferred pay shows that these were mainly unproductive (e.g. real estate and merchant activity) while it is reputed to have fuelled corruption among state officials. The Lesotho state has made no effort to control the emigration of skilled professionals from the country to South Africa. Although detailed figures are not available, circumstantial evidence shows that these must be high among teachers, professionals and high ranking civil servants. Dual citizenship is in theory illegal in Lesotho, yet it is common among members of the elite.

from the standpoint of the migrants. It seems that the migrant-peasants will continue to desire association with the industrial world of South Africa to the extent that such association enhances the benefits already established by their access to land and means of production, and the ability to satisfy those needs which can only be satisfied through the market. It would not make sense for the peasant migrants' partial and tenuous independence from the market, to be totally eliminated by a change in their status from that of semi-proletarians (part-proletarian and part-peasant) to fully-fledged proletarians. This would mean a total loss of their economic 'reserve base'— the loss of survival capacities under crisis conditions for some, and of possibilities of accumulation for others. The differentiated 'peasant side' of migrant life is therefore the more important determinant of their willingness to move permanently to South Africa.

We should not therefore be surprised to discover that recent survey data on migrant opinions show that only a minority of respondents wish to move permanently to South Africa. A survey undertaken by the Central Bank of Lesotho (CBL, 1995) finds that only 30 percent of Basotho migrant-peasants wish to become South African citizens, even though they may be members of the NUM which sees the move as beneficial to its members.[285] Another similar and more recent survey (1996) of 500 miners interviewed in the TEBA offices found that the proportion of miners wishing to move permanently to South Africa was just under 19 per cent. Some of the more important reasons mentioned for wishing to remain based in Lesotho concerned the facts that no land would be available in RSA and that migrants possess assets in Lesotho which they do not wish to lose. Coplan and Toahlane (1995:148) also note that the extent of the willingness of migrants, ex-migrants and their wives whom they interviewed, to leave Lesotho permanently for South Africa, varied in inverse proportion to "their social and material investment in their homesteads".

These data confirm both my analysis regarding the differentiation of the worker-peasantry in the region (Neocosmos, 1987, 1993a and 1993b; Levin and Neocosmos, 1989), and the view that migrants

---

285. Discussions with NUM officials in Lesotho reveal that their informal estimates of numbers wishing to take up South African residence and citizenship have regularly been over 50 per cent of their membership.

should be consulted before any transformation of the migrant labour system is undertaken. Clearly peasant-migrants do not wish to become permanent residents and South African citizens if this means they will be proletarianised as a result. This is confirmed by the low numbers who actually applied for permanent residence. The recent *South African Green Paper on International Migration* recognises this and notes that the figures of those applying for and receiving permanent residence were "much lower than anticipated and indicate that the scale of unauthorised migration might be smaller than originally estimated" (James, 1997:16). All these results fly in the face of the NUM's view (both in South Africa and in Lesotho) founded on a conception of miners as proletarians. The following quote from a miner illustrates the point:

> I have laboured under very difficult conditions to make South Africa what it is and so, have earned some reward. South Africans earn pensions at old age and blue card earnings for six months while looking for jobs. This blue card money is the money deducted from the salary while one works. Unlike in Lesotho where our deferred pay is not benefiting us as contributors, here at least there is something to wipe off one's tears...[Respondent has no intention to bring his family even if he is granted permanent residence] Life in South Africa is garbage...working here is like going to the cattle post where you take your livestock in summer and bring them back in winter. [He does not want to be a citizen of South Africa. He will only use the ID or permanent residence as a passport to getting his worked for benefits]...
> In sum, interviews with miners make it abundantly clear that, broadly speaking, those with asset (land, cattle, etc.) in Lesotho do not wish to move to South Africa, while those who own nothing in Lesotho are keen to secure permanent residence. (Sechaba Consultants, 1996:8)

Clearly migrants try to get the best of both worlds—the rural security and status of Lesotho and the access to cash in urban South Africa. However the majority make it absolutely clear that they are only interested in having access to South African benefits—jobs or IDs— temporarily. This response can be understood as being completely rational and seems to have two major reasons: first, because they have access to material resources (mainly land and cattle) in Lesotho, which they will never have access to in today's RSA; second, because the proletarianisation entailed by becoming permanently South African means a marked decline in living conditions, including moral standards, which are incomparably lower in urban areas from the perspective of rural dwellers. It is, in particular, this latter conception—recurring systematically in interviews—which is often expressed as an adherence to Sesotho cultural values (as expressed in songs, music etc.) and is interpreted by Coplan (1994) as an romantic attachment to national identity.

For Coplan, this national identity is a romantic attachment because it has no material basis as for him, following the nationalist assumptions of linear proletarianisation, there is no 'wealth' in Lesotho or any other 'labour reserve economy' in the Southern African periphery. Rather, to use Colin Murray's expression, the population of Lesotho is dismissively "described as a proletariat which scratches about on the land" (Murray, 1981:19). Basotho migrants are patronisingly portrayed in Coplan's book as people desperately clinging to an identity which alone can give their life meaning, given the appalling conditions in the mine compounds and shantytowns of South Africa and the desolate unproductive landscape of the Malotis (Neocosmos and Selinyane, 1996). Peasant-migrant statements tell a different story. Their access to resources such as land and cattle means that their socio-economic base is mainly in Lesotho. Those who do not have access to resources, of course, have nothing to lose, but all to gain by becoming South African residents and then citizens. In addition, the oft repeated comments regarding the corrupt and morally degrading life in urban South Africa is not just an effect of an attachment to Sesotho culture, but a common response of peasants all over the world when caught up in the confines of an urban culture within which they are largely isolated. It is thus as much to be seen as an articulation of the values of village life in general as an assertion of Sesotho nationalism. The 'good life' in rural Lesotho is often combined in statements with the possibilities of accumulation denied in South Africa to peasant-migrants in competition with many unemployed locals for jobs:

> Lesotho, poor as she is, is good for family life. [He thinks if he plays his cards well, he can still live decently with his family. He intends buying a taxi.] Lesotho has much to lose if her citizens decide to change [nationality—] but if enough jobs and skills could be created this problem could be averted (Sechaba Consultants, 1996).

Finally, it is important to refer to the evidence regarding the effects of 'internalisation' on Basotho migrants. This shows that, contrary to the arguments of Davies and Head (1995), these effects are anything but a 'democratisation' of economic relations and rather bear testament to the vulnerability of foreign peasant-migrants to crude manipulation and exploitation by unscrupulous mine and The Employment Bureau of Africa (TEBA) administrators. Coplan and Toahlane (1995) show that a whole "retrenchment industry" (the term is theirs) has developed around the laying off of Basotho mineworkers since 1987.

> Migrants said that bribery and nepotism at the recruiting offices were common, with a recall requiring a standard payment of R500 or a well-placed relative in the clerkdom of the mine or TEBA. Basotho found themselves at a disadvantage in this regard, as under present conditions TEBA no longer does much actual recruitment, the mines preferring to hire whoever they choose, whenever they choose, at the mine gates. Limited work-seeker permits and lack of funds for travel, food and accommodation at the mine site all make it especially difficult for repatriated Basotho to attempt to get their service bonuses or their jobs back...The mines themselves no longer use the term "retrenched" but prefer the euphemism "on leave". This allows them to perpetuate the fiction that the employee is only temporarily unengaged, remains eligible for recall and thus is not (yet) entitled to retrenchment benefits. (Coplan and Toahlane, 1995:142-3)

They continue:

> For senior management, the goals of the "retrenchment industry" include: 1) the downward restructuring of labour costs in the form of reduced wages, benefits, working conditions and employment security for workers; 2) the undermining of collective bargaining agreements signed with the NUM, and the extension of labour control and labour peace by the systematic retrenchments and victimisation of NUM members. Basotho were frequent targets of such victimisation because they are usually seen to be strong NUM supporters and because their foreign status makes them relatively easy to repatriate permanently to the sending area. (Coplan and Toahlane, 1995:145)

Finally they conclude that

> ...the varied strategies used by mine company clerks, TEBA officials and other administrative staff to avoid the payment of migrants' benefits or to redirect them to their own pockets range from the brutally simple to the Byzantine, but the amounts involved certainly exceed some millions of rands. The status of Basotho as foreigners and the policies of internalisation, union-busting and repatriation make them favoured targets of these corrupt practices. (Coplan and Toahlane, 1995:146)

There is little need to comment as these statements speak for themselves. What is worthy of comment is the intellectual myopia which conflates the gradual replacement of labour migrancy by the recruitment of South African nationals with a 'democratic' process. The ANC, the unions and their spokespersons are being increasingly accused of losing touch with their grassroots support, and perhaps this is an instance where this criticism is warranted. It could also be added that a conception of democracy restricted to universal suffrage and a liberal constitution is limited by its inability to address the issue of the independent self-organisation of the working people.

CONCLUSION: NATIONAL IDENTITY AND HUMAN RIGHTS

In conclusion it is not possible to avoid addressing, however briefly and boldly, the issue of democracy in post-apartheid South Africa, as the issue is brought up directly by the question of 'foreign' migrant labourers. Clearly the process of 'nation-building' (whether explicit or implicit), is not simply about the creation of 'national unity' around a common political project, it is also about demarcating that unity from others—from 'foreigners'. The opposition citizen-foreigner denotes both the creation of a new community as well as the exclusion of some from that community. As this community is based not only on a common 'identity' but also on legal prescriptions (rights and duties) and socio-economic benefits (access to social services, bank loans, etc.), it is certainly not 'imagined' but materially experienced. It is not only an ideological, but also a fundamentally socio-material object embedded in social relations and is experienced as such, most obviously by 'strangers'/'foreigners' who are excluded from community rights and access to resources.

How is this process of inclusion/exclusion arrived at? To what extent is it/has it been democratic? Clearly these are crucial questions, as the ability to sustain this community (the nation), including the ability to justify exclusion, is largely determined by the democratic nature of the process (both in its objective and subjective dimensions). The crisis of the state in Africa today is largely attributable to the fact that this process was constructed undemocratically during the post-colonial period in such a manner that the nation was reduced to the state (the 'nation-state') (Olukoshi and Laakso, 1996). Moreover it should really be questioned whether a concept of 'citizen' developed in 1789 in a context when nationhood and birthplace coincided, is still applicable in the 1990s when this correspondence ceased to exist some time ago, most notably in Africa. Perhaps it is time to replace such a concept by one of 'people from all walks of life' or 'persons from everywhere'.[286] Unfortunately South Africa has not yet reached this point. Arriving late in the realm of (bourgeois) democracy, the dominant view in that country is still one which sees concepts such as 'the market' and 'citizenship' as democratic. The contradictions to which this gives rise, can be seen in the recent *Draft Green Paper on International Migration* submitted in May 1997 to the Minister of Home Affairs (James, 1997).

The build-up to the publication of the Green Paper rightly gave the impression that this report would suggest the liberalisation of the existing law. Of course, given the extremely repressive character of current legislation, liberalisation was only to be expected, but at the same time the report is very disappointing from a democratic perspective. In fact the report is largely hamstrung by the assumptions internal to its discourse as well as by the external constraints of the new constitutionally enshrined Bill of Rights itself. These constraints can be seen in three different areas.

First, the report assumes without discussion that the reason for the "negative view of immigration" held by South Africans whereby immigrants are viewed as illegitimate competitors and as a security risk is simply a left-over from the period of apartheid (James, 1997:4). This is clearly absurd as the struggle against the apartheid state in the 1980s, linked oppressed South Africans with other Africans and especially those from the region very closely. Rather, the reasons for South African chauvinism should be sought elsewhere, particularly in the statements and actions of its state agents and politicians and in the failure of the state party, the ANC, to provide democratic leadership on the issue, within the context of its programme of 'nation-building'

---

286. This a translation of the French concept "les gens de partout" advocated by the political journal *La Distance Politique*. See Wamba-dia-Wamba (1994, 1995) for an explication of this idea.

and reconciliation. The Green Paper in fact confuses state policy especially in the Ministry of Home Affairs, which has indeed been influenced by apartheid on this issue, with popular attitudes. Even the new constitution as we shall see, makes important distinctions between the rights of "citizens" and those of "persons" (including foreigners), and as such provides the basis for 'legal' discrimination against foreigners.

Second, the Green Paper notes that the challenge in South Africa is to replace a racially-motivated policy on immigration (whereby immigration from Europeans was encouraged and African immigration prohibited under apartheid) by a "non-racial and rational" one—not it should be stressed by a *democratic* one. In other words, it is assumed, as with so much South African official/ANC reasoning, that 'non-racial' equals 'democratic', as if immigration policy cannot be non-racial, oppressive and undemocratic at the same time. For example, although the Green Paper is rightly concerned to restrict the hitherto arbitrary actions of Home Affairs officials with respect to migrants deemed to be 'illegal' by the state, it does not consider or encourage any form of self-empowerment by 'foreign' residents (or even people including 'foreigners') as a counterweight to the arbitrariness of state power. Rather, it merely stresses the importance of formal/legal "checks and balances in the form of appeal and review procedures and access to information", as a way of restricting the current "administrative discretion" given to the executive and bureaucracy in immigration matters. The point regularly made by democracy activists everywhere in relation to this is, of course, that poor people from whom most 'illegal' suspects come do not have the power or knowledge to use such legal avenues. Clearly, the self-empowerment of 'foreigners' raises the question of human and citizen rights along with the differences between them. This issue is posed directly by the Bill of Rights in the South African constitution.

The third point concerns the manner in which the Green Paper is hamstrung by the statements of the Bill of Rights on this matter. All foreigners (whether legally employed or not, or whether they pay taxes to the state or not), are denied all political rights, including voting at local, regional and national elections. They are also denied the "freedom to trade, occupation and profession" which is also restricted to citizens only. In these instances in particular, the most fundamental law of the land, constantly paraded in the media as 'one of the most democratic constitutions in the world', divides people resident in South Africa into 'citizens' and 'foreigners' regarding some of the most basic rights in existence, including the right to make a living and to survive. The logic behind this is quite incomprehensible given the regional history of Southern Africa and the regular patterns of migration and the arbitrariness of the drawing of borders which have characterised this history. Given this history, a large proportion (perhaps even a majority) of present-day South Africans or their forefathers have either been born or lived, often for several generations, outside the confines of South Africa's borders. Given this distinction in the constitution, the power to decide who is denied political and commercial rights now rests with that lower level legislation which defines citizenship! As in many other African countries, most recently Zambia, people can be denied their political rights simply by withdrawing their citizenship through legislation introduced for the purpose. Presumably people could even lose their right to work through similar methods. There is no sign of this happening at the moment, but the danger is there for the future.

Denying foreigners trading rights is clearly discriminatory. Reitzes (1997:17) comments that "all people should be assured of the necessary rights to engage in economic activity" as such a right is a human right—an attribute of human existence—which is "territorially transcendent" as "all human beings are rights bearers, when they cross borders they carry their rights with them". She argues that preliminary research suggests that these kinds of rights are the ones which immigrants claim; "their expectations of the state are primarily to be left alone to make their own way" in civil society. She continues:

> At present, in terms of the Aliens Control Amendment Act of 1995, the South African government fundamentally negates...[such]...rights by subjecting illegal immigrants to continual harassment, bribery and corruption; divesting them of their property and earnings; imprisoning them without trial, and deporting them. Furthermore, in granting the right to freedom of trade, occupation and profession exclusively to citizens, the revised bill of rights deprives migrants of a fundamental...human right. (Reitzes, 1997:17)

In this manner the *Green Paper on Immigration* is clearly restricted by both conceptual and legal constraints. It is this which ultimately accounts for the contradictions between its democratic intentions and genuine attempts to liberalise migration policy on the one hand and its fundamentally nationalist-statist preoccupations and concerns on the other. For example, while dismissing the SADC protocol on the free movement of persons, it attempts to suggest easier access to the South African labour market for SADC citizens in ways regulated by its narrow conception of South African 'national interest', i.e. regulation of migrants through quota systems and of immigrants through 'point systems' which again will give discretionary powers to the bureaucracy (Reitzes, 1997:11). While recognising that all available evidence shows that SADC migrants do not wish or intend to stay permanently in South Africa i.e. that they are migrants and not immigrants (Reitzes, 1997:16), it insists on restricting migration through quotas, and entry and trading permits. As a result the Green Paper is unable to address the issue of discrimination squarely and democratically and to suggest ways of overcoming it.

I have noted in this paper, and argued extensively elsewhere (Neocosmos, 1996), that a clear distinction is apparent in the way the process of national unification in South Africa was conducted in the 1980s from the way it is being conducted today. While during the former period this process was founded on concerted attempts to involve ordinary people (including many of those now deemed to be 'foreign') in its production so that a popular democratic process would be unleashed and sustained, today this process is exclusively state directed and controlled. National unity now means primarily unity 'at the top', within the state and its apparatuses and within the new 'non-racial elite' as the 'patriotic bourgeoisie' of Black accumulators now join their White counterparts in accumulating in the 'national interest'. While during the 1980s we could speak of a process (however flawed, however partial) of the construction of *national democracy*, it is difficult nowadays to refer to anything more than to *state democracy*. While the former involved a national debate within all sectors of the community regarding the nature of democracy, the latter no longer does so and is exclusively a state discourse (we have to watch Dennis Davis' TV programme *Future Imperfect* in order to experience any discussion on democracy; no such debate exists in communities). While distinct from the African experience in many ways, the South African process of 'nation-building' is fundamentally founded on the same conception that the state *is* the nation so that, for example, unity at state level is equated with national unity. Of course, this amounts to a clear substitution of the state for the people which can be said to be the main characteristic of statism throughout Africa (Gibbon, Neocosmos and Wamba-dia-Wamba, forthcoming).

The fact that the citizenry has the opportunity every five years to elect the party of its choice is not in itself an indication that this party represents in the intervening period, in all its pronouncements, the popular will. One way in which this will is expressed and which is regularly emphasised today, is through the existence of a 'vibrant' civil society. However, the latter is not itself a guarantee of democracy and is compatible with the existence of authoritarianism, but in any case civil society organisations in South Africa have been incorporated through a complex corporatist structure (NEDLAC etc.) into the state itself. As a result there are few avenues independent of the state, open for the expression of popular grievances and discontent. There are no longer popular controls over the people's representatives. The latter are controlled from above, by the party leadership, by patronage.

Recent examples of this are not simply the money spinning activities of ex-trade union leaders who we had been told would "represent workers' interests" in government, parliament and so on, but the revelations in which leading ANC women were said to be investing in a deportation centre for 'illegal immigrants' (*Mail and Guardian*, Vol. 13, No. 5, Feb. 1997). It is in this context that the recent *Green Paper on Immigration* must be situated and evaluated. While the liberalisation of the existing immigration laws was long overdue, the fact that such a review is taking place so late after the repeal of all other apartheid legislation is indicative of the fact that change in this area has not been a priority. As with previous government commissions on related issues, the authors of the Green Paper have not been concerned to go beyond a narrow conception of the 'national interest', and have not provided an opening to democratic popular perspectives. Clandestine migrants and 'foreigners' are the weakest members of any society, having few rights. It seems that the old concept of citizenship in Southern Africa is thoroughly outdated. In order to move forward to a new non-discriminatory vision in a democratic way, 'migrants' and 'foreigners' should be taken seriously and asked their opinions.

REFERENCES

Adelzadeh, A. and Padayachee, V. (1994) "The RDP White Paper: Reconstruction of a Development Vision", *Transformation*, No. 25.

African National Congress (1969) *Strategy and Tactics of the African National Congress*, adopted at the 1969 Morogoro Conference in Tanzania.

African National Congress (1994) *The Reconstruction and Development Programme*, Johannesburg: Umanyano publications.

Central Bank of Lesotho (1995) "Survey of Migrant Workers Attitudes to Permanent Residence in RSA", September, Maseru.

Centre for Socio-Political Analysis (1995) *A Research Review of the Policies Surrounding the Issue of the Free Movement of People across International Borders with Specific Reference to Southern Africa and the Particular Effect Thereof on South Africa*, Pretoria: HSRC.

Coplan, D. (1994) *In the Time of Cannibals: The Word Music of South Africa's Basotho Migrants*, Chicago: University Press.

Coplan, D. and T. Thoahlane (1995) "Motherless Households, Landless Farms: Employment patterns among Lesotho migrants", in Crush, J. and W. James (eds.) *Crossing Boundaries: Mine Migrancy in a Democratic South Africa*, Cape Town: IDASA/IDRC.

Crush, J. (1996) *Fortress South Africa? A Critique of Responses to the SADC Draft Protocol on the Free Movement of Persons in Southern Africa*, confidential unpublished report.

Crush, J. (1997a) *Contract Migration to South Africa: Past, Present and Future*, briefing paper to the Task Team on International Migration.

Crush, J. (1997b) *Temporary Work and Migration Policy in South Africa*, briefing paper to Task Team on International Migration.

Davies, R. and Head, J. (1995) "The Future of Mine Migrancy in the Context of Broader Trends in Migration in Southern Africa", *Journal of Southern African Studies*, Vol. 21, No. 3, September.

First, R. (1983) *Black Gold: The Mozambican Miner, Proletarian and Peasant*, Brighton: Harvester.

Friedman, S. (1997) "Migration Policy, Human Rights and the Constitution", Briefing Paper to the Task Team on International Migration.

Friedman, S. and Reitzes, M. (1996) "Democratisation or Bureaucratisation?: Civil Society, the Public Sphere and the State in Post-apartheid South Africa", *Transformation* No. 29.

Gay, J. (1997) *Riding the Tiger: Lesotho miners and attitudes to permanent residence in South Africa*, South Africa Migration Project Policy Studies No. 2, IDRC, Canada.

Gibbon, P, Neocosmos, M and Wamba-dia-Wamba, E (forthcoming) *The State and Civil Society in Africa: essays for a democratic politics*, Uppsala: Nordic Africa Institute.

Hermele, K. (1988) *Land Struggle and Social Differentiation in Southern Mozambique: A Case Study of Chokwe, ?? 1950–1987*, Research Report No 82, Uppsala: Nordiska Afrikainstitutet.

James, W. (1997) *Draft Green Paper on International Migration*. Presented to the South African Minister of Home affairs, May 13th.

Johnston, D. (1996) "The State and Development: An Analysis of Agricultural Policies in Lesotho, 1970–1993", *Journal of Southern African Studies*, Vol. 22, No. 1, March.

Levin, R. and M. Neocosmos (1989) "The Agrarian Question and Class Contradictions in South Africa", *Journal of Peasant Studies*, Vol. 16, No. 2, January.

Lodge, T. et al. (1991) *All Here and Now: Black politics in South Africa in the 1980s*, Cape Town: Ford Foundation, David Philip.

Mail and Guardian, Johannesburg

Mamdani, M (1996) *Citizen and Subject: Contemporary Africa and the legacy of late colonialism*, London: James Currey.

Marx, A.W. (1992) *Lessons of Struggle: South African Internal Opposition, 1960–1990*, Cape Town: Oxford.

Mbeki, G. (1996) *Sunset at Midday*, Braamfontein: Nolwazi Educational Publishers.

Morobe, M. (1987) "Towards a People's Democracy: The UDF View", *Review of African Political Economy*, No. 40, December.

Neocosmos, M. (1987) "Homogeneity and Differences on Swazi Nation Land" in Neocosmos, M. (ed.) *Social Relations in Rural Swaziland: Critical Analyses*, SSRU: UNISWA.

Neocosmos, M. (1993a) *The Agrarian Question in Southern Africa and 'Accumulation from below': Economics and politics in the struggle for democracy*, Uppsala: The Scandinavian Institute of African Studies.

Neocosmos, M. (1993b) "Towards a Political Economy of Adjustment in a Labour Reserve Economy: The Case of Lesotho" in P. Gibbon (ed.) *Social Change and Economic Reform in Africa*, Uppsala: The Scandinavian Institute of African Studies.

Neocosmos, M. (1995) *Towards a History of Nationalities in Southern Africa*, Centre for Development Research (Copenhagen) CDR Working Paper 95.6.

Neocosmos, M. (1996a) "From People's Politics to State Politics: Aspects of national liberation in South Africa, 1984–1994", *Politeia* Vol. 15, No. 3, special issue on "Opposition Politics in Africa", A. Olukoshi (ed.).

Neocosmos, M. (1996b) "Intellectual Debates and Popular Struggles in Transitional South Africa: Political discourse and the origins of statism" Nordic Africa Institute, mimeo.

Neocosmos, M. and Selinyane, N. (1996) "Labour Migration and Citizenship in Southern Africa: An analytical review". Paper presented at the seminar on *Constitutionalism in Southern Africa* organised by the Nordic Africa Institute, Uppsala and the Institute of Diplomacy and International Studies, University of Nairobi, December 13–16, 1996.

Olukoshi, A. O. and Laakso, L. (eds.) (1996) *Challenges to the Nation State in Africa*, Nordic Africa Institute and IDS, University of Helsinki.

Pae, Tiisetso (1992) *Labour Migration and the Differentiation of the Peasantry in a Lesotho Village*, B.Ed. Dissertation, National University of Lesotho.

Phimister, I. (1986) "Commodity Relations and Class Formation in the Zimbabwean Countryside: 1898–1920", *Journal of Peasant Studies*, Vol. 13, No. 4, July.

Reitzes, M. (1997) *Towards a Human Rights-Based Approach to Immigration Policy in South and Southern Africa*, Foundation for Global Dialogue Occasional Paper No. 7, January.

Republic of South Africa, President's Office (1995) *South African Citizenship Act, 1995*.

Republic of South Africa (1996) *Restructuring the Labour Market: Report of the Presidential Commission to Investigate Labour Market policy*.

Saul, J. and Gelb, S. (1986) *The Crisis in South Africa*, London: Zed.

Sechaba Consultants (1996) Interviews with Miners in Welkom, 27 August 1996. Maseru.

Sisulu, Z. (1986) "People's Education for People's Power", *Transformation*, No. 1.

Slovo, J. (1976) "South Africa: No middle road" in Davidson, B. et al. *Southern Africa: The new politics of revolution*, Harmondsworth: Penguin.

Swilling, M. (1988) "The United Democratic Front and Township Revolt" in Cobbett, W. and R. Cohen (eds.) *Popular Struggles in South Africa*, London: James Currey.

United Democratic Front (1985) *Isizwe, the Nation*, Vol. 1, No. 1.

United Democratic Front, Cape Town Area Committee (1986) *Broadening the Base*, discussion document.

United Democratic Front, Cape Town Area Committee (1986b) *Call for National Unity discussion paper* (85186).

United Democratic Front National Office (1986) *Proposed Joint Statement on 'Call for National Unity against Apartheid and the Emergency'* (leaflet).

Wamba-dia-Wamba, E. (1994) "Africa in Search of a New Mode of Politics" in Himmelstrand, Ulf, Kabiru Kinyanjui and Edward Mburugu (eds.) *African Perspectives on Development: Controversies, Dilemmas & Openings*, London: James Currey.

Wamba-dia-Wamba, E. (1995) *The state of all Rwandese: political prescriptions and disasters* paper presented at the Arusha conference on the Great Lakes Region, Sept. 4th–7th.

Winai-Ström, G. (1984) *Migration and Dependency*. Uppsala: The Scandinavian Institute of African Studies.

Wolpe, H. (1972) "Capitalism and Cheap Labour Power in South Africa: From Segregation to Apartheid", *Economy and Society*, Vol. 1, No. 4.

Advancing Non-Racialism in Post-Apartheid South Africa

Rupert Taylor and Don Foster

Following successful democratic elections in April 1994 and the formation of a new government, South Africa has entered an era in which non-racialism is official state policy. This is a rare situation. There can be few, if any, societies which have declared non-racialism as a central guiding policy. But while most people today proudly proclaim commitment to a non-racial society, there has been little in the way of a public conversation to seriously define the meaning of non-racialism. Moreover, the concept of non-racialism has not been particularly well-aired outside of South Africa, and the words 'non-racial' and 'non-racialism' do not even feature in standard dictionaries.

The notion of non-racialism was most firmly developed in the course of political action during the apartheid era in the 1980s, principally by the African National Congress (ANC) to combat racism. Here, non-racialism was developed to fight and correct the effects of apartheid as a Universal History in which 'race' was taken as the key and moving force to History. Non-racialism meant rejecting official racial categorization and racial segregation, and advancing integration through a united struggle to build a democratic society in which racial divisions would be swept away by the forging of a common South African identity (van Diepen, 1988). This was a time when people designated black and white grasped non-racialism as a lived experience. As Max Sisulu speaking in 1987, put it: 'You actively fight against racism: that is the essence of non racialism' (quoted in Frederikse, 1990:78); and as Papi Mokoena, also speaking in 1987, stated: 'The non-racialism of the ANC was positive because it involved a very clear analysis...One cannot eliminate apartheid with apartheid' (quoted in Frederikse, 1990:114).

With the end of apartheid, and the shifting terms of engagement after the relative demobilization of ANC social movement activity there has, however, come a greater need to define non-racialism. For as Joshua Lazerson has written: 'Where talk of a "non-racial, democratic society" had slipped easily off the tongue in the 1980s, there [*is*] greater necessity to define terms in the wake of the events of February 1990' (Lazerson, 1994:266). In fact, to some non-racialism now has 'the smell of failure' about it, to others it is 'just as woolly a concept as apartheid' (Marais, 1993; Giliomee, 1995). So, what should non-racialism be understood to mean today? Why is it still important? And how can it be advanced?

PRINCIPLES OF NON-RACIALISM

First of all, it is now necessary to develop clear and logically consistent principles of non-racialism. And here it must be stressed that the central point to non-racialism, by definition, is an acceptance of the scientific rejection of 'race', and hence a rejection of its status as an independent determining force in world history. Non-racialism begins with the recognition that the notion of 'race' does not have adequate scientific foundation; that there are no pure and distinct 'racial' entities, that there is no genetic or other deterministic basis to 'race' (Montagu, 1974; UNESCO, 1979). In this regard, as English and English have remarked, 'many authorities would abandon the term [*race*] as suggesting meanings contrary to fact' (English and English, 1958:435). In consequence, 'race' has to be seen as sociologically meaningless in terms of what it claims to be; 'race' cannot explain itself. To the extent that 'race' has been taken to exist, it must therefore be explained as an invented, socially constructed notion which does not exist outside meanings imputed by people.

Non-racialism then, at its core, questions and demands the reconceptualization of the relationship between science and 'race', it calls for a total reassessment of the meaning of 'race' in social scientific work and political practice. Why should 'race' be taken—as it invariably is—as some *thing* that we encounter in history when its objective existence has not been scientifically established? Everyday thinking, and much social scientific work, all too often operates *as if* this issue was settled; that 'race' can be taken as a tool of analysis, as some *thing* which can be picked up, listed, quantified, and coded to understand and analyze human behaviour. It is held that 'race' determines political behaviour; racial identity is taken as given and is seen to be tied to, and correlated with peoples attitudes and behaviour. But why should the notion that 'race' exists be presupposed prior to investigation of society?

Critical questioning on this issue has been insulated by the commonly held belief that science itself cannot be racist, but simply reveals the objective 'facts'. Science, however, is not innocent, because putatively objective generalizations formulated at the descriptive level cannot but fail to be conditioned by an *already* racialized social order. It has to be recognized that scientific inquiry *is* involved in 'the chain of reasoning from assumptions to findings to inferences' (Gardner, 1995:24), and that what is required is that the explanation needs to be retraced so that the process by which 'race' has been produced and become reified is opened to question. How is it that instead of being seen as the product of society, 'race' has actually come to confront one as an objectively given reality?

In truth, for those who look, it is not that hard to see that 'race' is not a 'given' fact inscribed in natural history but is an ideology. As Colette Guillaumin has noted, 'however far back one pushes the origin of the physical or "race" criterion, one ends up face to face with the social criteria underlying the invention of the idea of "race"' (Guillaumin, 1995:78).

What this means is that attention must be directed to investigating how society has worked to create the belief that there is such a *thing* as 'race'. This means that focus must shift to the social relations and material conditions which work to generate and reproduce 'race'. It has to be shown how 'race' has been socially constructed, especially through state-making imperatives, as a conceptual system for representing 'others' in terms of negatively evaluated content and establishing relations of power and forms of inequality (Miles, 1989).

To avoid any confusion it is imperative to stress that to say that 'race' has no factual basis in the natural history of humankind is not to deny the fact that a belief in 'race' has been part of history with real and severe historical consequences. It *is* to say, however, that the 'potent salience of "race" in the everyday thinking of many [*people*]...is only understandable in the light of an ideology of racism', and that what racial ideology does is that it inverts reality and thereby reverses cause and effect (Foster and Louw-Potgieter, 1991:386). This must be corrected. Non-racialism then, aware of the reality of racism, is concerned to rigorously expose the falseness of 'race' and to work towards a society in which eventually 'race' is no longer granted any meaning.

Acceptance of non-racialism calls forward some new principles for sociological method in dealing with 'race'. In particular, 'race' should not be taken-for-granted, it should not be understood to be some independent *thing* in itself. As Kwame Anthony Appiah in his book, *In My Father's House*, recognizes: 'the existence of racism does not require the existence of races...You don't have to believe in witchcraft, after all, to believe that women were persecuted as witches in colonial Massachusetts' (Appiah, 1992:283). Today, children believe that Santa Claus and the Easter Bunny exist, does that mean they are real (Fields, 1990:96)? The important point is that it is not the case that something called 'race' exists 'out there' as part of nature, rather 'race' is seen to be what it is because we have made it so.

Given this, it follows that to try to define and specify the effects of 'race' as a free-standing phenomenon on people's attitudes and behaviour is a fruitless, meaningless exercise. As causes cannot be attributed as being intrinsic to 'race', there is nothing essential to 'race' itself to be measured and it is therefore clearly impossible to control for 'race'. Given that social criteria underlie 'race'; 'controlling for "race" simultaneously controls for those variables with which race is correlated' (Fairchild, 1991:111).

Accepting that 'race' is not a primordial or pre-existing attribute of individuals or groups, points to the import of probing the extent to which racial thinking is actually upheld in people's sense of self-identity. Here there is a pressing need to rethink the nature of identity politics, to direct greater concern to developing new methods that recognize that 'political identities are always, everywhere relational and collective...[and that] they therefore alter as political networks, opportunities, and strategies shift' (Tilly, 1996). This constitutes making a shift away from an essentialist to a relational understanding of social processes, to a concern with how racial identities have been historically constructed; to thereby see racism as relational in the sense of power relations and dialogical or dialectical relations, between 'self' and 'other'. This does not require a turn away from empirical quantitative social research, rather it calls for work that incorporates more qualitative, contextual understanding that is more sensitive to issues of identity construction; as, for example, might be revealed through a continuous ethnography of associational life in the context of changing social structural conditions (consider Stanfield and Dennis, 1991). The important point in all this, is of course, that once it is understood just how 'race' has been constructed, strategies and tactics can be developed for it to be deconstructed.

RETHINKING SOUTH AFRICA

The importance of the above principles of non-racialism is that they point to the shortcomings of many analyses of South African society and towards how to develop a fundamentally new sociology of the country. Virtually all writing on South Africa succumbs to one or more failings in using 'race' as a tool of analysis, most notably: the uncritical use of racial terminology, assuming unproven 'race-behaviour' causal relationships, and not tracing the presumed effects of 'race' to social factors.

The misuse of 'race' has been and continues to be pervasive in everyday and social scientific understandings of South Africa. And the way in which this has prevented good analysis can be illustrated by two simple examples: interpretations of the recent political violence in KwaZulu-Natal (1986 to date) and on the Reef (1990–94), and of voting patterns in the April 1994 general election.

Many commentators have sought to assign racial explanations to the political violence primarily through viewing it in terms of 'black-on-black violence', in terms of 'tribal' fighting between the Xhosaorientated ANC and the Zulu-orientated Inkatha Freedom Party led by Chief Buthelezi (Johnson, 1990; Horowitz, 1991). To see the conflict as the result of the different nature of racial group identities, however, masks the socio-economic causes of the conflict, absolves the role of the Apartheid State, and ignores the fact that support from Zulu-speakers for the ANC is virtually indistinguishable from that of other African-language groups, including Xhosa-speakers. It is also hard to see how the violence in KwaZulu-Natal fits into any such explanation as the vast majority of those involved have actually been Zulu-speakers (Taylor, 1991).

Likewise, to see voting behaviour in the April 1994 election in terms of 'race' does not get one very far. It is a widespread view (upheld in virtually all media reporting) that the election was little more than a straight 'racial census', with whites voting for the National Party, and blacks voting for the ANC (Reynolds, 1994; Schlemmer, 1994). But why should 'race' be taken as the most important determinant of voting behaviour? Simply to show correlations between 'race' and people's voting behaviour can actually say nothing as to causation. Even in the case of the Western Cape, where it was held that racially-motivated fears among those whom apartheid designated 'Coloured' led to the electoral success of the National Party, voting patterns cannot be understood unless they are related to the social structural factors that shaped the outcome of the election, such as the old Coloured Labour Preference Policy, the differential access to social goods and services, and the crisis of the regional economy at the time (also consider Mattes, 1995).

In both these examples, the determining salience of 'race' has simply been inferred, never shown. Those advocating such analyses *through* 'race' make no attempt to even probe just how 'race' may be, or may not be, related to political violence and voting behaviour. In general, if 'race' is to be used as an analytic tool then it is vital that the socio-theoretical reasons for using 'race' be spelt out and its relationship to other forms of social differentiation explored, but what happens is that the category 'race' is *never* sufficiently called into question. Few of South Africa's leading social scientists have attempted to spin out a *fully specified* theory of the connections between 'race' and other variables, to thereby yield empirically testable predictions or propositions (Taylor and Orkin, 1995).

Those who continue to defend the use of racial categories on the grounds that 'race lies behind everything' and talk of the 'effects of race' have not started to provide an adequate explanation (see, for example, Klandermans, Roefs and Olivier, 1995). Further, to conduct survey research and opinion polls in which responses are primarily classified in terms of preassigned racial categories, is bad practice. Why should this be done? Consider, for example, the logic of a 1995 Human Science Research Council survey in which the sample was stratified by 'race' on basis of population census data prior to the conducting of the research (Bornman, 1995): the survey, through open-ended questions allowed respondents to describe their group memberships, which were nonetheless coded in terms of the preassigned racial stratification. Consider also, the case of the Institute for Democracy in South Africa's 1995 readership survey for their magazine *Democracy in Action*, which instead of simply asking 'To which group did apartheid legislation designate you?', asked respondents to answer 'Which group do you belong to?—*African, Coloured, Asian, White?*'. Similarly, whilst it is perhaps not surprising, given the apparent centrality of 'race' in South African society, that much social psychological research has been concerned for many years almost exclusively with racial attitudes pertaining to intergroup relations, especially of whites towards blacks, it needs to be asked why should what are in fact ideologically constituted 'groups' be taken as 'unquestioned objects of thought to which to apply attitude measures' (Foster and Louw-Potgieter, 1991:160). It is time for all this to change. The way in which 'race' has been objectified and used in 'explaining' South African society must (especially post-apartheid) be more thoroughly questioned.

The way for social research to proceed is to first of all accept the need to move away from the value placed on ascriptive social categories to focus on categories of self-identification, to give people their own *voice*, and understand the *process* and *structure* of ideological thinking (consider Billig, 1987; Sampson, 1993). As racial identities are not simply given, but are shifting political constructs, present conditions must be researched, through qualitative methods and more sophisticated statistical techniques, to find the extent to which racial thinking really does form part of people's social consciousness. To what extent and why have people internalized apartheid ideology and work within racial logic? In what ways, and to what extent is 'race'—including 'whiteness'—seen to be part of the structure of everyday life, experience and conduct? Is there, in everyday life, a formal consistency to racial thinking or is it marked by contradictions and dilemmas? And where is a belief in 'race' at its strongest in present-day South Africa? In the far-right Freedom Front? In the newly launched Coloured Liberation Movement (Kleurling Weerstandsbeweging)? Then the key questions which have to be answered are: how have these patterns of racial identity formation been produced and how have they been used in South African politics? What have been the varying and changing roles of science, religion, economics, culture, art and medicine in constructing racial 'selves' and 'others'? To what extent has there been a degree of collusion on the part of oppressed elites in the very manufacture and maintenance of racism? And, most importantly, how can all this be challenged, how can 'race' be unlearned?

To date, however, South African sociology has not distinguished 'itself as an intellectual, scholarly practice' (Sitas, 1996:2), and studies that discuss the question of 'race' have rarely risen above descriptive empiricism or a politics as current affairs idiom. Although a great deal has been written about apartheid, there is relatively little systematic work on how oppressed and oppressor construct the very concept of 'race', or how different political tendencies and parties such as Black Consciousness, Africanism, liberalism, nationalism construct 'race', and/or struggle against racism (although see, Alexander, 1979; Marx, 1992). As Jeremy Seekings has written, 'Orthodox social scientific research in South Africa has often been marked by intellectual poverty, regardless of its technical sophistication...I cannot think of any major study [*on race*] by a South African sociologist in the past fifteen years' (Seekings, 1994:13).

ADVANCING NON-RACIALISM

To further the potential for non-racial understanding, a new sociology of South Africa must also begin to fully chart and analyze the evidence for the presence of a non-racial outlook, with its alternative interpretation of self-identity which rejects and resists racial politics. That people are not in fact as racially predisposed as has often been claimed is evident in some attitude surveys. Vergnani (1985), most notably, pointed to the fact that: 'If "attitudinal colour bar" is taken as the criterion of racism, then blacks, strictly speaking, do not evidence a "racist" attitudinal pattern at all, in contrast to whites who do' (Foster and Nel, 1991:154).

There are many examples of the presence of non-racialism as subjective lived experience, especially for people located within organizations and institutions that have professed a non-racial standpoint: such as the ANC, South African Communist Party, Congress of South African Trade Unions, the South African Council of Churches and Southern African Catholic Bishops Conference, and the English-language universities (Foster, 1991). In the 1980s the emergence of new non-racial organizational forms—civics, youth groups, women's groups, alliances amongst student organizations, professional groupings in health, education, law, mental health—played a crucial role in the construction of non-racial identity. The presence of non-racialism is also shown in the rejection of the exclusive Zulu Nationalism of Inkatha and the poor electoral showing of the Pan-Africanist Congress.

That some South Africans have contested the 'collective selves' promoted by apartheid society and reject racial labelling is clear from a number of recent empirical studies. The pie chart below, which is adapted from the 1995 World Values Study (Mattes, 1997:18–19), shows that, in answer to the question 'Above all, I am a…', racial identification was relatively low—and here of course it should not be taken for granted that racial identification encapsulates the same meaning for those responding—and that a strong sense of a South African identity was present (also see Schlemmer, 1993; Adam, 1994; Bornman, 1995). That there has been a *growing* emphasis on a common South African civic identity is evident from surveys undertaken by the Institute for Democracy in South Africa which have found that those people identifying themselves as 'South African' have increased from 13 per cent in 1994 to 22 per cent in 1995, whereas those giving a racial answer decreased from 28 per cent to 21 per cent (Mattes, 1997:12).

'Above all, I am a...'

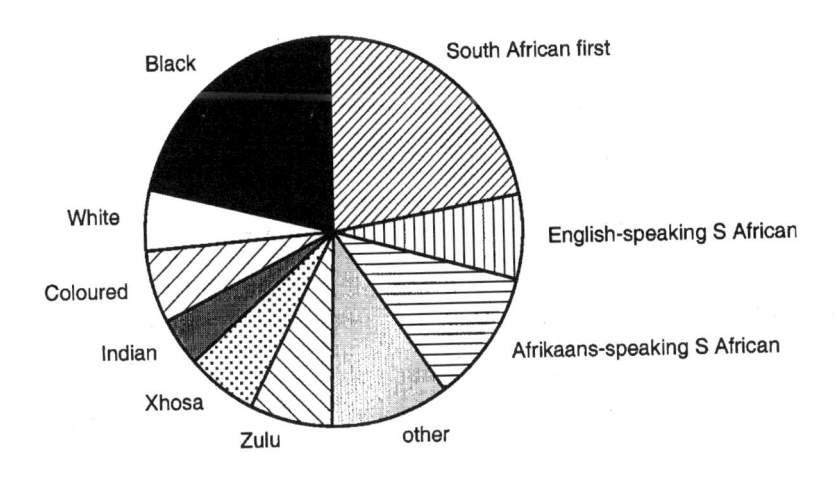

[Pie chart with segments: Black, White, Coloured, Indian, Xhosa, Zulu, other, Afrikaans-speaking S African, English-speaking S African, South African first]

Generally, as Neville Alexander has observed, 'identities have never been as fluid in South Africa as they are today' (Alexander, 1996:107). But all is not rosy for non-racialism, as there are countervailing pressures. Whilst the extensively propagated 'Rainbow Nation' metaphor does move beyond a rigid racial politics and is concerned to project an image of different racial groups coming together to live in peace and harmony, it is not a good metaphor. As Ashwin Desai has argued: 'To be a correct rainbow person one is actually encouraged to bring one's *racial separateness* and not one's common South Africaness out into the open, usually at appropriate media events' (Desai, 1996:119). And the colour-blind standpoint of the 'new' National Party—which now that apartheid (legislatively speaking) has gone, seeks to see racism as a thing of the past and a non-issue—is even more of a danger. This rather too conveniently obscures the racial realities of the present and misses the central point that non-racialism is an ideal which is far from realized. There is also the countervailing pressure of an essentialized Africanism. Such strains of Africanism are to some extent evident in the ANC's historic and symbolic appeals to African culture and African nationalism, as in talk of *ubuntu*, the transcendent *geist* of the African nation. It is also apparent in how the term 'black' is shedding its Black Consciousness umbrella connotation of referring to African, Indians, and Coloureds—such that more and more often 'black' is being used by Africans to refer to 'Africans' only (Bornman, 1995:9). In light of all these pressures, one commentator has gone so far as to state that: 'the long-cherished ideal of a nonracial South Africa [*is today*] under as much threat as at any time in [*South African*] history' (Schlemmer, 1996:27).

As part of developing a new sociology of South Africa, it is therefore time to advance a frame of reference regarding the promotion of non-racialism, so as to guide public policy and further the deracialization of society. Here, given that the legacies of racism are substantial and deep, and are likely to be reconstituted in numerous forms, the pursuit of non-racialism will require at least some of the following tasks:

- An active programme of civic nation-building to minimize the significance of erstwhile racialized identities and to enable new positive identity formations.
- Political opposition against those who aim to re-racialize or to reify the salience of 'race'.
- Challenging the very concept of 'race' while retaining attention to processes of racialization.
- Revision and challenge of the many forms that construct ongoing 'social representations' of racialized groupings: sport, education, media, advertising, curricula, textbooks, popular culture and everyday language.
- Rethinking racialized terminology itself, including the manner in which official statistics, census and research data are assembled, asked and deployed.

To carry all this forward requires addressing the unjust socio-economic conditions that lie behind 'race'. The above agenda is also dependent on developing strong and effective arguments and rhetorical strategies—at the level of people's everyday understanding—to turn around racial thinking. One cannot stop racism by simply proving that 'races' do not exist, appeals to science and logic alone are not good enough.

The full significance of non-racialism will prove difficult to put across and implement; for as Hilda Bernstein has argued, 'non-racialism is not an intrinsic part of political consciousness...It has to be learned by teaching, by experience, by example' (Bernstein, 1991:25).

A non-racial South Africa is still far from realized and it will take decades to reverse the psychological, social and economic damage caused by apartheid. Certainly non-racialism itself will constantly require vigilance, rethinking and revision; especially as the discourse about non-racialism finds little meaning or resonance in either Western Europe or in the Americas. Nonetheless non-racialism can provide the basis for a new humanism which strives eventually to move us beyond understanding South Africa *through* 'race'; it heralds a new vision—not just for South African politics but world politics.

ACKNOWLEDGEMENTS

The authors are grateful for the comments of: Adam Habib, Danielle Juteau-Lee, Robert Mattes, Mai Palmberg, Nora Räthzel and Per Strand.

REFERENCES

Adam, H. (1994) 'Nationalism, Nation-Building and Non-Racialism', in N.J. Rhoodie and I. Liebenberg (eds.), *Democratic Nation-Building in South Africa*, Pretoria: Human Sciences Research Council.

Alexander, N. [No Sizwe] (1979) *One Azania, One Nation: The National Question in South Africa*, London: Zed.

Alexander, N. (1996) 'The Great Gariep: Metaphors of National Unity in the New South Africa', in W. James, D. Caliguire and K. Cullinan (eds.), *Now*

That We Are Free: Coloured Communities in a Democratic South Africa, Cape Town: IDASA.

Appiah, K.A. (1992) *In My Father's House: Africa in the Philosophy of Culture*, London: Methuen.

Bernstein, H. (1991) 'The Breakable Thread', *Southern African Review of Books*, 4(2).

Billig, M. (1987) *Arguing and Thinking: A Rhetorical Approach to Social Psychology*, Cambridge, UK: Cambridge University Press.

Bornman, E. (1995) *Patterns of Group Identification in South Africa and Their Implications for Reconciliation*, Centre for Socio-Political Analysis, Human Sciences Research Council, Pretoria.

Desai, A. (1996) *Arise Ye Coolies: Apartheid and the Indian 1960–1995*, Johannesburg: Impact Africa.

English, H.B. and A.C. English (1958) *A Comprehensive Dictionary of Psychological and Psychoanalytical Terms*, New York: Longmans Green.

Fairchild, H.H. (1991) 'Scientific Racism: The Cloak of Objectivity', *Journal of Social Issues*, 47(3).

Fields, B. (1990) 'Slavery, Race and Ideology in the United States of America', *New Left Review*, 181.

Foster, D. (1991) *On Racism: Virulent Mythologies and Fragile Threads*, Inaugural Lecture, 21 August, University of Cape Town, New Series 161.

Foster, D. and J. Louw-Potgieter (eds.) (1991) *Social Psychology in South Africa*, Johannesburg: Lexicon.

Foster, D. and E. Nel (1991) 'Attitudes and Related Concepts', in Foster and Louw-Potgieter (eds.), op.cit.

Frederikse, J. (1990) *The Unbreakable Thread: Non-Racialism in South Africa*, Johannesburg: Ravan.

Gardner, H. (1995) 'Cracking Open the IQ Box', in S. Fraser (ed.), *The Bell Curve Wars: Race, Intelligence, and the Future of America*, New York: Basic Books.

Giliomee, H. (1995) Speech at an Institute for Democracy in South Africa (IDASA) Conference on National Unity and the Politics of Diversity. The Case of the Western Cape, Cape Town.

Guillaumin, C (1995) *Racism, Sexism, Power and Ideology*, London and New York: Routledge.

Horowitz, D. (1991) *A Democratic South Africa? Constitutional Engineering in a Divided Society*, Berkeley: University of California Press.

Johnson, R.W. (1990) 'Spears of the Nation', *The Independent on Sunday* [UK], 14 October.

Klandermans, D., M. Roefs and J. Olivier (1995) 'Political Protest and Political Transition in South Africa, 1994–1995', paper presented at the Annual Meeting of the American Sociological Association, Washington DC.

Lazerson, J. (1994) *Against the Tide: Whites in the Struggle against Apartheid*, Boulder: Westview Press.

Marais, H. (1993) 'Falling Down', *Work in Progress* [Johannesburg], 93.
Marx, A. (1992) *Lessons of Struggle: South African Internal Opposition, 1960–1990*, Cape Town: Oxford University Press.
Mattes, R. (1995) 'The (Limited) Impact of Race and Ethnicity on Partisan Identification in South Africa's First Open Election', paper presented to Colloquium of IPSA's Research Committee on Politics and Ethnicity, Johannesburg.
Mattes, R. (1997) 'The Role of Identity in Building a Common Democratic Culture in South Africa', paper presented at National Identity and Democracy Conference, University of the Western Cape, March 14–18, 1997.
Miles, R. (1989) *Racism*, London: Routledge.
Montagu, A. (1974) *Man's Most Dangerous Myth: The Fallacy of Race*, New York: Oxford University Press.
Reynolds, A. (1994) 'The Results', in Reynolds (ed.), *Election '94 South Africa*, Cape Town: David Philip.
Sampson, E.E. (1993) 'Identity Politics: Challenges to Psychology's Understanding', *American Psychologist*, 48(12).
Schlemmer, L. (1993) 'Ethnicity in Black Political Attitudes: An Uncertain Factor', in *Contemporary Social Realities in South Africa*, The Urban Foundation, Development Strategy and Policy Unit, Johannesburg.
Schlemmer, L. (1994) 'The Birth of Democracy', *Indicator South Africa*, 11(3).
Schlemmer, L. (1996) 'The Nemesis of Race in South Africa', *Frontiers of Freedom* [South African Institute of Race Relations], 10.
Seekings, J. (1994) 'Studying Political Sociology without Any Political Sociologists? Paradigms, Disciplines, and Research on Extra-Parliamentary Politics, 1974–1994', paper presented to *Journal of Southern African Studies* Twentieth-Anniversary Conference, University of York, UK.
Sitas, A. (1996) 'The Waning of Sociology in South Africa', paper presented to Annual Conference of the South African Sociological Association, University of Natal, Durban.
Stanfield, J.H. and R.M. Dennis (eds.) (1991) *Race and Ethnicity in Research Methods*, Newbury Park: Sage.
Taylor, R. (1991) 'The Myth of Ethnic Division: Township Conflict on the Reef', *Race & Class*, 33(2).
Taylor, R. and M. Orkin (1995) 'The Racialisation of Social Scientific Research on South Africa', *South African Sociological Review*, 7(2).
Tilly, C. (1996) 'Contentious Politics and Social Change', paper presented to Workshop on Social Movements and Social Change in South Africa, University of Natal, Durban.
UNESCO (1979) *Declaration on Race and Racial Prejudice*, Paris: UNESCO.
van Diepen, M. (ed.) (1988) *The National Question in South Africa*, London: Zed.
Vergnani, T. (1985) 'Social Distance Attitudes among White, Coloured, Indian and Black Population Groups in South Africa', unpublished report, Human Sciences Research Council, Pretoria.

Select annotated bibliography

These annotated references are compiled by Petra Smitmanis for suggested further reading. The bibliography is of course not exhaustive. See also the bibliographies at the end of each chapter.

Adam, Heribert and Hermann Giliomee, 1979. *Ethnic Power Mobilized: Can South Africa Change?* New Haven and London: Yale University Press. 308 pp.
    This book deals mainly with the at one time ruling Afrikaner group: focusing on the history of Afrikaner identity, their political and economic advance, and dimensions of their rise to power. The book also provides an analysis of the failure of political liberalism in South Africa. The book includes an index. Heribert Adam is Professor of Sociology at Simon Fraser University, Vancouver and Hermann Giliomee is Professor of Politics at the University of Cape Town.

Adam, Heribert and Kogila Moodley, 1993. *The Negotiated Revolution: Society and Politics in Post-Apartheid South Africa*. Johannesburg: Jonathan Ball. 277 pp.
    This book deals with the negotiation process for a democratic South Africa. The roles of the political actors are analysed, from the ANC to the political Right Wing. The book also analyses the salience of international intervention, the impact of regional relations and the prospects for the future of South Africa. The book includes a bibliography, a detailed index and reference suggestions for further reading on Southern Africa. Heribert Adam is Professor of Sociology at Simon Fraser University, Vancouver and Koogila Moodley is Associate Professor in the Department of Educational Studies at the University of British Columbia.

Alexander, Neville, 1990. *Education and the Struggle for National Liberation in South Africa*. Braamfontein: Skotaville. 226 pp.
    This book includes essays and speeches by Neville Alexander from the period 1985–1989. They all "address the relationship between education and national liberation struggle". Neville Alexander is a renowned activist and educationist who participated in the struggle for a democratic South Africa for more than 30 years. He was one of the Robben Island prisoners.

Alexander, Neville, 1993. *Some Are More Equal Than Others: Essays on the Transition in South Africa*. Cape Town: Buchu Books. 106 pp.
    This book includes six essays which deal with political developments in South Africa after 1990. The first essay deals with "the politics of national and institutional transformation", the second essay deals with "Africa and the new world order", the third essay deals with

"negotiations and the struggle for socialism in South Africa", the fourth essay deals with "problems of democratisation in South Africa" and the last essay deals with "fundamentals of education policy for a democratic South Africa".

Appiah, Kwame Anthony, 1992. *In My Father's House*. London: Methuen. 366 pp.

This book explores the meaning of African identity in the late 20th century. The book examines the role of racial ideology in the development of Pan-Africanism, and analyses how "questions about African identity figure in African literary life". Modern African philosophy is examined as well as humanism and the question of national identity. The book includes a bibliography and a brief index. Kwame Anthony Appiah is Professor of both African-American Studies and Philosophy at Harvard University, Massachusetts, USA.

Bazilli, Susan, 1991. *Putting Women on the Agenda*. Johannesburg: Ravan Press. 290 pp.

The 17 essays compiled in this volume were presented at the conference "Putting Women on the Agenda", organised by Lawyers for Human Rights at the University of Witwatersrand in 1990. The essays deal with the complexities of gender, race, gender oppression, violence against women and class in a South African context. The book provides examples drawn from South Africa, Namibia, Botswana, Zimbabwe and Canada. The book includes the "Statements of the National Executive Committee of the African National Congress on the emancipation of women in South Africa" and the "ANC Constitutional Guidelines". Susan Bazilli has degrees in sociology and law and was the organiser of the conference in question.

Chatterjee, Partha, 1993. *The Nation and Its Fragments: Colonial and Postcolonial Histories*. Princeton: Princeton University Press. 282 pp.

This book deals with the nation in relation to history, imagined communities, the colonial state, women, and communities. The book provides examples from colonial and postcolonial India particularly from Bengal. The book includes a bibliography and an index.

Davidson, Basil, 1992. *The Black Man's Burden: Africa and the Curse of the Nation State*. London: James Curry. 355 pp.

This book deals with the nation-state in Africa as a continuation of colonial rule. It examines the discourses concerning ethnicity and nations. Davidson draws a parallel between the situation in Africa and developments in Eastern Europe. The book includes an index.

van Diepen, Maria (ed.), 1988. *The National Question in South Africa*. London and New Jersey: Zed Books. 154 pp.

This volume of ten essays originates from a seminar series organised by the Dr Govan Mbeki Fund in Amsterdam. The essays deal with the discourse of nation, national identity and nationalism in South Africa in the context of the liberation movement's advances. The national question is discussed in relation to class, ethnicity, gender, minorities etc. The book includes a brief index.

Dijkin, Gertjan, 1996. *National Identity and Geopolitical Visions: Map of Pride and Pain.* London and New York: Routledge. 188 pp.

This book deals with the identification of territory in relation to history and geographical conditions. This is illustrated with examples taken from Germany, Britain, the United States, Argentina, Australia, Russia, Serbia, Iraq, and India. The book includes a bibliography and a detailed index. Gertjan Dijkin is Associate Professor of Political Geography at the University of Amsterdam.

Eriksen, Thomas Hylland, 1993. *Ethnicity & Nationalism: Anthropological Perspectives.* London and Boulder: Pluto Press. 179 pp.

This book deals with ethnicity and nationalism from a theoretical and a practical point of view. The concepts of ethnicity and nationalism are examined, as well as the history and the usage of the two concepts. The relationship between ethnicity, class and nationalism is exposed through examples from different parts of the world. The book includes a bibliography and an index. Thomas Hylland Eriksen is Senior Lecturer in Social Anthropology at the University of Oslo.

Frederikse, Julie, 1990. *The Unbreakable Thread: Non-Racialism in South Africa.* Johannesburg: Ravan Press. 294 pp.

This book deals with "the development of the theory and the practice of non-racialism in South Africa through the words and the writings of its people". The book focuses on resistance politics from 1950 to 1989. The book includes bibliographical updates on those interviewed in the book and an index.

Glickman, Harvey (ed.), 1995. *Ethnic Conflict and Democratization in Africa.* Atlanta: African Studies Association Press. 484 pp.

The contributors to this book were invited to write an essay in which they were to "report on evidence of ethnicity in politics in countries with which they were familiar". The examples provided are drawn from South Africa, Zimbabwe, Kenya, Somalia, sub-Saharan Africa in general, Cameroon, Gabon, Tanzania, Nigeria, and Zaire. The book includes a bibliography and an index. Harvey Glickman is Professor of Political Science at Haverford College.

Jackson, Peter and Jan Penrose (eds.), 1993. *Constructions of Race, Place and Nation.* London: UCL Press. 216 pp.

This volume of eight essays deals in different ways with the idea that "race and nation are social constructions rather than naturally occurring phenomena". The book is divided into four parts: the first examines the "construction of the nation", with examples drawn from Scotland, the United Kingdom and Canada. The second part deals with the "constructions of aboriginality", with examples drawn from Australia.

The third part analysis "places of resistance", and the last part deals with "politics and position". The book includes an index. Peter Jackson is Professor of Human Geography at the University of Sheffield and Jan Penrose is a Lecturer at the Centre of Canadian Studies.

James, Wilmot, Daria Caliguire and Kerry Cullinan (eds.), 1996. *Now That We Are Free: Coloured Communities in a Democratic South Africa*. Boulder and London: Lynne Rienner, in association with the Institute for Democracy in South Africa (Idasa). 147 pp.

The book is divided into six parts with the first giving the background to the discourse on Coloured identity and the second part analysing the "coloured vote". The third part deals with identity questions, the fourth part examines affirmative action and equity, the fifth part analyses non-racialism, and the last part provides comparative perspectives from Canada, Britain, Brazil and Malaysia. The book includes an index.

Kaarsholm, Preben and Jan Hultin, 1994. *Inventions and Boundaries: Historical and Anthropological Approaches to the Study of Ethnicity and Nationalism*. Occasional Paper no 11. Roskilde: International Development Studies. 327 pp.

This volume of essays includes thirteen essays presented in different forms at a Nordic Research training course at Sandbjerg Manor around the theme: "Ethnicity and Nationalism: Historical and Anthropological Approaches". The examples are drawn from Zimbabwe, South Africa, India, Ethiopia and Denmark. Crucial concepts discussed include race, nationalism and ethnicity. Preben Kaarsholm is from the University of Roskilde and Jan Hultin is from the University of Gothenburg.

Kaye, Jaqueline and Abdelhamid Zoubir, 1990. *The Ambiguous Compromise: Language, Literature, and National Identity in Algeria and Morocco*. London & New York: Routledge. 141 pp.

This book deals with the ambiguous situation in Algeria and Morocco where, despite the independence of their countries, novelists and poets continue to write in the former colonisers' language. The authors trace the problem to the "dilemma of the translation of a spoken language into fixed print". The book includes an index and a bibliography. Jaqueline Kaye is Lecturer in Literature at the University of Essex and Abdelhamid Zoubir is Maître de Conference at the University of Algiers.

King, Anthony D. (ed.), 1991. *Culture Globalization and the World System*. London: Macmillan. 186 pp.

This volume includes nine essays which were presented at a symposium held at the State University of New York at Binghamton in 1989, in a series called "Current Debates in Art History". The essays deal with the discourse on the globalisation of culture. The authors of the essays have at least two things in common; "the rejection of the nationally-constituted society as the appropriate object of discourse, or unit of social and cultural analysis, and a commitment to conceptualising the world as a whole". The book includes a name and subject index. Anthony D. King is Professor of Art History and Sociology at the State University of New York at Binghamton.

Lijphart, Arend, 1977. *Democracy in Plural Societies: A Comparative Exploration.* New Haven: Yale University Press. 248 pp.

This book deals with consociational democracy in which elite co-operation in sharing power is the primary distinguishing feature. The first part of the book deals with smaller European democracies such as Austria, Belgium and Switzerland, on which the empirical and normative model of consociational democracy is based. The second part deals with consociational democracy as a normative model of importance to the 'plural societies' of the world. The book includes an index.

Lodge, Tom and Bill Nasson, 1991. *All, Here, and Now: Black Politics in South Africa in the 1980s.* In South Africa Update Series. Cape Town: Ford Foundation, David Philip. 414 pp.

This book deals with resistance politics in South Africa during the 1980s. The United Democratic Front is analysed as well as Inkatha, Pan-Africanist Congress. The authors provide a national and regional perspective. The book includes the "Freedom Charter, June 26, 1955", "Forward to People's Power" by Zwelakhe Sisulu (1986), excerpts from "The Kairos Documents, 1986", "Manifesto of the Azanian People, 1983" and the "ANC Constitutional Guidelines for a Democratic South Africa". Also included are: a glossary of Black organisations, a selected bibliography on Black politics in South Africa, a selected annotated bibliography on South Africa, and a section listing key events in South African history.

Mazrui, Ali A., 1990. *Cultural Forces in World Politics.* London: James Currey. 262 pp.

This book includes essays dealing with culture and power in a worldwide perspective. The essays are divided into three parts, the first "the cultural sweep of history" deals with world history and is divided into three eras: the God era, the gold era and the era of glory. The second part deals with "ideology and power" in which ideologies are analysed together with race, youth, gender. The third part "in search of change" deals with aid relations from different angles. The book includes an index. Ali A. Mazrui is Professor of Political Science at the State University of New York, Binghamton.

Miller, David, 1995. *On Nationality.* Oxford: Clarendon Press. 210 pp.

This book aims to provide "a careful reflection on the nature of nationality, and the legitimacy of the claims that it throws up". Four questions are central; the first deals with "questions of boundaries", the second deals with national sovereignty, the third question analyses what nationality implies for the internal policy of a state. The last question is about the ethical weight that individuals should give to the demands of nationality. The book includes a bibliography and an index.

Ngugi wa Thiong'o, 1986. *Decolonising the Mind: The Politics of Language in African Literature*. London: James Currey. 114 p.
   This book includes four essays, three dealing with the relations between language and African literature, theatre and fiction, and the fourth analysing "the quest for relevance". All of the essays were first delivered as lectures. The essays deal with the struggle between an imperialist and a resistance tradition as two opposed forces. The book includes an index. Ngugi wa Thiong'o is one of the most important contemporary writers from Africa.

Parker, Andrew, Mary Russo, Doris Sommer and Patricia Yeager (eds.), 1992. *Nationalisms and Sexualities*. New York and London: Routledge. 451 pp.
   This volume of 23 essays brings together discourses concerning nationalism and sexualities, theoretically as well as practically. The book is divided into six parts: "(De)Colonising gender" which analyses the relationship between colonial and neo-colonial nations and sexualities; "Tailoring the nation" which examines the dress as a marker of national and sexual status; "The other country" analyses the projection of forbidden sexuality to nations outside; "Spectacular bodies" deals with the construction of national and sexual norms; "To govern is to populate" examines the creation of national citizens; and "Women, resistance and the state" examines the relationship between feminism and disparate nationalism.

Pütz, Martin (ed.), 1995. *Discrimination through Language in Africa: Perspectives on the Namibian Experience*. New York: Mouton de Gruyter. 338 pp.
   This volume of 17 essays deals with language policy planning in Africa. The book is divided into four parts with the first examining language contact and language conflict in Africa and the second part containing case studies from Africa dealing with language expansion and language engineering. The third and the fourth parts deals with different perspectives on language in the Namibian context. Language culture and nation-building are analysed as well as linguistic conflicts. The book includes a name and subject index. Martin Pütz is from the Gerhard-Mercator-University of Duisburg.

Sachikonye, Lloyd (ed.), 1995. *Democracy, Civil Society and the State: Social Movements in Southern Africa*. Harare: Sapes Books. 193 pp.
   This volume of eight essays deals with "the debates on the concept and process of Democracy, and on the relationship between state and civil society". The book provides case studies from South Africa, Swaziland, Mozambique, Zambia, and Zimbabwe. The book includes a select bibliography and a brief index.

Schrire, Robert (ed.), 1990. *Critical Choices for South Africa: An Agenda for the 1990s*. Cape Town: Oxford University Press. 465 pp.
   This volume of 24 essays deals with four critical issues. The first concerns "expanding the foundations of political participation while

structuring and controlling state power". The second issue is "balancing equalities and inequalities". The third issue is that of "managing resources in a context of relative scarcity". The last issue is "strategies of change". The book includes an index. Robert Schrire is Professor of Political Studies at the University of Cape Town.

Smith, Anthony D., 1973. *A Critique of the Functionalist Theory of Social Change*. London and Boston: Routledge and Kegan Paul. 198 pp.

This book deals with attempts to achieve an overall sociological theory of change. The author aims to make an evaluation of this theory from a neo-evolutionistic perspective, and to provide a methodological framework. The book has a three-fold structure, the first deals with "the background and outlines the main principles of neo-evolutionism", the second section provides a critical analysis of three problems of neo-evolutionist, namely "civilisation and its development, modernisation and revolution". The last section provides an "assessment and evaluation of neo-evolutionism". The book includes a bibliography and an index. Anthony D. Smith is Professor of Sociology at the London School of Economics.

Smith Anthony D., 1981. *The Ethnic Revival*. Cambridge: Cambridge University Press. 240 pp.

This book deals with the "theoretical interpretation of the causes, origin and significance of ethnic movements in the modern world". The author analyses the social roots of the development of the ethnic revival and documents its world-wide importance. The book includes a bibliography and an index.

Smith, Anthony D., 1983. *State and Nation in the Third World*. Brighton: Wheatsheaf Books. 171 pp.

This book deals with contemporary social change in Africa and Asia in relation to the political dimension of territorial states. Examples are drawn primarily from sub-Saharan Africa. The book includes a bibliography and a name and subject index.

Smith, Anthony D., 1991. *National Identity*. London: Penguin. 227 pp.

This book is a very good introduction to the discourses of national identity. The author attempts to "provide an historical sociology of national identity". National identities are discussed in relation to other identities, such as those based on language, religion, customs and pigmentation. The book includes a bibliography and an index.

Smith, Graham (ed.), 1995. *Federalism: The Multi-ethnic Challenge*. London and New York: Longman. 314 pp.

This volume of twelve essays deals with federal formations "where cultural differences—based around race, ethnicity, tribe, language or religion—provide their architectural focus" and the managing of these differences. The book is divided into three parts, the first deals with federation whose legitimacy is questioned by ethnic groups, the second analyses the break-up of the Soviet Union and the socialist bloc and their efforts to manage multi-ethnicity. The last part deals with federations as a solution to ethnic divisions. The book includes an index. Graham Smith is in the Department of Geography at the University of Cambridge.

Young, Crawford (ed.), 1993. *The Rising Tide of Cultural Pluralism: The Nation-State at Bay?* Madison: University of Wisconsin Press. 305 pp.

This volume of 13 essays deals with the transforming relations between cultural pluralism and the nation state in a global perspective. The essays provide examples drawn from the U.S., the Soviet Union, Iran, Ethiopia, Eritrea, Leninist States, South Asia, and the Modern Maya. The book includes a bibliography and a detailed index. Crawford Young is Professor of Political Science at the University of Wisconsin-Madison.

Young, Crawford, 1994. *The African Colonial State in Comparative Perspective.* New Haven and London: Yale University Press. 356 pp.

This book deals with the history of colonisation in Africa, from the genesis of the colonial state, its institutionalisation, the advent of independence, to the crises of postcolonial Africa. Examples are provided from a wide range of African countries. The book includes an index.

Werbner, Richard and Terence Ranger (eds.), 1996. *Postcolonial Identities in Africa.* London and New Jersey: Zed Books. 292 pp.

This volume of nine essays deals with postcolonial identity strategies and the reconfiguration of personal knowledge in relation to the postcolonial imagination. The book is divided into two parts; the first examines "crises, state decay and transitional identities" with examples drawn from Africa in general, West Africa, Zaire, Malawi, and South Africa. The second part analyses "identity degradation, moral knowledge and deconstruction", with examples drawn from Uganda, Cameroon, Nigeria, and Africa in general. The book includes a detailed index. Richard Werbner is Professor in African Anthropology at the University of Manchester and Terence Ranger is retired Professor of Race Relations and African Studies at Oxford University.

About the authors

Ousseina Alidou is from the Niger Republic. She has been teaching as a visiting lecturer at Abdou Moumouni University in Niger. Her research interests focus on linguistics, literature and the interplay between religion and gender politics in Francophone Africa. She works as lecturer of African languages and literature in the Department of African-American and African Studies at the Ohio State University.

Brendan Boyce has worked at the University of Durban Westville as tutor and associate lecturer in the Political department, and is a researcher in the Commission on the Restitution on Land Rights since 1996.

Horace Campbell is Professor of African American Studies and Political Science in at Syracuse University in New York. For the past twenty five years he has been studying and writing on the issues of militarism, transformation and peace in Africa.

Zimitri Erasmus is a lecturer in Sociology at the University of Cape Town. She completed her doctoral work in 1994 at the University of Nijmegen, the Netherlands. Her specific teaching and research interests are in the field of race, gender and identities in Africa with a focus on constructions of whiteness, blackness and creole identities.

Don Foster is Professor of Psychology at the University of Cape Town. He is a co-author of *Detention & Torture in South Africa* (1987) and *Social Psychology in South Africa* (1991).

Kimani Gecau is based at the English department of the University of Zimbabwe. He does research on popular song and the democratization process in Kenya, the making of a Zimbabwean community theatre, the history of the popular song in Kenya, and the context of the development of popular culture in Zimbabwe and Kenya.

Siri Lange (born 1966) is a Research Fellow at the Chr. Michelsen Institute in Bergen, Norway. She is currently working on a Ph.D. in Social Anthropology focusing on popular culture and identity in Dar es Salaam, Tanzania.

Svend Erik Larsen, b. 1946, dr. phil., professor of Comparative Literature, Aarhus University, Denmark. Director of the Humanities Research Center: Man & Nature, 1992–1997. Treasurer of the International Comparative Literature Association. Books and articles on literature, semiotics and cultural analysis. Recent publications are *Naturen er ligeglad* [Nature doesn't care] (1996), *La rue - espace ouvert* (1997), *Nature: Literature and its Otherness/La littérature et son autre* (1997).

Gerhard Maré is director of the Centre for Industrial, Organisational and Labour Studies and associate professor in the Sociology Department at the University of Natal Durban. He has published on the Inkatha movement and ethnicity.

Robert Mattes holds a Ph.D. from the Department of Political Science at the University of Illinois, Urbana-Champaign. Since 1995, he has been the Manager of the Public Opinion Service at Idasa (Institute for Democracy In South Africa). He has conducted research in the United States and in South Africa on the political impact of public opinion polling and more recently democratic culture and democratic consolidation in South Africa, with a particular focus on voting behaviour, political participation, and democratic values.

Alamin Mazrui is Associate Professor of African languages and literature in the Department of African-American and African Studies at the Ohio State University. He has written on language, literature, history and political economy. His two most recent latest books are *The Political Culture of Language: Swahili, Society and the State* (Binghamton: State University of New York, 1996, co-authored with Ibrahim Shariff), and *The Power of Babel: Language in the African Experience*, co-authored with Ali Mazrui, (University of Chicago Press 1998).

Michael Neocosmos is associate Professor of Sociology at the University of Botswana and has written extensively on rural relations and political economy as well as on issues of democracy, state and civil society in Southern Africa.

Maria Olaussen works as an Academy of Finland Research Fellow at Åbo Akademi University in Finland. She teaches African Literature and Critical Theory. 1998–1999 she spent at the University of Cape

Town in South Africa as a Postdoctoral Fellow working on South African women's autobiographies. She is the author of *Forceful Creation in Harsh Terrain: Place and Identity in Three Novels by Bessie Head* (1997) and *Three Types of Feminist Criticism and Jean Rhys's Wide Sargasso Sea* (1992). Her present contribution is part of a project on Transformations of Intimacy: Romance in African Women's Writing.

Mai Palmberg is a political scientist from Åbo Academy University in Finland, and works since 1984 at the Nordic Africa Institute. She has written, among other things, on political developments in southern Africa, aids in Africa, and the images of Africa in school books.

Edgar Pieterse is founder and director of the Isandla Institute, a policy research organisation specialising in urban development and anti-poverty strategies. Isandla is based in Cape Town and Johannesburg. Edgar completed his Masters degree at the Institute of Social Studies, the Hague. He is a part-time lecturer at the Graduate School of Public and Development Management, University of Witwatersrand.

Raisa Simola (Ph.D.) teaches at the University of Joensuu, Finland. She is the author of *World Views in Chinua Achebe's Works* Frankfurt am Main: Lang, 1995, and is currently working on a study of Ben Okri.

Rupert Taylor is Senior Lecturer in Political Studies at the University of the Witwatersrand, Johannesburg. Recent publications include articles in *Telos*, *Race & Class*, and *Ethnic and Racial Studies*.